STUDENT MOTIVATION, COGNITION, AND LEARNING

Essays in Honor of Wilbert J. McKeachie

Wilbert J. McKeachie

STUDENT MOTIVATION, COGNITION, AND LEARNING

Essays in Honor of Wilbert J. McKeachie

Edited by

Paul R. Pintrich
University of Michigan

Donald R. Brown
University of Michigan

Claire Ellen Weinstein
University of Texas

LAWRENCE ERLBAUM ASSOCIATES, PUBLISHERS
1994   Hillsdale, New Jersey   Hove, UK

Lawrence Erlbaum Associates, Inc., Publishers
365 Broadway
Hillsdale, New Jersey 07642

Library of Congress Cataloging-in-Publication Data

Student motivation, cognition, and learning : essays in honor of
  Wilbert J. McKeachie / edited by Paul R. Pintrich, Donald R. Brown,
  Claire Ellen Weinstein.
      p. cm.
    Includes bibliographical references and indexes.
    ISBN 0-8058-1376-4 (alk. paper)
    1. Learning, Psychology of. 2. Motivation in education.
  3. Cognitive learning. 4. College teaching. 5. McKeachie, Wilbert
  James, 1921-   . I. Pintrich, Paul R. II. Brown, Donald R., 1925-
  . III. Weinstein, Claire E. IV. McKeachie, Wilbert James, 1921- .
  LB1060.S876 1994
  370.15'4--dc20   94-22213
                                                      CIP

Books published by Lawrence Erlbaum Associates are printed
on acid-free paper, and their bindings are chosen
for strength and durability.

Printed in the United States of America

10 9 8 7 6 5 4 3 2 1

Contents

Preface

In Celebration of a Mentor, Colleague, and Friend

On an unusually warm and sunny Spring day in 1992 a group of more than one hundred current and former students, colleagues, friends, and family members gathered in Rackham Auditorium on The University of Michigan's Ann Arbor campus to celebrate Wilbert J. McKeachie's lifetime of contributions to psychology and higher education. The symposium speakers discussed how their own research on cognition, motivation, and instruction had been influenced by Bill's research and writing. That evening, more than 300 guests attended a special dinner in Bill's honor. The dinner guests heard from Bill's friends and his Psychology Department colleagues about Bill's contributions to the department during his term as chair as well as his many contributions to academic life at Michigan in general. The following year, at the 1993 Annual Meeting of the American Educational Research Association, an unprecedented invitational session was presented in honor of Bill's contributions to research on college teaching and learning.

The chapters in this volume were written by participants at these meetings and others who have worked closely with Bill over the years. These, and the many other honors Bill has received, are simply reflections of the tremendous esteem in which he is held as a scholar and as a person. Bill's leadership and contributions, particularly at the intersection of psychology and higher education, are unparalleled. His mentoring, warmth, and concern for other people, both students and colleagues, is legendary. It is with great pleasure that we are able to honor all of Bill's achievements with a Festschrift.

Bill has taught psychology at The University of Michigan since 1946, but his roots in the Michigan area go back even further. He grew up just 40 miles from Ann Arbor and married a local woman from the Detroit area who was to become his lifelong companion–Virginia (Ginny) McKeachie. He was always a voracious reader, and despite selecting mathematics as his college major at Michigan Normal College, his career goal focused on becoming a minister and an educator. In this way he was following in his parent's footsteps, both of his parents were teachers. In fact, Bill's father was his teacher in the local country school for the first 8 grades. Bill's career plans were interrupted by a stint as a Navy Lieutenant in World War II where his fascination with individual differences and learning began as he observed and tried to understand the many differences in the crew on his ship. When he returned from the war, Bill decided to continue his pursuit of a career in education but switched the focus to psychology from ministerial studies, although he continued to publish in the area of Christian education for many years. In 1945, he entered The University of Michigan, receiving his Master's degree in 1946 and his Doctorate in 1949.

It is impossible to even list all of the awards Bill has received or even his major accomplishments given that his curriculum vita is over 30 pages long, so we have provided an abstracted version of his vita at the end of the chapters in this volume. However, we would like to highlight a few of his most important accomplishments. Bill was involved in the creation of one of the first higher education teaching and learning centers in America. He established many of the early research collaborations among institutions of higher education. He was elected President of the American Psychological Association and the American Association of Higher Education. He has been a member of many curriculum review committees of the American Psychological Association, and his book entitled, *Teaching Tips: A guidebook for the beginning college teacher,* is in its 9th edition and has become a definitive text used in thousands of institutions of higher education. In addition, Bill's research, writing, teaching, and consulting work has had an enormous impact on conceptualization, theory development, research, faculty development, instructional practices, and student learning assistance programs, as witnessed by the diversity of the chapters in this volume.

Besides his scholarly work on college teaching and learning, Bill practices what he preaches through his efforts to improve education. Bill received his first teaching award in 1955—the Alumni Award for Distinguished Teaching at The University of Michigan. His first edited book, a set of readings for introductory psychology, came out in 1951 and the first edition of his book on teaching tips also came out in 1951. His first invited book chapter was in 1954 and it focused on past, present, and future relations of psychology to general education. The first journal article Bill wrote was published in 1950 and discussed anxiety in college students. It is interesting to note that 40 years later, Bill is still involved in curriculum development for psychology classes, the 9th edition of his 1951 book on teaching for college instructors, the implications of psychological theories and findings for educational practice, and the study of individual differences, such as the nature of anxiety and the mechanisms by which it debilitates performance. In addition, he was honored with a national teaching award from the American Psychological Association in 1992.

Bill McKeachie's legacy lies in his scholarly work, the work he has stimulated others to do, the thousands of students he has trained, the thousands of college teachers he has helped, and the lives he has touched with his wisdom, warmth, and support. This volume is designed to be a tribute to Bill and his accomplishments over the past forty-five years and the chapters reflect the diversity of his contributions.

First, Bill has worked in the area of cognition. A major focus of this work in the past decade has been on developing models and methods of understanding students' cognitive structures. This work is most closely reflected in the chapter by Moshe Naveh-Benjamin and Yi-Guang Lin, two long-time collaborators of Bill's. Their chapter discuss the research program that Bill, Moshe, and Yi-Guang have been involved in for several years on how to measure college students' cognitive structures for disciplinary knowledge. Janet Donald, one of Bill's many international colleagues, addresses how different disciplinary structures may influence students learning and cognition. Going beyond knowledge, Bill's own writings on college teaching have always stressed the importance of teaching for higher order thinking such as critical thinking and problem solving, not just recall of factual information. The two chapters by Kevin Biolsi and Edward Smith, and Scott VanderStoep and Colleen Seifert reflect current cognitive psychological research by Michigan Psychology faculty (Smith and Seifert) and recent Michigan graduate students (Biolsi and VanderStoep) on reasoning and problem solving. This work has important implications for our understanding of college student thinking and reasoning as well as our models of college instruction.

Besides cognition, Bill's research on college student learning also has been concerned with student motivation, in particular, test anxiety. Moreover, Bill's research program on anxiety has been in the forefront of efforts to link motivational constructs like anxiety to students' cognitive processing, memory, and use of learning strategies. The chapter by Paul Pintrich and Teresa Garcia reflects this integration of motivation and cognition by linking motivational beliefs to self-regulated learning. The work presented in this chapter grows out of Paul's collaboration with Bill over the last 12 years and Teresa's involvement during the last 6 years at Michigan and NCRIPTAL (National Center for Research to Improve Postsecondary Teaching and Learning). The chapter by Paul Schutz, a former student of Claire Ellen Weinstein's and through academic familial lineage, a "grandson" of Bill, also reflects this concern with the integration of motivational goals with other cognitive outcomes.

Another theme of Bill's work, and one that is reflected in a number of chapters, is how student motivation and cognition interact with instructional and classroom characteristics, the classic problem of aptitude-treatment interactions, or ATIs. Marty Covington, a long-time colleague of Bill's, and his graduate student Brent Roberts, propose a model of individual differences in terms of achievement strivings that connects need for achievement motives to current models of motivation. They then go on to link these individual differences in achievement to differential outcomes as a function of interactions with instructional and classroom characteristics. The confluence of classroom characteristics and individual differences is also reflected in Stuart Karabenick and Rajeev Sharma's paper on help-seeking. As colleagues of Bill's at NCRIPTAL, they began this research program on how and when college students will seek help and what classroom factors can influence help-seeking. They show that help-seeking behavior is related to both teacher behavior and student characteristics.

This concern for how student motivation, cognition, and learning is developed and "situated" in the ecologically valid setting of college classrooms has been a long-standing research focus of Bill's. In addition, he has not been content to just study college classrooms, he has been a leader in developing ways to change college teaching to improve students' learning. The chapter by Scott Paris, a Psychology Department colleague of Bill's, and his former student Julianne Turner, summarizes their research on how students' cognition and motivation are positively influenced by the classroom characteristics of choice, challenge, control, and collaboration. The chapter by Marita Inglehart, Donald Brown, and Mina Vida, all colleagues of Bill's at Michigan, also reminds us of the potential disadvantages of competition instead of collaboration. However, in keeping with the general cognitive approach and person-in-context perspective that characterizes Bill's research program, they find that it is students' appraisal of the situation which interacts with competition to influence achievement. The four "C's" also reflect Bill's own philosophy of teaching where he motivates his undergraduates and graduate students through the optimal use of choice, control, challenge, and collaboration, not competition. We often have been amazed at how much choice and control he gives students, but it reflects Bill's deep and abiding faith in students. In addition, anyone who has collaborated with Bill knows that they will have a great deal of choice, control, and challenge in any collaborative project, which will also facilitate their own motivation to learn.

Claire Ellen Weinstein's chapter continues with this theme of improving college classroom instruction by reviewing her research program on how to teach students to be more strategic learners, the assessment of students' learning strategies, and how college teachers can become more strategic teachers. Although she was not a graduate student of Bill's, Claire Ellen has been a "student" of Bill's since she began her professional career. Bill has been her mentor and colleague for many years and her research program has developed by building on Bill's insights and writings. Barry Zimmerman and his student, Rafael Risemberg, also discuss how to teach students to become more strategic and self-regulating learners. Barry was one of the invited speakers at the 1993 AERA symposium to honor Bill and Bill's contributions to the field of college student learning and teaching.

Besides teaching students how to become self-regulating learners in his "Learning to Learn" course at Michigan, Bill has been very interested in how to teach students to become more critical thinkers. The chapter by Susan Reiter, one of Bill's former students, presents a quasi-experimental study of dialogical teaching. This method of having students discuss and present ideas that are counter to their own view is designed to help them come to understand their own views better as well as opposing views. Again, anyone who has worked with Bill will realize that he often engages in dialogical teaching as he pushes you to think more clearly about your ideas. The final contribution in honor of Bill, by Marilla Svinicki, a colleague of Bill's in national efforts to improve college teaching and a speaker at the 1993 AERA symposium, challenges us all to think seriously about how research on cognition, motivation, and instruction can improve college teaching. In this way, Marilla's questions are not unlike Bill's own views as he constantly asks of himself and others, "how can this idea or research make a difference to college students and teachers?" We all know that Bill will continue using this questioning style to challenge existing ideas and blaze new trails as he suggests in his own final chapter in this volume.

We want to thank a number of other people and institutions that made the 1992 symposium and dinner at Michigan possible. First, the symposium committee was chaired by Donald Brown and had as members, Paul Pintrich, Charles (Tony) Morris, Daniel Weintraub, and Cheryl Israel. Tony and Dan were very helpful in planning the dinner and selecting the speakers for the symposium. Cheryl was instrumental in making sure all the administrative arrangements and details were taken care of and keeping a committee of academics grounded in the realities of the plans. We thank the chair of the Psychology Department, Pat Gurin, and Nancy Bates, administrative assistant in Psychology, for lending us Cheryl and for all their other financial and administrative support.

In terms of financial assistance, a number of departments and units at The University of Michigan made substantial contributions to our budget for the symposium speakers and their travel. The Office of the Vice President for Research, the Dean's Office of the Horace H. Rackham Graduate School, the Department of Psychology, the Center for Research on Learning and Teaching, and the Combined Program in Education and Psychology all contributed to our budget for the symposium and dinner. Without this help, we would not have been able to organize the symposium or plan this resulting Festschrift. In addition, Lawrence Erlbaum of Lawrence Erlbaum Associates provided us with our book contract and funding for typesetting so that this volume could be completed. Hollis Heimbouch of Lawrence Erlbaum Associates provided us with wonderful editorial support. Most importantly, we wish to thank Maria Huntley of the Center for Research on Learning and Teaching at Michigan for formatting and typesetting all the chapters in this volume. Without her skill and expertise in the use of desktop publishing, this volume would never have been finished. Moreover, she took on this difficult and time-consuming task with her usual good cheer and dedication to excellence. It was a great pleasure to have her work with us on this volume.

In summary, we want to take this opportunity to honor Bill with this Festschrift. In particular, we want to thank him for all his substantive contributions to the field and to his personal support for people in psychology and higher education. We are all much enriched for having known and worked with him. Moreover, we look forward to many more years of fruitful learning, collaboration, and friendship with Bill.

Paul R. Pintrich
Donald R. Brown
Claire Ellen Weinstein

1

The Automaticity of Similarity-Based Reasoning

Kevin Biolsi
Edward E. Smith
University of Michigan

A recurring theme in Bill McKeachie's writings about teaching and learning has been the importance of understanding students' cognition (e.g., McKeachie, 1980a, 1980b). For example, one line of McKeachie's work has focused on students' cognitive structures of key classroom concepts, and how the form and evolution of such structures reflect on student performance (Lin, McKeachie, Wernander, & Hedegard, 1970; Naveh-Benjamin, McKeachie, & Lin, 1989; Naveh-Benjamin, McKeachie, Lin, & Tucker, 1986). Other work on learning strategies (McKeachie, Pintrich, & Lin, 1985a) and learning to learn (McKeachie, Pintrich, & Lin, 1985b; Pintrich, McKeachie, & Lin, 1987) has emphasized the importance of teaching students key concepts of cognitive psychology along with the learning strategies that make use of these concepts. The importance of such considerations is underscored by the recent review of teaching and learning in the college classroom by McKeachie, Pintrich, Lin, Smith, and Sharma (1990); in this document, a considerable amount of space is devoted to student cognition, including such topics as knowledge structure, cognitive and metacognitive learning strategies, and thinking and problem solving. In this chapter we hope to contribute to such work on student cognition, focusing on issues that are relevant to probabilistic reasoning and to training such reasoning.

1

When people are asked to judge the probabilities of various events, rather than employing principles of probability theory they might have learned in academic settings, often they rely on a number of informal heuristics (e.g., Kahneman, Slovic, & Tversky, 1982; Nisbett & Ross, 1980). One such heuristic is *representativeness*, whereby an event is judged likely to the extent that it is "(i) similar in essential properties to its parent population; and (ii) reflects the salient features of the process by which it is generated" (Kahneman & Tversky, 1972, p. 431). When the problem elements are instances and categories, then the degree of representativeness reduces to the typicality of an instance in a category, or the degree to which the instance is similar to the prototype of the category (Shafir, Smith, & Osherson, 1990).

To illustrate the representativeness, or similarity, heuristic, consider the following description: "Bill is 34 years old. He is intelligent, but unimaginative, compulsive, and generally lifeless. In school, he was strong in mathematics but weak in social studies and humanities" (Tversky & Kahneman, 1983, p. 297). Given this description, subjects judge Bill more likely to be an accountant who plays jazz for a hobby than just someone who plays jazz for a hobby, presumably because of Bill's similarity to the prototypical (or stereotypical) accountant. Such a judgment violates the conjunction rule of probability, which specifies that the conjunction of any two events can be no more probable than either event by itself. In other judgment tasks, subjects have been shown to ignore or severely underweight prior probabilities or base rates of events in favor of similarity information, even though the use of such base-rate information is prescribed by normative theory (see Kahneman et al., 1982). Such reliance on similarity has been demonstrated in a number of domains with a number of different subject populations, including medical decision making (Travis, Phillippi, & Tonn, 1989), clinical judgment (Dawes, 1986), legal decisions (Saks & Kidd, 1986), and developmental studies with grade-school children (Agnoli, 1991; Jacobs & Potenza, 1991). In addition, the potential implications of the representativeness heuristic for school psychologists have been described by Burns (1990) and Fagley (1988).

In this chapter we build on the idea that the similarity heuristic is widely used because it is a type of "natural assessment" (Tversky & Kahneman, 1983). In what follows, we first interpret natural assessment as an "automatic" computation,[1] where the notion of automaticity is drawn from studies of attention and memory. We then describe two experiments that demonstrate that similarity assessments exhibit at least one important property of automatic processes, namely that their execution is obligatory, given that the appropriate inputs occur. Finally we tie these results to work in education.

As alluded to previously, automatic processes have been intensively studied in the domains of attention and memory (e.g., Schneider & Shiffrin, 1977; Shiffrin & Schneider, 1977). In these studies, automatic processes are generally characterized by some combination of the following properties: They are unavoidable or obligatory once the appropriate inputs occur, they are effortless or require relatively little of one's attentional capacities, they occur in parallel, and they are relatively fast. In the experiments described here, we focus on the first of these properties, namely the obligatory nature of similarity computations. This property of automatic processes is often studied within the paradigm pioneered by Stroop (1935; see MacLeod, 1991, for a comprehensive review of Stroop experiments).

In a variant of Stroop's original experiments, subjects are presented with lists of words printed in colored ink. The subjects' task is to name the color of the ink for all words in the list as quickly as possible. In one condition the words are neutral with respect to color (e.g., "take," "friend"), while in a second condition the words are color terms (e.g., "blue," "red") printed in ink colors different from the colors they named. For example, the word "blue" might be printed in red ink, whereas the word "brown" might be printed in green ink. In these experiments, color-naming times are found to be significantly longer and error rates higher in the second than in the first condition. Furthermore, when color words and ink colors are congruent (e.g., "blue" is printed in blue ink), facilitation occurs in the form of faster reading times and fewer errors as compared to control items. These results indicate that subjects are unable to suppress reading of the word, and that the encoding and interpretation of the color word can then interfere with or facilitate naming its print color. Thus, the encoding

---

[1]Our characterization of similarity assessment as an automatic process is similar in spirit to Garner's (1990) notion of "primitive routines that yield a product." The idea is that well-practiced, or automatic, routines may produce an output that can then inhibit the use of other learning or reasoning strategies.

and interpretation of a word is obligatory and, hence, an automatic process.

Like the encoding of a word, the assessment of similarity might be obligatory in the sense that it is manditorily performed whenever input information of the proper kind is presented. To test this hypothesis, we should be able to employ a variation of the Stroop paradigm in which information that automatically activates similarity computations is presented in a task that also requires computations of a second type, for example, computations of relative base rates or frequencies. By varying the degree to which the two processes lead to the same answer, we should observe both interference effects, in the form of increased response times and error rates, and facilitation effects, in the form of decreased response times and error rates, of similarity on frequency-based responses.

To illustrate, consider the description of Linda as "bright, outspoken and concerned with social issues" and the two categories bankteller and prominent feminist writer. If the task is to choose the category with the higher frequency, then bankteller should be chosen. However, Linda as described seems to be more similar to the typical prominent feminist writer than to the typical bankteller, so similarity leads to a different answer than does frequency. Thus, to the extent that the computation of similarity occurs more rapidly than that of frequency, and that the results of the similarity computation cannot be ignored, we should expect the response to such an item to be slower or less accurate when compared to an appropriate control. Similarly, if the two choices used with the Linda description are social worker and president of a cosmetics company, then both frequency and similarity lead to the same response, namely social worker, and we should expect facilitation in the form of faster and/or more accurate responses.

In our experiments, subjects were trained to make choices as just described using two different criteria: (a) base rates of the categories and (b) similarity of the descriptions to category prototypes. The predictions are displayed schematically in Fig. 1.1. Consider first those trials for which base rates are used as the criterion (the dashed line in Fig. 1.1). When the similarity and base-rate information agree (e.g., "Linda is a social worker" vs. "Linda is president of a cosmetics company"), we expect facilitation in the form of shorter response times and/or lower error rates than for suitable control items. When the two types of information conflict with each other (e.g., "Linda is a

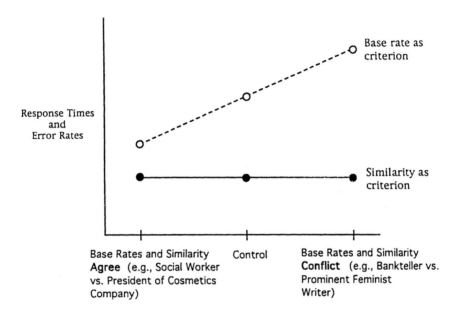

FIG. 1.1. Predicted patterns of error rates and response times for experimental conditions.

bankteller" vs. "Linda is a prominent feminist writer"), we expect interference in the form of longer response times and/or higher error rates relative to the control items.

Now consider those trials for which similarity to category prototype is used as the decision criterion. Because we do not predict automatic activation of base-rate computations, we do not expect such computations to intrude on similarity-based choices. Therefore, the response times and error rates should be relatively constant across the three conditions for the similarity-based trials, as indicated by the solid line in Fig. 1.1.

EXPERIMENT 1

Method

Procedure

Subjects were first given training materials that instructed them in judging relative likelihood using two different criteria: similarity to category prototype and frequency of category. The training materials briefly described the principles behind the two criteria and provided several examples with personality descriptions of the "Linda" type. Decisions based on similarities and frequencies are referred to as similarity decisions and probability decisions, respectively.

Following training, each subject performed the experiment seated at a computer terminal with a response panel. On each trial, a personality description was presented and remained on the screen until the subjects had read and understood it, and then pressed the appropriate response key. Following the description, either the word "Probability" or the word "Similarity" appeared on the screen for one second, instructing the subjects as to which criterion to use for their subsequent decision. Next, two category statements appeared on the screen, and the subjects' task was to indicate which category was more likely, based on the cued criterion (i.e., "Probability" or "Similarity"). The two categories remained on the screen until the subject responded by pressing one of two response keys. On each of 16 practice trials, subjects received feedback concerning the correct response. No feedback was given on the 72 experimental trials.

To summarize, a typical experimental trial would proceed as follows, where separate screen displays are indicated by the dashed lines:

Linda is bright, outspoken and concerned with social issues.

Probability

Linda is a prominent feminist writer.
Linda works as a bankteller.

< Subject's response >

Materials

We created 18 personality descriptions of the type illustrated here. For each description, we constructed four category statements that varied, factorially, in their base rate and their similarity to the description. Thus, for the Linda description, the four category statements were as follows:

Similarity	Base Rate	
	High	*Low*
High	Linda is a social worker.	Linda is a prominent feminist writer.
Low	Linda works as a bankteller.	Linda is president of a cosmetics company.

These statements were then combined into pairs to give the critical types of items. For the probability decisions, the three types of items were as follows:

Congruent items (i.e., similarity and frequency lead to same choice): high base rate, high similarity versus low base rate, low similarity (e.g., "Linda is a social worker" vs. "Linda is president of a cosmetics company").

Incongruent items (i.e., similarity and frequency lead to different choices): high base rate, low similarity versus low base rate, high similarity (e.g., "Linda works as a bankteller" vs. "Linda is a prominent feminist writer").

Probability control items (i.e., similarity held relatively constant): high base rate, high similarity versus low base rate, high similarity (e.g., "Linda is a social worker" vs. "Linda is a prominent feminist writer").

For the similarity decisions, we also used three item types. The first two were identical to the congruent and incongruent items just described. In addition, we included the following control:

Similarity control items (i.e., base rate held relatively constant): high base rate, high similarity versus high base rate, low similarity (e.g., "Linda is a social worker" vs. "Linda works as a bankteller").

Note that facilitation and interference are predicted only for the probability decisions and only when the similarity information agrees (congruent items) or disagrees (incongruent items), respectively, with the base-rate information.[2]

Subjects

Thirty-one University of Michigan undergraduates were paid for their participation in the study.

Results

Trials on which subjects' response times (RTs) exceeded their own mean response times by three standard deviations or more were excluded from all subsequent analyses.[3] Mean error rates and mean response times for correct trials are presented in Tables 1.1 and 1.2, respectively. In both tables, the data are broken down by two factors: (a) whether the operative criterion was probability or similarity, and (b) whether the base-rate information was congruent with the similarity information, incongruent with the similarity information, or independent of the similarity information (control).

To the extent that similarity assessments intrude on assessments of relative base rates or frequency, on probability-cued trials we expect increased error rates and response times on the incongruent trials relative to the control and decreased error rates and response times on the congruent trials relative to the control. For the most part, these

---

[2]In fact, a second type of control item was included for both probability and similarity trials. For these items, the noncriterial factor was held relatively constant at a low rather than high value; for example, for a probability trial, similarity was held constant at a low level. Probability trials corresponding to this item type had strikingly long latencies. An example of such a trial would be the Linda description followed by the choices "Linda is a bankteller" and "Linda is president of a cosmetics company." From a similarity point of view, neither choice really seems to have anything to do with Linda as described. This marked lack of "fit" between the description and the two choices might take subjects by surprise, perhaps even violating a conversational norm (Grice, 1975), which could be the cause of the increased latencies. To the extent that the absence of similarity affected subjects' responses on trials for which they needed only to attend to base-rate information, we have further support for the speed and naturalness of such similarity computations. In any case, this item seems inappropriate as a control for the phenomenon in question, and therefore analyses are reported for only the item types described in the body of the chapter.

[3]By this criterion, 48 of 2,232 or 2.2% of the trials were removed.

TABLE 1.1

Mean Error Rates in Experiment 1 as a Function of Criterion (Probability vs. Similarity) and Congruence of Base-Rate and Similarity Information

	Congruent	Control	Incongruent	Mean
Probability trials	.025	.032	.181	.079
Similarity trials	.022	.043	.055	.040
Means	.023	.037	.118	

TABLE 1.2
Mean Response Times in Experiment 1 as a Function of Criterion (Probability vs. Similarity) and Congruence of Base-Rate and Similarity Information

	Congruent	Control	Incongruent	Mean
Probability trials	3,180	3,444	3,754	3,459
Similarity trials	3,019	3,029	3,312	3,120
Means	3,099	3,237	3,533	

predictions were borne out. A criterion (probability, similarity) by item type (congruent, control, incongruent) ANOVA for the error rates revealed a marginally significant effect of type of criterion [probability $M = .08$, similarity $M = .04$, $F(1,30) = 3.18$, $p = .085$] and significant effects of both item type and the interaction [$F(2,60) = 12.49$, $p < .01$; $F(2,60) = 6.56$, $p < .01$, respectively]. Pairwise comparisons of means for probability trials reveal that the incongruent error rates were significantly greater than the error rates for both the congruent items [$F(1,60) = 27.97$, $p < .01$] and control items [$F(1,60) = 25.61$, $p < .01$]. In contrast, for the similarity trials, no pairwise differences of cell means were significant.

Turning to an analysis of the data summarized in Table 1.2, the pattern of response times supported both the interference and facilitation predictions. An ANOVA revealed significant effects of criterion [$F(1,30) = 7.36$, $p < .05$] and of item type [$F(2,60) = 5.94$, $p < .01$]. However, the interaction between the two factors was not significant [$F(2,60) < 1$, n.s.]. Individual contrasts for the probability trials revealed that the incongruent RTs were significantly longer than the congruent ones [$F(1,60) = 13.62$, $p < .01$] and marginally longer than the control RTs [$F(1,60) = 3.96$, $p = .051$]. For similarity trials, there were some borderline significant effects. The incongruent RTs were marginally higher than both the congruent and control RTs [$F(1,60) = 3.55$, $p = .06$; $F(1,60) = 3.30$, $p = .07$, respectively]. These latter effects were not predicted by our hypotheses.

Discussion

The pattern of error rates fits well with the hypothesis that similarity assessment is an obligatory process. As predicted, for probability trials, the greatest number of errors were made on incongruent items. We also expected fewer errors for congruent items than for control items, but with error rates around 3% we are likely encountering a floor effect. For the similarity trials, no differences across the three item types were expected, and none were observed.

Although the RT data were not as clear-cut, they provide some support for the hypothesis that similarity computations are automatic. For probability trials, RTs were greatest for incongruent items and smallest for congruent items, which is exactly as predicted. However, on the similarity trials, where no effects of item type were expected, the RTs for incongruent items were unexpectedly high; as a result, the predicted criterion-by-item-type interaction did not obtain. This unexpected result for incongruent items, however, may be artifactual. Consider the "similarity difference" associated with an item, which is the difference between the similarity of the description to one category and the similarity of the description to the other category. The smaller this difference, the harder it is to make a decision on a similarity trial, and there is independent evidence that similarity differences were inadvertently less for incongruent items than for other items. Specifically, when a new group of 16 subjects rated, on a 10-point scale, the similarity of each description to its associated categories, the average difference in similarity for pairs of statements in incongruent items (4.14) was less than that for congruent items (5.20) or control items (4.79). This unintended variation in similarity differences across conditions could account for the apparent interference effect.

Thus far we have hypothesized that similarity computations proceed in the following manner. When presented with any personality description and choice categories, people automatically compute the similarity of the described person to the prototypes of the categories. The results of these computations cannot be ignored, and these similarity computations are therefore capable of intruding on judgments of base rates. We refer to this as the *any-description* hypothesis. There is an alternative to this that does not assume that people inevitably compare any description to the categories. According to this alternative, when a description is presented, it will automatically activate a certain prestored category (or categories) if it is sufficiently rich and detailed. The activated category cannot be ignored, and it therefore intrudes on judgments of base rates. We refer to this as the *sufficient-description* hypothesis. Thus, the sufficient-description hypothesis, like the any-description hypothesis, assumes that interference and facilitation effects arise because the outcomes of a fast similarity process cannot be ignored. The two hypotheses differ, however, in that the sufficient-description hypothesis assumes that the similarity computation of interest is between a rich description and prestored categories, whereas the any-description hypothesis assumes the computation is between any description and categories explicitly presented.

The sufficient-description hypothesis seems plausible in light of the fact that research on the similarity heuristic has frequently used rich descriptions. For example, in a well-known study, Tversky and Kahneman (1983) provided subjects with the following description: "Linda is 31 years old, single, outspoken, and very bright. She majored in philosophy. As a student, she was deeply concerned with issues of discrimination and social justice, and also participated in anti-nuclear demonstrations" (p. 297). This description may, in fact, automatically activate the category of feminist for many people. If one of the subsequent category choices then exactly or closely matches the activated category of feminist, then ignoring it in favor of something like base-rate information in a speeded task may be quite difficult, if not impossible, which should lead to intrusions of similarity information on probability trials.

EXPERIMENT 2

We contrasted the any-description and sufficient-description hypotheses in the second experiment. Half of the trials used "sufficient" descriptions, that is, rich descriptions that when presented alone tend to elicit a particular hobby, occupation, or lifestyle category. The other half of the trials used "insufficient" descriptions, that is, descriptions that are not sufficiently rich to elicit a particular category. According to the sufficient-description hypothesis, interference and facilitation effects should be considerably stronger for the sufficient than insufficient items. According to the any-description hypothesis, interference and facilitation effects should be comparable for sufficient and insufficient items.

Method

Materials

Eight sufficient and eight insufficient descriptions were chosen based on the responses of a separate group of 12 subjects who had been asked to give the three most likely hobbies, occupations, lifestyles, and so on, for each of a number of described persons. Descriptions that elicited identical or very similar responses from at least half of the subjects were designated "sufficient"; all other descriptions were "insufficient."

For each of the 16 descriptions, three types of categories were used. One was similar to the description (for sufficient descriptions these were the categories provided by the group of 12 subjects), one was dissimilar and of lower frequency than the similar category, and the third was dissimilar and of higher frequency than the similar category. The similar and high/dissimilar category statements were combined to form an incongruent item, whereas the similar and low/dissimilar category statements were combined to form a congruent item.

Associated with each description, then, were four types of trials, resulting from the fact that incongruent or congruent items could occur on either probability or similarity trials. To illustrate, consider the following sufficient description: "Linda was a philosophy major. She is bright and concerned about issues of discrimination and social justice and has participated in anti-nuclear demonstrations." The congruent and incongruent categories used with this description are given here (the same items were seen on both probability and similarity trials):

Congruent	*Incongruent*
Professional activist	Professional activist
versus	versus
Radio sportscaster	Bankteller

Procedure

Except for the specific materials, the procedure for Experiment 2 was identical to that of Experiment 1. Subjects saw all four trial types associated with each description, for a total of 64 trials (16 descriptions by 4 trials per description). Trials were presented randomly, with the constraint that the same description was separated by at least eight intervening trials.

Subjects

Thirty University of Michigan students were paid for their participation in the study.

Results and Discussion

Trials on which RTs exceeded individual subject means by more than three standard deviations were excluded from the subsequent analyses.[4] Mean error rates for sufficient and insufficient description trials are shown in Table 1.3. As before, the data are broken down by whether the criterion was probability or similarity, and whether the similarity and base-rate information were congruent or incongruent. In

---

[4]By this criterion, 36 of 1,920 or 1.9% of the trials were removed.

addition, the sufficiency of the description is also a factor. If the sufficient-description hypothesis is correct, then for trials with sufficient descriptions we would expect patterns of error rates and response times very much like those in Experiment 1, whereas for the insufficient trials the error rates and response times should be roughly equal for the congruent and incongruent items. The data in Table 1.3 clearly support these predictions of the sufficient-description hypothesis.

An ANOVA on the error rates for sufficient descriptions revealed significantly higher rates for probability than similarity trials $[F(1,29) = 35.88, p < .01]$ and for incongruent than congruent items $[F(1,29) = 6.38, p < .05]$. The interaction between these two factors was also significant $[F(1,29) = 4.57, p < .05]$. Thus, the error rates for sufficient trials strongly support the hypothesized intrusion effects. A comparable ANOVA on the error rates for the insufficient descriptions again shows that the error rates were higher on probability than similarity trials $[F(1,29) = 23.11, p < .01]$. However, the error rates were only marginally higher for incongruent than for congruent items $[F(1,29) = 3.16, p = .09]$ and the critical interaction between the two factors was not significant $(F < 1)$.

The mean RTs for sufficient and insufficient description trials are presented in Table 1.4.[5] An ANOVA on sufficient descriptions revealed that RTs were longer on probability than similarity trials $[F(1,28) = 77.64, p < .01]$ and longer for incongruent than congruent items $[F(1,28) = 6.01, p < .05]$. The interaction effect was also highly significant $[F(1,28) = 15.70, p < .01]$. This pattern of mean RTs is precisely as predicted by the obligatoriness of similarity.

For insufficient descriptions, the pattern of RTs is quite different. Although RTs were still longer for probability than similarity trials $[F(1,29) = 17.04, p < 01]$, there was no overall effect of congruent versus incongruent items $[F(1,29) = 1.50, p = .23]$, and no interaction between criterion and item type $(F < 1, n.s.)$.

---

[5]Before being submitted to statistical analyses, the RTs were adjusted for unwanted variation in similarity differences and relative base rates between pairs of categories making up the experimental items. Ratings of similarity differences and relative base-rates were provided by an independent group of 15 subjects.

TABLE 1.3
Mean Error Rates in Experiment 2 as a Function of Criterion (Probability vs. Similarity) and Congruence of Base-Rate and Similarity Information

a) *Sufficient Descriptions*

	Congruent	*Incongruent*	*Mean*
Probability trials	.098	.230	.164
Similarity trials	.008	.025	.017
Mean	.053	.127	

b) *Insufficient Descriptions*

	Congruent	*Incongruent*	*Mean*
Probability trials	.080	.139	.109
Similarity trials	.008	.034	.021
Mean	.044	.086	

TABLE 1.4
Mean Response Times in Experiment 2 as a Function of Criterion (Probability vs. Similarity) and Congruence of Base-Rate and Similarity Information

a) *Sufficient Descriptions*

	Congruent	Incongruent	Mean
Probability trials	2,073	2,530	2,301
Similarity trials	1,544	1,519	1,531
	1,808	2,024	

b) *Insufficient Descriptions*

	Congruent	Incongruent	Mean
Probability trials	2,380	2,220	2,300
Similarity trials	1,905	1,854	1,880
	2,142	2,037	

Note. One subject was removed from the analysis of sufficient items because he provided no correct responses in the probability-congruent cell.

The results of Experiment 2 strongly support the idea that intrusions of similarity on frequency-based judgments will occur when the descriptions are rich enough so as to activate specific categories. However, when the personality descriptions are insufficient to elicit such categories, no intrusion effects are observed.

GENERAL DISCUSSION

Summary

By employing a variation of the traditional Stroop paradigm, we have shown that similarity information can intrude upon the use of base-rate or frequency information in judgments of probability. The patterns of response times and error rates in Experiments 1 and 2 reveal the facilitating and interfering effects of early arriving similarity information. Taken together, these results provide evidence for the idea that at least certain kinds of similarity computations are obligatory. The results of Experiment 2 suggest that the critical kinds of computations are those in which a prestored category is activated by a sufficiently rich description. A topic for future research is identifying other possible triggering conditions for obligatoriness. For example, are there cases in which even insufficient descriptions will lead to obligatory similarity computations?

With regard to the typical studies of the representativeness heuristic (e.g., Tversky & Kahneman, 1983), it has been argued that people disregard more formalistic, probability-based information in favor of similarity, because computations of the latter are in some sense easier or more natural. We now have partly unpacked this notion of "naturalness"; assessments of similarity are natural, in part, because they occur spontaneously in the presence of certain triggering conditions and because the results of such computations are readily accessible. In contrast, computations of base rates or more complicated Bayesian probabilities presumably are not obligatory and therefore require additional effort. Under these circumstances, then, it is not surprising that individuals rely heavily on similarity information when making "probability" judgments.

There is, however, more to naturalness than obligatoriness and speed. If we identify naturalness with automaticity, then another property of automatic processes is that they require relatively little attentional capacity. We expect to focus on the reduced attentional requirements of automatic processes in future research. That is, to the extent that similarity-based judgments are relatively more automatic than probability-based judgments, we should expect that subjects should be more successful on similarity trials than probability trials in attending to some secondary task requiring attentional resources.

Educational Implications

In closing, we briefly describe several implications of our findings for learning and education. The first and most obvious implication of our results is that students, even college-level ones, may continue to use similarity as a reasoning strategy even when it is inappropriate, simply because they cannot stop the strategy and hence cannot stop its output from entering consciousness. This kind of difficulty is easiest to envision for situations involving simple probabilistic inference tasks, along the lines of the types of problems we have used in our experiments. When information is present that allows for quick and easy similarity assessments, the outputs of such assessments might be used regardless of their normative value. Similarity-based reasoning can likely occur in any domain, however, and certainly there are reports of it in domains as disparate as medicine (Travis et al., 1989) and school psychology (Burns, 1990).

Given the prevalence of the similarity strategy, the question arises of how an instructor can best offset a student's reliance on it. One possibility is to try and automatize competing strategies that may be more appropriate for the domain. The importance of automatizing procedures that are initially effortful has been recognized by educational researchers (see, e.g., Hasselbring, Goin, & Bransford, 1988; Pellegrino & Goldman, 1987; Samuels, 1988). Carnine (1989) described a set of practice activities designed to enhance the automation of certain types of procedures. He gave as examples of automatized responses "the answer to 9 + 7, the sound that the letter m represents, or the name of a country on a map" (p. 603). Although the procedures to be "automatized" in the typical problems encountered in statistical reasoning may not be as simple as "9 + 7 = 16," it is still quite possible that people can be trained to the point where, when faced with a certain type of probability problem, they will recognize the need to determine such things as base rates or set/subset relationships. In their discussion of the development of automaticity, Shiffrin and Dumais (1981) emphasized that, with the exception of a few general principles, "little is known about the limits of automatism" (p. 130).

Likewise, the potential of training to automaticity in statistical reasoning seems relatively untapped. For example, in the context of our work, extensive practice with base-rate computations might increase the relative automaticity of such computations, making these computations faster and, consequently, less susceptible to intrusion by similarity information.[6]

Even in situations where training on competing heuristics does not lead to automating these heuristics, the training can reduce reliance on simplifying heuristics such as representativeness. This has been demonstrated in a number of recent studies. For example, Agnoli and Krantz (1989) showed that adults can be trained to represent probability problems in terms of Venn diagrams, which helps them to not succumb to the representativeness heuristic. Agnoli and Krantz described these training effects in a general framework that fits very well with the approach we have taken here:

> From our perspective, which we label the competing-heuristic framework, even if natural assessments are made automatically and strongly influence probability judgment, they nonetheless compete with other problem-solving strategies. Thus, strengthening alternative strategies by training in the classroom, the laboratory, or by practical experience ought to affect probability judgments. (p. 519)

Agnoli (1991) extended this work to show that such training is effective even for grade school-aged children.

Training in statistical reasoning has also been shown to be effective by Nisbett and his colleagues (Fong, Krantz, & Nisbett, 1986; Nisbett, Fong, Lehman, & Cheng, 1987; Nisbett, Krantz, Jepson, & Kunda, 1983). These authors have shown that training can increase the use of "statistical heuristics" (e.g., an intuitive version of the law of large numbers) in everyday reasoning problems. They found beneficial effects of both short-term training of subjects in the laboratory context and long-term training, such as that received by graduate students in psychology. Thus, the potential of training students to use more formal

---

[6]In fact, for Stroop-like stimuli, practice on the color-naming task has been shown to lead to a reverse Stroop effect, where the ink color can interfere with word reading (see MacLeod, 1991). It remains to be seen whether analogous effects will obtain with the base-rate/similarity tasks.

reasoning procedures instead of (or in addition to) simple heuristics seems promising.

Finally, we note that construing similarity assessment as an automatic, almost primitive process has additional implications as it relates to the cognitive effort required in reasoning. For example, Fagley (1988) noted that "one of the principles that seems to be followed in cognition is that strategies reducing mental effort are preferred" (p. 314). In this vein, automatic heuristics like similarity offer a path of least resistance in that they are simple, indeed, nearly effortless to carry out.

This idea is related to work on cognitive effort in judgment and choice (e.g., Bettman, Johnson, & Payne, 1990; Payne, Bettman, & Johnson, 1990). Work by these researchers suggests that, other things being equal, decision makers tend to choose strategies that minimize the mental effort involved. We might expect this to be particularly true when there is a stressor involved, such as time pressure. For example, with the experimental tasks discussed in the chapter, reliance on the similarity heuristic might be greater under time pressure (e.g., when using a deadline procedure in which the subject is required to respond within a specified amount of time), thereby leading to even stronger intrusion effects. Tendencies (deliberate or otherwise) toward minimization of effort may lead to greater reliance on simpler (i.e., less cognitively effortful) strategies, which may be suboptimal for the particular problem situation. Again, in such situations, prior training of more appropriate strategies to automatic stature may be a partial solution.

By way of conclusion, we have attempted to show in this chapter that reasoning by similarity is an automatic thinking strategy. Even when trained in more formal (statistical) reasoning procedures, people still simultaneously engage in similarity-based reasoning. Although it is still unclear how the results for our specific materials generalize to the types of problems students typically encounter, we have suggested some educational implications of the work. In particular, we have focused on notions of automaticity in education and research specific to training in statistical/probabilistic reasoning. The concept of automatic strategies in reasoning seems relatively untapped, and may offer a useful way to talk about what the student brings to new learning situations.

ACKNOWLEDGMENTS

This research was supported by Air Force Contract No. AFOSR-92-0265 to Smith and a National Science Foundation Graduate Fellowship to Biolsi. We are indebted to John Jonides for his helpful suggestions about the research.

REFERENCES

Agnoli, F. (1991). Development of judgmental heuristics and logical reasoning: Training counteracts the representativeness heuristic. *Cognitive Development, 6*, 195–217.

Agnoli, F., & Krantz, D. H. (1989). Suppressing natural heuristics by formal instruction: The case of the conjunction fallacy. *Cognitive Psychology, 21*, 515–550.

Bettman, J. R., Johnson, E. J., & Payne, J. W. (1990). A componential analysis of cognitive effort in choice. *Organizational Behavior and Human Decision Processes, 45*, 111–139.

Burns, C. W. (1990). Judgment theory and school psychology. *Journal of School Psychology, 28*, 343–349.

Carnine, D. (1989). Designing practice activities. *Journal of Learning Disabilities, 22*, 603–607.

Dawes, R. M. (1986). Representative thinking in clinical judgment. *Clinical Psychology Review, 6*, 425–441.

Fagley, N. S. (1988). Judgmental heuristics: Implications for the decision making of school psychologists. *School Psychology Review, 17*, 311–321.

Fong, G. T., Krantz, D. H., & Nisbett, R. E. (1986). The effects of statistical training on thinking about everyday problems. *Cognitive Psychology, 18*, 253–292.

Garner, R. (1990). When children and adults do not use learning strategies: Toward a theory of settings. *Review of Educational Research, 60*, 517–529.

Grice, H. P. (1975). Logic and conversation. In D. Davidson & G. Harman (Eds.), *The logic of grammar* (pp. 64–75). Encino, CA: Dickenson.

Hasselbring, T., Goin, L., & Bransford, J. (1988). Developing math automaticity in learning handicapped children: The role of computerized drill and practice. *Focus on Exceptional Children,* 20(6), 1–15.

Jacobs, J. E., & Potenza, M. (1991). The use of judgment heuristics to make social and object decisions: A developmental perspective. *Child Development, 62,* 166–178.

Kahneman, D., Slovic, P., & Tversky, A. (Eds.). (1982). *Judgment under uncertainty: Heuristics and biases.* New York: Cambridge University Press.

Kahneman, D., & Tversky, A. (1972). Subjective probability: A judgment of representativeness. *Cognitive Psychology, 3,* 430–454.

Lin, Y.-G., McKeachie, W. J., Wernander, M., & Hedegard, J. (1970). The relationship between student-teacher compatibility of cognitive structure and student performance. *Psychological Record, 20,* 513–522.

MacLeod, C. M. (1991). Half a century of research on the Stroop effect: An integrative review. *Psychological Bulletin, 109,* 163–203.

McKeachie, W. J. (1980a). Implications of cognitive psychology for college teaching. In W. J. McKeachie (Ed.), *New directions for teaching and learning: Learning, cognition, and college teaching* (pp. 85–93). San Francisco: Jossey-Bass.

McKeachie, W. J. (1980b). Improving lectures by understanding students' information processing. In W. J. McKeachie (Ed.), *New directions for teaching and learning: Learning, cognition, and college teaching* (pp. 25–35). San Francisco: Jossey-Bass.

McKeachie, W. J., Pintrich, P. R., & Lin, Y.-G. (1985a). Learning to learn. In G. d'Ydewalle (Ed.), *Cognition, information processing, and motivation* (pp. 601–618). Amsterdam: Elsevier.

McKeachie, W. J., Pintrich, P. R., & Lin, Y.-G. (1985b). Teaching learning strategies. *Educational Psychologist, 20,* 153–160.

McKeachie, W. J., Pintrich, P. R., Lin, Y.-G., Smith, D. A. F., & Sharma, R. (1990). *Teaching and learning in the college classroom: A review of the research literature* (2nd ed.). Ann Arbor, MI: The Regents of the University of Michigan, National Center for Research to Improve Postsecondary Teaching and Learning.

Naveh-Benjamin, M., McKeachie, W. J., & Lin, Y.-G. (1989). Use of the ordered-tree technique to assess students' initial knowledge and conceptual learning. *Teaching of Psychology, 16,* 182–187.

Naveh-Benjamin, M., McKeachie, W. J., Lin, Y.-G., & Tucker, D. G. (1986). Inferring students' cognitive structures and their development using the "ordered tree technique." *Journal of Educational Psychology, 78,* 130–140.

Nisbett, R. E., Fong, G. T., Lehman, D. R., & Cheng, P. W. (1987). Teaching reasoning. *Science, 238,* 625–631.

Nisbett, R. E., Krantz, D. H., Jepson, C., & Kunda, Z. (1983). The use of statistical heuristics in everyday inductive reasoning. *Psychological Review, 90,* 339–363.

Nisbett, R. E., & Ross, L. (1980). *Human inference: Strategies and shortcomings of social judgments.* Englewood Cliffs, NJ: Prentice-Hall.

Payne, J. W., Bettman, J. R., & Johnson, E. J. (1990). The adaptive decision maker: Effort and accuracy in choice. In R. M. Hogarth (Ed.), *Insights in decision making* (pp. 129–153). Chicago: University of Chicago Press.

Pellegrino, J. W., & Goldman, S. R. (1987). Information processing and elementary mathematics. *Journal of Learning Disabilities, 20,* 23–32.

Pintrich, P. R., McKeachie, W. J., & Lin, Y.-G. (1987). Teaching a course in learning to learn. *Teaching of Psychology, 14,* 81–86.

Saks, M. J., & Kidd, R. F. (1986). Human information processing and adjudication: Trial by heuristics. In H. R. Arkes & K. R. Hammond (Eds.), *Judgment and decision making* (pp. 213–242). New York: Cambridge University Press.

Samuels, S. J. (1988). Decoding and automaticity: Helping poor readers become automatic at word recognition. *Reading Teacher, 41,* 756–760.

Schneider, W., & Shiffrin, R. M. (1977). Controlled and automatic processing: I. Detection, search, and attention. *Psychological Review, 84,* 1-66.

Shafir, E. B., Smith, E. E., & Osherson, D. N. (1990). Typicality and reasoning fallacies. *Memory & Cognition, 18,* 229–239.

Shiffrin, R. M., & Dumais, S. T. (1981). The development of automatism. In J. R. Anderson (Ed.), *Cognitive skills and their acquisition* (pp. 111–140). Hillsdale, NJ: Lawrence Erlbaum Associates.

Shiffrin, R. M., & Schneider, W. (1977). Controlled and automatic human information processing: II. Perceptual learning, automatic attending, and a general theory. *Psychological Review, 84,* 127–190.

Stroop, J. R. (1935). Studies in interference in serial verbal reactions. *Journal of Experimental Psychology, 18,* 643–662.

Travis, C. B., Phillippi, R. H., & Tonn, B. E. (1989). Judgment heuristics and medical decisions. *Patient Education & Counseling, 13,* 211–220.

Tversky, A., & Kahneman, D. (1983). Extensional versus intuitive reasoning: The conjunction fallacy in probability judgment. *Psychological Review, 90,* 293–315.

2

Problem Solving, Transfer, and Thinking

Scott W. VanderStoep
Colleen M. Seifert
University of Michigan

OVERVIEW

The essence of a critical thinker is not simply the acquisition of knowledge, but the application of knowledge across time and circumstance. Many studies have shown that students often have difficulty abstracting a principle from examples, encoding information into flexible memory representations, and accessing the appropriate principle in new problem contexts. How can we help learners maximize potential use of what they have learned?

This chapter reviews literature in cognitive and educational psychology on problem solving, transfer, and critical thinking. In the first section, we review research on schema induction and analogical transfer. We review factors found to affect people's ability to solve problems by analogy. In the second section, we examine the extent to which certain cognitive skills are domain-general, and can therefore be applied in many different contexts. In the third section, we present an overview of three experiments that attempt to facilitate learning and transfer in a problem-solving context. We see these experiments as one way to illustrate the instructional implications of the research on problem solving and transfer. Although the studies were conducted in the laboratory, we think the results have implications for instruction. We appreciate the opportunity to present these studies in this volume honoring Bill McKeachie. We feel it appropriate to present our work in this volume because of the assistance he gave us in developing the experiments, in particular, and also because of his positive influence on our professional lives, in general.

The experiments we report in this chapter are the result of many conversations we had with Bill over the last couple of years. The conversations were focused broadly on the question: "So why don't students transfer more in the classroom?". Bill's work has been largely devoted to understanding the correlates of effective thinking and transfer. Bill's approach to teaching has always been that a teacher must make it clear to the learner why it is important to learn something, and when the information might be useful in the future. We tried to test this idea experimentally in these studies. Our data are largely consistent with this intuition. Thus, we are excited about the chance to report the findings here, given that Bill played such an integral role in the idea's inception. This is our "thank you" for all of those enjoyable and stimulating conversations!

We conclude the chapter with a discussion of ways in which learning and thinking skills can be taught in classroom settings. Teaching-thinking programs provide the best example of a classroom application of the research on transfer. Bill has been influential and innovative in the development of a teaching-thinking program for college students. We describe the program he initiated (and continues to be active with) at the University of Michigan. This program represents one of many ways in which Bill's teaching and research have bridged the gap between the laboratory and the classroom, defining new paradigms for studying "cognition in the wild"—actual classroom learning.

SCHEMA INDUCTION AND ANALOGICAL TRANSFER

Research in cognitive psychology has devoted significant attention to the study of analogical transfer. Solving problems by analogy involves recognizing the higher order relationships that exist between two domains, even though the two domains share very few similar surface features or characteristics (Gentner, 1983, 1989).

The work by Gick and Holyoak (1980, 1983) and others introduced the modern paradigm of analogical transfer. In their experiments, Gick and Holyoak (1980, 1983) presented subjects with the following story:

A small country was ruled from a strong fortress by a dictator. The fortress was situated in the middle of the country, surrounded by farms and villages. Many roads led to the fortress through the countryside. A rebel general vowed to capture the fortress. The general knew that an attack by his entire army would capture the fortress. He gathered his army at the head of one of the roads, ready to launch a full-scale direct attack. However, the general then learned that the dictator had planted mines on each of the roads. The mines were set so that small bodies of men could pass over them safely, since the dictator needed to move his troops and workers to and from the fortress. However, any large force would detonate the mines. Not only would this blow up the road, but it would also destroy many neighboring villages. It therefore seemed impossible to capture the fortress.

However, the general devised a simple plan. He divided his army into small groups and dispatched each group to the head of a different road. When all was ready he gave the signal and each group marched down a different road. Each group continued down its road to the fortress so that the entire army arrived together at the fortress at the same time. In this way, the general captured the fortress and overthrew the dictator.

Gick and Holyoak (1980, 1983) referred to the general's plan as the "convergence solution," because it spreads a large amount of force (troops) over several paths (roads) from multiple directions, and these forces converge simultaneously. After subjects read the "General story," they were presented with Duncker's (1945) "radiation problem":

Suppose you are a doctor faced with a patient who has a malignant tumor in his stomach. It is impossible to operate on the patient, but unless the tumor is destroyed the patient will die. There is a kind of ray that can be used to destroy the tumor. If the rays reach the tumor all at once at a sufficiently high intensity, the tumor will be destroyed. Unfortunately, at this intensity the healthy tissue that the rays pass through on the way to the tumor will also be destroyed. At lower intensities the rays are harmless to healthy tissue, but they will not affect the tumor either. What type of procedure might be used to destroy the tumor with the rays, and at the same time avoid destroying the healthy tissue?

Early experiments examined subjects' ability to access the solution-relevant information to solve the radiation problem (pre-hint condition). That is, were subjects able to recognize the relationship between the analog and the target problem? If subjects were unable to recognize the solution, they were given a "hint" to use the information from the General's solution to solve the problem. They found that subjects had a higher solution rate after they were given a hint than before they were given a hint. This suggests that subjects had encoded the information in a usable fashion, but were unable to access it, perhaps because they failed to see the relevance of the General story to the radiation problem. This inability to use previous knowledge to solve novel problems is known as the *transfer problem* in cognitive psychology. These transfer failures often seem surprising because the relatedness of the previous knowledge and the novel problem appears intuitively obvious.

Other experiments have also indicated that transfer is often difficult to achieve (e.g., Gick & Holyoak, 1983) or may be somewhat ephemeral or context dependent (Spencer & Weisberg, 1986). A variety of factors have been found to affect people's ability to transfer. We provide here a summary of several of the factors shown to affect analogical transfer. These factors can affect different thinking processes: *access* and *use*. Access refers to the ability to recognize the relevant similarities between the example analog and the target problem, and use refers to the ability to apply the relevant principle to the particular problem.

One factor found to affect transfer is the number of example analogs a learner studies. Transfer rates were higher when subjects were exposed to multiple examples prior to solving a target problem than when subjects were exposed to only one example. Gick and Holyoak (1983) showed that subjects who read two story analogs produced a higher pre-hint solution rate than subjects who read one story analog plus a disanalogous control story. Gick and Holyoak concluded that two examples are necessary for abstracting the appropriate solution schema (schema induction). When subjects had represented the basic principle of the analog(s) (e.g., multiple forces of small intensity converging simultaneously), they were more likely to transfer this principle to the radiation problem. When subjects were given a summary statement of the solution principle with two analogs, the spontaneous transfer rate was even higher than the transfer rate of two analogs without a summary statement of the principle (Gick & Holyoak, 1983). This improvement in spontaneous transfer was not often found after subjects were given the "hint" to use the General story. The fact that the differences between the transfer rates between the one-analog and two-analog conditions diminished after the hint was given suggests that being exposed to two examples enhances the memory access of solution-relevant information, but it has less effect on subjects' ability to use the information.

Second, a positive relationship has been found between the quality of the schema induced by the subjects (as measured by the extent to which subjects were able to identify solution-relevant similarities between the story and the target problem) and the solution rate, again suggesting that schema induction is critical in facilitating analogical transfer (Gick & Holyoak, 1983).

Third, transfer was more likely when learners were asked to compare examples in terms of their solution-relevant features. Catrambone and Holyoak (1989) found that two analogs facilitated analogical transfer only when subjects were given an explicit instruction to compare how the two stories were similar, thereby facilitating schema induction. Similarly, Dellarosa (1985) found that subjects who were asked to answer questions that facilitated problem comparison performed better at sorting mathematics problems in terms of structural features than those who did not answer such questions. Reed (1987) also found that the correlation between subjects' ability to match corresponding concepts of two algebra problems and problem-solving performance was .77. Dellarosa's (1985) question-asking and Reed's (1987) matching task are similar to the comparison manipulation of Catrambone and Holyoak (1989). These studies used learning activities that appear to foster greater understanding of the underlying principle(s).

Perhaps this kind of problem comparison is more likely to result in what Salomon and Perkins (1989) called "mindful abstraction." Mindful abstraction is necessary for what they refer to as "high-road transfer." High-road transfer involves the effortful use of learned material in a new situation, the "decontextualization of a principle" (p. 126). This is in contrast to "low-road transfer," which is use of an acquired skill in a similar situation. The essence of low-road transfer is when learned material is introduced in a variety of learning situations until it becomes fairly automatic, and then a transfer situation is introduced that is similar to one or more of the learning situations, and the material is used properly in this relatively similar circumstance.

Fourth, similarity among problems has been found to affect transfer (Anderson, 1987; Gentner, 1983, 1989; Hammond, Seifert, & Gray, 1991; Holyoak & Koh, 1987; Seifert & Gray, 1990). Thorndike and Woodworth (1901) concluded that the degree to which two domains shared "identical elements" determined the extent to which transfer occurred. Modern approaches to studying problem solving also consider similarity to be a crucial determinant; for example, Anderson's (1987) production-system model (ACT*) predicts that transfer will occur to the extent that two tasks involve similar productions. Supporting this notion, Seifert and Gray (1990) found that spontaneous transfer is more frequent if learners' representations of the analog are more similar to the solution-relevant features that are needed to solve the target problems.

Most of the work on similarity and transfer has made a distinction between two types of features: superficial and structural. In the problem-solving context, superficial features are aspects of the problem that are not relevant to the solution principle, such as the story line of the problem (e.g., a story about a general) and the objects described in the problem (e.g., roads, fortress). Structural features are aspects that are essential to solving the problem, such as the formula, procedure, or algorithm used to solve the problem. An example problem and target problem are superficially similar if they are similar in story line, objects, or some other irrelevant feature. They are structurally similar if the same solution procedure can be applied to both problems to solve them successfully.

Holyoak and Koh (1987) varied both the surface and structural features of the test problem, and found that both types of similarity between the story analogs and test problem affected spontaneous transfer (access). A test problem that had high surface similarity with the story analog had a higher solution rate than a test problem with low surface similarity. Also, a test problem that had high structural similarity with the story analog had a higher solution rate than a test problem with low structural similarity. However, after the hint was given about the relevance of the previous knowledge to the current problem (use), transfer was affected only by structural features.

Gentner's (1983, 1989) research shows that access to past examples sharing superficial similarities occurs more frequently than access based on structural similarities. That is, even though people may judge structural similarity to be important in making analogies, memory access to the material is often influenced by superficial features (Gentner & Landers, 1985). Furthermore, superficial features may affect retrieval prior to (or independent of) the effect of structural features (Hammond et al., 1991). Hammond et al. found that when superficial similarity was preserved while all identifiable structural similarity was removed, retrieval based on available superficial features still occurred, suggesting that retrieval based on superficial features may act alone in accessing prior knowledge.

Ross (1984) demonstrated that the similarity between examples plays a major role in problem solving as well, particularly in novices. He showed that when learners were reminded of an earlier problem that was solved (successfully) with a similar formula, performance was higher on a test problem than when learners were reminded of an earlier problem that involved a different formula. Learners seemed likely to rely on superficial similarity between earlier problems and current test problems when trying to solve problems.

Ross (1987, 1989) also showed that a more detailed understanding of superficial similarity is necessary. He distinguished between two types of superficial similarity: story-line similarity and object correspondences. These have differential effects on (a) memory access and (b) formula use. Using probability problems, he found that when the story lines of the example problem and test problem were similar, *memory access* was affected. So, when subjects had an example problem and a test problem that shared a similar story line (e.g., subjects studied a practice problem about IBM and solved a test problem about IBM as well), greater access to the formula used in the example occurred than when an example problem and a test problem had different story lines (e.g., subjects studied a practice problem about IBM and solved a test problem about a golf tournament). However, story-line similarity had little effect on formula use.

In contrast, when the object correspondences (i.e., whether objects referred to in the problem were used in the same way in each problem) of the example and test problem were similar, *formula use* was affected. So, subjects who were given an example and a test problem that had similar object correspondences (e.g., people being assigned to objects in both the example and test problem) used the formula correctly more often than when the object correspondences were reversed in the example and test problems (e.g., people being assigned to objects in the example problem and objects being assigned to people in the test problem). However, this reversal of object correspondences had little or no affect on memory access. The important point this research makes is that problem solving involves several cognitive processes, and these processes may be affected in different ways by different factors. We return to this distinction when we discuss our empirical studies.

To summarize, novice learners seem to be affected by superficial similarity when they solve problems. Learners will often base their decisions about how to solve a problem on features that are not relevant to the solution. Because novices are not aware of what features of problems are important, they must rely on whatever features are most salient and accessible, which often happen to be superficial features.

The major implication of this research for understanding transfer is that people do not access previous knowledge to help them solve novel problems as frequently as they could. Furthermore, work on superficial similarity suggests that when people do get reminded of previous problems, it is not always for the "right" reasons. The fact that transfer is difficult to achieve may suggest an important role for instruction in facilitating transfer. Specifically, how can instruction be designed to decrease the reliance on superficial similarity and other features of problems that are not relevant to understanding the solution principles? We return to this issue when we discuss our empirical studies. Next, we discuss the issue of transfer more broadly, specifically, by examining the extent to which basic cognitive skills are domain-independent.

GENERALITY OF PROBLEM-SOLVING SKILL

Are people's cognitive skills limited to the contexts in which they were acquired, or can they be used in a variety of situations? Evidence that problem-solving skills are, in fact, domain-independent would offer hope that education can play a role in facilitating transfer. In contrast, if skills are bound to the context in which they are learned, then it is not likely that transferable skills can be taught. The contrast seems to be between teaching specific content knowledge or teaching transferable skills or, as Perkins and Salomon (1989) have said, "educating memories versus educating minds" (p. 23). (For other reviews on skill generality, see Larkin, 1989 and Perkins & Salomon, 1989.)

The question addressed in this section is whether the knowledge used to solve problems can be represented in memory at a level of abstraction that is domain-general. Those who take a domain-general view would argue that knowledge can be represented in a fashion such that it can be used in a variety of different contexts and domains. Those who take a domain-specific view would argue that knowledge is largely limited to the domain in which it was learned, and that it is unlikely that skills from one domain will be used in another domain. Empirical attempts to answer the question appeared early in psychology (e.g., Thorndike & Woodworth, 1901). Thorndike and Woodworth found that improvement in one skill domain as a result of training in another skill domain occurred only if the two domains shared similar features (i.e., "identical elements"). This research contradicted the idea of formal discipline, which stated that training the mind by studying disciplines like mathematics was beneficial to improving all aspects of human thinking (see Nisbett, Fong, Lehman, & Cheng, 1987).

Early work in problem solving in cognitive psychology and artificial intelligence posited a domain-general view of cognitive skill acquisition. This work was predicated on the notion that problems could be solved with effective general strategies and heuristics (e.g., Newell & Simon, 1972). In this approach, solving a problem is seen as a process of moving from an original state, in which the solution to a problem is not apparent, to an end (solution) state. General strategies and heuristics serve as the mechanisms by which problems are solved. In this paradigm, content knowledge of the particular domain is less important than applying these general strategies effectively.

More recently, Cheng and colleagues (Cheng & Holyoak, 1985; Cheng, Holyoak, Nisbett, & Oliver, 1986) found evidence that some types of rule-based reasoning are domain-independent. They found that people use neither completely specific knowledge nor completely domain-independent rules, but instead use "pragmatic reasoning schemas." These reasoning schemas are developed as a function of everyday-life experiences, and are defined in terms of goals for understanding events such as permission, obligation, and causation. As people experience everyday phenomena, such as events involving causation, their pragmatic reasoning schemas become more sophisticated. For example, with respect to understanding causation, people's ability to understand what is necessary to infer causation becomes more complete and refined as they experience situations involving causation. Cheng and colleagues found that purely abstract training in deductive reasoning did little to improve deductive reasoning performance, unless examples were also provided. However, training based on pragmatic reasoning schemas such as permission did improve subjects' deductive reasoning performance. These rules could be applied in different content domains. This research provides evidence that thinking in one domain can transfer to another. Similarly, Smith, Langston, and Nisbett (1992) argued that people use abstract rules in several areas of human reasoning, and put forth a hybrid model of human thinking containing both rule-based and instance-based mechanisms.

For the past several years, Nisbett, Fong, and their colleagues have examined people's ability to reason about everyday-life events using knowledge of statistical and methodological principles. They argue that people possess an inferential rule system that is similar to the statistical notion of the law of large numbers (Nisbett, Krantz, Jepson, & Kunda, 1983). (The law of large numbers refers to the fact that as a sample becomes larger, it more accurately estimates the population parameter. Thus, the more times an event takes place—for instance a baseball team playing baseball games—the more likely it is that the outcome of that event truly reflects the population parameter—whether or not the baseball team is a good team.) Nisbett and others argued quite convincingly that this rule system is domain-independent, and that it can be applied to a variety of content domains.

Fong, Krantz, and Nisbett (1986), for example, found that training in the law of large numbers improved subjects' ability to reason using that statistical principle. When subjects were given examples of applications of the law of large numbers, subjects were able to abstract the general principle underlying the concept and apply the law of large numbers to several other content domains. This experimental training has been shown to persist over time delays of up to two weeks (Fong & Nisbett, 1991).

Undergraduate and graduate training has also been found to have an effect on statistical and methodological reasoning. Students who had taken an undergraduate statistics course used statistical principles to reason about everyday life events more often. Lehman, Lempert, and Nisbett (1988) studied the effects of graduate-school training on statistical and methodological reasoning. To study methodological reasoning they examined students' ability to reason about evidence from real-life scenarios in light of methodological concerns. For example, Lehman et al. studied graduate students' ability to understand concepts such as spurious correlations and the lack of an appropriate control group as they occur in real-life situations. They studied first-year and third-year graduate students in law, medicine, chemistry, and psychology. They employed both longitudinal and cross-sectional designs, and tested subjects' statistical and methodological reasoning as well as formal logical reasoning (e.g., if p then q). They found that students in medicine and psychology showed significant improvement in both statistical and methodological reasoning from the first to the third year of graduate school. Law students improved significantly in logical reasoning. Training in chemistry did not improve performance in any of the three domains. Lehman et al. (1988) concluded that different graduate disciplines foster the use of certain inferential rule systems—for example the law of large numbers—and that training in other disciplines (e.g., chemistry) does not require the use of these schemas and thus does not lead to improvement in these types of reasoning.

Lehman and Nisbett (1990) studied the effects of undergraduate education on students' statistical and methodological reasoning. They gave students real-life problems and measured the extent to which they used statistical or methodological reasoning in their answers. Subjects answered these questions at the beginning of their first year and the end of their fourth year of college. They found that social science majors showed large improvement in statistical and methodological reasoning from first year to fourth year. Humanities and natural science majors showed smaller but still significant improvement. In addition, natural science and humanities majors, unlike social science majors, showed large improvement in formal logic.

In summary, the research by Fong, Nisbett and their colleagues shows that (a) people possess an inferential rule system that employs knowledge of statistical and methodological principles, (b) people can reason about everyday-life problems using this knowledge, (c) this ability is domain-independent and can be applied in a range of contents, and (d) this ability can be improved by training.

Another set of skills that has been consistently shown to operate at a high level of domain-generality is the metacognitive components of learning (Larkin, 1989; Sternberg, 1986). These skills are often referred to as *self-regulative activities* (Zimmerman, 1989) and include both cognitive components such as comprehension monitoring and motivational components such as goal setting (see also, McKeachie, Pintrich, & Lin, 1985; Pintrich, McKeachie, & Lin, 1987). Similarly, Naveh-Benjamin and Lin (this volume) studied the ability of students to think "flexibly" about course topics. Cognitive flexibility is also thought to be a skill that can be employed in a variety of different domains.

However, other work has been less sanguine about the generality of cognitive skills. In particular, many educational researchers are now putting forth the notion of *situated cognition,* which posits that knowledge acquisition is a function of the "activity, context, and culture in which it is developed and used" (Brown, Collins, & Duguid, 1989, p. 32). This approach places greater emphasis on tasks and contexts as important factors in understanding human learning. This is in contrast to traditional cognitive theories that tend to emphasize the role of people's mental representations, and search for universal laws of human information processing. The rationale for viewing cognition as bound to culture and contexts is in part motivated by frequent failures to transfer in cognitive research (as discussed in the first section) and a general contention that cognitive theories have not sufficiently informed educational practice. Research on similarity, problem representation, memory access or other components discussed by cognitive psychologists do little to help understand or improve school learning. As Brown et al. (1989) forcefully contend: " . . . educational practice is the victim of an inadequate epistemology. A new epistemology might hold the key to a dramatic improvement in learning and a completely new perspective on education" (p. 41).

Thus, the research on the generality of cognitive skills is mixed. The work by Nisbett and colleagues (e.g., Nisbett et al., 1987) argues for generality in thinking. This research perhaps represents the best evidence that people can transfer knowledge to a variety of contexts. Cheng and Holyoak (1985) also showed that pragmatic reasoning schemas can be applied to a variety of content domains These two lines of research suggest that people can use rules or knowledge in a variety of contexts. On the other hand, the work by Brown et al. (1989) and others points out the failure of cognitive theories to account for contextual factors in knowledge acquisition. They argue that the generality of cognitive skills is more limited than what has been previously believed.

What should be concluded from the work on skill generality? We argue that either extreme position is insufficient to explain human learning. A domain-general approach to learning and transfer is inadequate because of research that highlights failures to transfer. On the other hand, a domain-specific approach makes generalizations about learning and transfer difficult to construct; developing theories of learning, thinking, and problem solving will be difficult if one considers only the role of activity, contexts, and culture. Clearly contextual factors affect knowledge acquisition, but so do general learning strategies such as self-regulation, metacognition, and certain domain-general thinking mechanisms. More helpful, we feel, is what we call *learning to transfer*. Learning to transfer can be understood as learning to identify what types of information, rules, or strategies are relevant across different learning situations. For example, a student may have learned some declarative knowledge in a particular content domain, but the student is going to be unlikely to transfer that knowledge to a new situation unless she/he can identify when and why that information might be useful again.

We discuss this idea of learning to transfer in the next two sections. First, we describe three experimental studies that examined the effect of teaching learners how to identify when knowledge might be relevant. In the final section, we describe McKeachie's teaching-thinking program. This is an excellent working example of a learning-to-transfer approach.

THREE EMPIRICAL STUDIES: LEARNING "HOW" VERSUS LEARNING "WHEN"

In this section we present an overview of three experimental studies on learning to transfer (VanderStoep & Seifert, 1993). Our original research question was: How do people recognize how to solve a novel problem when more than one principle may be applicable? We hypothesized that if people are learning principles that appear very *similar* to each other, they will need instructional information about the conditions under which each principle applies, and why a principle should be applied in those situations (what we call *applicability instructions*). In other words, learners need to know which principle applies to different types of problems. However, if people are learning principles that are very distinct from each other, information about the conditions under which each principle applies will not be needed. In this case, when problems are distinguishable based simply on the format, content, or structure, it is not necessary to provide learners with information about when and why each principle applies to different situations. Learners will be able to determine which principle to use based simply on obvious characteristics of the problem they are trying to solve, and additional instructional information will not be helpful. We tested the extent to which instructional differences facilitated problem solving in a series of studies.

In our first experiment, subjects studied two of three principles of elementary probability theory: combinations, permutations, or conditional probability. Subjects in the *similar* condition learned combinations and permutations. Combinations and permutations are similar in the kinds of problems to which they apply and how those problems are worded. Subjects in the *distinct* condition learned combinations and conditional probability. Combinations and conditional probability can be distinguished easily from one another based solely on differences in what the problems ask for and how the problems are worded. All subjects received instruction at the beginning of the experiment on each of the two principles. This included a statement of the principle, the formula, an example problem, and a detailed explanation of its solution. After the subjects studied the formulas, half of the subjects in each of the conditions received a review of how to solve the problems (procedural review). The other half of the subjects received information about when and why each principle should be applied (applicability instructions). Subjects were then given test problems to solve.

Results showed that subjects who studied the distinct problem pair solved more problems correctly than those who studied the similar problem pair. With respect to the instructional manipulation, for the distinct pair, as expected, there was no difference between the procedural-review and the applicability-instructions conditions. For the similar pair, the procedural-review and applicability-instructions conditions also did not differ in terms of the number of problems they solved correctly. However, in the similar pair, those who received applicability instructions made *fewer* confusion errors (i.e., solved a combinations problem with a permutations formula or vice versa) than those who received procedural-review instructions.

The first experiment suggests that problem solving involves several cognitive steps. First, learners must *identify* which rule or procedure (in this case, a mathematical formula) they should use to solve a particular problem. Second, they must *access* the specific contents of that formula correctly from memory. Third, they must correctly *apply* the formula to the current problem. Given that subjects in the applicability-instructions condition made fewer errors than those in the procedural-review condition, but did not solve more problems correctly, it appears that the applicability instructions may have an effect on the first stage of the problem-solving process—identifying the appropriate formula—but may not affect memory access or the ability to apply the formula.

This hypothesis was tested explicitly in our second experiment in which we asked subjects to identify the proper formula for each test problem, but did not require them to solve the problems. The results showed no difference between applicability instructions and procedural review for the distinct pair, but for the similar pair, subjects who received the applicability instructions correctly identified the formula marginally more often than subjects who received procedural review.

The second experiment provides more direct evidence that teaching learners the applicability conditions of a principle improves problem solving at the level of improving the ability to *identify* the appropriate solution procedure (the first step in the problem-solving process). However, providing applicability instructions does not appear to affect the performance at the level of *accessing* the contents of formula or *applying* the formula correctly to the present problem.

We conducted a third experiment to replicate the finding of the second experiment, and also to test whether the differences between procedural review and applicability instructions were due to the information subjects received or the way in which they received it. In the first two experiments, the procedural-review instructions were presented to subjects on two separate study sheets, whereas the applicability instructions were presented on one study sheet. It may be that if learners are allowed to study the information on one study sheet, they perhaps may be more likely to form an integrated representation and to induce the differences between combinations and permutations on their own. This was tested by creating two different procedural-review conditions. In the *separate-review* condition, subjects received the review information in the same way as they did in the first two experiments. In the *combined-review* condition, subjects were given the same information as separate-review, but it appeared on one study sheet. If subjects are able to induce the differences between the two principles, and by doing so improve their ability to recognize when the principles should be used, then the combined-review condition should do better than separate-review. The applicability-instructions condition was the same as the first two experiments. Only the similar problem pair was used in this experiment. Two (orthogonal) contrasts indicated that (a) the applicability condition identified the appropriate formula significantly more often than the two review conditions and (b) the review conditions were not different from one another. This suggests that it is important for the instructional material to include the important information about when to apply the principles, because learners are unlikely to induce the important distinctions on their own. This replicates the main finding from the previous two experiments: Learning applicability conditions improves the first stage of problem-solving process (identification), but has no effect on the final two stages of access and application.

Taken together these three experiments suggest one way in which transfer to novel problems can be improved. Specifically, if learners are taught the applicability conditions of the principles they are studying, their ability to recognize when to use the principles is improved. However, it appears unlikely that teaching applicability conditions improves learners' memory for the content of the formula or their ability to instantiate the formula to a problem. In fact, when learners were asked to recall the formulas, at the end of the experiment there was no difference between the two instructional conditions. Apparently, teaching applicability conditions helps learners just in the first phase of the problem-solving process—identifying which formula is relevant to a particular problem.

Although it may seem intuitively obvious that teaching applicability conditions will be helpful, it may not always be the case that instruction is designed like this. For example, in a probability textbook permutations might be taught in one section and then combinations taught in the next section. Students could become proficient at solving the two different types of problems; however, without explicit instruction on when to apply each principle, learners may have little knowledge of when each should be applied.

As another example, consider the different methods of integration taught in calculus. Textbook sections devote attention to different ways functions can be integrated. Students likely will solve problems using the integration-by-parts method, integration by substitution, and certain "rules" for integrating specific trigonometric functions. However, without adequate knowledge of when to apply each of these different procedures, students will have difficulty applying the different methods to new problems.

As a final example, consider a pre-service student teacher taking educational psychology. She receives instruction on, among other things, how students learn most effectively, how and why students are motivated, how individual differences play a role in classroom behavior, how to manage her classroom, and how to discipline problem behavior. What is potentially lacking from this student's repertoire of knowledge is information about when and where these different pieces of knowledge are relevant. The student has been given lots of rules and heuristics, but they will not help her be a better teacher unless she receives training about when, where, and how to apply these rules. In general, instruction on the applicability conditions of the knowledge, rules, strategies, and skills students learn during school should be an essential part of the instruction they receive.

Future research in this area would seem most interesting in one of two general areas. First, the generality of the instructional method—teaching applicability conditions—is not known. Did we simply hit upon a content domain (probability problems) that is particularly amenable to this instructional approach? Or, is the distinction we make between learning "how" and learning "when" a robust and theoretically interesting one? Our hunch is that the how-versus-when distinction is relevant to other content domains (cf. Paris, Lipson, & Wixson, 1983).

Second, the generality of the problem-solving process—identification, access, application—is not known. It is possible that mathematical problem solving is the only content domain in which these particular cognitive operations occur in this fashion. However, it may be that problem solving in other domains such as social science problem solving occurs similarly. Related to this idea, there is an implicit assumption in this work that these cognitive operations occur serially. Empirical research or cognitive modeling taking a parallel-processing approach may provide a different perspective from which to understand how instruction is affecting the cognitive operations involved in problem solving and transfer.

TEACHING STUDENTS HOW TO THINK

Several programs have been developed for teaching thinking skills to students. These interventions represent one way in which the experimental research on transfer has been used as a basis for designing instruction. We present two examples of thinking-skills programs, one designed for middle school-aged children and the other for college students. (For more extensive reviews of several other successful programs, see Bransford, Sherwood, Vye, & Reiser, 1986; Glaser, 1984; and Polson & Jeffries, 1985).

First, Nickerson and colleagues (Herrnstein, Nickerson, de Sanchez, & Swets 1986; see also Nickerson, Perkins, & Smith, 1985) designed a thinking-skills course for seventh-grade students in Venezuela. The five-component course taught students fundamental principles in five broad cognitive domains: foundations of general reasoning, verbal reasoning, problem-solving strategies, decision making, and inventive thinking (creativity). Fifty-six different lessons were taught. Researchers assessed students on previously validated tests of general cognitive ability (e.g., General Abilities Test). They also constructed their own test (Target Abilities Test—TAT) to assess improvement on the processes they attempted to teach in their course. They found significant gains for the experimental classrooms that used the thinking-skills course compared to control classrooms that did not. The largest effect was the improvement the experimental students showed on the TAT. Even though the experimental group had higher pretest means on four of the five components of the TAT, the effect sizes showed significant improvement for the experimental group over the control group. This research provides evidence that general higher-order skills can be taught via traditional instructional means and that the improvements in performance can be quite large.

Second, McKeachie and colleagues designed a thinking-skills course (called *Learning to Learn*) for college students at the University of Michigan (McKeachie et al., 1985; Pintrich et al., 1987). The course introduces students to basic concepts in cognitive and motivational psychology, and teaches them how these concepts can be used to improve their own learning in college. Students who have taken the course have shown significant improvement in their study habits and moderate improvement in their achievement in subsequent college courses. McKeachie and colleagues have found that students who are high in anxiety about learning have been helped the most by taking the course (McKeachie et al., 1985).

This course differs from traditional "study-skills" courses. Study-skills courses typically provide students with a variety of techniques to improve their memory and other skills. The Learning to Learn course offers students these tips as well, but also covers several basic concepts in psychology such as attention, memory, problem solving, decision making, and motivation. The purpose of this approach is first to give students a rationale for the study strategies discussed in the course. It is thought that if students have elementary knowledge of the information-processing system, then their understanding of how best to use their cognitive skills will be increased. Furthermore, it is hoped students will understand that different approaches to learning and studying are appropriate under different circumstances. This understanding is what has been referred to as *conditional knowledge:* knowledge of when to apply particular cognitive strategies (e.g., Paris et al., 1983). The goal is for students to understand that the cognitive strategies they employ should differ as a function of their goals, the time available to them, and the nature of the course. As was stated earlier, the course has been found to be effective in improving students' future use of study strategies. Recently, VanderStoep (1992) found that students who took Learning to Learn showed significant improvement from the beginning to the end of the course in their statistical and methodological reasoning about real-life events. This suggests that students were developing thinking and reasoning skills they could apply in nonschool domains.

People's beliefs about the efficacy of teaching-thinking programs have often centered around a debate as to whether thinking should be taught in the disciplines or whether thinking-skills courses should be taught apart from any particular course content. We believe that both teaching thinking in the curriculum and as a separate course can be effective, although each may serve different purposes. We have just shown two examples of how general skills training can be effective. However, each discipline has its own approach to addressing problems, interpreting and analyzing evidence, and presenting findings. Modeling how professionals in the particular disciplines think about problems is a way to teach students how to approach problems, handle evidence, and present findings in that discipline. This kind of domain thinking cannot be taught very effectively in a general-skills course. At its best, teaching thinking in the disciplines can foster the appropriate critical thinking skills needed to be successful in a particular domain. At the same time, however, general thinking skills such as planning, monitoring, goal setting, memory strategies, elaboration strategies, and general problem-solving methods also can serve a valuable role in the development of students' critical thinking. General thinking skills cannot replace teaching thinking in the disciplines. However, it is also unlikely that content courses in the disciplines will have the time or resources to teach domain-general thinking strategies, which we view as equally valuable. We encourage both efforts to teach students to think.

As in many other areas, Bill McKeachie has been a leader in the area of teaching thinking. We estimate that almost 1,500 Michigan students have taken his Learning to Learn course since its inception in 1982. That number continues to grow, as he continues to teach Learning to Learn as a "retired" professor. Ten years ago, the phrase "Learning to Learn" was not part of the vocabulary of those who were interested in student cognition and motivation. Today, thanks largely to McKeachie's contribution, this phrase has become more common. His approach to teaching students how to learn and think has given the new generation of researcher-educators a firm ground on which to conduct our research and to teach our students. He has set a demanding standard for all of us interested in cognition and instruction, in the way that he has integrated the study of how people think with the techniques to help them do so.

REFERENCES

Anderson, J. R. (1987). Skill acquisition: Compilation of weak-method problem solutions. *Psychological Review, 94,* 192–210.

Bransford, J., Sherwood, R., Vye, N., & Reiser, J. (1986). Teaching thinking and problem solving. *American Psychologist, 41,* 1078–1089.

Brown, J. S., Collins, A., & Duguid, P. (1989). Situated cognition and the culture of learning. *Educational Researcher, 18,* 32–42.

Catrambone, R., & Holyoak, K. J. (1989). Overcoming contextual limitations on problem-solving transfer. *Journal of Experimental Psychology: Learning, Memory, and Cognition, 15,* 1147–1156.

Cheng, P. W., & Holyoak, K. J. (1985). Pragmatic reasoning schemas. *Cognitive Psychology, 17,* 391–416.

Cheng, P. W., Holyoak, K. J., Nisbett, R. E., & Oliver, L. M. (1986). Pragmatic versus syntactic approaches to training deductive reasoning. *Cognitive Psychology, 18,* 293–328.

Dellarosa, D. (1985). Abstraction of problem-type schemata through problem comparison (Tech. Rep. No. 146). Boulder: University of Colorado, Institute of Cognitive Science.

Duncker, K. (1945). On problem solving. *Psychological Monographs, 58* (Whole No. 270).

Fong, G. T., Krantz, D. H., & Nisbett, R. E. (1986). The effects of statistical training on thinking about everyday problems. *Cognitive Psychology, 18,* 253–292.

Fong, G. T., & Nisbett, R. E. (1991). Immediate and delayed transfer of training effects in statistical reasoning. *Journal of Experimental Psychology: General, 120,* 34–45.

Gentner, D. (1983). Structure-mapping: A theoretical framework for analogy. *Cognitive Science, 7,* 155–170.

Gentner, D. (1989). The mechanisms of analogical transfer. In S. Vosniadou & A. Ortony (Eds.), *Similarity and analogical reasoning* (pp. 199–241). Cambridge: Cambridge University Press.

Gentner, D., & Landers, R. (1985). Analogical reminding: A good match is hard to find. *Proceedings of the International Conference on Cybernetics and Society* (pp. 607–613), Tucson, AZ.

Gick, M. L., & Holyoak, K. J. (1980). Analogical problem solving. *Cognitive Psychology, 12*, 306–355.

Gick, M. L., & Holyoak, K. J. (1983). Schema induction and analogical transfer. *Cognitive Psychology, 15*, 1–38.

Glaser, R. (1984). Education and thinking: The role of knowledge. *American Psychologist, 39*, 93–104.

Hammond, K. J., Seifert, C. M., & Gray, K. C. (1991). Functionality in analogical transfer: A hard match is good to find. *Journal of the Learning Sciences, 1*, 111–152.

Herrnstein, R. J., Nickerson, R. S., de Sanchez, M., & Swets, J. A. (1986). Teaching thinking skills. *American Psychologist, 41*, 1279–1289.

Holyoak, K. J., & Koh, K. (1987). Surface and structural similarity in analogical transfer. *Memory and Cognition, 15*, 332–340.

Larkin, J. H. (1989). What kind of knowledge transfers? In L. B. Resnick (Ed.), *Knowing, learning, and instruction: Essays in honor of Robert Glaser* (pp. 283–305). Hillsdale, NJ: Lawrence Erlbaum Associates.

Lehman, D. R., Lempert, R. O., & Nisbett, R. E. (1988). The effects of graduate training on reasoning: Formal discipline and the thinking about everyday-life events. *American Psychologist, 43*, 431–442.

Lehman, D. R., & Nisbett, R. E. (1990). A longitudinal study of the effects of undergraduate training on reasoning. *Developmental Psychology, 26*, 952–960.

McKeachie, W. J., Pintrich, P. R., & Lin, Y.-G. (1985). Teaching learning strategies. *Educational Psychologist, 20*, 153–160.

Newell, A., & Simon, H. A. (1972). *Human problem solving*. Englewood Cliffs, NJ: Prentice-Hall.

Nickerson, R. S., Perkins, D., & Smith, E. E. (1985). *The teaching of thinking*. Hillsdale, NJ: Lawrence Erlbaum Associates.

Nisbett, R. E., Fong, G. T., Lehman, D. R., & Cheng, P. W. (1987). Teaching reasoning. *Science, 238,* 625–631.

Nisbett, R. E., Krantz, D. H., Jepson, C., & Kunda, Z. (1983). The use of statistical heuristics in everyday inductive reasoning. *Psychological Review, 90,* 339–363.

Paris, S. G., Lipson, M. Y., & Wixson, K. K. (1983). Becoming a strategic reader. *Contemporary Educational Psychology, 8,* 293–316.

Perkins, D. N., & Salomon, G. (1989). Are cognitive skills context bound? *Educational Researcher, 18,* 16–25.

Pintrich, P. R., McKeachie, W. J., & Lin, Y.-G. (1987). Teaching a course in learning to learn. *Teaching of Psychology, 14,* 81–86.

Polson, P. G., & Jeffries, R. (1985). Instruction in general problem-solving skills: An analysis of four approaches. In J. W. Segal, S. F. Chipman, & R. Glaser (Eds.), *Thinking and learning skills Vol. 1: Relating research to practice* (pp. 417–455). Hillsdale, NJ: Lawrence Erlbaum Associates.

Reed, S. K. (1987). A structure-mapping model for word problems. *Journal of Experimental Psychology: Learning, Memory, and Cognition, 13,* 124–139.

Ross, B. H. (1984). Remindings and their effects in learning a cognitive skill. *Cognitive Psychology, 16,* 371–416.

Ross, B. H. (1987). This is like that: The use of earlier problems and the separation of similarity effects. *Journal of Experimental Psychology: Learning, Memory, and Cognition, 13,* 629–639.

Ross, B. H. (1989). Distinguishing types of superficial similarities: Different effects on the access and use of earlier problems. *Journal of Experimental Psychology: Learning, Memory, and Cognition, 15,* 456–468.

Salomon, G., & Perkins, D. N. (1989). Rocky roads to transfer: Rethinking mechanisms of a neglected phenomenon. *Educational Psychologist, 24,* 113–142.

Seifert, C. M., & Gray, K. J. (1990). Representational issues in analogical transfer. *Proceedings of the Twelfth Annual Cognitive Science Society* (pp. 30–37). Hillsdale, NJ: Lawrence Erlbaum Associates.

Smith, E. E., Langston, C., & Nisbett, R. E. (1992). The case for reasoning by rules. *Cognitive Science, 16,* 1–40.

Spencer, R. M., & Weisberg, R. W. (1986). Is analogy sufficient to facilitate transfer during problem solving. *Memory and Cognition, 14,* 442–449.

Sternberg, R. J. (1986). *The triarchic mind: A new theory of human intelligence.* New York: Penguin Press.

Thorndike, E. L., & Woodworth, R. S. (1901). The influence of improvement in one mental function upon the efficiency of other functions. *Psychological Review, 8,* 247–261, 384–395, 553–564.

VanderStoep, S. W. (1992, August). Effects of a learning and thinking skills course on everyday reasoning and problem solving. In W. J. McKeachie (Chair), *Learning, thinking, and problem solving—Issues in teaching and transfer.* Symposium conducted at the meeting of the American Psychological Association, Washington, DC.

VanderStoep, S. W., & Seifert, C. M. (1993). Learning "how" versus learning "when": Improving transfer of problem-solving principles. *Journal of Learning Sciences, 3,* 93–111.

Zimmerman, B. J. (1989). A social-cognitive view of self-regulated academic learning. *Journal of Educational Psychology, 81,* 329–339.

3

Measuring and Improving Students' Disciplinary Knowledge Structures

Moshe Naveh-Benjamin
Ben-Gurion University of the Negev, Israel

Yi-Guang Lin
University of Michigan

This chapter features background information relevant to the assessment of students' cognitive structures. Two new methods of assessment are presented, followed by a report of a series of studies that embody the implementation of these methods. Finally, practical suggestions, focusing on the application of the methods in classroom situations, are discussed. Having insights about college student learning, using assessment techniques to empirically investigate these insights, and applying the results to improve college student learning and teaching, all characterize Bill McKeachie's distinguished career. This chapter, like many others in this book, is based on research that Bill encouraged, and actively participated in.

BACKGROUND

One of the major goals of college education is teaching the content of a course in such a way that students can see relationships among concepts and facts. Instructors hope that students will develop conceptual structures that will enable them to remember and apply the facts and theories learned and that will establish a solid basis for continued learning. In recent years, educational and instructional psychologists have emphasized the importance of meaningful learning (Ausubel, 1963, 1968; Greeno, 1980). The main focus is on the question of how students organize and represent knowledge and the role of students' cognitive structures in learning. It is generally agreed that cognitive structure or knowledge structure may be considered as an organized mental configuration of knowledge stored in a learner's memory (Ausubel, 1963; Ausubel, Novak, & Hanesian, 1978; Shavelson, 1974). As a hypothetical construct, cognitive structure refers to the organization of different kinds of knowledge and information in long-term memory (Shavelson, 1972). We use the terms *cognitive structure* and *knowledge structure* interchangeably.

Although cognitive structure is an internal representation of conceptual structure, it is nevertheless a "student's public understanding of a discipline" (Shavelson, 1983, p. 81). It is public in the sense that the cognitive structure can be inferred and described by objective measures and compared with some objective criteria.

The purpose of assessment is to reveal and infer a representation of the subject's cognitive structure. Based on the assessment procedure employed, the techniques can be classified into two categories: indirect and direct. The indirect approaches require two procedures: data gathering and scaling. For data gathering, these techniques first use key concepts to present a task to subjects for their responses; they then score or transform subjects' responses into proximity or distance measures as an indication of the relationships between the stimuli or key concepts. Scaling methods are used to yield the representation of cognitive structures from the distance matrices. Several such methods were used in the past, including word association, card sorting, interviews, preference judgments, and similarity ratings (see McKeachie, Pintrich, Lin, Smith, & Sharma,1990, pp. 15–26). Results of studies using these methods (e.g., Geeslin & Shavelson,1975; Shavelson, 1972) indicated developments in students' cognitive structures during learning periods.

In the direct approaches, subjects are asked to arrange key concepts and propositions and to construct some kind of spatial diagram or hierarchical structure to indicate the relationships among the key concepts and propositions as well as the overall framework or structure of the text material and passage. The spatial diagrams produced by the subjects may be considered representations of subjects' cognitive structures. Among the methods used were tree construction, graph building, and concept mapping. These methods were able to capture cognitive structures in various academic disciplines (e.g., Donald, 1983) and yield meaningful representations of students' cognitive structures (e.g., Champagne, Hoz, & Klopfer, 1984; Novak & Gowin, 1984; Shavelson & Stanton, 1975).

OUR RESEARCH

Measurement

Problems with previous methods

Although these studies add to our understanding of structural changes as a result of learning subject matter, Naveh-Benjamin, McKeachie, Lin, and Tucker (1986) addressed issues that were not settled. First, many of the studies (especially those using the indirect methods) transform the data into distance matrices in which the analysis is already removed several steps from the original data and can miss some regularities in the data because of the averaging techniques used. Second, some of these studies (again, mostly those using indirect methods) provide only one measure of structure development—the distance of a student from a standard structure (usually the instructors' structure). Distance alone may not be very helpful in diagnosing a student's problems in learning. Third, in many of the methods the tasks performed by the students involve retrieving the concepts themselves. Reliance of the task on such retrieval processes might obscure the underlying cognitive structure. Fourth, many of the techniques do not reveal dynamic properties of the structure and most provide only static structures without indications of the processes that serve as the basis for their use. Finally, many of the studies use a relatively small amount of information, such as a chapter from a book or a short instructional period.

In trying to solve some of these problems, we have used a modification of the "ordered-tree" technique introduced by Reitman and Rueter (1980) as an indirect method to infer students' cognitive structures. Later we devised a fill-in-the-structure technique as a direct method to infer students' structures (Naveh-Benjamin, Lin, & McKeachie, 1994). The latter provides easy-to-score quantitative and qualitative characteristics of a student's structure. In the following sections we describe each of these methods and then provide a sample of studies in which we have used them.

The "Ordered-Tree" Technique (an indirect method)

Description

This technique is based on a theory of mental organization that assumes that single concepts or sets of concepts are mentally organized into a hierarchy whose lowest level terminal nodes represent single concepts and higher level nodes represent more abstract categories or concepts. The technique capitalizes on people's tendency to list all items in one chunk of information before moving on to the next chunk. From a set of cued and uncued trials, an algorithm efficiently finds the set of all chunks for each subject and represents this set as an ordered tree, that represents a subject's knowledge structure from a course.

This technique solves some of the problems raised about previous techniques. First, it is more faithful to the original data than other techniques because it does not use averaging procedures to create distance matrices. Second, it enables us to derive several different measures of the cognitive structure, including the amount of organization in a given cognitive structure, the similarity between the instructor's knowledge structure and students' structures, and order information, which can be used to infer the traversal rules along the structure used by the students. Finally, the task is fairly easy to use and can be administered to groups of subjects.

Task

The administration of the task varied slightly from one study to another (e.g., number of concepts used, which varied between 16 and 20). We describe here a prototypical way of administering the task.

The knowledge structure task is presented to each of the students in a test booklet with four pages. Each page has the same set of concepts chosen by the staff members of the course as important concepts representing the major content areas covered in the course. (An example of an instructor's cognitive structure, which includes the concepts used in a Psychology of Aging class, appears in Fig. 3.1). The concepts appear in columns; vertical blanks are provided on the right side of the page where students list the concepts. The order of the concepts in the columns is different on each page to avoid the effects of response set.

Students are asked to arrange the concepts vertically in such a way that concepts closely related in terms of their meaning in the course appear close to each other. They are alternating between two cued trials (in which they are told to start with a specific concept) and two uncued

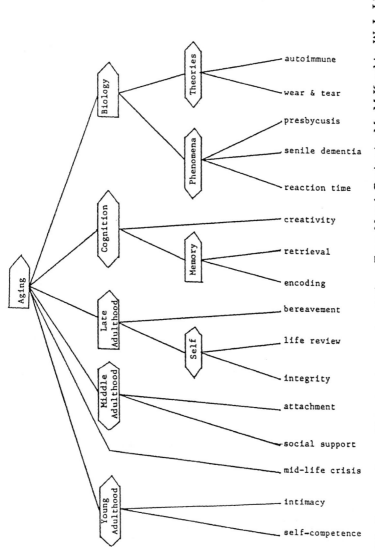

FIG. 3.1. Instructor's cognitive structure representation. From Naveh-Benjamin, M., McKeachie, W. J., Lin, Y.-G., & Tucker D. G. (1986). Inferring students' cognitive structures and their development using the "ordered tree technique." *Journal of Educational Psychology, 78*, 130–140. Copyright 1986 by the American Psychological Association. Reprinted by permission.

trials (in which they can start with any of the concepts) with periods of unrelated activity in between (for details see Naveh-Benjamin et al., 1986).

Measures

For each student, four measures can be extracted from this task:

1. *Amount of organization:* This measure, which is possible recall orders (PRO), is the natural logarithm of the number of different written orders that could contain its chunks. In general, the smaller the PRO, the more organized the structure (Reitman & Rueter, 1980).

2. *Depth:* Another measure of structure is the average hierarchical depth (number of levels in each chunk). *Depth* is defined as "the average number of nodes between root and terminal items" (McKeithen, Reitman, Rueter, & Hirtle, 1981, p. 311). Larger average depths would indicate more structure.

3. *Similarity:* This measure gives us an index of similarity of a student's structure to that of the instructor. It is defined by McKeithen et al. (1981) as the natural logarithm of the total number of chunks two trees have in common plus one, divided by the natural logarithm of the total number of chunks in both trees plus one. A high value on this measure indicates similarity in a student cognitive structure to the structure of the instructor.

4. *Directionality:* A cluster of concepts can be nondirectional, bidirectional, or unidirectional. A nondirectional cluster has three or more concepts that occur together consistently, but in no consistent order; in a bidirectional cluster the concepts are consistently ordered but the student may start from either end of the cluster; in a unidirectional cluster, the cluster is consistently traversed in a given direction. The directionality measure thus seems to indicate how a student is traversing his or her cognitive structure. (See Naveh-Benjamin et al., 1986, for details.)

The Fill-in-the-Structure Technique—FITS (a direct method)

Task

In this technique students receive the instructor's hierarchical graphic representation of course materials in which some of the concepts are missing from different parts of the representation. (See Fig. 3.2 for an example.) These concepts appear at the bottom of the page intermixed with distractor concepts. Students' task is to place the concepts in the appropriate position in the representation while marking down the order in which they use the concepts. Students usually need about 15 to 20 minutes to complete this task.

Measures

For each student, various measures can be extracted from this task, including the total number of concepts that are correctly filled in as well as more analytic measures, such as the number of concepts that are placed correctly at each of the levels of the hierarchy, and various types of errors that students make. In addition, the order in which the concepts are filled in can be used to infer the model that could describe how the student accesses the structure. Various models are possible here including top-down access, random access, and so on (see Yekovich & Thorndyke, 1981).

Let us elaborate on each of these measures:

1.   The total number (or percentage) of concepts that are correctly put in the appropriate place according to the instructor's structure. This measure provides an overall index of a student's cognitive structure similarity to that of the instructor.

2.   The number of concepts that are placed correctly at each of the levels of the hierarchy. These measures provide information about the similarity of each level of a student's structure (from the upper—more general, to the lower—more specific) to that of the instructor.

3.   The *order* in which the concepts are placed can be used to infer the model, which could describe students' access of the structure. This can be achieved by calculating, for each level of the hierarchy, the average ordering. Generally, smaller averages of orderings at the lower levels of the hierarchy relative to upper levels imply that students access their structure in a bottom-up fashion (from the specific to the more general concepts). In contrast, smaller averages of orderings at the upper levels of the hierarchy relative to the lower levels imply that students access their structure in a top-down fashion (from the general to the specific).

4.   A final group of measures can be obtained by looking at the *type of errors* that students committed. Two students could misplace the same number of concepts, but at different places in the structure. Several measures of both vertical and horizontal errors can be computed (for details, see Naveh-Benjamin, Lin, & McKeachie, 1994).

Characteristics of Cognitive Structures

In the following, we describe several studies that have used one of the described techniques. Although almost all studies were intended to

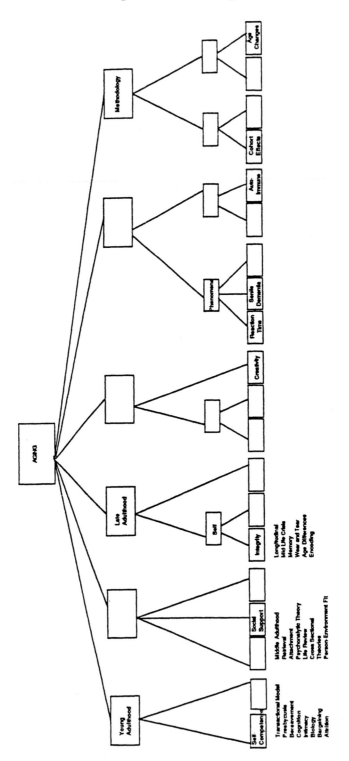

FIG. 3.2. Fill-in-the-structure task (FITS).

reveal students' cognitive structures in a given domain, each addressed a different question.

Study 1: Knowledge at the beginning of a course

To help students develop conceptual structures, instructors can benefit from information about the extent of the students' knowledge when they enroll in a course. We usually assume that students come to a new course with some prior knowledge. This level of knowledge at the beginning of a course, and especially the organization of that knowledge, is in many cases only assumed by the instructor. Each student's initial knowledge could be composed of accurate, relevant knowledge, reflecting what has been learned previously, as well as inaccurate knowledge, reflecting, among other things, stereotypes prevailing in our society. Having information about students' initial knowledge may enable the instructor to develop materials for the course, to improve organization of the different topics, and to dispel misconceptions or stereotypes.

We have used the ordered-tree technique to assess students' knowledge at the beginning of a Psychology of Aging course (Naveh-Benjamin, McKeachie, & Lin, 1989). One hundred nineteen students were asked to perform the ordered-tree task using 16 concepts in the first meeting of the course. Analysis of students' structures revealed little organization of the concepts. This finding is not surprising because students have not yet studied the material. As a result, they are not expected to see many relationships among concepts.

The question still remains about the type of relationships students perceive even at such an early stage of the course. Looking at students' organization at that time across all students in the class, enables one to identify some local organization based on three separate sources. First, these structures reflected some prior, general, common-language understanding of the relationships among the concepts. For example, *attachment* and *intimacy* tended to appear together, reflecting the fact that these two concepts are associated in everyday life. The initial structure also represented knowledge gained in previous psychology courses. This was illustrated by the frequency of the cluster containing *encoding* and *retrieval*, two concepts that appear together frequently in discussions of current cognitive psychology. The third type of knowledge represented by the initial structure was stereotypes students have about the subject matter. Their belief in steep decline during middle age (a decline not supported by evidence) was indicated by the cluster containing the concepts *mid-life crisis* and *wear and tear*.

To summarize, the use of this technique at the beginning of the course allowed us to assess the students' organization of the material, including areas of possible conflict with the instructor's organization.

Study 2: Development of knowledge throughout a course and its relationships to course performance

As with any other measuring instrument, we would like to evaluate its sensitivity. Within the context of measuring cognitive structures of students there are basically two important questions: One is whether the measures indicate some changes and development during a course. The other is the relationships between achievement of students in the course and their cognitive structures of the material. Some answers to these questions were obtained in a study in which we asked 154 students to perform the ordered-tree task three times—at the beginning of a course, in the middle of it, and at the end (Naveh-Benjamin et al., 1986).

First, we looked at whether there was a development during the course in measures of the cognitive structures of the students. Table 3.1 presents these results. Evidently there was an increase in the amount of organization in students' structures from the beginning to the end of the course (smaller PRO indicates more structure). In addition, there was an increase in the depth measure over the course, indicating an increase in the elaboration of the students' structures. Finally, the similarity index increased throughout the semester, indicating that students' structures became more similar to the instructor's as a result of learning.

Next, we looked at the relationships between measures of the cognitive structure and course performance. These correlations were positive, some of them (especially for the similarity measure, $r = 0.51$) reaching statistical significance. Such results indicate that all three measures of the cognitive structure capture aspects of students' knowledge of the subject matter. It should be noted that the correlations between the cognitive structure measures with performance on the final examination were lower than those with the final course grades, reflecting the fact that grades on term papers, assignments that usually require deeper knowledge, contributed to the correlation with the final course grades.

TABLE 3.1

Cognitive Structure Measures at Different Points in the Semester[1]

Period	N	PRO[2]		Depth		Similarity	
		Mean	SD	Mean	SD	Mean	SD
Beginning of course	119	26.22	12.27	1.15	.88	0.07	.11
Mid-term	85	23.98	11.22	1.27	.87	0.12	.13
End of course	82	22.35	10.96	1.26	.85	0.15	.15

[1]From Naveh-Benjamin, M., McKeachie, W. J., Lin, Y.-G., & Tucker D. G. (1986). Inferring students' cognitive structures and their development using the "ordered-tree technique." *Journal of Educational Psychology, 78,* 130–140. Copyright 1986 by the American Psychological Association. Reprinted by permission.

[2]The ranges of structure measure scores were: PRO, 0–44; Depth, 0–3.81; Similarity, 0–0.53.

We also looked at the combined effects of the PRO (amount of organization) and similarity measures in relation to course performance. Fig. 3.3 presents the multiple-choice scores in the final examination as a function of similarity and PRO measures. The results indicate that students with more highly organized structures do well if their structures are similar to the instructor's, but they do not do well if their structures are different. For the latter type of students, high organization could reflect a tendency toward repetition and stereotyping in their four productions of the concepts and not conceptual understanding. For students with low organization, similarity matters less. These students lack the necessary condition for matching the instructor's structure, namely a well-organized structure, to begin with.

The next issue studied was how the order of information in the structure can indicate the way in which students traverse the structure. To address this, we analyzed the directionality information provided by the algorithm. We looked at the direction of the major chunk (the outer chunk that includes all concepts) for several groups of students that differed on several standard course performance measures (Table 3.2). Generally, performance was the best for the unidirectional group and poorest for the nondirectional group. A t test compared the scores of students with an outer unidirectional chunk (indicating a more tight structure) with those with an outer bidirectional chunk. It showed that those with a unidirectional outer chunk had significantly higher scores on the take-home exam and the GPA. The same trend held for course grades. Similar results were obtained when the analysis was done on directionality of all chunks and not only the outer ones.

Next, we looked at the development of cognitive structure measures for students with different performance in the course. We divided the students into three groups: (a) those with A grades, (b) those with B grades, and (c) those with C and D grades. The results that are tabulated in Table 3.3 indicate that whereas the A students, and to a lesser extent the B students, gained on all measures of organization throughout the course, the C and D students either showed no change in the measures or a slight decrease. Results also show that the differences between the strong and the weak students develop throughout the course and are not a result of previous differences in knowledge structures. There were no initial differences between good and poor students on all measures (the trend even shows a slight advantage for the C and D students on the initial test).

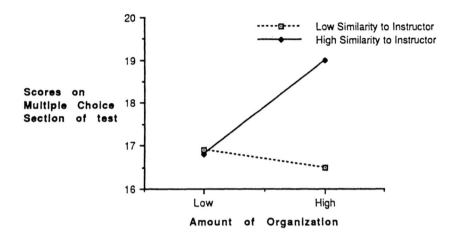

FIG. 3.3. The interaction of organization and similarity in affecting test scores.

Finally, in order to determine the usefulness of the ordered-tree technique in several academic disciplines, we assessed the development of cognitive structures created in several university courses (Naveh-Benjamin, Lin, & McKeachie, 1989). The three courses, chosen to represent courses from different fields (natural sciences, social sciences, and humanities), included a biology course, a psychology course, and an English course. There were 157 students involved in this study. All the subjects took the ordered-tree task twice, once at the beginning of the semester and once at the end of it.

Results indicate that the trends in both the amount of organization and the similarity measures were in the expected direction. There was an increase in both measures from the beginning to the end of the course, indicating that the cognitive structures of students developed in the amount of organization they contained throughout the course, and that these structures became more similar to that of the instructor as the course progressed.

TABLE 3.2

Take-Home Exam, Final Course Grade, and GPA Scores for Each of the Outer Chunk Type Groups

Type of Outer Chunk	Take-home Exam			Course Grade			GPA		
	N	Mean	SD	N	Mean	SD	N	Mean	SD
Unidirectional	21	72.7	10.2	21	3.22	.48	13	3.32	.31
Nondirectional	49	66.7	11.4	49	3.04	.51	25	3.09	.29

From Naveh-Benjamin, M., McKeachie, W. J., Lin, Y.-G., & Tucker D. G. (1986). Inferring students' cognitive structures and their development using the "ordered-tree technique." *Journal of Educational Psychology, 78,* 130–140. Copyright 1986 by the American Psychological Association. Reprinted by Permission.

TABLE 3.3
Development of Cognitive Structure for Students With Different Performance in the Course[1]

Students' Course Grade		PRO						Depth						Similarity					
		I		II		III		I		II		III		I		II		III	
Period[2]	N	Mean	SD	Mean	SD	Mean	SD	Mean	SD	Mean	SD	Mean	SD	Mean	SD	Mean	SD	Mean	SD
A	22	28.9	9.2	21.5	11.7	19.3	10.4	1.0	0.8	1.2	0.8	1.3	0.8	0.08	.11	0.16	.16	0.18	.16
B	42	25.9	12.5	24.7	10.6	23.3	11.1	1.1	0.8	1.3	0.9	1.3	0.9	0.07	.11	0.12	.13	0.16	.14
C+D	5	24.6	14.8	22.0	15.3	30.4	10.9	1.2	1.0	1.6	1.6	1.0	1.1	0.09	.18	0.10	.11	0.04	.09

[1]From Naveh-Benjamin, M., McKeachie, W. J., Lin, Y.-G., & Tucker D. G. (1986). Inferring students' cognitive structures and their development using the "ordered-tree technique." *Journal of Educational Psychology, 78,* 130–140. Copyright 1986 by the American Psychological Association. Reprinted by Permission.

[2] I—Beginning of semester
II—Middle of semester
III—End of semester

In addition, both the amount of organization and similarity measures were, as expected, positively related to course performance in the psychology and the biology courses (significantly so for the psychology course, $r = 0.55$ and 0.68, for the amount of organization and the similarity measures, respectively). Order information analyses indicated that in all three classes the proportion of nondirectional chunks decreased from the beginning to the end of the course, implying more systematic traversal of the structure as the courses progressed.

Nevertheless, there were some differences between the different courses. Whereas the biology and psychology courses revealed positive relationships between measures of cognitive structures and academic performance, the English literature course did not (it even showed a slightly negative relationship). A possible reason for that is that, whereas the courses in the natural and the social sciences were characterized by their instructors as disciplines consisting of sets of concepts and principles tied together in an organized fashion, the courses in composition or literature were characterized by their instructors not as disciplines but rather as interrelated sets of values or interests (see also Donald, 1983). These instructors tend to see their role as promoting students' growth, skill acquisition, or personal enrichment, rather than as teaching sets of interrelated concepts and principles (Stark et al., 1988).

To summarize, the answer to the two questions that we raised at the beginning of this section are clearly positive. First, the various measures of the ordered-tree task are sensitive to and develop during university course in several disciplines. Second, they are related to course performance.

Study 3: Assessment of course goals

Assessing students' knowledge organization at the end of the course could help instructors evaluate the course's outcomes in relation to their objectives. To make such an assessment, we asked 82 students (Naveh-Benjamin, McKeachie, & Lin, 1989) to perform the ordered-tree task, using 16 concepts, on the last day of a Psychology of Aging course.

We performed global evaluations of students' cognitive structures throughout the course. We did so by searching students' ordered-trees for clusters that reflected major aspects of the course in the instructor's cognitive structure (Fig. 3.1). These aspects included young, middle, and late adulthood as developmental aspects, and biology and cognition as topical aspects. A major aspect was considered to exist if there was at least one chunk in a student's tree that was identical to one of the instructor's chunks. Inspection of students' common clusters with the instructor revealed differences in the consolidation of knowledge about different facets of the course, both in terms of whether these facets were developed and when they developed. For example, students' structures at the end of the course revealed that they were aware of separate cognitive and biological aspects (topical facets), but their structures did not reflect as much the developmental facets (young adulthood, middle adulthood, and old age).

The dominance of the topical over the developmental dimension comes partly from the way the course was taught. Although the instructor intended to combine these two dimensions, in practice it proved difficult. For example, it was difficult to discuss cognition in young adulthood without comparing young adult cognition to that in middle and old ages. As a result, although intended to be presented from a combined topical-developmental perspective, the course actually presented each topic somewhat independently of a given stage of development.

Study 4: Knowledge and flexibility

This study goes a step further in this line of research. It evaluates the feasibility of unfolding another aspect of students' cognitive structures— their flexibility. Cognitive flexibility is defined as the number of available alternative strategies or processes in the learner's repertoire and the ability to select one or more of these alternatives to perform a task appropriately (Battig, 1979).

In this study (Naveh-Benjamin, Lin, McKeachie, & Neely, 1994) we assessed the degree to which students in a regular biology course developed alternative cognitive structures using the fill-in-the-structure (FITS) task. That is, we were interested in their ability to use different underlying dimensions when evaluating the relationships among various concepts in the course. In addition, we evaluated the relationships between course performance and flexible use of knowledge. Subjects were 30 students who took an ecology course at a comprehensive four-year university during the fall 1988 semester.

To measure flexibility, we asked the instructor of the course to devise two different hierarchical ways to represent important concepts in the course and their relationships to each other from two different points of view. Some of the concepts in each structure were common to the two structures while others were distinctive to each structure. Some of the common concepts appeared in different places in each of the two knowledge representations.

Students performed the FITS task twice in one class meeting held during the last week of the semester. They sequentially received the two instructor's hierarchical graphic representations of course materials (half of the class in one order and the other half in an opposite order), where some concepts were missing. There was an interval of about 20 minutes between the administration of the two structures. Students found the tasks meaningful and interesting.

For each student, a measure of flexibility that combines information from both structures was computed. The rationale for this index is that flexibility is best reflected not in the total amount of structured information that a student has but in the ability to see alternative relationships among concepts. This should be reflected particularly in correctly choosing common concepts; that is, those concepts that appear in both structures even though these concepts fit in different places in each structure, depending on the underlying dimension of the structure.

The analysis revealed reasonable range and spread of the flexibility score. In addition, there was a fairly high positive correlation between the flexibility measure and students' course performance ($r = 0.53$). This should be expected if part of students' grades is based on their ability to manipulate the information they study in a given course. The ability to perceive relationships flexibly is especially important in solving new problems related to the materials learned; that is, in transfer of the knowledge studied. It should be noted that when the effects of the total correct responses for each structure were partialled out, the flexibility measure still correlated positively with course grade ($r = 0.32$), implying their independent contributions to grade variance. This study adds to our previous studies on the assessment of students' cognitive structures, and it represents a first step in measuring flexibility of students' cognitive organization in a full-scale university course.

Use of Cognitive Structures as a Learning Tool

Study 5: Explicit teaching of structure

So far we have discussed and showed examples of using the techniques for assessment of student cognitive structure of course materials. The next study went a step further in this line of research by evaluating the use of the instructor's knowledge structure not only as an assessment tool for measuring students' organization of the materials but as *a teaching tool,* as well. Specifically, we assessed the effects of explicitly teaching students the knowledge structure of the instructor at the beginning of a given unit in the course. We looked at the effects on students' development of knowledge structure for this unit as well as for a consecutive unit. The hypothesis tested was that teaching, in advance, the instructor's organization scheme for a given unit would help students organize concepts in this unit. Furthermore, such explicit teaching of the instructor's structure could be assimilated into students' repertoire of cognitive skills as a structural schema to be used in guiding the structuring of materials in another unit. This should happen without any explicit guidance by the instructor.

Subjects were 72 students who took an introductory psychology course at a community college. They were divided into three groups, an experimental group and two control groups. Such a design allowed us to assess the net effects of explicitly teaching the instructor's cognitive structure, controlling for the amount of exposure to the tests in the two units. Two units in the course were chosen for the study. The first unit was on neuropsychology, and it dealt with physiological and biological aspects of behavior. The second unit was on personality, and it dealt with major theories and phenomena in personality. These units were studied consecutively around the middle of the semester and took about a week and a half each. At the beginning of Unit 1 (neuropsychology), the instructor presented students in the experimental section with his knowledge structure of the materials for this unit. This knowledge structure was presented as a hierarchical tree, relating major concepts in the unit to each other. The instructor went through the structure and explained the major concepts to be learned in the unit and their relationship to each other. Students in the two control groups did not receive this introduction. At the end of the unit, both the experimental and the first control group received a FITS task on this unit. The second unit (on personality) was taught uniformly in all groups without any reference to the knowledge structure of the materials. At the end of this unit, students in both the experimental and the two control groups were given, without warning, a FITS task on this unit.

Results indicate that the experimental group had a higher percentage correct on the total fill-in score for Unit 1, implying a better organization of the material (at least in relation to the instructor's organization) than the first control group. In addition, for Unit 2, the percentage of the total score was the highest for the experimental group, the next highest for the first control group, and lowest for the second control group. To summarize the results obtained, first, students who, at the beginning of a unit of studies, are explicitly taught the instructor's cognitive structure of that unit, show organization of materials at the end of the unit closer to that of their instructor. Second, such students tend to hierarchically organize materials learned in a different unit. These results are related to several reports in the literature about the effects of providing initial organization on learning (e.g., advance organizers, Ausubel, 1968).

To summarize, this series of studies shows that using the ordered-tree and the FITS techniques can increase our knowledge about students' organization of course materials at the beginning of a course and the development of this knowledge throughout courses in different disciplines. It also enables us to assess course goals and to measure flexibility in students' knowledge. Finally, we have shown that knowledge representation techniques can be used as learning tools to help students organize course materials.

Comparison of the Two Techniques

There are both similarities and differences between the two knowledge structures techniques. Both techniques use a notion of a knowledge structure represented as a group of concepts interrelated in a hierarchical fashion. In addition, both techniques provide several characteristics of student structure. These characteristics provide analytic tools for assessing student knowledge.

There are, however, some differences between the techniques. First, as mentioned earlier, the ordered-tree is an indirect method of inferring structure, because we learn indirectly about a subject's hierarchical structure from his or her orderings of concepts. The students are not necessarily aware of the hierarchical nature of the relationships. The FITS task, in contrast, is a direct technique where students are aware that they deal with hierarchical representation of the material. Second, the ordered-tree is less flexible in that it requires strict hierarchical relationships, whereas the FITS allows deviations from strict hierarchical relationships (e.g., two "parent" concepts can be both related to a mutual "sibling"). Third, in the ordered-tree technique the subject is less constrained by the type of relationships he or she may show, whereas in the fill-in-the-structure technique, the subject's responses are constrained by the graphic representation, which includes some predetermined relationships (those of the instructor). Finally, the ordered-tree task is more time consuming.

Limitations on the Use of the Two Techniques

While there are some limitations on the use of these techniques, most of these limitations are not unique to these techniques but rather characterize most of the techniques discussed at the beginning of this chapter.

First , there is the issue of the domain sampled. The domain of the assessed cognitive structure is defined and restricted by a limited number of key concepts (e.g., in the case of the ordered-tree, 14 to 20 concepts). Although the FITS technique allows the use of more concepts, the concepts used are usually only a subset of concepts in the whole area of the subject matter.

Second, there is the issue of choice of concepts. There is a question about the kind of concepts to be used in the tasks. The criteria for selecting the key concepts to describe the cognitive structure have not been always well defined. Although most studies usually choose key concepts for defining the domain of cognitive structure, the choice of these key concepts, which should vary in terms of their generality, is still a judgment task that needs to be further illuminated through research.

Finally, multiple representations of cognitive structures should be considered. We should recognize that there may be more than one way to represent cognitive structure (Shavelson, 1981). An individual's representation of cognitive structure constructed or inferred by any technique may be viewed as a representative structure or a dominant structure (Naveh-Benjamin et al., 1986). Multiple representations and the complexity and varieties of cognitive structure, therefore, cannot be adequately assessed or described by any single task or measure. The assessment-of-flexibility study was a step toward dealing with multiple representations.

PRACTICAL SUGGESTIONS

Assessment

Assessing students' initial knowledge to improve teaching and learning

We would like to encourage instructors to use either of the techniques at the beginning of their courses. In many cases college instruction, although guided by a general curriculum, is relatively insensitive to the prior knowledge that students bring with them to the course, especially of the subject matter to be learned in it. Using these techniques (among other instruments, such as quizzes or questionnaires) might provide the instructor with information about his or her students' backgrounds for the materials. The instructor may find that parts of the knowledge structure are well known to the students, so more attention can be paid to less well known parts. If biases and stereotypes show up, as happened in our first study reported previously, the instructor might pay special attention and dedicate more time to teaching the materials related to these stereotypes. While teaching, he or she could contrast these biased, initial relationships with more appropriate ones.

Assessing development of knowledge to evaluate and improve teaching and learning

The techniques enable us to follow the development of students' cognitive structures throughout a course. The methods show specific changes that occurred in different stages of the course. The techniques also captured the alignment of the students' structures with the instructor's structure. Gaining information about students' knowledge development at various points in a course could help instructors improve students' learning. For example, if parts of students' structures in midcourse do not correspond with the teacher's expectations, remedial measures could be taken, such as using review, further elaboration of relevant relations, or explicit reference to the instructor's knowledge structure.

Another valuable feature for teachers is the characteristic organization of students' overall knowledge at the end of the course. Teachers can use such information to assess the degree and the exact manner in which planned conceptual learning outcomes were achieved. If instructors find that their planned conceptual learning outcome were not achieved, they could take corrective measures based on the picture of students' knowledge revealed by these techniques. We believe that these are objective tools that can add to the knowledge that instructors have about their students' performance, which is usually based on test performance.

Use as a Learning Tool

Teaching the structure

Teaching students the knowledge structure of the course explicitly might benefit learning. Results indicate that teaching students the knowledge structure explicitly in the beginning of a course (or a unit in the course) can help students assimilate these relationships and learn the materials. This can be done easily, for example, when introducing the course in the first meeting. Instead of going over the syllabus, as many instructors do, the instructor could use handouts of the knowledge structure of the course and go over it in explaining the major units, concepts, and relationships between them. Because the structure is limited in the amount of information it contains, the instructor could elaborate on it. Beyond the benefit in terms of course content, such a presentation might develop in students a general tendency for looking at relationships between concepts, as indicated by the results of the fifth study, which showed that learning a structure in one unit can make students more aware of a structure in another unit.

Teaching flexibly

As previously mentioned, having a flexible knowledge structure is important in enabling one to relate concepts differently and to perceive relationships in different ways. Although we have only *measured* flexibility in the study reported earlier, instructors can use the notion of *teaching* flexibility in a more direct way. For example, during the course the instructors might stress different points of view for the same topic, showing how the same group of concepts can be related, each time from a different viewpoint.

Instructors might combine this notion of teaching flexibly with teaching the structure explicitly, as mentioned above. The instructor could go over alternative structures, and show the similarities and differences between them. He or she can elaborate on the different dimensions underlying each of the structures. This would help students anticipate alternative relationships during the course and might develop in them a tendency to look at the materials from different perspectives.

Providing feedback to students

Using the techniques could provide information not only to the instructor but to the students as well. For example, if administered at the beginning of the course, the instructor can provide his or her own structure of the materials to the students and ask them to compare their structures. This could give students information about how the way they see the relationships between concepts differ from the instructor's view. It could also prepare and help students' learning later in the course. (We have created a computerized on-line version of the ordered-tree task which can be used by each student in an interactive manner during class; Naveh-Benjamin & Lin, 1991.)

Alternatively, if the task is administered at mid-term and looked at individually, it would let the instructor provide individual students with feedback about their performance. Those students who showed significant deviations in their structure from that of the instructor could learn about the mismatches so they could concentrate on these aspects in their studying. Finally the instructor could use the tasks at the end of the course for review. After asking the students to do the task, he or she can provide them with his or her structure so they can evaluate their knowledge in relation to the ideal. We have used this exercise in the past, and students reported being helped by it while thinking about the materials and studying for the final examination.

Increasing instructors' awareness

While working with the instructors of the different courses as part of our research program on cognitive structures, we realized that in many cases preparing a knowledge structure task for their classes made the instructors aware of the organization of concepts in their courses. Some instructors teach without thinking about the elaborate relationships between different parts of it too much. They skillfully teach, in many cases, each unit of the course but do not pay much attention to the relationships between concepts and issues. Using these techniques, which require the instructor to come up with a knowledge structure of the course, might help the instructors, as well, to think more about conceptual relationships in their course.

SUMMARY

Instructional psychologists have realized during the last twenty years that any development of any curriculum and consideration of instructional methods must take into account how knowledge is initially organized and represented in students and how their knowledge representations are modified by new information.

Several methods have recently been offered for measuring students' conceptual structures. After reviewing some of the techniques used by other investigators, we described two methods we developed for measuring students' cognitive structures, an indirect one (the ordered-tree task) and a direct one (the FITS task). We then reviewed part of our research program to study characteristics of students' cognitive structures as they are measured in a variety of classroom situations.

Altogether, using these techniques enabled us to identify sources of information contributing to students' cognitive structures at the beginning of a course and the development of these structures throughout courses in different disciplines. In addition, we evaluated the degree to which these structures are flexible and modifiable. Finally, we have shown the impact of using these knowledge structures as a learning tool to help students study the information learned. We then discussed some practical considerations of the possible uses of these techniques in classroom settings.

We think that these techniques, in addition to others suggested, can be a major aid toward understanding student learning and toward advancing a framework for designing strategies for teaching. Still, further research is required in order to establish and extend the reported results. First, a process model, which describes how students acquire these conceptual structures, is needed. Second, we need to study how these knowledge structures are related to students' beliefs systems, and their perception of the logic of a given discipline. Finally, research is needed to assess the degree to which teaching students about the importance of organization can be transferred not only within a given domain, but also across fields and disciplines. The study of the formation and modification of knowledge structures and their assessment continues to be a significant task for the cognitive psychology of learning and teaching, and will benefit both instructors and students.

ACKNOWLEDGMENTS

The research reported in this chapter was partially supported by Grant Number G0086900100 from the Office of Educational Research and Improvement (OERI), U. S. Department of Education. The work does not necessarily represent the positions or policies of OERI or the Department of Education. The research was also partially supported by Grant Number 87-00100 from the United States-Israel Binational Science Foundation (BSF) to the first author and to Wilbert J. McKeachie.

REFERENCES

Ausubel, D. P. (1963). *The psychology of meaningful verbal learning.* New York: Grune & Stratton.

Ausubel, D. P. (1968). *Educational psychology: A cognitive view.* New York: Holt, Rinehart & Winston.

Ausubel, D. P., Novak, J. D., & Hanesian, H. (1978). *Educational psychology: A cognitive view* (2nd ed.). New York: Holt, Reinhart & Winston.

Battig, W. F. (1979). Are the important "individual differences" between or within individuals? *Journal of Research in Personality, 13*, 546–558.

Champagne, A. B., Hoz, R., & Klopfer, L. E. (1984, April). *Construct validation of the cognitive structure of physics concepts.* Paper presented at the meeting of the American Educational Research Association, New Orleans.

Donald, J. G. (1983). Knowledge structures: Methods for exploring course content. *Journal of Higher Education, 54*, 31–41.

Geeslin, W. E., & Shavelson, R. J. (1975). An exploratory analysis of the representation of a mathematical structure in students' cognitive structures. *American Educational Research Journal, 12*, 21–39.

Greeno, J. G. (1980). Some examples of cognitive task analysis with instructional implications. In R. E. Snow, P. A. Federico, & W. E. Montague (Eds.), *Aptitude, learning, and instruction* (Vol. 2, pp. 1–21). Hillsdale, NJ: Lawrence Erlbaum Associates.

McKeachie, W. J., Pintrich, P. R., Lin, Y.-G., Smith, D. A. F., & Sharma, R. (1990). *Teaching and learning in the college classroom: A review of the research literature.* Ann Arbor, MI: The University of Michigan, National Center for Research to Improve Postsecondary Teaching and Learning.

McKeithen, K. B., Reitman, J. S., Rueter, H. H., & Hirtle, S. C. (1981). Knowledge organization and skill differences in computer programmers. *Cognitive Psychology, 13*, 307–325.

Naveh-Benjamin, M., & Lin, Y.-G. (1991). *Assessing students' organization of concepts: A manual for measuring course-specific knowledge structures.* Ann Arbor, MI: The University of Michigan, National Center for Research to Improve Postsecondary Teaching and Learning.

Naveh-Benjamin, M., Lin, Y.-G., & McKeachie, W. J. (1989). Development of cognitive structures in three academic disciplines and their relations to students' study skills, anxiety, and motivation: Further use of the ordered-tree technique. *Journal of Higher Education Studies, 4*, 10–15.

Naveh-Benjamin, M., Lin, Y.-G., & McKeachie, W. J. (1994). Inferring students' cognitive structures and their development using the "fill-in-the-structure" (FITS) technique. In P. Nichols, S. F. Chipman, & R. Brennan (Eds.), *Cognitively diagnostic assessment*. Hillsdale, NJ: Lawrence Erlbaum Associates.

Naveh-Benjamin, M., Lin, Y.-G., & McKeachie, W. J., & Neely, R. K. (1994). Assessing the flexibility of cognitive structures created in university courses. Submitted.

Naveh-Benjamin, M., McKeachie, W. J., & Lin, Y.-G. (1989). Use of the ordered-tree technique to assess students' initial knowledge and conceptual learning. *Teaching of Psychology, 16,* 182–187.

Naveh-Benjamin, M., McKeachie, W. J., Lin, Y.-G., & Tucker, D. G. (1986). Inferring students' cognitive structures and their development using the "ordered tree technique." *Journal of Educational Psychology, 78,* 130–140.

Novak, J. D., & Gowin, D. B. (1984). *Learning how to learn.* Cambridge, England: Cambridge University Press.

Reitman, J. S., & Rueter, H. H. (1980). Organization revealed by recall orders and confirmed by pauses. *Cognitive Psychology, 12,* 554–581.

Shavelson, R. J. (1972). Some aspects of the correspondence between content structure and cognitive structure in physics instruction. *Journal of Educational Psychology, 63,* 225–234.

Shavelson, R. J. (1974). Methods for examining representations of a subject matter structure in students' memory. *Journal of Research in Science Teaching, 11,* 231–250.

Shavelson, R. J. (1981). Teaching mathematics: Contributions of cognitive research. *Educational Psychologist, 16,* 23–42.

Shavelson, R. J. (1983). On quagmires, philosophical and otherwise: A reply to Phillips. *Educational Psychologist, 18,* 81–87.

Shavelson, R. J., & Stanton, G. C. (1975). Construct validation: Methodology and application to three measures of cognitive structure. *Journal of Educational Measurement, 12,* 67–85.

Stark, J. S., Lowther, M. A., Ryan, M. P. S., Bomotti, S., Genthon, M., Haven, C. L., & Martens, G. (1988). *Reflections on course planning: Faculty and students consider influences and goals* (Tech. Rep. No. 88-B-

002). Ann Arbor, MI: University of Michigan, National Center for Research to Improve Postsecondary Teaching and learning.

Yekovich, F. R., & Thorndyke, P. W. (1981). An evaluation of alternative functional models of narrative schemata. *Journal of Verbal Learning and Verbal Behavior, 20,* 454–469.

4

Science Students' Learning: Ethnographic Studies in Three Disciplines

Janet Gail Donald
McGill University
Montreal, Quebec, Canada

To understand how students learn at the postsecondary level has been a lifelong quest for Bill McKeachie. In 1974 his review of the field of instructional psychology brought together studies on the factors that influence the effectiveness of instruction: the learner, the teacher, and the instructional process (McKeachie, 1974). The principles of learning and instruction enunciated at that time reflected a change from an associationist approach to an information-processing approach to learning. One of the questions asked in this article interested me greatly as a young researcher at McGill University's Centre for Learning and Development: "What was the effect of content structure and information processing strategies on the teaching and learning process?" Little was known about representations of knowledge at that time, but I began to investigate methods for representing course content and disciplinary differences in student learning. Twenty years later, McGill's Centre for University Teaching and Learning has evolved as has our program of research to a cognitive and constructivist approach to postsecondary learning and thinking. Over the years, Bill has provided wise counsel to members of our centre as an invited speaker, symposium participant, discussant, and external reviewer. This study of student learning in three scientific disciplines—physics, engineering, and psychology—is a "thank you" to Bill for his help over a time span of some two decades.

In the study, professors selected for their expertise as teachers and researchers, from universities in Australia, Canada, the United Kingdom, and the United States, were interviewed to determine their perceptions of student learning in their courses. A class in which the professor taught the course was observed; then, students from the course were interviewed for their perceptions of what and how they learn in their courses. Emphasis in the interviews was on meaningful learning and thinking. This chapter is an attempt to capture the learning experience in physics, engineering, and psychology courses, beginning with an analysis of major influences on learning according to the literature in each of these fields. Three kinds of interacting influences on student learning are: the disciplinary structure; student characteristics including ability, motivation, and preparation for their programs; and the instructional process.

THE DISCIPLINARY STRUCTURE

How does the discipline affect student learning? Disciplines are defined by their knowledge structures, methods, and validation processes (Donald, 1986; Franklin & Theall, 1992; Hirst, 1974; Schwab, 1962, 1978). The literature on teaching and learning in the university suggests that there are major differences across disciplines, although the ways in which these differences might affect learning need further examination. Of the disciplines studied here, physics, the oldest and most paradigmatic, is described as structured, hard, or restricted, because the field of phenomena is limited, methods are tightly defined, and research is highly replicable (Becher, 1989; Biglan, 1973; Pantin, 1968). Engineering has many aspects of the pure physical sciences, but must, in addition, apply knowledge in designs and systems (Sparkes, 1989). The knowledge and skills needed in engineering will therefore consist of both a high degree of theoretical structure and the procedures and strategies for applying them. The field of psychology is similar to physics in that it is considered to be a hard or structured science, but it has areas, such as mathematical or physiological psychology, that are more structured, and others that are less structured.

The validation processes used in the three fields imply different goals and methods. The validation process in physics and engineering is one of logical empiricism with reproducibility and consistency as important criteria for validity (Donald, 1990). Physicists and psychologists reported using conflicting evidence, counterexamples, or alternative explanations in the process of validating their work, but no engineering professor suggested using such deductive processes. Their reported test of validation is, "Does it work?" These findings are consistent with the fact that engineers deal with unstructured problems with many unknowns, and thus tend to use inductive and means-ends methods in their problem solving. In contrast to the physicists and engineers, psychology professors considered coherence or internal consistency the criterion for validity more often than external consistency. Psychologists talked about building theories at least as much as testing them, whereas the physical scientists focused on testing theories.

Disciplinary differences in goals, knowledge structures, and methods affect learning task characteristics that in turn affect student learning. Although all three fields are structured, or "hard," requiring logic and mathematical skills, the research literature suggests that there would be more emphasis on deductive logic in physics and psychology programs, and more design and synthesis in engineering programs. We could expect that physicists and engineers would find physical or empirical proof of their theories more easily than psychologists would, and that psychologists would spend more time developing theories than physical scientists would. Physics is the most convergent field of the three. Engineering is the most applied. Psychology could be expected to be the most immediately relevant field to students because it studies human behavior.

How would disciplinary differences affect student learning and motivation? The discipline directly influences the formation of the instructional goal: physics and engineering professors must teach students how to problem solve; engineering professors must also teach students how to design (Donald, 1990). Asked to describe what their competent students will be able to do, physics professors speak of interpreting and analyzing experimental data (Entwistle, 1984). According to the literature, physics professors expect students to relate experiences in the physical world to theoretical concepts, visualizing and seeing the relationships among the equations (Ramsden, 1992). Physics and engineering students are expected to acquire a concept of orders of magnitude, so that they can estimate within what range an answer should lie.

Psychology professors must teach students a variety of inferential methods, how to measure human characteristics, and how to conceptualize and represent human and animal activity. Psychology professors describe their competent students as becoming concerned about the nature of evidence and scientific argument (Entwistle, 1984). Seeing coherence and pattern is important—in the words of one professor, "how things hang together" (Hounsell & Ramsden, 1978). Although the match may be made before students reach the postsecondary level, for example, in student preference for mathematics and physical sciences in high school, the discipline creates an ethos or tradition (Becher, 1989) within which the student must operate.

STUDENT CHARACTERISTICS

What student characteristics affect science students' learning? Psychometrically, the greatest influence on student learning is student aptitude, consisting of ability and preparation for the program undertaken. Previous achievement in a field of study is the strongest predictor of student success. Students could be expected to come to physics and engineering programs with relatively homogeneous backgrounds in physical sciences and mathematics, compared to psychology students. It is not necessarily the case, however, that physics or engineering students form a homogeneous group, and comparisons of students are made by their professors as standard practice. Physics students are most likely to be compared on their ability to think logically, although mathematical insight, problem-solving ability, and the ability to think in terms of visual images are also considered important (Peltzer, 1988). In engineering, grades in calculus in the first and second year are most strongly related to success in coursework (Pike, 1991). Reasoning skills rated most important or critical for engineering graduates include breaking down complex problems into simpler ones, reasoning or problem solving in situations where all the needed information is not known, and identifying all the variables in a problem (Powers & Enright, 1987).

Psychology students have heterogeneous backgrounds compared to students in the physical sciences primarily because they may have either arts or science backgrounds. Students entering psychology programs are normally required to have had at least functions if not calculus as a mathematics prerequisite, but science majors are perceived to have an advantage over arts students in psychology courses (Donald, 1992b). Most professors in psychology courses expect their students to be able to think logically, independently, and abstractly, whereas the majority of physics professors expect only that their students will think logically (Donald, 1988). Taking psychology courses has been correlated with increased analytical reasoning and mathematics scores on the Graduate Record Examination (Ratcliff, 1988). Graduate psychology students appear to make major gains in intellectual skills in statistical and methodological reasoning compared to students in physical and health sciences and law (Lehman, Lempert, & Nisbett, 1988; Nisbett, Fong, Lehman, & Cheng, 1987). Over two years of graduate school, students in psychology were shown to make the largest increases in inferential skills, in statistical reasoning, and in methodological reasoning dealing with different types of confounded variable problems, and in their ability to solve problems. Initial differences across fields of study were minimal for all types of reasoning, but after two years, psychology students had made the greatest gains in inferential skills, followed by medical students, with law and chemistry students showing slight but insignificant improvement.

Students' beliefs and attitudes about the subject matter affect their orientation to learning. Physics students' beliefs about the structure and content of physics knowledge, and about how one develops that knowledge, affect how they use new information, how they work on problems, and whether or not they develop a coherent understanding of course material (Hammer, 1991). Earlier experiences in secondary school may lead students to adopt either a surface (reproduction oriented) or deep (meaning oriented) approach to learning (Ramsden, 1992). Students have varying perceptions of causality, stability, and controllability that affect their judgment (Russell, 1982) as well as varying epistemological standards or requirements (Ryan, 1984; Tobias, 1990). Tobias found that humanities students who had the prerequisites to do science but had chosen not to, wanted a challenging intellectual experience that they felt was not provided in the physical science courses they took. Psychology and natural science students were found to have lower levels of belief in unsubstantiated (e.g., paranormal) phenomena than humanities students, but the absolute level of belief was high even among advanced undergraduate students (Gray & Mill, 1990). It is widely accepted that introductory psychology students enter the classroom with misconceptions about the subject matter (Brown, 1983, 1984; Vaughan, 1977). Introductory psychology students' epistemological beliefs were significant predictors of course grades (Ryan, 1984). Students' varying beliefs and attitudes render the relationship between instruction and learning more complex.

Motivational and personality characteristics also affect the learning milieu. In a study of engineering personality characteristics, young British civil engineers were found to be tough, practical, realistic, aggressive, and participative (Barker, 1989). Their personality profiles suggested that, relative to arts and science students, they are self-reliant, willing to take responsibility, act on practical logical evidence, and keep to the point. Although there has been little research within disciplines on the effect of motivation on learning, the general literature (Corno & Snow, 1986; Pintrich, Cross, Kozma, & McKeachie, 1986) suggests its importance. In one study, natural science students had higher intrinsic goal motivation and metacognitive strategies than social science students (Garcia & Pintrich, 1992). Intrinsic goal orientation was a significant predictor of critical thinking, however, for both natural and social science students.

According to the research literature in the three domains, as a minimum we could expect that students in these fields would be able to think logically, with psychology students being more heterogeneous and engineering students more practically oriented. We could also expect that student motivation would affect learning in these domains, although whether physics, engineering, or psychology students would be more intrinsically goal oriented is unknown.

THE INSTRUCTIONAL PROCESS

How does the instructional process affect learning? What students learn is also dependent on how they are taught, and the discipline determines to some extent what methods will be used. For example, physical science courses usually have assignments and labs associated with them. Do problem solving courses in the physical sciences have the same effect as experimental courses in psychology? What is the ratio of "knowledge-based" courses to methods courses? How is the learning process perceived by those responsible for instruction? To what extent is meaningful learning fostered? In an Australian study, professors reflecting on their teaching in weekly interviews talked about communicating aims, expectations, and ideas to their students twice as often (62%) as they talked about intellectual development (32%) (Andresen, Barrett, Powell, & Wieneke, 1985). One professor noted that it was not only difficult to judge if students understood but inappropriate in large lectures. To be sure that students understood, the instructor felt it would be necessary to sit down with a small group of students and take them through the idea step by step, then verify by asking if the students understood. At the same time, professors have been shown to overestimate their students' learning in a course by approximately 15% (Fox & LeCount, 1991).

Studies of different teaching methods generally show that lectures are at least equal to and often more effective than discussion for immediate recall of factual knowledge on course examinations, but discussion tends to be superior for long-term retention (McKeachie, 1990). To increase knowledge, students have been provided with advance organizers for text or analogies so that the rate of recall is increased (Glover, Dietzer, & Bullock, 1990; Halpern, Hansen, & Riefer, 1990). Teaching students generative learning strategies, for example, self-questioning or summarizing methods, also aids comprehension and retention (King, 1992). Concept mapping has proved helpful in facilitating meaningful learning in a variety of subject matter areas and at different levels (Novak, 1990; Pankratius, 1990). Students taught to use a concept mapping procedure had greater success in novel problem solving situations.

Specific teaching methods such as using examples and analogies (Brown, 1992), and adding explicit detail to the elements in diagrams (Winn, 1988) facilitate analytic processing and tasks associated with it in physics courses. Brown (1992) found that a bridging explanation that made use of concrete situations from the students' experience, starting with an anchor example and moving through intermediate situations to the target situation, aided students in constructing a new conceptual model of a physical situation. In psychology, students' structural knowledge has been assessed by having them rate the relatedness of important concepts in statistics and research design; their scores correlated significantly (.74) with examination performance (Goldsmith, Johnson, & Acton, 1991).

For intellectual development to occur, active methods of learning that require students to think, problem solve, synthesize, or evaluate are needed. In the physical sciences, much attention has been paid to learning how to problem solve (Adams, 1986; Reif, Larkin, & Brackett, 1976). Although instruction in problem solving methods in physics has yielded mixed results (Pankratius, 1990), specific problem solving strategies have been taught to physics students with positive results (Reif, Larkin, & Brackett, 1976; van Weeren, de Mul, Peters, Kramers-Pals, & Roossink, 1982). In these studies, instruction became a process in which students systematically wrote down all their actions when problem solving until the process became automatic. Course grades increased significantly in the courses.

Ferguson and de Jong (1991), studying learning in engineering courses, found that higher percentages of integrating and connecting activities occurred in problem solving classes than in lectures. To aid in integrating new knowledge, the role of the teacher was to stimulate students to construct meaning and structure for themselves by indicating main issues, relating elements, comparing situations or laws, drawing conclusions, or giving explicit arguments for choices. Instruction to aid thinking would, therefore, require different activities from those usually seen in lectures, with greater emphasis on integrating and connecting activities. Another approach, "route mapping" problems to be solved, was developed by van Weeren (1983) for physics students. It consists of requiring students to summarize in a schematized route their way of solving the problem, then indicating in the route which results of the analysis and which key relations are associated in the problem. This procedure helps the student to form an adequate and accessible representation of knowledge.

In a study of quality in engineering education, Sparkes (1989) drew a distinction between engineering and pure science, in content, purpose, and process, since the differences entail very different approaches to teaching. A key difference between scientific processes and engineering processes lies in the fact that scientific processes are concerned with the analysis, generalization, and synthesis of hypotheses, whereas engineering processes are involved with the analysis and synthesis of designs, and reaching decisions based on incomplete data and approximate models. Engineering processes and skills, either manual or intellectual, are learned mainly through practice.

Thus the knowledge structure of the discipline, the characteristics of the students who elect to study in the field, and the instructional processes used will affect students' learning experience, so that although to the layperson it may appear that students in different programs have all "gone to university," in fact their learning experiences may be singularly different. To examine the extent to which this is so, ethnographic studies in three scientific disciplines, physics, engineering, and psychology, were carried out. Particular emphasis in the studies was placed on the kinds of meaningful learning activities carried out by students in these fields of study. Professors were first asked about the knowledge structure in their field. To describe student characteristics, the professors were asked what their expectations were of students' knowledge and intellectual skills. Next, professors described the instructional process and their perceptions of students' motivation to learn. Students' perceptions of learning in their courses provide comparative data.

METHOD

The procedures used in the studies are summarized here. A more detailed explanation of the procedures is provided in articles written previously by the author (Donald, 1991, 1992a, 1992b, 1993).

To establish professors' perceptions of student learning in their disciplines, 24 expert teachers and researchers were selected to be interviewed—8 from each field of study, and 2 each from the University of Western Ontario in Canada, Cambridge University in the United Kingdom, Stanford University in the United States, and Monash University in Australia. Pilot studies were carried out at McGill University. The professors were interviewed during the period from 1986 to 1989 by the author, using a tape-recorded semi-structured interview format with questions on the learning task in the discipline, the thinking skills developed (Donald, 1992a), student characteristics, and the instructional processes used to aid learning. Reports of the interviews were sent to the professors who were asked to comment on the report and the extent to which it represented their discipline; their comments were included in the final version of the report. To analyze the protocols across disciplines, a similarity grouping procedure on the important phrases excerpted from the reports was used (Miles & Huberman, 1984; Miller, 1971). Reports on each field of study were sent to the participants for their comments.

To establish student perceptions of learning, 89 students—23 physics students, 45 engineering students, and 21 psychology students—in the courses of the professors who had taken part in the previous studies were interviewed during 1989 and 1990. The general procedure was to: (a) observe a class in which the professor taught the course in order to better situate and understand the students' comments in the interview, then (b) interview a group of student volunteers who would be willing and able to articulate what they had learned in the course.

In the interview room, the students were asked to independently fill in a questionnaire form of 12 questions with their own views on what and how they learned in their course. They were asked to describe what the course was about, what they had learned (knowledge and thinking skills), and how they learned (lectures, readings, assignments, discussion), whether they felt the course had helped them to think and in what way (problem solving, developing arguments, analyzing, changing perspective, evaluating). A group discussion about learning in their course followed. In addition, a small number of students were interviewed individually to establish their perceptions, using the same questionnaire but with a semi-structured interview format.

In reporting the results of these studies, the professors' and students' perceptions of learning are used as recorded. Quotes were taken from the reports to the professors and from the students' questionnaires and were selected to show the most frequently voiced views. The findings, however, are insights that would need to be tested over a larger sample, rather than measures of central tendency. Although the professors are models and experts in their fields, they are not necessarily typical professors. Their perceptions of knowledge in the field, expectations of students, their views of the instructional process and of students' motivation to learn are presented by field. Students' perceptions of learning in their courses follow. Perceptions of learning in the three domains are then compared.

LEARNING PHYSICS

The eight professors of physics highlighted the particular role of physics as a discipline, and underlined the pressure that professors feel themselves under to meet the knowledge requirements of the discipline. They were also, however, very aware of students' attitudes and spent a considerable amount of time describing how they dealt with students' motivation to learn.

Perceptions of Knowledge in the Field

The approach that physics professors took to instruction in their discipline was highly intellectual, even at the introductory level. One professor recommended that all university students study physics if the course were taught as an intellectual enterprise instead of one where the professor tries to transmit knowledge:

"What is special about physics as opposed to philosophy, is that when you are all done, you have a physical world to compare the output of your thought process to."

"The general course goal is to help students develop critical objective skills in solving novel situations. Students are expected to think for themselves; at freshman level this is done by problem solving."

"Physics is a very highly disciplined thought process that has strict connections with logic and mathematics."

Instructors' Expectations of Students

Students are expected to have a specific physics vocabulary acquired in their high school courses. For example, they are expected to know what is meant by distance, velocity, acceleration, force, molecule, and atom. They would also know some mathematics, such as solutions of quadratic equations and the differentiation and integration of power functions and trigonometric functions. Students may, however, not know how to use this vocabulary. Physics professors expect their students to think logically, but not necessarily independently or abstractly (Donald, 1988). One professor explained that because physics is an ancient discipline, students could not be expected to discover something new. Physics students, however, are expected to reason with abstract propositions. According to the professors, the attitudes toward learning that students bring with them to university are pervasive and play a large role in determining how well students will achieve. These attitudes include not only general motivation, but also willingness to participate, commitment, a tendency to plan or organize their work, and industry or self-discipline.

Instructors' Views of the Instructional Process

The primary instructional and evaluation methods tend to be traditional, that is, lectures and formal examinations, but great emphasis is placed on learning how to problem solve. Introductory courses are given by means of lectures, although laboratories or problem sets are assigned each week. All of the introductory courses use some edition of Halliday and Resnick (1988), *Fundamentals of Physics*, as a text, suggesting strong disciplinary convergence. The development of understanding in physics is seen to rely heavily on building upon previous knowledge. Pressure to cover the course material results from the professors' view of physics as sequential in nature: instructors stated that they cannot skip some part of the subject as might occur in other disciplines but must provide the appropriate foundation on which students will be able to build future knowledge. Evaluation of student learning takes a variety of forms: homework assignments, laboratories, tutorial tests, mid-term quizzes, and final examinations. Multiple-choice questions, in which problems are subdivided, often take the place of longer problems. Laboratory reports require students to place their work in context, identify important aspects of the measurements, assess the significance of results, and analyze and interpret them. As courses progress from the introductory level to more advanced courses, which are more experimental, independence, creativity, and the ability to build and test models are more expected.

Instructors' Perceptions of Students' Motivation to Learn

In the development of positive attitudes toward learning, participation in class appeared to be the most general problem. With large class sizes, professors felt that participation can be promoted in a very limited way. To get feedback to know how much students are understanding, one professor tries to get one or two of the "natural extroverts" to be active in class. He tells students to stop him and ask him if they have a question, because if they save it until the end of the class, they may forget the rest of the lecture.

The professors noted that student attitudes vary from course to course and from program to program. For example, in physics courses taught to medical students, students are already highly motivated. In another course, students have problems in making decisions about how to organize their time and what priority to give to their studies. In a third course, the professor tries to develop students' ability to make an objective evaluation of what they have done and to not be afraid to come to the conclusion that what they have done is not so good. He has seen students hurt themselves strictly through fear of failing. He therefore tries to get students to evaluate their grades as a realistic assessment of what they have done. The laboratory serves as a place where students can sort out material and participate more in discussion with partners or the demonstrator.

Students' Perceptions of Learning in Physics Courses

In spite of the opportunity to study physics at secondary school, students' backgrounds in university level introductory courses were heterogeneous; some had taken no previous physics courses or related courses, whereas others had taken three. Their level of felt preparation for the course was correspondingly varied, from poorly or not at all prepared to being very well prepared. Students said that they learned the major course concepts through a combination of lectures, laboratory sessions, readings and practice problems, but that they learned to think primarily through problem solving. In learning to think, students most frequently cited the identification of critical elements and relations as most important, although in one course, five of the six students emphasized the importance of stating assumptions, which had not been noted by any of the eight professors. One student described the learning process in the following manner: "Much time has been spent wrestling with different methods of solving a difficult question, and examining what worked, and why. Once I know *why*, I feel confident about having actually learned it."

Asked how they know when they know something in physics, students gave a variety of answers. One group talked about things "flowing together." Students tended to write or talk about learning as "acquiring knowledge" rather than "learning methods or skills," but said that physics is not like history or political science; there is more application and it is more interconnected. Another line of response was, "If you can prove something mathematically, then you know it." One student replied that people in higher physics know that they don't know. Other students said:

"The ability to apply the knowledge successfully to unfamiliar situations/problems is the real test of understanding."

"Attempting to teach the subject is a good test!"

"You can see which problems that idea applies to, you can discuss its limitations, you can explain it to someone else. Other people who have learned it before use the idea in a similar way to you."

"Because I can deduce it from other things which I think I 'know,' using inferences which I 'know' to be true."

When asked what it is most important to know to be a good teacher, students replied in terms of their own limitations, starting with the importance of knowing the perspective of the students or starting at the students' level—"or else students will be lost at the beginning." The students suggested that instructors should take nothing for granted, and stressed the importance of going through things thoroughly. Students appreciated well-prepared lectures and demonstrations, and the professor's taking a serious attitude toward the subject: the professor's level of motivation was very important to the students.

Asked what advice they would give to other students about learning physics, one replied: "First of all, they should know under what conditions they learn best, then utilize all resources, e.g., go to lectures, use the reference room which is open all day with tutors to answer questions, use different textbooks to get different views, then when they get confused, that shows something is happening (not to be discouraged)."

One student noted that often the sheer volume of work is frightening and it seems impossible to remember everything that is taught. His advice was that although this is true, many of the general principles "stick," although the details are forgotten, and that the general principles are the important part. More practical advice included sharing problem solving with another person of similar ability and knowledge in order to prevent going up too many blind alleys. "Try to find worked examples using the idea you want to learn. Do plenty of exercises and applications of the idea on your own. Don't believe that the lecturer's way of doing it is the best, look in books to find alternative approaches."

Summary

Because the discipline of physics is highly defined and developed in relation to other scientific fields, it might be expected that the learning task would be clearer and thus easier than in other disciplines. This study suggests that, on the contrary, the learning task in physics is difficult, due to the sheer weight of the theory, and the fact that it is often counterintuitive. This means that the learning pattern for students is intensive, requiring concentration to restructure knowledge. Instructors are aware of the importance of problem solving tutorials, reference rooms, and study groups. Perhaps because the discipline is considered to be well-structured and sequential, in class, emphasis is on covering course material and not leaving anything out. The professors take a highly intellectual, content-oriented view to instruction. Professors recognized the importance of problem solving skills, mentioning them most frequently when they talked about the evaluation of learning. Direct teaching of problem solving skills, of representational (diagramming) skills, or of integrating and connecting activities did not tend to occur in class. Instead, it was the role of assignments, tutorials, or laboratories to develop these skills. In response to this situation, students commented that their "learning" took place in laboratories or supervisions rather than in the classroom.

The students in introductory courses, who had highly varied backgrounds in physics, recognized the emphasis put on problem solving skills in their courses, and were aware of the varied instructional modes used in their courses. They also recognized the importance of application and connections in physics courses compared to courses in other disciplines, but they did not note an emphasis on the development of thinking skills in their classes. They tended to think of learning in the course as a matter of acquiring knowledge, perhaps because they recognized their own inadequacies in the knowledge structures needed to solve problems. More advanced students made a distinction between learning concepts in lectures and developing thinking processes through problem solving. They were highly aware of the volume of work and recommended using all of the resources available for learning.

LEARNING ENGINEERING

The eight engineering professors spoke primarily of the problem solving process, and in particular of developing the skills of solving problems with incomplete information. As courses advanced, the learning goals shifted to design issues. In contrast to physics, the engineering professors' views of instruction were very student-centered. Helping students to acquire learning strategies was an important goal. The professors expected, however, that students were already highly motivated to learn.

Perceptions of Knowledge in the Field

The approach that engineering professors took to their discipline was very practical. Course goals are highly specified, with problem solving the most prominent overall goal. One professor pointed out that the course goal "is more than trying to teach students to solve well-posed problems, because ultimately they are going to have to solve ill-posed problems, that is, where there is too little or too much information. . . . Furthermore, the results of their analysis must be interpreted: students more than ever need a feel for the subject which will enable them to make these interpretations."

Instructors' Expectations of Students

Students are expected to have a specific vocabulary, for example, in mechanics, a technical understanding of velocity, force, and acceleration. In mathematics, they will know some calculus, integration, algebra, and linear algebra. Students are expected to think logically or analytically; this kind of thinking is often called *rule driven*. Most engineering professors expect students to be able to think independently. Professors consider that their students think along well-oiled grooves, conventionally but not unconventionally. They have the least expectation that students will be able to think abstractly (Donald, 1988). Some professors considered that abstract thinking was of great importance, but several stated that in engineering, abstract thinking is not as important as thinking logically and independently, and that the person who can only think abstractly will be unhappy as an engineer.

Instructors' Views of the Instructional Process

Professors spoke most about the development of problem solving skills, noting that, unguided, students use an efficient metacognitive approach to problem solving in which they first look at the problem assignment to see if they can do it unaided. If they cannot, they refer to the worked examples (sample problems) and see if they can then do it. Only as a very last resort would they read the theory from their lecture notes or textbook.

Ideally, students develop problem solving skill by first selecting information that is pertinent to the problem when they rewrite the problem. Students are taught to write down the law they are using, systematically set down the equations, and to have axes, diagram, equations, and a check as parts of their solution. Particularly important to the engineering professors is the development of a concept of orders of magnitude to guide their students' thinking, for example, to provide context and verification of their problem solutions. Another important ability to be developed is report writing, for which students must select information, organize it, and draw inferences. In projects, students have to synthesize, and the write-up of their projects is evaluated on how successfully they have done all these things including verification.

As the level of the course advances, a shift in emphasis occurs from problem solving to synthesis and design issues. Professors expect students to have the means, when confronted with a problem, to be able to analyze the problem into its essential parts, to know there are ways and means of solving those parts and of connecting the solutions with all other prior knowledge. From an engineering perspective, unless students can put the parts of a problem back together, they do not have a solution. Another goal is to make the students observant about what constitutes an engineering project, what are the difficulties faced, and what are the solutions. Students are asked to deal with broader issues that are much closer to the kinds of questions they will be expected to answer as professionals in the field. Communication skills increase in importance. In contrast to introductory courses, which equip students to solve problems and to start to relate their knowledge, upper level courses broaden perspective and equip students with synthesizing and explanatory skills. Students are selected for their mathematical rather than their verbal ability, but must develop their communication skills, first through participation in problem solving groups, then through projects and reports.

Instructors' Perceptions of Students' Motivation to Learn

Learning to learn is one of the most important attitudes for engineers, and it is considered to be as important as actual knowledge, since knowledge may become obsolete in five years. One professor suggested that not enough attention has been paid at any level in the school or university to learning to learn, and to see the logical pattern in engineering topics. Some professors were concerned that engineers could get through four years of study without speaking in class. They felt that although sometimes students work in groups, they should be participating in classroom discussion more than they do.

Students' Perceptions of Learning in Engineering Courses

The large groups of engineering students (45 students) who elected to be interviewed confirm a high level of interest in learning in this field. The first-year students came from various subfields of engineering, for example, mechanical or civil, but appeared to be relatively homogeneous in background. They identified themselves as engineers, were open and empirically oriented (practical) and were aware of the demands of the field. For the students, the main goal of the course was most frequently described as the learning of mathematical methods or methods of analysis that could be applied to solve problems. Students also made frequent reference, particularly at the end of term, to the more immediate goal of passing their examinations. Although many of the students had worked on engineering projects before coming to university, some felt they were not at all prepared for the course, whereas others felt very well prepared. Students reported that they had learned the major course concepts mostly from lectures, and more particularly from the set question or example papers for the course, considered an "intensive but effective way to learn," coupled with supervisions. Several of the students mentioned that they had also learned to think in the lectures, by observing the problem solving process in class, but generally students referred to problem solving in the regular example papers.

Students described the skill-learning process in the following manner:

"By example. The lecturer would describe a course of action to solve a problem which illustrates a particular technique/concept/ convention, then compares the result to earlier results or common sense. Attention to detail and comment upon the obvious (which in the student's mind is usually far from obvious) has also helped greatly."

"In mechanics in particular it is necessary to step behind what is taught and to try to follow the lecturer's methods and ways of viewing the problems."

In advanced courses, students were more insistent than first-year students that the goal was to develop thinking processes and gain techniques in problem solving. Students showed greater independence in their learning, describing the learning of concepts through doing follow-up or clarification reading of the text and doing the assigned problems. The textbook assumed greater importance for these students. The students also recognized that their problem solving skills had been enhanced, that their perspective had been changed, that it was now "easier to conceptualize what a problem solution would be like," and that they must now "look more at the overall picture and combine concepts." Several mentioned that the course had reinforced work skills. Again, students pointed to the value of the textbook sample problems and examples. In design courses, students noted that in their project, which requires putting a design into an environment in a systematic manner, they had to change perspective frequently. Advanced students used more discussion in their learning, and they tended to ask more questions, and engage in more report writing. One student noted that discussion leads to insight.

Asked how they know when they know something in engineering, first-year students talked about having a feel for something, finding you can apply something new, or being able to explain the ideas or techniques to someone else in a different way or angle from that prescribed to you. Some students, however, responded by saying that knowing something is merely a matter of remembering and being able to recall it, as a microprocessor would. Some students therefore have an understanding of learning in terms of its meaning and application, whereas others are still using a rote or reproduction learning model. Second-year students gave a variety of answers to the question, from careful answers such as "double checking all calculations" or "re-analyzing the process," to "knowing within a certain acceptable error." Students tended to rely on the course manual, or on consulting others. Others remarked that "You know you're right when you are capable of developing a concept from first principles and then applying it to what you need to find or evaluate," and "If you look at it practically speaking, if the answer is obviously unrealistic, you should recheck your answer. Otherwise, check the solution."

Advanced students' replies included "if others support," "peer support," and "try it and see if it works—difficult to know because long term and so much is going on at the same time." These responses echo the engineering personality profile found by Barker (1989), in which engineering students are portrayed as practical and dependent on group approval.

Asked what advice about learning they would give to future students, some students suggested ways of dealing with the learning process itself, and others spoke more generally:

"Make sure to start with that you are learning in the right way, i.e., you are not here to learn facts, but to learn an approach. This is important—it is far more useful to be able to analyze a problem logically and get a feel for it than to remember equations."

"Try to keep relating things to the real world."

"Do *Not* do all night sessions; establish regular and sufficient sleep patterns and keep them."

"Enjoy your work and make use of the time you have but do other things to relax your body and mind."

Summary

Professors' and students' views of the learning process in engineering were highly consistent, focusing on the problem solving process. This was due in some part to the professors' being very student-centered in their approach to instruction and to their focus on students' acquisition of learning strategies. As courses advanced, design and communication skills were added to the repertoire.

In response to their program, in their first year, engineering students tended to talk about survival skills. These developed from "not doing all night sessions" to checking solutions, then to gaining perspective. If students enter their engineering programs with a shallow or limited view of the learning task, by the second year they can enunciate clear and meaningful learning goals, and by the third and fourth years they have acquired considerable perspective. They are more aware of their limitations but are developing the broader strategies they will need as engineering team members. Their professors' emphasis on "learning to learn" appears to gain in effect over the four years of the program.

The time frame for advanced students was much longer, and they appeared more inclined to reflect than their younger colleagues. The instructional methods also had changed, with greater emphasis on discussion and greater opportunity to ask questions. Feeling less rather than more prepared for their courses than first- and second-year students, the third- and fourth-year students were more attuned to possible "managerial" solutions, in which one reflects, then tries out a solution on a colleague, and if that has a good result, talks until "something feasible comes out."

LEARNING PSYCHOLOGY

The eight psychology professors had varying views of the learning process, and noted that different courses supplied students with different intellectual skills. Instructional methods were equally varied, even within a course. Introductory courses were primarily vocabulary oriented, as students were entering a new field. As courses advanced, the learning goals were influenced by whether courses were in a specific area within psychology or were methods courses. Professors discriminated between honors and general courses, and spoke more about graduate training than physics or engineering professors had. Apprenticeship, and metacognitive skills, became more important at the graduate level.

Perceptions of Knowledge in the Field

The course objectives as stated in the course syllabus for one of the introductory courses are:

to provide a general introduction to the scientific investigation of behavior, to examine basic psychological processes such as sensation, perception, and learning, as well as to introduce more complex psychological phenomena such as the effects of early childhood experience, conflict, aggression, altruism, hypnosis, behavior pathology, and psychotherapy. Therefore, you will be exposed to an introduction to selected issues and concepts in psychology along with a relatively complete survey of the field. The emphasis taken is an experimental one, stressing scientific methodology in the study of behavior—human and animal. An additional goal of this course is to emphasize the applicability of psychology to everyday life, and in so doing perhaps enrich your insight into your own and others' behavior.

Because this is the first course that students take in this discipline, it must equip them with a general vocabulary and an overview of the field. In contrast to the engineering courses, because only a small portion of the students in the introductory course will pursue studies in psychology, the instructor is providing a "service" course to most, as many as 400 students, but at the same time introducing the subject to the small portion who will pursue it for some seven years in order to become psychologists. In introductory psychology courses, the tendency is to use texts that are in their 6th to 12th edition, but there are seven or eight different introductory texts with different approaches, in contrast to physics, which uses one textbook. There is thus content continuity but limited convergence.

Instructors' Expectations of Students

Students entering psychology do not have a specific vocabulary or background knowledge in psychology, but are expected to be able to understand what they read, read quickly, and memorize much of what they read. One professor pointed out that in introductory courses, the development of vocabulary requires a dictionary or textbook glossary: in a glossary of 1,500 words, students will not have heard of 1,000. Other words will have more technical meanings.

"Many of the words they know they must learn to use more precisely, like schizophrenia and depression or multiple personality. Because psychology is part of the popular culture, students hear these words which are used inconsistently or vaguely, and they have to learn to use them precisely. For example, to behaviorists there is a huge difference between reward and reinforcement, where people are rewarded and responses are reinforced. You do not reward a response. Punishment is of responses, not people; punishing people is wrong and punishing responses modifies behavior, and therefore may be good under judiciously chosen circumstances."

The ability to think abstractly is as necessary for psychology students as logical and independent thinking, and a large percentage of psychological concepts are abstract or higher order abstract in nature (Donald, 1983, 1988).

Instructors' Views of the Instructional Process

Although most introductory courses are taught using lectures, several variants to the introductory psychology course were described by the professors. The variants included a year-long course with three hours of lectures and a three-hour lab each week where eight members of staff teach different topics, a personalized mastery system of instruction (PSI), and a first-year honors seminar organized around newly developed computer software and limited to 12 students. In this course the students do experiments on the computer and have 36 written assignments that put the students in different situations as a therapist, the head of a design company, or Pavlov's research assistant. Often it is a policy of the psychology department to have each student in the introductory course serve as a subject in several psychological experiments sponsored by the faculty and/or graduate students.

Thinking skills are developed in different kinds and levels of courses; professors thought that no one course would concentrate on most of the skills. As one remarked, "some courses, particularly those dealing with methods, would be more heavily focused on inference and verification, while higher level courses would focus more on selection and synthesis."

In first- and second-year courses, learning is evaluated by means of multiple-choice tests designed to require thought, as well as essays and lab reports, but primarily by means of formal written examinations. Final examinations usually cover the work of the entire course.

Examinations given earlier in the term may or may not be cumulative, are most frequently multiple-choice, and require a thorough knowledge of the facts and details as well as an overview of the material. In courses that have laboratories, work is marked throughout the year. Students are expected to talk and participate in seminars, and although participation is not formally evaluated, in one course students are told that they will not get credit for the course unless the teaching assistant knows their name. Evaluation of learning reflects the course organization and goals, which are highly varied.

Instructors' Perceptions of Students' Motivation to Learn

At the undergraduate level, the development of positive attitudes toward learning is promoted through classroom discussion and demonstration experiments. But psychology professors paid more attention to the promotion of learning strategies at the graduate level than at the undergraduate, particularly to planning and organization skills. At the undergraduate level, the professor gets a product, a paper, or a report. At the graduate level, in an apprenticeship relationship, students are taught how to plan better and organize ideas, and how to organize their time. Other attitudes that are important for graduate students are demonstrable industry and self-discipline, which are considered essential if students are to be productive and to be recommended for good academic jobs. Thus, attitude development assumes greater importance at the graduate level, both because it is more critical for the student's work, and because it is possible to attend to it.

Students' Perceptions of Learning in Psychology Courses

On entry to the introductory course, students had had little background in psychology, although one of them noted that his high school science courses had prepared him in terms of the skills necessary for the course. Although students had had little preparation for the course, no one felt poorly prepared, because a background in psychology was not expected of them. Students interpreted the goal of the course to be to give them one possible approach to the understanding of human and animal behavioral studies, that is, a scientifically, biologically based approach. They spoke of having learned processes (writing up experiments, models proposed for encoding of audio frequencies, how to think critically) more than concepts. Learning took place through a combination of lectures, labs, specified reference material and discussion. The introductory psychology students felt that they had learned to think, particularly to analyze and evaluate, through the use of experimental reports, statistical procedures, and by participating in research projects. Inferential skills, especially discovering new relations between elements and hypothesizing, were ˒ the most frequently mentioned skills developed through report writing. One student noted that "the report writing required a great many of the skills and since this work was regular, it was possible to improve them."

One student pointed out that the experimental sessions are often not understood until the writing of the report. Thus report writing was central to the development of thinking. When asked what were the most important things they had learned as psychology students, advanced students gave general answers.

"That there isn't always a right answer. Different theories can account for the same results with the same validity. How to think analytically—in other words—don't believe everything you read, try to understand what the writer is saying and does he follow through."

"There are no black and white answers. For example, in therapy, there is more than one way, and different ways may be equally successful."

"To identify and test all assumptions, to evaluate theoretical material carefully, to construct experiments that rigorously test relationships that occur in a complicated process or system."

One graduate student was more explicit, remarking, "my experience in coursework and research, and the guidance I have had from advisors has equipped me to examine theories and data critically, and to design my own research to isolate and investigate carefully processes which interest me."

Students gave a greater variety of answers to the question, "How do you know when you know something in psychology? How do you know when you're right?" One student replied that as an experimentalist, you never know. This reply was similar to one given by a physics student, that people in higher physics know that they don't know. Other responses included the following:

"I never know when I am right. All I can know is when I am wrong, and I test hypotheses to find that out."

"No absolute truth."

"One perspective may work better than another."

"Counsellor's (clinician's) viewpoint: happiness, turning a person around from being unhappy."

COMPARISON ACROSS STUDIES

Perceptions of Knowledge in the Field

Physics professors' approach to their discipline was as an intellectual endeavor; engineering professors focused on teaching their students how to learn and to problem solve; psychology professors saw a variety of abilities being developed in different courses in the program. Physics students sensed that knowledge was crucial in their field, engineering students that problem solving was central, and psychology students spoke in terms of the thinking processes they had acquired. The contrast between physics professors' views of learning in their discipline and that of their students was the greatest of the three. Physics students entered a plea for their professors to recognize the limitations of student knowledge and to be thorough in their explanations. It would appear that students are not prepared for the focus on the discipline that is found in physics. The most paradigmatic discipline is least oriented to students' learning needs, although the physical resources for learning are substantial.

Because the approach to learning in engineering courses is practical, with "Does it work?" as the ultimate criterion, knowledge and skills are learned in context. Students recognize this and there appears to be no conflict between professors' and students' perceptions of knowledge in the field. Professors and students work toward the same goals, and have a number of external checkpoints for verification of their thinking. In psychology, professors are introducing students to a scientific approach to understanding behavior. The psychological processes that professors consider central to the discipline, according to the interviews of the students in this study, are learned by the students. If the theory construction that psychology professors consider so important in the discipline was not discussed as a learning task by professors or students, the inferential skills needed for building theories were recognized as predominant learning outcomes by the students.

Instructors' Expectations of Students

There is a close match between professors' expectations of students' ability in this study and in the literature. Professors in physics and engineering are, however, more specific in the knowledge expected of their students than in their skills, whereas psychology professors expect students to not have encountered the vocabulary but to have the ability to learn quickly. This expectation is consistent with the gains in analytical reasoning and intellectual skills reported by Ratcliff (1988) and the Lehman et al. (1988) and Nisbett et al. (1987) studies. The question we are left with is whether the disciplinary demands select the students or the students are trained according to expectations.

Physics professors were most likely to be attributional in their thinking, that is, they compared students on their ability to learn rather than putting the onus on the program or the instructional process. This approach extends to students' beliefs and attitudes, with physics professors comparing students' attitudes toward learning, whereas engineering and psychology professors are more general in their expectations of positive attitudes. Thus, although students' backgrounds in the physical sciences were more homogeneous than in psychology, physics professors discriminated among students more than engineering and psychology professors did. Attitude development was discussed in terms of class participation by physics and engineering professors; psychology professors thought it important at the graduate level, although participation in discussion and experiments is required at the undergraduate level. Perhaps because knowledge and intellectual skills are viewed as varied across courses and this variation is accommodated, attitudes toward learning are more positive and there is less angst than is found among physics students.

The Instructional Process

Across the three disciplines, instruction is designed to promote thinking processes. Although introductory courses tend to be knowledge-based in the lectures, students are required to problem solve or think in their assignments and reports. Students were highly aware of the value of assignments in their learning and relatively unclear about the value of lectures. This could be explained by the relatively passive role assigned to students in lectures, or by students' lack of recognition that lectures can be important for learning. A review of the role of lectures in aiding learning might clarify their contribution, for example, in providing context or scaffolding for learning, or examples of thinking for students. If students are capturing from 11% in first-year courses to less than 40% generally of available lecture information in their notes (Hartley & Cameron, 1967; Hartley & Marshall, 1974; Howe, 1970), strategies for learning from lectures should also be provided to students.

Students did not seem to be aware of different teaching methods used in classes. Engineering students mentioned observing how lecturers approached problems in order to develop problem solving skills, but knowledge about research on the learning process was rarely encountered. Awareness of learning appeared to be overshadowed by the course workload. Across disciplines, more problems with workload were experienced by physics and engineering students than by psychology students, perhaps because the psychology program is introduced at university and therefore students are not expected to have had previous experience in the area. One of the physics professors in the study stated that physics should be learned by all university students as an intellectual enterprise. However, students appeared to be overwhelmed by the amount of work, and therefore had adopted a surface, rote approach to learning rather than searching for meaning. In engineering, students began by adopting survival skills, but soon learned strategies to handle the intellectual demands of problem solving.

Psychology students quickly recognized that they were learning thinking processes, particularly in writing reports. Because introductory psychology courses serve students entering a variety of programs, it could be expected that there would be great heterogeneity of attitude and response to introductory courses, but this did not appear to be the case. One explanation could be the greater openness of students to a subject matter area that is new and personally meaningful to them. They are likely to have developed theories of their own that they have not yet had a chance to test, in contrast with students' testing of physical science theories in secondary school.

One of the most notable insights gained from this study is the attention paid to learning skills in the engineering program. One physics professor talked about loading introductory students with problems until they were forced to go to the tutorial lab for assistance, but engineering professors adopted a more benign attitude of instructing their students in how to solve problems. They seemed more able to put themselves in the students' place. Students recognized this and became team players; their learning strategies by their senior year were collegial. All students had learned important intellectual and metacognitive strategies, but the engineering students appeared to have developed the widest variety of them.

Future Directions for Research

The research reported in this chapter is part of a program of research at the Centre for University Teaching and Learning. Its goal is greater understanding of the relationships between perceptions of the learning process, expert knowledge, and instructional methods and how they affect the quality of learning. Three perspectives guide the research and constitute a set of specific objectives. The first objective is to apply what has been learned to date of professors' and students' perceptions of the learning process to the analysis of student learning behavior and development in their courses; it focuses on the student. The second objective is to elucidate the relationship between explicit expert knowledge and student learning. The focus here is on pedagogical expertise. The third objective is to investigate the effectiveness of selected instructional methods on learning in the courses, with the focus on the methods.

To address the first objective, studying the learning process, we are carrying out three cross-disciplinary studies of the relationship between learning and student characteristics. To do this, a comparative study of what is learned in the classroom at different levels in selected pure and applied fields of study in physical sciences (physics and engineering), social sciences (psychology and education), and humanities (English literature and English language) is underway. In conjunction with this study, a second study focuses on students' declared needs in relation to their developmental level. Studies of intrinsic goal motivation and the challenges that students face will be undertaken to provide comparative information across disciplines about how students learn and develop. In these studies, we are using participant-observation techniques (Tobias, 1990) supplemented by an in-depth interview process. Student research assistants audit a course and keep a record of their experiences as students. A classroom observation matrix is used to examine the kind of intellectual skills and learning strategies developed in class. In-depth interviews and questionnaires are used to establish motivations and challenges.

To address the second objective, of elucidating the relationship between explicit expert knowledge and student learning, a model of explicit knowledge representation encompassing both content knowledge and pedagogical knowledge is being used to delineate the type and level of expert knowledge used to teach in lectures and in interactive settings. In the initial phase, the focus is on the discipline of physics, exploring the scope of expert explicit knowledge in dealing with identified pedagogically difficult (hard to learn) situations, for example, instruction on electrical potential in circuits, in two instructional settings: cognitive apprenticeship and traditional lecture. The focus will then shift to psychology and English literature so that comparisons can be made across disciplines.

The third objective, to investigate the effectiveness of selected instructional methods on learning, is being addressed by studies that focus on specific instructional and learning methods and their effectiveness in different disciplines. In one set of studies, professors at the university level are testing methods used to aid learning for their effectiveness in specific courses. In a second set, professors at the college level are working as a team to identify the intellectual skills that students need to develop, then devising a method for teaching these skills across their courses. Measures are being taken of the effect on student learning and motivation. We invite collaboration in these studies.

ACKNOWLEDGMENTS

This chapter is based on research funded by the Social Science and Humanities Research Council of Canada, the Quebec Fonds pour la Formation de Chércheurs et l'Aide a la Recherche and by Monash University, Australia. The author wishes to express particular appreciation to the professors and students who participated in this project.

REFERENCES

Adams, J. L. (1986). *Conceptual blockbusting.* San Francisco: Freeman.

Andresen, L., Barrett, E., Powell, J., & Wieneke, C. (1985). Planning and monitoring courses: University teachers reflect on their teaching. *Instructional Science, 13,* 305–328.

Barker, D. (1989). Personality profiles and selection for courses. *Assessment and Evaluation in Higher Education, 14*(2), 87–94.

Becher, T. (1989). *Academic tribes and territories*. Milton Keynes: Open University Press.

Biglan, A. (1973). The characteristics of subject matter in different academic areas. *Journal of Applied Psychology, 57*(3), 195–203.

Brown, L. T. (1983). Some more misconceptions about psychology among introductory psychology students. *Teaching of Psychology, 10,* 207–210.

Brown, L. T. (1984). Misconceptions about psychology aren't always what they seem. *Teaching of Psychology, 11*(2), 75–78.

Brown, D. E. (1992). Using examples and analogies to remediate misconceptions in physics: Factors influencing conceptual change. *Journal of Research in Science Teaching, 29*(1), 17–34.

Corno, L., & Snow, R. (1986). Adapting teaching to individual differences among learners. In M. Wittrock (Ed.), *Handbook of research on teaching* (pp. 605–629). New York: Academic Press.

Donald, J. G. (1983). Knowledge structures: Methods for exploring course content. *Journal of Higher Education, 54*(1), 31–41.

Donald, J. G. (1986). Knowledge and the university curriculum. *Higher Education, 15*(3), 267–282.

Donald, J. G. (1988). Professors' expectations of students' ability to think. *Higher Education Research and Development, 17*(1), 19–35.

Donald, J. G. (1990). University professors' views of knowledge and validation processes. *Journal of Educational Psychology, 82*(2), 242–249.

Donald, J. G. (1991). The learning task in engineering courses: A study of professors' perceptions of the learning process in six selected courses. *European Journal of Engineering Education, 16*(2), 181–192.

Donald, J. G. (1992a). The development of thinking processes in postsecondary education: Application of a working model. *Higher Education, 24*(2), 413–430.

Donald, J. G. (1992b, August). *Learning psychology: Ethnographic studies of professors' and students' perceptions*. Paper presented at the annual meeting of the American Psychological Association, Washington, DC.

Donald, J. G. (1993). Professors' and students' conceptualizations of the learning task in introductory physics courses. *Journal of Research in Science Teaching, 30*(8), 905-918.

Entwistle, N. J. (1984). Contrasting perspectives on learning. In F. Marton, D. Hounsell, & N. Entwistle (Eds.), *The experience of learning* (pp. 1-18). Edinburgh: Scottish Academic Press.

Ferguson, M., & de Jong, T. (1991, April). *A model of the cognitive aspects of physics instruction.* Paper presented at the annual meeting of the American Educational Research Association, Chicago.

Fox, P. W., & LeCount, J. (1991, April). *When more is less: Faculty misestimation of student learning.* Paper presented at the annual meeting of the American Educational Research Association, Chicago.

Franklin, J., & Theall, M. (1992, April). *Disciplinary differences: Instructional goals and activities, measures of student performance, and student ratings of instruction.* Paper presented at the annual meeting of the American Educational Research Association, San Francisco.

Garcia, T., & Pintrich, P. (1992, August). *Critical thinking and its relationship to motivation, learning strategies, and classroom experience.* Paper presented at the annual meeting of the American Psychological Association, Washington, DC.

Glover, J. A., Dietzer, M. L., & Bullock, R. G. (1990). Advance organizers: Delay hypotheses. *Journal of Educational Psychology, 82*(2), 291–297.

Goldsmith, T. E., Johnson, P. J., & Acton, W. H. (1991). Assessing structural knowledge. *Journal of Educational Psychology, 83*(1), 88–96.

Gray, T. & Mill, D. (1990). Critical abilities, graduate education (Biology vs. English), and belief in unsubstantiated phenomena. *Canadian Journal of Behavioral Science, 22*(2), 162–172.

Halliday, D. & Resnick, R. (1988). *Fundamentals of physics.* New York: Wiley.

Halpern, D. F., Hansen, C., & Riefer, D. (1990). Analogies as an aid to understanding and memory. *Journal of Educational Psychology, 82*(2), 298–305.

Hammer, D. M. (1991). *Defying common sense: Epistemological beliefs in an introductory physics course.* Unpublished doctoral thesis, University of California, Berkeley.

Hartley, J., & Cameron, A. (1967). Some observations on the efficiency of lecturing. *Educational Review, 20,* 3–7.

Hartley, J., & Marshall, S. (1974). On notes and note-taking. *Universities Quarterly, 28,* 225–235.

Hirst, P. H. (1974). *Knowledge and the curriculum: A collection of philosophical papers.* London: Routledge & Kegan Paul.

Hounsell, D. J., & Ramsden, P. (1978). Roads to learning: An empirical study of students' approaches to coursework and assessment. In D. Billing (Ed.) *Course design and student learning* (pp. 132–139). Guildford: Society for Research in Higher Education.

Howe, M. J. (1970). Using students' notes to examine the role of the individual learner in acquiring meaningful subject matter. *Journal of Educational Research, 64,* 61–63.

King, A. (1992). Comparison of self-questioning, summarizing, and note-taking review as strategies for learning from lectures. *American Educational Research Journal, 29*(2), 303–323.

Lehman, D. R., Lempert, R. O., & Nisbett, R. E. (1988). The effects of graduate training on reasoning. *American Psychologist, 39*(4), 421–427.

McKeachie, W. J. (1974). Instructional psychology. *Annual Review of Psychology, 26*(2), 161–193.

McKeachie, W. J. (1990). Research on college teaching: The historical background. *Journal of Educational Psychology, 82*(2), 189–200.

Miles, M. B., & Huberman, A. M. (1984). *Qualitative data analysis: A sourcebook of new methods.* Beverly Hills: Sage.

Miller, G. A. (1971). Empirical methods in the study of semantics. In D. D. Steinberg & L. A. Jakobovits (Eds.), *Semantics: An interdisciplinary reader in philosophy, linguistics, and psychology* (pp. 569–585). Cambridge: The University Press.

Nisbett, R. E., Fong, G. T., Lehman, D. R., & Cheng, P. W. (1987). Teaching reasoning. *Science, 238,* 625–631.

Novak, J. D. (1990). Concept maps and Vee diagrams: Two metacognitive tools to facilitate meaningful learning. *Instructional Science, 19,* 29–52.

Pankratius, W. J. (1990). Building an organized knowledge base: Concept mapping and achievement in secondary school physics. *Journal of Research in Science Teaching, 27*(4), 315–333.

Pantin, C. (1968). *The relations between the sciences.* Cambridge: Cambridge University Press.

Peltzer, A. (1988). The intellectual factors believed by physicists to be most important to physics students. *Journal of Research in Science Teaching, 25*(9), 721–731.

Pike, G. (1991). The effects of background, coursework, and involvement on students' grades and satisfaction. *Research in Higher Education, 32*(1), 15–30.

Pintrich, P. R., Cross, D. R., Kozma, R. B., & McKeachie, W. J. (1986). Instructional psychology. *Annual Review of Psychology, 37,* 611–651.

Powers, D., & Enright, M. (1987). Analytical reasoning skills in graduate study: Perceptions of faculty in six fields. *Journal of Higher Education, 58*(6), 658–682.

Ramsden, P. (1992). *Learning to teach in higher education.* London: Routledge.

Ratcliff, J. L. (1988). *Developing a cluster-analytic model for identifying coursework patterns associated with general learned abilities of college students.* Paper presented at the annual meeting of the American Educational Research Association, New Orleans.

Reif, F., Larkin, J. H., & Brackett, G. C. (1976). Teaching general learning and problem solving skills. *American Journal of Physics, 44*(3), 212–217.

Russell, D. (1982). The causal dimension scale: A measure of how individuals perceive causes. *Journal of Personality and Social Psychology, 42*(6), 1137–1145.

Ryan, M. P. (1984). Monitoring text comprehension: Individual differences in epistemological standards. *Journal of Educational Psychology, 76*(2), 248–258.

Schwab, J. J. (1962). The concept of the structure of a discipline. *The Educational Record, 43,* 197–205.

Schwab, J. J. (1978). *Science, curriculum and liberal education.* Chicago: University of Chicago Press.

Sparkes, J. J. (1989). Quality in engineering education. *Engineering Professors' Conference, Occasional papers, No. 1,* p. 11.

Tobias, S. (1990). *They're not dumb, they're different.* Tucson, AZ: Research Corporation.

van Weeren, J. H. P. (1983, July). *Route mapping and reflection in the process of learning problem solving.* International summer workshop: Research on physics education, La Londe les Maures, France.

van Weeren, J. H. P., de Mul, F. F. M., Peters, M. J., Kramers-Pals, H., & Roossink, H. J. (1982). Teaching problem solving in physics: A course in electromagnetism. *American Journal of Physics, 50*(8), 725–732.

Vaughan, E. D. (1977). Misconceptions about psychology among introductory psychology students. *Teaching of Psychology, 4,* 138–141.

Winn, W. (1988). Recall of the pattern, sequence, and names of concepts presented in instructional diagrams. *Journal of Research in Science Teaching, 25*(5), 375–386.

5

Self-Regulated Learning in College Students: Knowledge, Strategies, and Motivation

Paul R. Pintrich
The University of Michigan

Teresa Garcia
University of Texas at Austin

Our research the past five to eight years has focused on self-regulated learning in college students and has been conducted in close collaboration with Bill McKeachie on a number of different grants and research projects. The first project that brought Paul Pintrich and Bill McKeachie together was a National Science Foundation grant to develop and research a Learning to Learn course (see McKeachie, Pintrich, & Lin, 1985; Pintrich, McKeachie, & Lin, 1987). From this early collaboration on how to teach college students learning strategies and improve their motivation, we then moved on to a program of research on college student learning in general, funded through a five-year OERI grant to the National Center for Research to Improve Postsecondary Teaching and Learning (NCRIPTAL). It was then that Teresa Garcia joined the research team as a graduate student and has since been an active collaborator throughout these studies of college student learning. We did a number of correlational field studies of college student learning during this program of research (see Pintrich, 1989; Pintrich & Garcia, 1991), as well as developed a general model of college student motivation and self-regulated learning (see McKeachie,

Pintrich, Smith, Lin, & Sharma, 1990; Pintrich, 1988a, 1988b) upon which the Motivated Strategies for Learning Questionnaire (MSLQ) is based (see Pintrich, Smith, Garcia, & McKeachie, 1993). More recently, our College Student Research Group has been continuing its research on college student learning by investigating the role of intraindividual differences in motivation and self-regulation over time (see Pintrich & Garcia, 1994) and the application of our general model to specific classroom contexts like chemistry and calculus courses (e.g., Garcia, Yu, & Coppola, 1993).

Although Bill McKeachie and Paul Pintrich have been co-directors of our College Student Research Group, it has been Bill McKeachie who has provided the intellectual inspiration for our research program and the personal leadership and example that has fostered our collaborative research community. We have also learned a great deal from our colleagues in the College Student Research Group, and we would like to acknowledge the invaluable contributions made by Moshe Naveh-Benjamin, Yi-Guang Lin, Stuart Karabenick, David Smith, Scott VanderStoep, Robert Doljanac, Donna Kempf, Susan Reiter, Barbara Hofer, and Shirley Yu. The purpose of this chapter is to review several general themes that have characterized Bill McKeachie's research as well as our own research in the College Student Research Group, and to propose future directions for research on self-regulated learning in college students. We have identified three general themes that reflect both Bill's contribution to the field and to own our research program: the role of knowledge; the role of general learning and thinking strategies; and the role of motivation, emphasizing the integration of motivation and cognition.

THE ROLE OF KNOWLEDGE

In his famous paper "The Decline and Fall of the Laws of Learning," McKeachie (1974) noted how the law of effect (reward correct responses) and the law of exercise (practice correct responses) proposed by Thorndike (1932) and Skinner (1965) are not easily applied to the classroom because "meaningful learning is much more robust and complex" than suggested by these two general laws of learning based on behavioral theory. In contrast, Bill has always taken a more cognitive view of learning, and as he observed in *Teaching Tips*, (McKeachie, 1994), "human beings are learning organisms—seeking, organizing, coding, storing, and retrieving information all their lives; building on cognitive structures to continue learning throughout life, (certainly not losing the capacity to learn); continually seeking meaning" (p. 289).

This quote has served as an important assumption in all of our research on college students. Our colleagues Moshe Naveh-Benjamin and Yi-Guang Lin (this volume) have been investigating the role of college students' cognitive structures and how the organization of students' knowledge influences their learning. At the same time, however, we have become convinced that just as there are cognitive structures that represent content knowledge, there are cognitive structures that represent self-knowledge and that these structures—self-schemas—can influence learning. Although we are just beginning our research on the role of self-schemas and self-regulated learning (Garcia, 1993; Garcia & Pintrich, 1994), we would like to briefly review the structure and functions of self-schemas, then highlight how self-knowledge plays a role in student learning.

As mentioned earlier, the idea of self-schemas (see Markus & Nurius, 1986; Markus & Wurf, 1987) assumes that we have declarative knowledge about ourselves that operates in a fashion similar to declarative knowledge about a content area. Structurally, this knowledge is stored dynamically in cognitive representations (schemas) that are activated in different situations or tasks. For example, an individual may activate a positive self-schema in a math class because she has a past history of success and believes that she is "generally good at math." On the other hand, this student may not have done well in science class: In contrast to her math self-schema, she may be more likely to activate a negative self-schema about her ability in science. Moreover, in certain situations (e.g., an important math test), a less positive, more anxious self-schema could be activated even for a person with a generally positive math self-schema. The notion that self-schemas are differentially activated in different situations provides a more dynamic, situation-specific view of the self-concept, one that represents an "on-line" or "working" self-concept (Garcia & Pintrich, 1994; Markus & Wurf, 1987).

Besides this general assumption about the dynamic nature of the self-concept, there seems to be four dimensions of the self-schema: affective, temporal, efficacy, and value. The affective dimension refers to the fact that we can have both positive and negative self-schemas and that we generally strive to approach or enact the positive self-schemas and avoid or try to prevent attainment of the negative self-schemas. In this sense, this affective dimension provides "motivational force" that can provide the impetus for behavior, including self-regulation (Garcia & Pintrich, 1994). In addition, it should be noted that these positive and negative self-schemas are personal construals of the individual, so that one person's positive self-schema ("I'm good at schoolwork") may not necessarily be seen as positive by another student who does not value school or whose peer group does not value school.

The temporal dimension represents the idea that self-knowledge not only includes knowledge about oneself at the present, but also knowledge about what one may become in the future (present and possible selves; Garcia & Pintrich, 1994; Markus & Nurius, 1986). Possible selves can represent goals to strive for and can serve the same guiding function as distal and proximal goals in goal theory. For example, a student who is able to envision herself as a scientist and eventually completing a doctoral degree may demonstrate higher motivation and greater cognitive engagement in her science class, compared to a student who cannot imagine herself as a scientist or going on to graduate school. We would expect that these two students would differ in their motivation and use of self-regulatory strategies in their science classes, although there is a great need for empirical evidence for this hypothesis.

The other two dimensions of self-schemas that have been implicit in our discussion to this point are efficacy and value. Efficacy refers to the beliefs about what we can do to become or avoid particular self-conceptions, thereby including perceptions of instrumentality and control. For example, a student may have a "scientist" possible self yet believe there is little she can do to obtain that goal. We assume that these perceptions of efficacy operate in the same manner as self-efficacy and control beliefs do in self-efficacy theory (Bandura, 1986; Schunk, 1991) and self-determination theory (Deci & Ryan, 1985).

The value dimension concerns the centrality of the self-schema to the individual and parallels the notion of attainment value in expectancy-value theory (Eccles, 1983; Feather, 1982). The value dimension represents a way to tap the centrality of different self-schemas. For example, there may be certain self-conceptions that are more central or more important to our sense of self than other self-beliefs (Garcia & Pintrich, 1994). For example, to continue the science example, if the student with a scientist possible self holds this self-belief as highly important, this self-schema will be chronically accessed and she may be more likely to attend to information regarding it, compared to a self-schema for which she holds lower value, perhaps her "athlete" self-schema. In addition, although there are a multitude of self-schemas that we may hold, the value dimension provides a mechanism that ensures that some self-schemas are more important to us than others and are more likely to be activated in different situations.

We are just beginning our research on self-schemas and self-regulated learning with college students, but the results are promising. For example, Garcia (1993) found that students' self-schemas were related to their motivational beliefs and strategies for learning. The various self-schemas generated by the students (e.g., "intelligent," "keeps up with course work," "procrastinates," "unhappy with major") were differentially related to motivational beliefs and learning strategies. For example, the "keeps up with course work" self-schema was positively related to an intrinsic goal orientation, task value, and cognitive, metacognitive, and resource management strategies, whereas the "intelligent" self-schema was positively related to motivational beliefs but unrelated to strategies for learning. These distinct patterns of correlations suggest that different levels of self-regulated learning may be partially accounted for by students' self-beliefs. That is, what we believe we are like and what we believe we may become help provide the impetus for regulating behavior; we have found similar results in a sample of seventh-grade adolescents, lending an encouraging cross-validation of these relations (Garcia & Pintrich, 1993).

Nevertheless, there are many unresolved issues for future research. First, a problem we have struggled with is the assessment of self-schemas, not unlike our colleagues Naveh-Benjamin and Lin (this volume) with the assessment of knowledge structures. We have used open-ended formats ("We would like to know what you think is possible for you to become as a student. Imagine yourself at the beginning of your senior year of college. What positive ways could you be like? What do you hope to be like in terms of academics?"), and although the responses do represent the students' own language, coding these data is problematic. An open-ended protocol results in a number of idiographic codes that make data analysis difficult. On the other hand, having students respond to a standardized protocol forces the respondents to use an organization constructed by the researcher, which may or may not correspond to the individual's personal organization (Deutsch, Kroll, Weible, Letourneau, & Goss, 1988). Another problem with measuring self-schemas using closed-ended, Likert-scaled items is that extremity is generally confounded with descriptiveness. That is, rating a descriptor as moderately true of oneself should not preclude having an elaborate structure of knowledge with regard to that descriptor. For example, a student may rate the "I am quite good at mathematics" item as moderately true, yet hold an elaborate and salient network of knowledge of himself in the mathematics domain (e.g., of himself with regard to different topics in mathematics, of the objective value of being proficient in mathematics, etc.). Another problem arises as to the most appropriate way to integrate the multiple dimensions of self-schemas (affective, temporal, efficacy, and value) into one scale or pattern variable that can capture their unique contribution, but represent self-schemas in their totality. Multidimensional scaling techniques may be helpful in this regard, but we need more research on the assessment of self-schemas.

Besides this basic research on self-schemas and self-regulated learning, there are three general future directions for research on knowledge structures, both content-based knowledge structures and self-knowledge or self-schemas. First, it has become commonplace in cognitive psychology to note that students' prior knowledge influences their learning. In some ways, this general principle has probably replaced the law of effect and law of exercise as a basic principle of learning. Although this a very powerful and useful axiom, the first future direction we offer is that we still need more research on how students actually acquire these cognitive structures. Cognitive psychology's descriptions of expert–novice differences have been very important to our field, but we have yet to fully examine how exactly a novice becomes an expert. We need longitudinal studies of college students that trace the acquisition and development of their cognitive structures over their college careers, not in terms of general stages or styles, but in terms of their understanding of discipline-specific concepts. In the same fashion, the self-schema literature has not really examined how individuals come to acquire and form their self-schemas, instead focusing on the influence self-schemas have on self-perception, motivation, and affect (e.g., Fong & Markus, 1982; Markus, 1977; Markus, Hamill, & Sentis, 1987; Ruvulo & Markus, 1992). Accordingly, we need research that traces the intraindividual development of self-schemas over the course of a college career. This research would be developmental in nature, tracing the acquisition and change in self-schemas for individuals over time, not just cross-sectional studies of self-schemas in different age groups (e.g., Cross & Markus, 1991).

A second general issue concerns research on the transfer of these knowledge structures across tasks and situations. In the cognitive domain, this involves examining how knowledge structures are used across different tasks. For example, how does a knowledge structure formed in an introductory psychology course transfer to an upper level psychology course taken a year later? The work by Bill and our colleagues Naveh-Benjamin and Lin (this volume) suggests that these knowledge structures can be transferred to new domains, or at least the idea that knowledge can be organized in a particular fashion seems to transfer for some students. Accordingly, although knowledge-based models of learning and research on expert–novice differences seem to suggest the difficulty of transfer, we need more research on how students transfer their knowledge as they learn within a discipline. One aspect of this future research on transfer will be the development of a taxonomy of tasks or situations that college students actually confront as they learn in college courses (e.g., types of exams, papers, labs, projects, etc.). The research on these tasks will also have to examine how these tasks are embedded in different content areas and disciplines and try to untangle task from domain effects on students' learning. By developing this taxonomy of actual classroom tasks, we will be able to examine how different knowledge structures map onto these tasks and be able to define the range of applicability of different knowledge structures across tasks and domains. In addition, the development of this taxonomy will help us become more aware of how to specifically teach for transfer across tasks and domains and encourage the use of tasks and specific instructional strategies that help us accomplish the goal of transfer of learning.

In the same fashion, we need research on the "transfer" of self-schemas. Although the term *transfer* is usually not used in the social and personality literature, the issue of the situational specificity of self-schemas is analogous to the issue of transfer of knowledge. We need research that examines the domain-specificity of self-schemas. Although Markus and her colleagues have taken a domain-specific view of self-schemas, their domains (e.g., personal relationships, careers, health) reflect larger aspects of life. In contrast, we are interested in the self-schemas students have for different academic domains and how these course- or discipline-specific self-schemas are organized and their functions in self-regulated learning. Of course, Marsh and his colleagues (Marsh, 1990; Marsh, Byrne, & Shavelson, 1988; Marsh & Gouvernet, 1989) have suggested that self-concept is hierarchically organized with different self-concepts for different academic domains (cf. Wigfield & Karpathian, 1991). This may also be the case with self-schemas, but we still need to examine how domain-specific self-schemas are related to self-regulated learning in different academic domains.

Moving beyond self-schemas and knowledge structures, a third direction for research on knowledge concerns students' understanding of the logic and epistemological assumptions of different disciplines, what Perkins and Simmons (1988) called "epistemic frames." This type of knowledge represents a "higher" level of thinking about a discipline in terms of reasoning, evidence, and beliefs about thinking that are discipline-specific, but not focused on specific concepts. Donald (1990, this volume) showed that university faculty do think and reason somewhat differently about the nature of evidence and the logic of argument, depending on their discipline. In our own research program, we are beginning to explore how students' personal epistemological beliefs are related to their motivation and self-regulation. It appears that students who are less committed to an absolutist view of knowledge (e.g., "there is only one right answer and authorities should tell it to me") are more likely to be mastery-oriented and use deeper processing strategies (Schutz, Pintrich, & Young, 1993). There is a need for more descriptive research on this type of disciplinary thinking and how students acquire it over the course of their college careers, and how it is linked to their specific knowledge structures as well as self-schemas. Moreover, there is a need for research on the best methods for teaching students the disciplinary frames of thinking. Most faculty members believe that by teaching the content and methods of their discipline, students will develop the appropriate epistemic beliefs and thinking frames, but Donald's work (this volume) suggests that this may not be the case. Accordingly, we need to think about different ways of explicitly teaching this type of disciplinary thinking along with our discipline's content and methods.

THE ROLE OF GENERAL LEARNING AND THINKING STRATEGIES

Although knowledge is important, as Bill has noted in his introduction to one of our NCRIPTAL publications (McKeachie, Pintrich, Smith, & Lin, 1986), "Students should continue to learn and use their learning in more effective problem solving for the rest of their lives. When one takes life-long learning and thinking as the major goal of education, knowledge becomes a means rather than an end, and other formerly implicit goals become more explicit" (p.1). The emphasis on the role of general learning and thinking strategies is a second area in which Bill's research has had a major impact on the field of college student learning and one that we have examined extensively in our program of research.

In our research on college students' use of general learning strategies, we have worked from a general model of learning strategies based on the framework suggested by Weinstein and Mayer (1986). We have examined the different roles that rehearsal, organizational, elaboration, and self-regulatory strategies play in college students' learning. The correlational studies we carried out during the five years of funding for NCRIPTAL on more than 2,000 students show fairly consistent results (see Pintrich, 1989; Pintrich & Garcia, 1991). In general, students who use more deep-processing strategies like elaboration and organization are more likely to do better in the course in terms of grades on assignments, exams, and papers, as well as overall course grade. In addition, students who attempt to control their cognition and behavior through the use of planning, monitoring, and regulating strategies also do better on these academic performance measures.

We believe that one of the major contributions of this work for the field of college student learning is its reliance on a theoretically-based model of the active, constructive learner as well as its focus on the actual cognitive and metacognitive strategies that students might use when they try to learn and study, rather than general learning or personality styles (e.g., introversion–extroversion; field dependence or independence; Myers–Briggs profiles). Much of the research on college student learning has concentrated on these general personality styles and it is not clear how they are linked to students' actual study behavior or their cognitive processing of lecture or text information. Our model assumes that these cognitive and metacognitive strategies are not "traits" of the learner, but rather that these strategies can be learned and can be brought under the control of the student. By focusing on strategies that can be controlled and learned by students, our model presents a much more optimistic view of learning to both faculty and students. Students can be taught these strategies directly and faculty can help students learn how to use them. In contrast, models of personality styles assume that these traits of students are stable and domain-general and that students do not have much control over them. Accordingly, models that focus on cognitive styles suggest that faculty adapt their class and teaching style to the diversity of student learning styles—a rather difficult and impractical suggestion.

Besides these general substantive findings, a second more practical contribution of this research has been the development of a self-report instrument for assessing learning strategies and motivation, the Motivated Strategies for Learning Questionnaire or MSLQ (Pintrich, Smith, Garcia, & McKeachie, 1993). The MSLQ can be used for both research and classroom purposes, thereby serving both substantive and practical concerns. Faculty members can use it in their classrooms because it is relatively easy to fill out and does not take much time. Faculty can then use the MSLQ to obtain feedback on their students that may be used to make adjustments in their course. Students can use it for self-diagnosis of their strengths and weaknesses in any course or in specific learning to learn or study skills courses. It seems to be a reliable and useful tool that can be adapted for a number of different purposes for researchers, instructors, and students.

In terms of future directions for research in this area, there are a number of directions; the one that seems most important concerns the contextualization of general learning strategies. For example, we have found that for certain courses and certain types of exams, rehearsal strategies actually work quite effectively, or at least are correlated highly with students' grades on the exam. These courses and exams stress the simple recall of facts, names, and labels as in many biology courses that focus on memorizing terms. These results have made us realize that good strategy use in the classroom may be more conditional and contextual than is suggested by experimental research. That is, students need to understand the conditions under which certain learning strategies might be more or less effective, rather than just assuming that all deeper processing strategies like elaboration are better. We need more research on the conditional knowledge of strategy use, not unlike the research discussed earlier on the range of applicability of knowledge structures. This would include studies of the range of applicability of learning strategies for different tasks and different domains. In addition, as part of understanding conditional knowledge we need research on students' understanding of the goals of the task (e.g., memorization vs. understanding), their own personal goals and criteria used to judge success (performance vs. mastery), and how these goals are coordinated with actual strategy use.

THE ROLE OF MOTIVATION AND BUILDING INTEGRATIVE MODELS OF COGNITION AND MOTIVATION

This focus on conditional knowledge and personal goals brings us to our third theme, involving the role of student motivation in learning and the building of integrative models of cognition and motivation. Traditionally, cognitive research has focused on learners in an experimental setting and not dealt with motivation, thereby portraying a "motivationally inert" learner. At the same time, motivation theory and research has concentrated on students' beliefs, goals, and quantitative notions of effort, but have not addressed issues of how students might actually go about enacting their goals through the use of qualitatively different cognitive and self-regulatory strategies. In effect, these motivational models describe a "cognitively empty" learner. However, in the last few years we have seen a great increase in research that attempts to integrate motivation and cognition and this trend will continue in research in higher education.

Bill's research on how anxiety and information-processing interact to influence learning is an excellent exemplar of research that attempts to link a motivational construct, test anxiety, to students' encoding and retrieval of information (McKeachie, 1951). Bill's research in this area, again with his colleagues Naveh-Benjamin and Lin, shows that the attentional interference model of anxiety and the cognitive skills deficit model may both be valid descriptions depending on the student. They found that there are some test-anxious students who do show deficits in performance because test anxiety interferes with their performance during the exam, even though these students have reasonable cognitive strategies for encoding and learning. However, they also found a second group of high-anxious students who did not have a very good repertoire of learning strategies and were accordingly less well-prepared for the exam and rightfully anxious about their test performance.

This research has had a significant impact on our models of student learning in the college classroom because of its emphasis on the integration of student motivation and cognition. More recently, our research has shown that other motivational beliefs such as goal orientation and self-efficacy are linked in important ways to the use of cognitive and self-regulatory strategies. For example, it seems to be a fairly reliable finding that students who adopt a general intrinsic orientation, have interest in and value the task, and have high self-efficacy for learning beliefs are more likely to be cognitively engaged in learning through the use of cognitive and metacognitive learning strategies (Pintrich & Schrauben, 1992). At the same time, we found that both intrinsic and extrinsic orientations can interact to influence college students' self-regulated learning (Pintrich & Garcia, 1991). This study showed that there was an intrinsic by extrinsic orientation interaction such that students who were high in intrinsic and low in extrinsic orientation were the most cognitively engaged, as would be predicted by goal theory (Ames, 1992) and intrinsic motivation theory (Deci & Ryan, 1985). However, students who were low in intrinsic and high in extrinsic were more cognitively engaged than those low in both types of goal orientations (Pintrich & Garcia, 1991). Accordingly, for some college students, particularly those with little or no intrinsic interest in or value for the course (as might be expected in many required as opposed to elective college courses), extrinsic goals of getting a good grade are "beneficial" in the sense that these goals lead uninterested students to become somewhat more cognitively involved in the course. We need more research that examines these types of multiplicative relations in college classrooms between both motivational and cognitive components of learning.

At the same time, in terms of future directions for research, we need to develop models for representing exactly how these different components interact and are related to the tasks and situations students confront. This is both a theoretical and a unit or level of analysis issue. For example, in Bill's research on test anxiety and information processing, he was able to work at two different levels of analysis, one focused on the constructs themselves in a traditional correlational between-subjects analysis, the other level focused on within-individual differences. If Bill had just examined the correlational results without looking for different types of individuals who showed different patterns of anxiety and strategy use, he would not have found the two types of test anxious students, both supporting different models of test anxiety. In our own research, we also have found differences in our between-subject analyses and our within-subject cluster analyses focused on creating different types of individuals (Pintrich, 1989; Pintrich & Garcia, 1993). For example, although we generally find that self-efficacy and intrinsic goal orientation are positively correlated with cognitive strategy use at about the .40 level, in our cluster analyses we do find certain groups of individuals where self-efficacy and cognitive strategy use are not related to one another.

The unraveling of these differences and the unit of analysis problem will receive a great deal of attention in future research on motivation and cognition. We obviously need some larger unit of analysis beyond just the constructs. After all, college faculty deal with whole students, not an array of motivational and cognitive constructs. Bereiter (1990) argued that a focus on the individual is too large and not context-specific enough. He suggested the use of "modules" that are "carried" by the individual, thereby allowing for individual differences and avoiding problems of strong contextualism; but at the same time, he noted that these modules are assembled and activated differentially depending on the situation.

The construct of self-schemas discussed earlier represent one type of module that may be activated in different situations and guide student cognition and motivation. Another construct that may serve the same function is what we have termed *motivational strategies* (Garcia & Pintrich, 1994), and we have just begin research on these strategies (Garcia, 1993). Motivational strategies are thoughts and behaviors in which students engage during evaluatively "risky" situations, helping to maintain self-worth or to harness anxiety. Our preliminary research has shown that two motivational strategies, self-handicapping and defensive pessimism, influence students' cognitive engagement (Garcia, 1993).

The strategy of self-handicapping involves the deliberate withdrawal of effort in order to create an attributional ambiguity in the event of a failure outcome (Baumeister & Scher, 1988; Berglas, 1985; Covington, 1992; Covington & Beery, 1976; Jones & Berglas, 1978). Self-Handicapping grows out of the realization of the effort-ability link, in which the highest ability evaluations are attached to success paired with low effort, and the lowest ability evaluations are attached to failure paired with high effort. Self-handicapping by withdrawing effort therefore ensures a "safe" outcome, whether the outcome be a success or failure: a failure may be attributed to low effort, whereas one's ability is maximally enhanced by a success following low effort. We have found that this anticipatory strategy is indeed related to lower levels of resource management strategies (i.e., managing time, effort, and study environment) and greater levels of rehearsal, a surface-processing strategy (Garcia, 1993).

In contrast, the strategy of defensive pessimism is a pattern in which individuals use anxiety to fuel effort (Norem & Cantor, 1986). Defensive pessimism involves setting unrealistically low expectations that create anxiety; this anxiety is then used to promote greater efforts whose dividends are generally superior performance. Defensive pessimism is easily recognizable; individuals who engage in this strategy show tremendous worries and believe themselves to be underprepared, yet work terribly hard and have an infuriating tendency to achieve well despite those anxieties. Our empirical work indicates that defensive pessimism is related to high levels of resource management strategies; lower levels of rehearsal strategies; and perhaps not unexpectedly, higher levels of test anxiety (Garcia, 1993).

Although self-regulated learners are generally portrayed as intrinsically motivated, low-anxious, cognitively engaged individuals, the strategy of defensive pessimism demonstrates how performance concerns and anxiety can actually promote cognitive engagement. The strategy of self-handicapping suggests that low motivation and low cognitive engagement may not necessarily be evidence of failure to self-regulate one's learning. Indeed, self-handicapping students' regulation instead involves engaging in low effort, effectively creating an attributional ambiguity which maximizes ability evaluations.

Constructs such as self-schemas and motivational strategies highlight the integration of motivation and cognition in academic settings such as the college classroom. However, we still need more research on how these constructs interact with other motivational and cognitive components and how an individual student regulates his or her knowledge, strategy use, motivation, and volition. As Zimmerman (1989, this volume) and others like Corno (1993) pointed out, students' ability to control their cognition, motivation, and volition can have a dramatic influence on learning. This is especially true for college students who, when you talk to them, are very motivated and concerned about doing well, but often have a very difficult time enacting their intentions, given all the internal and external distractions they confront in college life. So, although the ability to regulate cognition and volition may be important in K–12 education, we think it is even more important for college students. Not only are they developmentally more likely to have the capability to be metacognitive and self-regulating, the classroom and general college environments they confront offer them more choice and control and demand more self-regulation and motivational and volitional control.

On a final note, the focus on students' motivation and cognition and individual differences brings to light another domain in which Bill has made a contribution to research on college student learning: adapting instruction to diversity. Bill's work and writings, best represented by his book *Teaching Tips*, has been reminding us since the first edition in 1951 and continues to remind us now in the 1994 ninth edition, that teaching is not algorithmic. As he notes in his 1974 article on the laws of learning, "this complexity, so frustrating to those who wish to prescribe educational methods, is a reminder of the fascinating uniqueness of the learner" (p. 7).

Bill has been a champion of aptitude-treatment interactions in research on college teaching. At the same time, as Bill pointed out in his 1990 *Journal of Educational Psychology* article on the history of research on college teaching, he does not feel we have to fall into Cronbach's "hall of mirrors" of interactions. In that article, he noted that we do know quite a bit about the main effects of certain types of instruction like the use of small groups or how to teach learning strategies, and that we also have much better theories and data to explain the interactions that do emerge from this research.

One area that will be important for future research on college student instruction is research on diverse groups of students, including gender, ethnic, and class differences. Bill has been a pioneer in diversity research. His work on the college classroom in the 1950s was some of the first to examine gender differences. Throughout his career, he has consistently been concerned with gender and ethnic differences, including the development of special programs and courses to help different students adapt to college life. Although this type of work is important, we believe that as the demographic profile of the United States evolves, becoming comprised of greater numbers of women and persons of color, future research on gender, ethnicity, and class will need to become even more psychological and focus on the within-group individual differences. As Bill would say, we need to understand the psychological mediators of the differences that emerge, not try to understand that all women or African Americans learn the same way or are motivated in the same way. It is this respect for the individual student and teacher that is a hallmark of Bill's career. As he noted in his 1974 article, "most educational situations are interactive situations in which a developing, learning human being engages with a situation in ways designed to meet his needs. Part of that situation is another human being who has some resources for instruction and some capacity to adapt to the learner. It is this that makes education both endlessly challenging and deeply humane" (p. 10).

We believe that our task of understanding cognition, motivation and learning is endlessly challenging and look forward to continued research and the development of our knowledge on these issues. At the same time, given that we both have benefited greatly from the mentorship of Bill, we realize the importance of being deeply humane in our educational efforts. With Bill as an ideal possible self, we hope we can make a contribution to the education of college students in the manner of Bill McKeachie.

REFERENCES

Ames, C. (1992). Classrooms: Goals, structures, and student motivation. *Journal of Educational Psychology, 84,* 261–271.

Bandura, A. (1986). *Social foundations of thought and action: A social cognitive theory.* Englewood Cliffs, NJ: Prentice-Hall.

Baumeister, R. F., & Scher, S. J. (1988). Self-defeating behavior patterns among normal individuals: Review and analysis of common self-destructive tendencies. *Psychological Bulletin, 104,* 3–22.

Bereiter, C. (1990). Aspects of an educational learning theory. *Review of Educational Research, 60,* 603–624.

Berglas, S. (1985). Self-handicapping and self-handicappers: A cognitive/attributional model of interpersonal self-protective behavior. In R. Hogan & W. H. Jones (Eds.), *Perspectives in personality: Theory, measurement, and interpersonal dynamics* (pp. 235–270). Greenwich, CT: JAI Press.

Corno, L. (1993). The best laid plans: Modern conceptions of volition and educational research. *Educational Researcher, 22,* 14–22.

Covington, M. V. (1992). *Making the grade: A self-worth perspective on motivation and school reform.* Cambridge: Cambridge University Press.

Covington, M. V., & Beery, R. G. (1976). *Self-worth and school learning.* New York: Holt, Rinehart & Winston.

Cross, S., & Markus, H. (1991). Possible selves across the life span. *Human Development, 34,* 230–255.

Deci, E. L., & Ryan, R. M. (1985). *Intrinsic motivation and self-determination in human behavior.* New York: Plenum.

Deutsch, F. M., Kroll, J. F., Weible, A. L., Letourneau, L. A., & Goss, R. L. (1988). Spontaneous trait generation: A new method for identifying self-schemas. *Journal of Personality, 56,* 327–354.

Donald, J. (1990). University professors' views of knowledge and validation processes. *Journal of Educational Psychology, 82,* 242–249.

Eccles, J. S. (1983). Expectancies, values, and academic behaviors. In J. T. Spence (Ed.), *Achievement and achievement motives* (pp. 75–146). San Francisco: Freeman.

Feather, N. T. (1982). *Expectations and actions: Expectancy-value models in psychology.* Hillsdale, NJ: Lawrence Erlbaum Associates.

Fong, G. T., & Markus, H. (1982). Self-schemas and judgments about others. *Social Cognition, 1,* 191–204.

Garcia, T. (1993). *Skill and will for learning: Self-schemas, motivational strategies, and self-regulated learning.* Unpublished doctoral dissertation, University of Michigan, Ann Arbor.

Garcia, T., & Pintrich, P. R. (1993, August). *Self-schemas as goals and their role in self-regulated learning.* Paper presented at a symposium, "New directions for goal theory in achievement contexts" at the 101st annual meeting of the American Psychological Association, Toronto, Canada.

Garcia, T., & Pintrich, P. R. (1994). Regulating motivation and cognition in the classroom: The role of self-schemas and self-regulatory strategies. In D. H. Schunk & B. J. Zimmerman (Eds.), *Self-regulation of learning and performance: Issues and educational applications* (pp. 127–153). Hillsdale, NJ: Lawrence Erlbaum Associates.

Garcia, T., Yu, S. L., & Coppola, B. P. (1993, April). *Women and minorities in science: Motivational and cognitive correlates of achievement.* Paper presented at the annual meeting of the American Educational Research Association, Atlanta, GA.

Jones, E. E., & Berglas, S. (1978). Control of attributions about the self through self-handicapping strategies: The appeal of alcohol and the role of underachievement. *Personality and Social Psychology Bulletin, 4,* 200–206.

Markus, H. (1977). Self-schemata and processing information about the self. *Journal of Personality and Social Psychology, 35,* 63–78.

Markus, H., Hamill, R., & Sentis, K. P. (1987). Thinking fat: Self-schemas for body weight and the processing of weight-relevant information. *Journal of Applied Social Psychology, 17,* 50–71.

Markus, H., & Nurius, P. (1986). Possible selves. *American Psychologist, 41,* 954–969.

Markus, H., & Wurf, E. (1987). The dynamic self-concept: A social-psychological perspective. *Annual Review of Psychology, 38,* 299–337.

Marsh, H. W. (1990). The structure of the academic self-concept: The Marsh/Shavelson model. *Journal of Educational Psychology, 82,* 623–636.

Marsh, H. W., Byrne, B., & Shavelson, R. J. (1988). A multifaceted academic self-concept: Its hierarchical structure and its relation to academic achievement. *Journal of Educational Psychology, 80,* 366–380.

Marsh, H. W., & Gouvernet, P. J. (1989). Multidimensional self-concepts and perceptions of control: Construct validation of responses by children. *Journal of Educational Psychology, 81,* 57–69.

McKeachie, W. J. (1951). Anxiety in the college classroom. *Journal of Educational Psychology, 45,* 153–160.

McKeachie, W. J. (1974). The decline and fall of the laws of learning. *Educational Researcher, 3,* 7–11.

McKeachie, W. J. (1994). *Teaching tips: Strategies, research and theory for college and university teachers.* Lexington, MA: Heath.

McKeachie, W. J. (1990). Research on college teaching: The historical background. *Journal of Educational Psychology, 82,* 189–200.

McKeachie, W. J., Pintrich, P. R., & Lin, Y.-G. (1985). Teaching learning strategies. *Educational Psychologist, 20,* 153–160.

McKeachie, W. J., Pintrich, P. R., Smith, D. A. F., & Lin, Y.-G. (1986). *Teaching and learning in the college classroom: A review of the research literature.* Ann Arbor, MI: National Center for Research to Improve Postsecondary Teaching and Learning.

McKeachie, W. J., Pintrich, P. R., Smith, D. A. F., Lin, Y.-G., & Sharma, R. (1990). *Teaching and learning in the college classroom: A review of the research literature.* Ann Arbor, MI: NCRIPTAL, The University of Michigan.

Norem, J. K., & Cantor, N. (1986). Defensive pessimism: Harnessing anxiety as motivation. *Journal of Personality and Social Psychology, 51,* 1208–1217.

Perkins, D., & Simmons, R. (1988). Patterns of misunderstanding: An integrative model of misconceptions in science, mathematics, and programming. *Review of Educational Research, 58,* 303–326.

Pintrich, P. R. (1988a). A process-oriented view of student motivation and cognition. In J. S. Stark & L. Mets (Eds.), *Improving teaching and learning through research: New directions for institutional research* (Vol. 57, pp. 55–70). San Francisco: Jossey-Bass.

Pintrich, P. R. (1988b). Student learning and college teaching. In R. E. Young & K. E. Eble (Eds.), *College teaching and learning: Preparing for new commitments* (Vol. 33, pp. 71–86). San Francisco: Jossey-Bass.

Pintrich, P. R. (1989). The dynamic interplay of student motivation and cognition in the college classroom. In C. Ames & M. L. Maehr (Eds.), *Advances in motivation and achievement: Motivation-enhancing environments* (Vol. 6, pp. 117–160). Greenwich, CT: JAI Press.

Pintrich, P. R., & Garcia, T. (1991). Student goal orientation and self-regulation in the college classroom. In M. L. Maehr & P. R. Pintrich (Eds.), *Advances in motivation and achievement: Goals and self-regulatory processes* (Vol. 7, pp. 371–402). Greenwich, CT: JAI Press.

Pintrich, P. R., & Garcia, T. (1993). Intraindividual differences in students' motivation and self-regulated learning. *Zeitschrift fur Padagogische Psychologie, 7,* 99–107.

Pintrich, P. R., McKeachie, W. J., & Lin, Y. G. (1987). Teaching a course in learning to learn. *Teaching of Psychology, 14,* 81–86.

Pintrich, P. R., & Schrauben, B. (1992). Students' motivational beliefs and their cognitive engagement in classroom tasks. In D. H. Schunk & J. Meece (Eds.), *Student perceptions in the classroom: Causes and consequences* (pp. 149–183). Hillsdale, NJ: Lawrence Erlbaum Associates.

Pintrich, P. R., Smith, D. A. F., Garcia, T., & McKeachie, W. J. (1993). Reliability and predictive validity of the Motivated Strategies for Learning Questionnaire (MSLQ). *Educational and Psychological Measurement, 53,* 801–813.

Ruvulo, A., & Markus, H. (1992). Possible selves and performance: The power of self-relevant imagery. *Social Cognition, 10,* 95–124.

Schunk, D. H. (1991). Self-efficacy and academic motivation. *Educational Psychologist, 26,* 207–231.

Schutz, P. A., Pintrich, P. R., & Young, A. J. (1993, April). *Epistemological beliefs, motivation and student learning.* Paper presented at the annual meeting of the American Educational Research Association, Atlanta, GA.

Skinner, B. F. (1965). *Science and human behavior.* New York: Free Press.

Thorndike. E. L. (1932). *The fundamentals of learning.* New York: Teachers College.

Weinstein, C.E., & Mayer, R. (1986). The teaching of learning strategies. In M. Wittrock (Ed.), *Handbook of research on teaching and learning* (pp. 315–327). New York: Macmillan.

Wigfield, A., & Karpathian, M. (1991). Who am I and what can I do? Children's self-concepts and motivation in achievement situations. *Educational Psychologist, 26,* 233–262.

Zimmerman, B. J. (1989). A social cognitive view of self-regulated academic learning. *Journal of Educational Psychology, 81,* 329–339.

6

Goals as the Transactive Point Between Motivation and Cognition

Paul A. Schutz
University of Akron

The relationship between cognition and motivation is an issue that is receiving increased attention in both education and psychology (Ford, 1992; Kuhl, 1986; McKeachie, 1990; McKeachie, Pintrich, & Lin, 1985; Pintrich & Garcia, 1991; Pintrich & Schrauben, 1992; Sorrentino & Higgins, 1986). This attention is the result of an interest on the part of theorists and researchers to understand the combined influences of motivation and cognition on self-directed behavior. As indicated by McKeachie et al. (1985), knowledge of learning strategies does not necessarily lead to better academic performance; students must also develop the motivation to use those strategies. Therefore, if we are going to understand and be able to facilitate the self-directed behavior needed to reach academic as well as other life goals, we must understand the combined influences of motivation and cognition on those processes.

As the theoretical and empirical work continues, we must remember that motivation and cognition in thought and behavior are two transactive[1] dimensions of the same self-directed process. They are not separate entities. Theoretical and empirical convenience and bias has resulted in them being studied as different constructs (Ford, 1992; Locke

---

[1]The term *transaction* is used in this chapter to indicate the relationship is one where exchange or mutual change takes place with the factors involved in the relationship (Dewey & Bentley, 1949; Rosenblatt, 1978).

& Latham, 1990; McKeachie, 1990; Sorrentino & Higgins, 1986). Thus, conceptually, it is important that we begin not by trying to put two existing, yet separate, constructs together but by finding a point where the transactions between cognition and motivation during self-directed processes can be seen. The question related to this issue is not, "What is the relationship between cognition and motivation?" but "Where is the transactive point between the processes of thinking, the content of thought, and the direction of thought and behavior?"

To answer that question it will be helpful to begin by clarifying how the constructs cognition and motivation are used in the literature. For example, *cognition* is often referred to as "all the ways in which people think" (Gage & Berliner, 1992) as well as the cognitive strategies used to facilitate learning and thinking (Pintrich & Garcia, 1991). From these definitions, the relevant questions that emerge for our discussion are: "What are we thinking about?" and "What are the cognitive strategies used for?" The assumption in this chapter is that our cognitions are about something; there is an object or content to thought. This is not to say that we are always thinking. There are times when we act or react with little or no awareness of any thoughts that may be occurring. But when we think, we think about something. In terms of learning and thinking strategies, we use them for a purpose; there is an intent or an end-point the strategies are directed toward. For example, our thoughts may be about a test next week and the strategies used may be directed toward learning the material to do well on the test.

Motivation in the literature tends to be discussed in terms of the direction of thought and behavior and the regulation of thoughts and behaviors[2] (Campbell & Bickhard, 1986; Ford, 1992; Schutz & Lanehart, 1994). From this definition, the relevant questions that emerge are, "What are our thoughts and behaviors directed toward?" and "What are our thoughts and behaviors regulated in relationship to?" The assumption in this chapter is that our thoughts and behaviors are directed toward something; they are intentional. This does not mean that we are always conscious of that intent, only that there is a direction

---

[2]Some theories also discuss motivation in terms of what energizes human behavior. The contention of the author is that we are always doing something. Hence, the discussion of what energizes behavior appears to be a vestigial concern from the perspective that humans are machinelike and, therefore, need, like all good machines, something to get them going (see Bickhard, 1980; Campbell & Bickhard, 1986; Ford, 1992).

to our thoughts and behaviors (Ford, 1992; Klinger, 1977). In addition, regulation implies a standard to judge where you are in relationship to where you would like to be. To regulate means that you are comparing something to something else and adjusting or not adjusting your thoughts and behaviors accordingly. Thus, the decision may be to study for the test next week and not watch a TV show, thereby maintaining a standard of being a good student.

From the perspective presented here, the answer to the questions "What are we thinking about?," "What are the cognitive strategies used for?," and "What are our thoughts and behaviors directed toward and regulated in relationship to?" is: the goals and standards we attempt to attain and maintain. Our thoughts are about something and are directed toward some purpose or end. That something is the goals and standards we attempt to attain and maintain. For example, ask yourself, "Why am I reading this chapter?" For some, the answer may be a prelude to looking for something else to do. For others, the answer may be their interest in motivation or goals. Whatever answer you give is, in essence, a goal for reading the chapter. In addition, as you read you use strategies and make judgments about the content, the logical flow of the arguments, and the perceived relevancy of what is said. In order to make those judgments you use personal standards, which have been developed through past experiences, related to the content being discussed and how it is presented. Those goals and standards direct and regulate your thoughts (motivation) and the strategies you use while reading (cognition). Your goals and standards influence whether or not you decide to continue to read the chapter (cognition) and influence if and when you stop reading the chapter (motivation). Therefore, one of the premises of this chapter is that in order to understand the transactions between motivation and cognition, you must find the point where cognition and motivation merge. The argument here is that goals and standards are that transactive point.

THE COMBINED INFLUENCES OF MOTIVATION AND COGNITION

There is a growing number of researchers and theorists who have attempted to investigate the combined influences of motivational and cognitive variables on self-directed behavior (Ford, 1992; McKeachie, 1990; McKeachie, Pintrich, & Lin, 1985; Pintrich & Garcia, 1991; Pintrich & Schrauben, 1992; Schutz, 1993a; Schutz & Lanehart, 1994; Sorrentino & Higgins, 1986; Weinstein, 1988). For example, M. Ford (1992), who has based his work, in part, on D. Ford's (1987) person-in-context model, presented an integrated view that attempts to deal with the transactions between motivation and cognition within an environmental context. The cornerstone of that model and the focus of the transactions between motivation and cognition are the core goals and standards that we attempt to attain and maintain. He referred to core goals as a small set of personal goals that are so important that a large portion of our strong feelings of satisfaction and frustration can be traced to these central organizing concerns (Ford, 1992).

In addition, the research focus of the National Center for Research to Improve Postsecondary Teaching and Learning (NCRIPTAL) that was housed at the University of Michigan under the direction of Wilbert J. McKeachie and Paul R. Pintrich was the interaction of motivational and cognitive characteristics (McKeachie, 1990). This project produced a number of findings indicating that academic performance is enhanced when both motivational and cognitive strategies are employed by students (McKeachie, 1990; McKeachie et al., 1985; Pintrich & Garcia, 1991; Pintrich & Schrauben, 1992).

These results are similar to our research findings with both college and high school students that indicate that motivation in and of itself does not insure successful academic performance. Motivation must be accompanied by the cognitive learning strategies needed for successful academic performance (Schutz, 1993b; Schutz & Lanehart, 1994; Weinstein, 1988; Weinstein & Mayer, 1986). Our program of research has been developed with the assumption that goals and standards are the key dimensions to understanding self-directed behavior (see Fig. 6.1).

Goals and Standards

Goals, as they are defined here, are cognitive representations of what we would like to have happen and what we would like to avoid in the future (Ford, 1992; Markus & Nurius, 1986; Wentzel, 1991). Standards, on the other hand, are developed throughout the process of goal clarification and provide additional information about the nature of what it would take to accomplish the goals. In other words, part of the thoughts related to the goal of becoming a teacher are the characteristics of the "ideal" teacher that we would like to become as well as the characteristics of the teacher that we would like to avoid becoming (e.g., "I want to be a caring teacher" or "I don't want to be an unorganized teacher"). These standards are based on the person's current level of

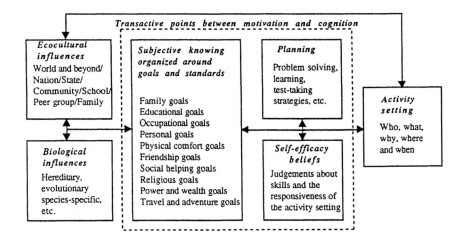

FIG. 6.1. A model representing the transactions between motivation and cognition.

knowing related to the nature of the goal and they are also used in the goal attempt to compare one's present position to the goal's accomplishment.

The depth and richness of our current level of knowing related to the goal develops throughout the process of attempting to reach the goal. For example, my goal of becoming a professor started with a vague notion that I wanted to become a college teacher. When I was in college it looked like a good job—you got to meet and talk to students in a learning environment and the hours "seemed" good. I had no clue of what it took to get there or what you did besides teach if you did get there. In addition, since I was a first-generation college student, I had no idea that graduate school existed.

From the time of that vague notion until I got my first position, my goal did not change: "I wanted to become a college teacher." What changed was my level of knowing related to becoming a college teacher. Throughout the process of becoming or attempting to attain the goal, various standards have developed (e.g., I wanted a teaching job that provided me the opportunity to do research, I wanted to become a teacher who is organized in the classroom, and I wanted to become a teacher who is willing to help others develop professionally). Thus, part of the representation of a goal that we are pursuing is the standards that we develop throughout the goal attempt and which, in this example, differentiate the nature and type of teacher that I am continually becoming. For example, I consider myself of the second-generation when it comes to the ecocultural influences of Dr. McKeachie (see Fig. 6.1). Thus far, I have had the opportunity to work with two first-generation people: Dr. Claire Ellen Weinstein, who has helped me through graduate school and into the beginnings of my professional career, and Dr. Paul Pintrich, who I have more recently gotten to know both professionally and personally. I can think of no greater tribute to Dr. McKeachie than when I hear Claire Ellen and Paul talk about how he has helped them develop professionally. I hear and see them doing the same things not only for me but for many others as well.[3] In other words, helping others to develop professionally is a standard related to the goal of becoming a college teacher. That standard has developed through transactions within an ecocultural niche where helping is considered part of the goal. Therefore, it also becomes one of the criteria that I use to determine whether or not I am attaining the personal goal of becoming a college teacher.

Current Research on Goals

Presently, our investigations focus on the identification of the content of the goals that are developed within the transactions between cognition and motivation. This approach is somewhat different from many of the current investigations of goals in education and psychology where the emphasis has tended to focus on two major lines of this research (Ford, 1992; Schutz 1991; Schutz & Lanehart, 1994). One line has focused on how the characteristics of goals, such as specificity, difficulty, and measurability, effect performance in the classroom as well as a variety of other settings (see Locke & Latham, 1990). These characteristics, when

---

[3]I once heard Coach Bear Bryant say that when they won, he attributed it to what his players and assistant coaches did; when they lost, he attributed it to what he should have done differently. At this point I know that Bill will be trying to use Bear's philosophy (or Bear was using Bill's philosophy) and say that Claire Ellen and Paul are the ones that deserve the credit. Well, there are at least three people who know that is not completely true.

looked at in conjunction with goal commitment, informational feedback, and self-efficacy beliefs related to goal attainment, have been shown to influence the direction of thought and behavior, the regulation of thought and behavior, and the level of performance on academic as well as other tasks (Locke & Latham, 1990).

The other line of research focuses on the orientation of the goals that we set (Ames & Ames, 1984; Ames & Archer, 1988; Dweck & Leggett, 1988; Nicholls, 1984; Pintrich & Schrauben, 1992). The major focus in this line of research is on the distinction between intrinsically oriented goals, such as mastery, challenge, learning, or curiosity, and extrinsically oriented goals, such as grades, rewards, or approval from others (Pintrich & Schrauben, 1992). This research shows that one's goal orientation may influence the direction of thought and behavior, the regulation of thought and behavior, and the level of performance on academic tasks (Ames & Archer, 1988; Dweck & Leggett, 1988; Nicholls, 1984; Pintrich & Garcia, 1991; Pintrich & Schrauben, 1992).

Goal orientation is a similar construct to what has been referred to in this chapter as a standard; a particular type of standard that helps to inform the person about the nature of the goal and what it would mean to the person to attain that goal. The goal for becoming a teacher could have standards that were intrinsically oriented as well as extrinsically oriented. Goals, as they are being defined here, and goal orientation are orthogonal constructs. For example, part of the reason that a person may want to become a teacher could be related to the challenge and interest they find in working with people. On the other hand, they could also want to become a teacher because of the perceived recognition they would receive from family and friends. Thus, you could have a goal to become a teacher, yet have different standards or orientations as to what that means.

Goal Content

Our investigations into the content of goals have identified 10 interdependent goal domains (see Fig. 6.1):

1. personal well-being (e.g., "to acquire self-knowledge" or "to have a happy outlook on life");
2. social helping (e.g., "to be a community leader" or "to work helping others");
3. educational (e.g., "to earn a bachelor's degree" or "to earn a high grade point average");

4. religious (e.g., "to be active in religious affairs" or "to help others develop religiously");
5. family (e.g., "to develop or continue to develop a fulfilling intimate relationship" or "to get or stay married");
6. occupational (e.g., "to improve your occupational skills throughout your career" or "to have a job that you truly enjoy");
7. material wealth and recognition (e.g., "to be rich" or "to be seen as being powerful and important");
8. physical comfort (e.g., "to have financial stability" or "to own a home");
9. friendship (e.g., "to continue my friendships" or "to make new friends"); and
10. travel and adventure (e.g., "to travel to foreign countries" or "to sky dive or climb a mountain").

These domains are similar to other models (see Astin & Nichols, 1964; Buhler & Massarik, 1968; Cross & Markus, 1991; Ford & Nichols, 1987; Wicker, Lambert, Richardson, & Kahler, 1984; Winell, 1987). However, unlike other models, which tended to be developed from the theory of the experimenter, these domains were developed from the responses of students in previous studies to the question: "Think about all you would like to achieve, obtain, and/or experience during your life. List as many as you can." With an interrater reliability of .85, we have been able to categorize 98% of the goals stated by 348 students in one study and 95% of the goals of 120 students in a second study (see Table 6.1). Therefore, the model may provide more ecological validity to the study of goals than previous models.

Goal Development

The goals and standards that are represented in those domains emerge from the transactions between (a) biological influences, (b) ecocultural influences, and (c) our present level of subjective knowing (see Fig. 6.1). The biological influences include hereditary and evolutionary species-specific influences (e.g., genetic factors and life cycle processes such as growth, puberty, maturity, and physical decline). These influences provide a basic framework that allows for a range of developmental potentialities during the life cycle of the human system. The ecocultural influences include environmental as well as cultural influences from

TABLE 6.1

Percent of the Subjects Who Listed at Least

One Goal in a Domain

		Study 1	Study 2
		N = 348	N = 120
		M = 8.7	M = 13.2
		SD = 3.7	SD = 6.6
1.	Occupational goals	94.3%	86.7% (3)
2.	Family goals	85.3%	90.0% (2)
3.	Educational goals	77.0%	91.7% (1)
4.	Travel and adventure goals	54.6%	74.2% (4)
5.	Personal well-being goals	50.3%	70.8% (5)
6.	Physical comfort goals	40.2%	58.3% (6)
7.	Power and wealth goals	35.9%	36.7% (7)
8.	Social helping goals	21.8%	25.0% (9)
9.	Friendship goals	9.8%	29.2% (8)
10.	Religious goals	8.9%	13.3% (10)

family, friends, community, nation, etc. (Berry, 1988; Smith, 1991; Smith & Schutz, 1991; Tharp & Gallimore, 1988). The ecocultural influences, working within the perimeters of the biological influences, can facilitate the potentialities of the human system or allow the potentialities to deteriorate. For example, a person can be born with the potential to grow to be seven feet tall. This potential, however, can be hindered by a lack of adequate nutrition during important periods of development and, thereby, not reached.

Out of the potentialities of the biological influences and the experiences provided within the ecocultural influences, we begin to emerge and develop our subjective view of the world or our subjective knowing. This subjective knowing is organized around what Winell (1987) referred to as ultimate goals (values) and Ford (1992) referred to as core goals. These core goals emerge out of the dynamic interplay of the biological, ecocultural, and subjective knowing influences. It is within that dynamic interplay that self-directed attempts at the attainment of our goals occur. These goals are cognitive representations of what we would like to have happen and what we would like to avoid in the future. In addition, our thoughts and behaviors are directed toward and regulated in relationship to these goal representations.

Goals in Organizing and Representing the Content of Thought

This perspective is consistent with a number of researchers and theorists that have emerged from a variety of areas who discuss goals and standards as a key organizational process that influences our thoughts, memories and interpretations of what we see in the world (e.g., Abbott & Black, 1986; Barsalou, 1983; Bickhard, 1980; Campbell & Bickhard, 1986; Ford, 1992; Lenddo & Abelson, 1986; Pervin, 1991; Read, 1987; Trzebinski, 1989).

For example, Trzebinski (1989) investigated the nature of goals in thoughts as related to the attributions we make while explaining or talking about someone's behavior. In several studies he and his colleagues were able to demonstrate that goals influence how we perceive the behavior of others and how we represent that knowledge in memory (Trzebinski, 1985; Trzebinski & Richards, 1985). These findings indicate that when we view the behavior of others, one of the primary factors involved in our interpretive thought process and the resulting behavior is an attempt to determine the goal we perceive the person to be attempting to attain. For example, if we know that John studied one hour for a major test, we may ask ourselves, "What is John trying to accomplish by only studying one hour?" We may conclude that John is not particularly interested in school or the class he has the major test in. But, what if we add the information: "It is two weeks before the test and it is Thanksgiving day." Does our perception of John's intentions for the class change? If we were John's teacher, how might that knowledge change how we interact with John as a student?

In a different, but related, series of studies, Barsalou (1983, 1988) provided evidence that people organize their thoughts around the information, skills, and strategies needed to move them closer to a particular goal or a combination of goals. So, the goal of getting an "A" on a math test could result in the process of developing cognitive representations of the "ways to prepare for the math test." This goal-derived organization of information, skills, and strategies could be useful in developing a plan for achieving the goal of an "A" on the test.

Conway (1990), in similar research, concluded that goal-derived categories speed memory retrieval. He suggested these results indicate that goal-derived categories are closely associated in long-term memory with memories of specific experiences. A similar view is held by Ford (1992) who discussed the concept of a *behavior episode schema* which he referred to as an integration of thought, feeling, perceptual activities, biological processes, and knowledge related to a particular context. He further stated that *behavior episode schemata* are organized and integrated around the goals we attempt to attain within a particular context. Thus, when going home from work, the behavior episode schema for going home is invoked and the strategy for being in the right lane at the right time, as well as our standard for how long it should take, becomes active and is used to judge our progress. Our thoughts and behaviors are organized around the goal of getting home. This theory and research indicates that knowing, at the very least, may be situationally organized around the goals and standards that we attempt to attain and maintain within a specific context.

The perspective being explicated here takes a stronger position: Knowing is successful, goal-directed, interactive process. To know something is to interact successfully according to some goal or standard (Bickhard, 1980; Campbell & Bickhard, 1986; Schutz, 1991). To know how to manage a classroom means that you have developed some standards related to what a well-managed classroom is like. It would include knowing the information, skills, and ways of doing things, as well as being able to determine when and why to use the information, skills, and strategies to move closer to the overall goal of a well-managed classroom (Paris, Lipson, & Wixson, 1983; Schutz & Smith, 1991). This personal knowing is developed through our experiences while interacting within the world from our subjective view of the world in attempts to develop, reach, and maintain our goals and standards (Schutz, 1991). Consequently, the organizing processes related to the representation of our subjective knowing are the goals and standards that we attempt to attain and maintain.

Goals and Learning

It would therefore follow that learning is also centered around the goals and standards that we attempt to attain and maintain. Learning, as it relates to subjective knowing and our subjective view of the world, is a process of organizing and reorganizing our interactive experiences. Human learning is a constructive process that involves, among other things, making errors, detecting errors, and attempting to correct them (Bickhard, 1980; Campbell & Bickhard, 1986; Popper, 1965, 1972; Schutz, 1991). It is constructive because the process involves the generation of new attempts and theories aimed at eliminating past errors and moving one closer to one's goals or helping one to maintain standards. Learning can also be reflective in the sense that, if learning is to occur, at some level there is awareness of the goals as well as where the interactive attempt is in relationship to those goals. The intended result of the learning process is an improvement in the way one interacts according to a particular goal or combination of goals. In other words, one knows how to interact at a level in which one previously was unable to interact (Schutz, 1991).

One area of research that has provided results related to how goals influence learning is the study of the comprehension of story grammars (Abbott & Black, 1986; Rumelhart & Ortony, 1977; Thorndyke, 1977). This research has demonstrated that while learning how to read stories, students develop hierarchical standards for what stories are expected to contain. Students who develop these standards read stories with certain expectations that facilitate their thoughts and behaviors towards the overall goal of comprehending the story. Thus, while reading the story, certain things are expected and looked for within the context of the story. For example, one important characteristic of a story is the goal the main character is trying to attain. That goal has been shown to be an important factor in determining the level of understandability of the story (Abbott & Black, 1986; Bartlett, 1932; Kintsch & Green, 1978; Thorndyke, 1977). This research has indicated that recall of the story is adversely affected when the goal of the main character is missing, introduced late, or written in obscure language. This research has also shown that successful paths to the main goal tend to be remembered better than unsuccessful paths (Abbott & Black, 1986) and goal-directed actions tend to be remembered better than non-goal-directed actions (Lichtenstein & Brewer, 1980).

Core Goals

Although the research from our program of work has discussed 10 interdependent goal domains, most students we researched tended not to have important goals in all domains. As indicated earlier, the goals that students report having tend to be centered around a smaller number of core goals that are of primary concern at any point in time (Ford, 1992; Klinger, 1977; Winell, 1987). For most of the subjects we have studied (i.e., college students), the three domains that are most likely to be represented when they are asked to list their goals are family, educational, and occupational domain goals. Table 6.1 shows the percent of the students that listed at least one goal in a domain in the aforementioned studies. From the table you can see that with two different samples, even though the second sample stated more goals (i.e., $M = 13.2$ compared to $M = 8.7$), similar patterns emerged. Basically the relative percent of students who listed a goal in a domain remained the same. The top three goal domains changed places but still remained the most mentioned of the goal domains. In fact, the gap between the top three core domains and the fourth most mentioned goal was 22% in Study One and 12% in Study Two. Therefore, at least at this point in their lives, for most of the undergraduate college students that we asked, their core goals revolve around their perceived family, educational, and occupational future.

It is out of these core goals and standards that subgoals emerge. Often these subgoals are goals that have the potential to help in the attainment of multiple goals (Ford, 1992; Pintrich & Garcia, 1991; Wentzel, 1991). For example, the subgoal of getting an "A" in a class can help with the educational goal of getting a degree, the occupational goal of getting a good job, and the personal goal of self-development. On the other hand, subgoals in one domain may also have the potential to conflict with goals in another domain (e.g., the parent who has the subgoal to get an "A" in a class but also has a sick child who must be taken care of) (Argyle, Furham, & Graham, 1981; Dodge, Asher, & Parkhurst, 1989; D. Ford, 1987; M. Ford, 1992). In that situation, decisions will need to be made; the "A" may not be as important as was once thought.

Planning, Self-Efficacy and the Activity Setting

It is from our goals and subgoals that plans are developed for their attainment. The success of this planning is dependent in part on the level of reflection about the relevant situational variables that may be involved or that may affect the attempt. *Developing awareness* as it is used here is similar to Flavell's (1987) conception of metacognition but is closer in nature to the concept of *reflective abstraction* used by Bickhard (1980), Campbell and Bickhard (1986), and Piaget (1976). This process involves reflective thinking and collecting information about: (a) the environmental constraints as well as information about the specific task; (b) the person relevant to the development and use of the goals; and (c) the potential tactics and strategies that could be used to help deal with the situational characteristics and, therefore, help to attain one's goals. Thus, as the information is collected, the person is in the process of planning and predicting when particular tactics and strategies would be effective and when they would not be effective. Through this process of considering one's present level of knowing related to oneself, the task, and potential tactics and strategies, one begins to develop plans to move closer to the attainment of one's goal(s).

Considerable theory and research has indicated that students who use effective learning strategies in their plans tend to be more successful academically (King, 1992; McKeachie, Pintrich, & Lin, 1985; Pressley et al., 1992; Schutz, 1993a; Schutz & Lanehart, 1994; Weinstein, 1988; Weinstein & Mayer, 1986). In other words, students who get themselves to the learning situation and know what to do when they get to that situation tend to perform better academically. Yet, what has also come out of this research is that knowing how to use effective learning strategies does not insure they will be used. There are other factors involved. Goals, strategies, and plans must be combined with confidence in the ability to reach the goals by developing and using a plan with effective strategies.

The confidence needed for the success of plans and strategies emerges from our beliefs about our ability to accomplish goals and use strategies successfully as well as the perceived willingness of the activity setting to facilitate the goal attempt (Bandura, 1986; Ford, 1992; Pervin, 1991; Schunk, 1991; Schutz, 1993b). These personal agency beliefs and/or self-efficacy judgments have been found to influence the plans developed, the strategies considered, the goals attempted, and successes at the goal attempts (Bandura, 1986; Ford, 1992; Schunk, 1991; Schutz, 1993b). These cognitive judgments have emotional and motivational influences on the thoughts and behaviors that occur. For example, we can have a goal we are confident in and committed to, as well as effective strategies we believe will work; yet, placed in a situation where we believe the activity setting will not facilitate goal attainment, we may avoid the attempt. This may be dealt with by anger, depression, or a plan that takes into account the aspects of the activity setting that are perceived to be the problem (Schutz, 1991). In any event, these judgments, which are related to goals and goal attempts, involve the combined influence of both cognitive and motivational variables and have a strong influence on self-directed behavior.

As indicated, our goal attempts take place in various activity settings that tend to be patterned and repetitive places where individuals interact (Smith, 1991; Smith & Schutz, 1991; Tharp & Gallimore, 1988). In education the activity setting is often the classroom. The activity setting in the classroom is defined by who is present and available, what they are doing and why, and where and when they are doing it (Smith, 1991; Smith & Schutz, 1991). Even though individuals have the potential to influence what transactions occur in the setting, what occurs is mostly influenced by the goals and standards of the ecoculture. For example, in our society, one of the prevalent ideologies of many school systems is a belief in the importance of an external goal orientation (Maehr & Midgely, 1991). This is manifested in the activity setting by such things as grades, gold stars, or honor rolls. These goals and standards influence the activities that are developed and used in the classroom. In this example, grades tend to become the standard by which students are judged, and, therefore, activities tend to be designed so judgments can be made.

Thus our goals and standards emerge and change in the midst of continual transactions within ourselves as well as between ecocultural and biological influences. The ecocultural and biological influences help to create the activity setting in which our goal attempts take place. Before, during, and after participating in these activity settings, we think about our experiences. Through this thought process, we develop a subjective view of the world that is the platform from which we base our interactive attempts at reaching or maintaining our goals and standards. Our perceptions of the ecocultural and biological influences, our perceptions of ourselves, and our feelings about our interactive attempts in various activity settings are influenced by and help in the continual development of our subjective view of the world that, in turn, provides the basis for the continual development and pursuit of our goals and standards. Therefore, if we want to investigate the combined influence of motivation and cognition on self-directed behavior, that discussion begins with the goals and standards that we attempt to attain and maintain.

CONCLUSIONS

The assumption of this chapter was that in order to understand the transactions between motivation and cognition, you must find the point where cognition and motivation merge. The chapter attempted to explicate a perspective where goals and standards were that point. The combined influence of motivational and cognitive variables in Table 6.1 occurs within the transactions between the development of goals, the planning developed to reach those goals and the self-efficacy beliefs about our skills and the responsiveness of the ecoculture. The goals we develop provide the context around which our thoughts are organized and represented in memory (cognition). In addition, those representations are what our thoughts and behaviors are directed toward and regulated in relationship to (motivation).

On the other hand, we must also remember that although goals provide direction, in and of themselves, they do not insure successful performance. For example, students can have goals to do well in school and a facilitatory activity setting, but if they lack useful strategies to plan and learn, their academic performance can be adversely affected (Schutz, 1993a; Schutz & Lanehart, 1994). In other words, it is not sufficient to just have a goal to, for example, get a high school diploma or a college degree; goals must be accompanied by strategies, plans, and self-efficacy beliefs within a facilitatory activity setting.

As indicated, our current research has focused on developing a model to represent the multidimensional nature of the goals and standards that we develop and attempt to attain and maintain. Although that work has answered some of our questions it has also raised many more. The next phase of our research will focus on three main questions. The first of those questions is: "What is the nature of the transactions between goals and subgoals?" It would seem that our subgoals, or short-term goals, develop out of core goals. It would also seem the continual pursuit of one's goals will be related to the success or lack of success of one's subgoals. Yet the nature of that transaction, to my knowledge, has not been explicated.

A second related question is: "How do ecocultural factors influence the development and pursuit of the goals and standards that we attempt to attain and maintain?" For example, what factors in an activity setting influence a person to develop a goal to become a teacher or to develop an extrinsic goal orientation in the classroom? Although it is quite common for theories to indicate there are ecocultural influences, the study of the nature of those influences will need to continue.

The third main question that our research is investigating is: "How are goals represented in memory and how does that representation change over time?" One of the major premises of the theoretical perspective presented here is that much of the organizational quality for the representation of content in memory involves the core goals that we develop and attempt to attain and maintain. The research that was presented in this chapter indicates that goals and standards at the least influence the organization and representation of the content of thought. Questions remain related to the nature of that organization and representation.

ACKNOWLEDGMENT

I would like to thank Paul Pintrich, Sonja Lanehart, and the other editors for their comments on previous versions of this chapter. Their comments were very useful and the chapter is better because of their time and effort.

REFERENCES

Abbott, V., & Black, J. B. (1986). Goal-related inferences in comprehension. In J. A. Galambos, R. P. Abelson, & J. B. Black (Eds.), *Knowledge structure* (pp. 123–142). Hillsdale, NJ: Lawrence Erlbaum Associates.

Ames, C., & Ames, R. (1984). Systems of student and teacher motivation: Toward a qualitative definition. *Journal of Educational Psychology, 76,* 535-556.

Ames, C., & Archer, J. (1988). Achievement goals in the classroom: Students' learning strategies and motivation processes. *Journal of Educational Psychology, 80,* 260-267.

Argyle, M., Furham, A., & Graham, J. A. (1981). *Social situations.* New York: Cambridge University Press.

Astin, A. W., & Nichols, R. C. (1964). Life goals and vocational choice. *Journal of Applied Psychology, 48*(1), 50–58.

Bandura, A. (1986). *Social foundations of thought and action: A social cognitive theory.* Englewood Cliffs, NJ: Prentice-Hall.

Barsalou, L. W. (1983). Ad hoc categories. *Memory and Cognition, 11,* 211–227.

Barsalou, L. W. (1988). The content and organization of autobiographical memory. In U. Neisser & E. Winograde (Eds.), *Remembering reconsidered: Ecological and traditional approaches to the study of memory* (pp. 193–243). Cambridge, England: Cambridge University Press.

Bartlett, F. C. (1932). *Remembering: A study in experimental and social psychology*. London: Cambridge University Press.

Berry, J. W. (1988). Cognitive values and cognitive competence among the bricoleurs. In J. W. Berry, S. H. Irvine, & E. B. Hunt (Eds.), *Indigenous cognition: Functioning in cultural context*, (pp. 9–20). Dordrecht, The Netherlands: Martinus Nijoff.

Bickhard, M. H. (1980). A model of developmental and psychological processes. *Genetic Psychology Monographs, 102*, 61–116.

Buhler, C., & Massarik, F. (1968). *The course of human life: A study of goals in the humanistic perspective*. New York: Springer.

Campbell, L. R., & Bickhard, M. H. (1986). *Knowing levels and developmental stages*. Basel, Switzerland: Karger.

Conway, M. A. (1990). Association between autobiographical memories and concepts. *Journal of Experimental Psychology: Learning, Memory, and Cognition, 16*(5), 799–812.

Cross, S., & Markus, H. (1991). Possible selves across the life span. *Human Development, 34*, 230–255.

Dewey, J., & Bentley, A. F. (1949). *Knowing and the known*. Boston: Beacon Press.

Dodge, K. A., Asher, S. R., & Parkhurst, J. T. (1989). Social life as a goal-coordination task. In C. Ames & R. Ames (Eds.), *Research on motivation in education: Goals and Cognition* (pp. 107–135). San Diego, CA: Academic Press.

Dweck, C. S., & Leggett, E. L. (1988). A social-cognitive approach to motivation and personality. *Psychological Review, 95*, 256–273.

Flavell, J. H. (1987). Speculations about the nature and development of metacognition. In F. E. Weiner & R. H. Kluwe (Eds.), *Metacognition, Motivation, and Understanding* (pp. 21–29). Hillsdale, NJ: Lawrence Erlbaum Associates.

Ford, D. H. (1987). *Humans as self-constructing living systems: A developmental perspective on behavior and personality.* Hillsdale, NJ: Lawrence Erlbaum Associates.

Ford, M. E. (1992). *Motivating humans: Goals, emotions and personal agency beliefs.* Newbury Park, CA: Sage.

Ford, M. E., & Nichols, C. W. (1987). A taxonomy of human goals and some possible applications. In M. E. Ford & D. H. Ford (Eds.), *Humans as self-constructing living systems: Putting the framework to work* (pp. 261–287). Hillsdale, NJ: Lawrence Erlbaum Associates.

Gage, N. L., & Berliner, D. C. (1992). *Educational Psychology: Fifth edition.* Boston: Houghton Mifflin.

King, A. (1992). Comparison of self-questioning, summarizing, and notetaking-review as strategies for learning from lectures. *American Educational Research Journal, 29(2),* 303–323.

Kintsch, W., & Green, E. (1978). The role of culture-specific schemata in the comprehension and recall of stories. *Discourse processes, 1,* 1–13.

Klinger, E. (1977). *Meaning and void: Inner experience and the incentives in people's lives.* Minneapolis: University of Minnesota Press.

Kuhl, J. (1986). Motivation and information processing: A new look at decision making, dynamic change, and action control. In R. M. Sorrentino & E. T. Higgins (Eds.), *Handbook of motivation and cognition: Foundations of social behavior* (pp. 404–434). New York: Guilford.

Lenddo, J., & Abelson, R. P. (1986). The nature of explanations. In J. A. Galambos, R. P. Abelson, & J. B. Black (Eds.), *Knowledge Structure* (pp. 103–122). Hillsdale, NJ: Lawrence Erlbaum Associates.

Lichtenstein, E. H., & Brewer, W. F. (1980). Memory for goal directed events. *Cognitive Psychology, 12,* 412–445.

Locke, E. A., & Latham, G. P. (1990). *A theory of goal setting and task performance.* Englewood Cliffs, NJ: Prentice-Hall.

Maehr, M. L., & Midgley, C. (1991). Enhancing student motivation: A school wide approach. *Educational Psychologist, 26,* 399–427.

Markus, H., & Nurius, P. (1986). Possible selves. *American Psychologist, 41(9),* 954–969.

McKeachie, W. J. (1990). Learning, thinking, and Thorndike. *Educational Psychologist, 25*(2), 127–141.

McKeachie, W. J., Pintrich, P. R., & Lin, Y. (1985). Teaching learning strategies. *Educational Psychologist, 20,* 153–161.

Nicholls, J. G. (1984). Concepts of ability and achievement motivation. In R. Ames & C. Ames (Eds.), *Research on motivation in education, Vol. 1: Student motivation* (pp. 39–73). Orlando, FL: Academic Press.

Paris, S. G., Lipson, M. J., & Wixson, K. K. (1983). Becoming a strategic reader. *Contemporary Educational Psychology, 8,* 293–316.

Pervin, L. A. (1991). Self-regulation and the problem of volition. In M. Maehr & P. R. Pintrich (Eds.), *Advances in motivation and achievement, Vol. 7: Goals and self-regulatory processes* (pp. 1–20). Greenwich, CT: JAI.

Piaget, J. (1976). *The grasp of consciousness: Action and concept in the young child.* Cambridge: Harvard University Press.

Pintrich, P. R., & Garcia, T. (1991). Student goal orientation and self-regulation in the college classroom. In M. Maehr & P. R. Pintrich (Eds.), *Advances in motivation and achievement, Vol. 7: Goals and self-regulatory processes* (pp. 371–402). Greenwich, CT: JAI.

Pintrich, P. R., & Schrauben, B. (1992). Students' motivational beliefs and their cognitive engagement in classroom academic tasks. In D. Schunk & J. Meece (Eds.), *Student perception in the classroom* (pp. 149–183). Hillsdale, NJ: Lawrence Erlbaum Associates.

Popper, K. (1965). *Conjectures and refutations.* New York: Harper.

Popper, K. (1972). *Objective knowledge.* New York: Harper.

Pressley, M., Wood, E., Woloshyn, V. E., Martin, V., King, A., & Menke, D. (1992). Encouraging mindful use of prior knowledge: Attempting to construct explanatory answers facilitates learning. *Educational Psychologist, 27*(1), 91–109.

Read, S. J. (1987). Constructing causal scenarios: A knowledge structure approach to causal reasoning. *Journal of Personality and Social Psychology, 52*(2), 288–302.

Rosenblatt, L. M. (1978). *The reader, the text, the poem: Transactional theory of the literary work.* Carbondale: Southern Illinois University Press.

Rumelhart, D. E., & Ortony, A. (1977). The representation of knowledge in memory. In R. C. Anderson, R. J. Spiro, & W. E. Montague (Eds.), *Schooling and the acquisition of knowledge*. Hillsdale, NJ: Lawrence Erlbaum Associates.

Schunk, D. H. (1991). Goal setting and self-evaluation: Asocial cognitive perspective on self-regulation. In M. Maehr & P. R. Pintrich (Eds.), *Advances in motivation and achievement, Vol. 7: Goals and self-regulatory processes* (pp. 85–113). Greenwich, CT: JAI.

Schutz, P. A. (1991). Goals in self-directed behavior. *Educational Psychologist, 2*(1), 55–67.

Schutz, P. A. (1993a). *The relationship between long-term goals, learning strategies, and academic performance for high school students*. Paper presented at the annual meeting of the American Educational Research Association, Atlanta, GA.

Schutz, P. A. (1993b). Additional influences on response certitude and feedback requests. *Contemporary Educational Psychology, 18,* 427-441.

Schutz, P. A., & Lanehart, S. L. (in press). The relationship between long-term educational goals, learning strategies and academic performance. *Learning and Individual Differences*.

Schutz, P. A., & Smith, B. (1991). The future of teacher education: The relationship between knowing, learning, and teacher training. In J. J. Van Patten (Ed.), *Human Energy Shaping the Future* (pp. 45–48). College of Education: University of Arkansas.

Smith, B. (1991). *The influence of context on teachers' classroom management decisions*. Paper presented at the annual meeting of the American Educational Research Association, Chicago, IL.

Smith, B., & Schutz, P. A. (1991). The future of teacher education: An ecocultural perspective. In J. J. Van Patten (Ed.), *Human Energy Shaping the Future* (pp. 49–58). College of Education: University of Arkansas.

Sorrentino, R. M., & Higgins, E. T. (1986). Motivation and cognition: Warming up to synergism. In R. M. Sorrentino & E. T. Higgins (Eds.), *Handbook of motivation and cognition: Foundations of social behavior* (pp. 3–19). New York: The Guilford Press.

Tharp, R. G., & Gallimore, R. (1988). *Rousing minds to life: Teaching, learning, and schooling in social context.* Cambridge: Cambridge University Press.

Thorndyke, P. W. (1977). Cognitive structures in comprehension and memory of narrative discourse. *Cognitive Psychology, 11*, 82–106.

Trzebinski, J. (1985). Action-oriented representations of implicit personality theories. *Journal of Personality and Social Psychology, 48*(5), 1266–1278.

Trzebinski, J. (1989). The role of goal categories in the representation of social knowledge. In L. A. Pervin (Ed.), *Goal concepts in personal and social psychology* (pp. 363–411). Hillsdale, NJ: Lawrence Erlbaum Associates.

Trzebinski, J., & Richards, K. (1985). The role of goal categories in personal impression. *Journal of Experimental Social Psychology, 22*, 216–227.

Weinstein, C. E. (1988). Executive control processes in learning: Why knowing how to learn is not enough. *Journal of College Reading and Learning, 21*, 48–56.

Weinstein, C. E., & Mayer, R. E. (1986). The teaching of learning strategies. In M. Wittrock (Ed.), *Handbook of research on teaching* (pp. 315–327). New York: Macmillan.

Wentzel, K. R. (1991). Social and academic goals at school: Motivation and achievement in context. In M. Maehr & P. R. Pintrich (Eds.), *Advances in motivation and achievement, Vol. 7: Goals and self-regulatory processes* (pp. 185–212). Greenwich, CT: JAI.

Wicker, F. W., Lambert, F. B., Richardson, F. C., & Kahler, J. (1984). Categorical goal hierarchies and classification of human motives. *Journal of Personality, 52*(3), 285–305.

Winell, M. (1987). Personal goals: The key to self-direction in adulthood. In M. E. Ford & D. H. Ford (Eds.), *Humans as self-constructing living systems: Putting the framework to work* (pp. 261–287). Hillsdale, NJ: Lawrence Erlbaum Associates.

7

Self-Worth and College Achievement:
Motivational and Personality Correlates

Martin V. Covington
Brent W. Roberts
University of California at Berkeley

> The world can be divided into two kinds of people: those who believe the world can be divided into two kinds, and those who do not.—Benchley

The tendency to categorize people is irresistible; so are attempts to define our uniqueness as individual human beings. This chapter addresses both preoccupations, especially as they relate to establishing individual and group differences among college students. Nowhere is the dictum, "the whole is greater than the sum of its parts," more apt than when we try to describe the nature of human variation. The assumption that the whole (whether it be an individual student or a corporation) carries excess meaning not detectable in the separate parts presents a special challenge to those investigators wishing to provide a rational basis for understanding individual differences. First, they must ask what parts are important—in short, what are the most salient dimensions along which to categorize people? And, second, where is the individual person in this web of impersonal variables—in effect, what theories serve best as the conceptual glue that establishes the whole as contrasted to the mere sum of its parts?

As a psychologist concerned with instructional issues, Bill McKeachie has been posing these questions throughout his career, indeed, beginning long before it was widely recognized as important to do so—in effect, he has asked in one form or another what are the educationally relevant dimensions along which student differ. Additionally, as a motivational theorist, Bill has repeatedly drawn our attention to the heuristic value of describing individual differences among learners in dynamic nonstatic terms. Moreover, as a cognitive psychologist, Bill has always sought out the interface between thoughts and actions and their close kinship with feelings and motives. In short, Bill McKeachie has pioneered much of the conceptual and empirical basis on which modern instructional psychology rests. And so it is that we honor him here by reporting research that is clearly in his debt.

This chapter is divided into three sections. In the first section we review the research conducted under the auspices of the Berkeley Teaching/Learning Project (Covington, 1989, 1992) dealing with the identification of individual difference factors important to college achievement. As to the first question posed above concerning the most appropriate dimensions to consider, we have chosen to study the intersect between two factors: the tendency of students to approach success and to avoid failure. As to the matter of conceptual glue, we have adopted a self-worth interpretation of achievement behavior (Beery, 1975; Covington & Beery, 1976; Covington & Omelich, 1979b). Thus, our approach is driven largely by motivational concerns, that is, identifying students on the basis of their *reasons* (motives) for learning. For example, some individuals strive to succeed in order to avoid failure; others learn for the sake of self-mastery and for the satisfaction of curiosity; while still others seek to demonstrate superior ability either by out-performing others or by achieving notable successes with little or no effort.

In the second section of this chapter, we present data from our most recent efforts to extend a self-worth analysis by considering the personality attributes of those student types we initially identified by motive alone. Here we are especially interested in describing those characteristic styles of coping, the dynamics of well-being and levels of personal adjustment associated with the various types.

In the third and final section, we explore briefly the educational implications of our student typology and how best to accommodate the variety of needs and reasons for learning represented in the college classroom.

MOTIVES FOR LEARNING

The development of college student typologies is something of a cottage industry. One of the first major typologies was developed by Clark and Trow (1960, 1966), who differentiated students in terms of their subculture membership—vocational, collegiate, nonconformist, and the like. Another early example is the Omnibus Personality Inventory, which was used by its developers, Heist and Yonge (1968), to study changes in student coping styles over the course of their college careers. Other examples include the classification of college students based on broad occupational choices including enterprising, artistic, and intellectual (investigative) types (Folsom, 1969; Holland, 1966, 1973; Osipow, Ashby, & Wall, 1966). More recently Katchadourian and Boli (1985) classified college students on two dimensions, one reflecting a preference/nonpreference for career preparation and the other a preference/nonpreference for an intellectual life of discovery. Thus, the four types of college students resulting from this 2 x 2 matrix are based on an interplay between careerism and intellectualism variables. We, too, like Katchadourian and Boli, catalog students in terms of two independent dimensions, those of approach and avoidance, polar opposites that served as the bedrock of John Atkinson's original need achievement model.

Atkinson's Theory of Need Achievement

Atkinson's (1957, 1981; McClelland, 1961, 1980, 1985) theory of need achievement holds that achievement behavior is the result of an emotional conflict between a tendency to approach success and a disposition to avoid failure. As originally conceived, Atkinson's theory featured an orthogonal, two-dimensional system (of the kind portrayed in Fig. 7.1) in which individuals could be located not only high or low with respect to either approach or avoidance tendencies, but also described by their relative placement on the two dimensions— that is, for example, those individuals driven simultaneously by excessive hope and fear or, conversely, those persons best described as indifferent to achievement events, that is, scoring low on both approach and avoidance dimensions. This quadripolar model has the advantage of allowing for the presence of conflicting tendencies as in the case of those students who are simultaneously attracted to and

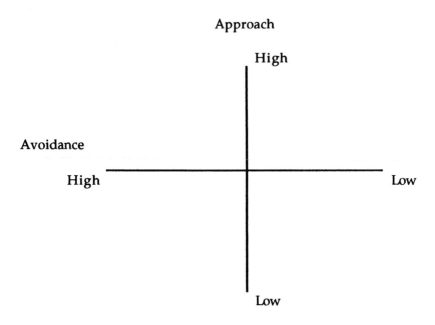

FIG. 7.1. Quadripolar model of need achievement

repelled by academic challenges. Yet despite the importance of this feature of the model, the majority of subsequent research inspired by Atkinson's theory has abandoned the quadripolar model in favor of a simpler unidimensional, bipolar interpretation of achievement motivation in which approach and avoidance tendencies represent extreme polar opposites on only one dimension. By this reckoning approach and avoidance tendencies become blended within the same person so that everyone can be placed somewhere along a single continuum. For example, one group of studies has focused solely on describing the differential achievement behavior of individuals rated as high in approach versus high in avoidance, while disregarding altogether the lower and middle range of both dimensions (e.g., Feather, 1961). Although some researchers have explored the middle ground of this single continuum, that is, a modal degree of both approach and avoidance—usually by dividing their sample distribution by thirds—they have generally failed to recognize that approach and avoidance tendencies are likely to operate in opposition within each level (e.g., Moulton, 1965). By far the most frequent strategy for exploring the implications of Atkinson's model has been to treat achievement motivation as a *resultant* phenomenon in which individuals whose approach tendencies exceed their avoidance dispositions are considered success-oriented, and those persons expressing a preponderance of inhibition are classified as failure-avoiding (e.g., Feather, 1963; Littig, 1966; Litwin, 1963). Not only does this treatment of data disregard the possibility of conflicting tendencies, but it also renders ambiguous the meaning of the zero point midway between high avoidance and high approach. Does it represent the complete absence of motivation or simply the result of canceling two extreme motives? Obviously genuine indifference is not the same, psychologically, as apparent indifference in which placidity may mask extreme and opposite forces held in uneasy check.

Self-worth Theory

Recent developments in the self-worth theory of achievement motivation (e.g., Covington, 1984a, 1984b, 1989, 1992) attest to the potential heuristic value of maintaining Atkinson's original quadripolar model. In essence, self-worth theory argues that the need for self-acceptance is the highest human priority and that, in reality, the dynamics of school achievement largely reflect attempts to aggrandize and protect self-perceptions of ability. Because ability (or its lacking) is often perceived as the major cause of success (or failure), ability becomes a central part of student self-definition. In short, one is only as worthy as one's ability to achieve competitively. Indeed, when students equate their worth with the ability to achieve competitively, the maintenance of feelings of competency becomes of paramount importance even when self-protective strategies may cause the very failures that individuals are trying to avoid (Birney, Burdick, & Teevan, 1969). For instance, when individuals jeopardize their standing in school by procrastinating in their studies or by taking on too heavy a course load—thereby virtually ensuring failure—at least it is failure with honor, that is, failure that reflects little on ability because no one could be expected to do very well when the academic burdens are so great, when time is so short, or the opportunities for study so few (Berglas & Jones, 1978; Snyder, 1984; Solomon & Rothblum, 1984).

From this self-worth perspective only those students who occupy the upper right quadrant of the quadripolar model, so-called success-oriented students (after Atkinson), are likely to be relatively immune to the kinds of stress that triggers defensive, failure-oriented strategies such as procrastination and unrealistically high goal-setting. Indeed, the accumulated evidence suggests that the defining characteristic of success-oriented individuals is a willingness to set realistic learning objectives—goals slightly beyond the person's current capacity to achieve yet still within reach if he or she will only study harder next time.

According to self-worth formulations, the remaining quadrants in Fig. 7.1 represent three distinctive and ultimately self-defeating responses to the threat of failure. The first maladaptive reaction is that of so-called *overstrivers* (high approach/high avoidance) who experience a classic approach/avoidance conflict, a highly stressful condition that typically is alleviated by a defensive strategy of avoiding failure by succeeding.

A second mode of dealing with failure, or at least with the implication of failure—that one lacks ability—is to create excuses either in advance of falling short, thereby actually increasing the likelihood of failure (recall the example of procrastination) or after the fact of failure by making excuses retrospectively. These actions describe the defensive posturing of *failure-avoiders* (high avoidance/low approach). A third defensive style is that of *failure-acceptors* who, according to self-worth theory, reflect the final stages of resignation among those initially failure-avoiding students whose efforts to protect a sense of competency have failed. As failures mount, the increasing implausibility of their self-serving explanations finally force some individuals to conclude (usually erroneously) that they are, in fact, incompetent and hence unworthy. In terms of Atkinson's model, these individuals are low in both approach and avoidance tendencies.

Guided by the expectation that individual differences in achievement motivation are best characterized by a two-dimensional, quadripolar model, and by the prospects of extending our understanding of self-worth dynamics, we developed two orthogonal scales designed to measure the behavioral correlates of need achievement (Covington & Omelich, 1988), which we christened the Approach/Avoidance Achievement Questionnaire (AAAQ). The first scale reflects those dispositions characterized in Atkinson's original model as the approach motive. It consists of a composite of five empirically derived factors including realistic goal setting, degree of self-confidence, level of intrinsic engagement, persistence on task, and risk-taking propensity. The avoidance scale is composed of four factors: fear of failure, doubts about one's ability, self-criticism versus self-rewards following success, and unrealistic achievement standards.

Following the initial psychometric refinement of these factor measures, the scales were administered to some 400 Berkeley undergraduates at the beginning of an introductory psychology course (Covington & Omelich, 1991). Then before each course examination various additional measures were administered to assess the quality and quantity of student test preparation including self-reported estimates of time spent studying and the extent to which egocentric thoughts may have interfered with proper study concentration. Students also provided periodic ratings of perceived levels of both general apprehension and specific test-related anxiety. They also rated changes in self-perceived ability following either success or failure feedback on each test as well as indicating the perceived causes of these achievement outcomes.

The results of this study can be summarized succinctly. The findings overwhelmingly favored Atkinson's original quadripolar model. A series of stepwise discriminant analyses indicated that not only were the traditional success-oriented and failure-avoiding profiles in clear evidence, but two other groups also emerged as behaviorally distinct, coinciding with our initial descriptions of overstrivers and failure-acceptors. Approach tendencies were associated with increasing levels of self-confidence regarding ability as well as with the presence of superior study skills, whereas avoidance tendencies were associated with increasing levels of anxiety, and to a lesser, but still significant degree with increasing amounts of time devoted to test preparation. Thus, in this latter connection, it appears that anxiety drives many failure-threatened students to study more. But in the absence of good study strategies, such effort no matter how seriously undertaken will likely prove ineffectual. Moreover, failure-avoiding students rated themselves far lower in ability than did success-oriented students and they held these disabling views with considerable certainty. As a consequence failure-avoiders experienced greater amounts of anxiety both during study and during test-taking itself.

According to the assumptions of a quadripolar model, the two remaining groups—overstrivers and failure-acceptors—represent hybrid combinations of the orthogonal approach and avoidance dimensions. Thus overstrivers should share to varying degrees, and in different combinations, the behaviors, attitudes, and dispositions of both success-oriented and failure-avoiding individuals. This is precisely what occurred. For instance, because overstrivers share approach tendencies, they rated their ability high, equal, in fact, to the self-ratings of success-oriented individuals. But because overstrivers are also plagued by avoidance tendencies, they too, like failure-avoiders, were uncertain about these self-ratings of ability and feared being unmasked as intellectual impostors. As a result, overstrivers experienced high levels of achievement anxiety throughout the course, equal in intensity to that reported by failure-avoiders. This conflicting combination of approach and avoidance is the hallmark of overstrivers. They hold out hope because success, when it occurs, reassures them of their worth; yet at the same time, they live in constant fear knowing that they cannot succeed indefinitely because their goal is not merely excellence, but perfection.

By similar logic, failure-accepting students are also hybrids. The relative absence of approach tendencies implies that this group would rate their ability to compete successfully in school as low, and also hold these dismal judgments with a high degree of certainty. This is what happened. Also, failure-acceptors were found to be highly ineffectual in their study habits. At the same time, the relative absence of avoidance tendencies suggests that these students would be largely unconcerned about their negative self-evaluations; a hypothesis also borne out by the data. At best these individuals were only mildly apprehensive about their self-perceived deficits, and they spent relatively little time preparing for tests, less time in fact than did any of the other groups. *Indifference* is a term that readily comes to mind in the case of failure-acceptors. Although subject to many interpretations (a point raised later), indifference was initially interpreted by us as reflecting resignation and withdrawal, an inevitable reaction to repeated failure and growing suspicions of inability.

As a final step in our evaluation of the quadripolar model, we estimated the extent of the behavioral separation among these four groups by means of a composite, centroid analysis (Covington &

Omelich, 1991). Two factors were found to maximize group separation. The first was an avoidance function or dimension comprising trait anxiety, fear of being revealed as incompetent, and, to a lesser extent, total study time, which, as will be recalled, depended on the degree of avoidance tendencies present. The second function, representing a general approach tendency, was comprised of an effective study skills factor, perceptions of personal control over events, and an adequate self-concept of ability.

Causal Analysis by Type

Although the results of the centroid analysis provided considerable encouragement for the development of psychologically meaningful student typologies, more information was needed if we were to understand fully the unique dynamics of each group. As centroids, the groups remain static entities—distinctly different, to be sure—but lacking animation and offering only partial answers to the question of how they cope differently with the stresses of actual achievement demands. For this information we needed to undertake a *causal* analysis of how variations in the adequacy of study strategies, individual differences in anxiety level, and changes in self-perceived ability influence one another over time, and impact jointly on distant achievement outcomes (test scores). To this end a series of multivariate achievement studies was conducted. The time frames involved ranged from an analysis of a single study/test cycle (Covington & Omelich, 1981) to the study of several successive mid-term examinations within the same college class (Covington & Omelich, 1979a, 1984, 1988, 1990; Covington, Omelich, & Schwarzer, 1986). As previously described we gathered a variety of data from students including self-ratings of current anxiety levels at several points in time prior to an upcoming test, self-estimates of their ability to deal with the course material, and following each test, student explanations (attributions) for their successes or failures. In all cases the resulting data were analyzed according to multiple prediction procedures (Anderson & Evans, 1974). We proposed a testable model in advance of actual data collection, thus, we felt justified in interpreting the results of these multiple prediction analyses in causal path analytic terms.

Failure-avoiding students

Failure-avoiding individuals entered the achievement arena harboring considerable doubts about their ability, fearful of being exposed as incompetent and feeling highly anxious—results that merely reaffirmed our earlier findings gathered in the process of validating the quadripolar approach/avoidance measures, as well as replicated by numerous other investigators (Carver & Scheier, 1988; Hagtvet, 1984; Laux & Glanzman, 1987; Salamé, 1984; Schmalt, 1982). But how does this legacy of fear and self-recrimination reflect itself in actual achievement behavior over time? Basically, ability-linked worries dogged failure-avoiding students throughout the class, first and foremost, by diverting their attention from their studies. For example, these youngsters spent disproportional amounts of their study time (compared to success-oriented students) preoccupied with efforts to seek relief from anxiety by indulging in magical thinking ("I wish the test would somehow go away"), in minimizing the importance of anticipated failure ("This course is less important than I originally thought"), and by actively rehearsing excuses that would place responsibility for future failure on others ("If I had a better teacher, I might do better"). As a result these students were simply going through the motions of study, and emerged basically unprepared despite their reports of having spent a great deal of time at the books. Second, doubts about ability further handicap failure-avoiding students during test taking itself by interfering anew, this time by disrupting the recollection of what little they had learned in the first instance. Thus, as far as the dynamics of performance anxiety are concerned failure-avoiding students appear to suffer from both a *skill-deficit* (Culler & Holahan, 1980) and a *retrieval-deficit* (Deffenbacher, 1977, 1986; Liebert & Morris, 1967; Mandler & Sarason, 1952). In the first instance, anxiety is thought to be the byproduct of recognizing that one is unprepared and likely to fail, or as the old saying goes, "anxiety is the interest paid on trouble before it is due." In the second instance during test-taking negative arousal interferes directly with the recall of what was previously learned. Some investigators have argued that skill-deficit and retrieval-deficit interpretations of test anxiety are incompatible (e.g., Kirkland & Hollandsworth, 1980). But our data suggests that both kinds of deficiencies can operate simultaneously or separately depending on the type of students studied. Both deficiencies are present among failure-avoiding students, and as we are about to see, overstrivers are relatively more handicapped by the failure to retrieve than by the failure to learn.

Overstrivers

As already documented, overstrivers possess certain redeeming characteristics including both superior study skills and the ability to apply them effectively despite (or because of) high levels of anxiety and nagging self-doubts. For overstrivers, anxiety actually acts to mobilize and intensify a study focus, but ironically enough, making for the least effective kind of test preparation. Fear arouses a condition of inflexible, superficial overlearning in which information is rehearsed as a collection of isolated events. This kind of rote learning is less resistant to forgetting, especially in the face of retrieval anxiety, than is the case when material is organized around a deeper understanding of basic principles. Little wonder, then, that overstrivers often suffer a failure to recall during testing, yet they are quite capable of remembering in detail what was learned originally as soon as the pressure of testing is over (Covington & Omelich, 1987a). The oft-heard lament, "but I knew it cold before the exam," is an apt description of overstrivers.

Failure-acceptors

The resulting data is consistent with the proposition that failure acceptors have abandoned efforts to maintain a sense of dignity via a reputation for ability. In all respects these students appeared resigned or at least passive in the face of academic challenges. They studied far less than did any of the other groups and reported little anxiety at the various points sampled in the study/test cycle (Covington & Omelich, 1991). Nor did they express much in the way of affect—neither much pride over their infrequent successes nor much shame in failure (Covington & Omelich, 1985). An overall picture of failure-acceptors emerges—students performing poorly not so much because of a failure to recall what was learned originally (retrieval deficit), as in the case of overstrivers, but rather (like failure-avoiders) because of a failure to learn in the first place (skill deficit).

Success-oriented Individuals

Success-oriented students are unique among all the groups in that they elude description at least in terms of the variables included in our research. Although the essential nature of the three failure-prone groups can be captured by the competitive dynamics of classroom life, not so with success-oriented students whose test scores bore little relationship to other variables. Even self-estimates of ability were only minimally related to the achievement of success-oriented students. It appears that these students have moved beyond concerns about ability status and the conventional meaning of success and failure competitively defined. For example we know that when individuals learn for its own sake, variations in perceived ability are less important to success than when they enter the competitive game.

PERSONALITY AND THE QUADRIPOLAR MODEL

A self-worth perspective has proven a valuable starting point for our inquiries into the nature of individual difference factors in college achievement dynamics. Yet we were intrigued to learn more about the quadripolar typology, and believed the assessment of personality variables to be an essential complement to the work that until recently had followed largely the dictates of motivation theory. For the most part, these fresh inquiries concerned issues of student well-being and personal adjustment. Four questions readily came to mind.

First, a picture of success-oriented students emerged largely as individuals motivated for positive reasons, valuing learning for its own sake and for the sake of curiosity, and who were able to adapt successfully to a variety of academic demands (Roberts & Covington, 1991). However, does this apparently healthy academic commitment extend to the personal lives of success-oriented individuals as well? Second, and conversely, does the defensive posture that so dominates the scholastic life of failure-avoiders disrupt their sense of personal well-being and jeopardize their relations with others? Third, we also hoped to penetrate further the nature of the conflict experienced by individuals who are simultaneously drawn to success and repelled by failure, that is, the overstrivers. Surely there must be considerable psychic costs to holding such stress in check. But so far our analysis had revealed basically model students—hard workers to be sure, and perhaps to a fault—but nonetheless highly successful by the numbers. Would an analysis of personality factors reveal a darker side of the kind hinted at in the findings of Depreeuw (1990)? Depreeuw discovered that *active avoiders* (akin to our overstrivers) often risk their health by taking excessive amounts of tranquilizers and other drugs before examinations to control the stress associated with study. Fourth, and finally, although the behavior of failure acceptors was generally consistent with a self-worth interpretation of inaction born out of resignation and a loss of personal control over events, they nonetheless remained ciphers because of the difficulty, if not impossibility, of proving a negative. What, then, is the true meaning of not only one, but of a double negative—in this case, the relative absence of both approach and avoidance tendencies?

Our main source of personality measures was the California Psychological Inventory (CPI; Gough, 1987). The CPI emphasizes the assessment of well-being and effective interpersonal functioning at the college level. It also enjoys long-standing preeminence as a tool for the study of personality and school achievement dynamics. For example, those personality theorists who view success and failure in school as the result of a match or mismatch, respectively, between task demands and the individual's preferred work style have found support for their position using various subscales of the CPI. More specifically, substantial positive correlations have been demonstrated between a preference for achievement by conformance (preference for tasks that are clearly defined) and grade point average (GPA) in high school, a context in which students can often do well simply by applying rote learning strategies. Conversely, the same work style is essentially uncorrelated with GPA in college where greater stress is placed on settings that encourage freedom and individual initiative (Gough, 1957, 1964, 1966, 1968, personal communication, 1983).

The CPI has 20 primary scales broken into four classes. Class I scales measure social poise and assertiveness. Class II scales measure adherence to norms and maturity. Class III scales measure achievement and intellectual style as well as degree of intellectual efficiency. Class IV scales measure personal style and role behavior.

We administered the CPI to 220 Berkeley undergraduates along with the AAAQ (described previously) as part of a larger study of adaptation and coping among college students. In conjunction with a previous study of vocational aspirations (Roberts & Covington, 1992), we also administered several vocational measures including the Vocational Identity Scale from the Holland My Vocational Situation (MVS; Holland, 1966, 1973) and several work value scales. The MVS measures the strength, clarity, and confidence of a person's career plans. High scorers are thought to have a stable and clear sense of self, a sophisticated knowledge of one's strengths and weaknesses, and an understanding of whether they match one's career aspirations (Holland, Gottfredson, & Power, 1980). The work value scales were based on importance ratings of 18 different job characteristics that were clustered into three scales: challenge, status, and social work values.

Approach and Avoidance Concepts Refined

To begin with, we examined data for the two groups traditionally identified by the bipolar perspective on achievement motivation: success-oriented students (high approach/low avoidance), on the one hand, and failure-avoiding individuals (low approach/high avoidance), on the other. In effect, we asked the question, "How are the pure motivational extremes of approach and avoidance related to underlying dimensions of personality and overall psychological functioning?" This query was answered simply by correlating the approach and avoidance dimensions with various subscales of the CPI. Table 7.1 presents these correlational data. The findings are straightforward and require little by way of explanatory interpretation. In general, success-oriented students are associated with those personality traits that reflect a healthy adjustment (e.g., self-control), whereas a failure-avoiding stance is associated with a dearth of these same characteristics. In effect, those subjects who strive for success enjoy a "profile elevation," that is, overall high scores on the CPI, which generally is taken as a global indicator of good psychological adjustment (Gough, 1987).

If we are to judge from those scales on which success-oriented individuals load highest, they are best described in personality terms as norm-adhering, concerned with the impression they make on others and wishing to please (Good Impression scale), sensitive to the needs of others (Psychological Mindedness), and preferring to achieve in traditional ways (Achievement by Conformance). From a personality perspective, success-oriented students are highly functioning, and relatively free of adjustment problems. They tend to be outgoing, socially poised, conscientious, tolerant of their fellow students and psychologically sophisticated. These personality data add to an already positive motivational picture of success-oriented persons as intrinsically focused, that is, seeking knowledge for its own sake (Roberts & Covington, 1991); persons, moreover, who are confident in their ability to succeed and harbor little in the way of achievement anxiety. As reported in Roberts and Covington (1992), success-oriented students as a group are also confident in their chosen career path, having scored highest of all the four groups on the Vocational Identity

TABLE 7.1
Correlations Between Approach and Avoidance Tendencies
and Selected Scales From the California Psychological
Inventory (CPI)

CPI Scales	Hope-of-Success	Fear-of-Failure
Class I		
Capacity-for-status	.21*	-.30*
Social presence	.20*	-.34*
Class II		
Self-control	.28*	-.17*
Tolerance	.21*	-.27*
Good impression	.41*	-.26*
Well-being	.29*	-.28*
Class III		
Achievement via conformance	.35*	-.27*
Achievement via independence	.15*	-.18*
Intellectual efficiency	.24*	-.26*
Class IV		
Psychological mindedness	.38*	-.26*
Flexibility	-.04	-.15*

Note. $N = 216$
* $p < .05$

Scale, and value challenging careers. Their combined qualities of high interpersonal functioning, self-control, and mature career identity give the impression of persons quite capable of succeeding in society; indeed, of taking a leadership role. Thus, as to our first inquiry, clearly the healthy posture of success-oriented students extends beyond academics to include a wide range of personal attributes.

Conversely, individuals high in avoidance tendencies score in a diminished direction on such positive attributes as Capacity-for-Status, meaning that they tend to be unsure of themselves and dislike direct competition. Yet despite evidence of a subdued countenance, these failure-avoiders show little tolerance for the behavior or ideas of others (low Tolerance). Moreover, they are concerned, if not often preoccupied, with personal and health problems and worried about the future (low Well-being), and probably as a result of such worry have a hard time starting tasks and seeing them through to completion (low Intellectual Efficiency). Finally, students who manifest substantial avoidance tendencies are unlikely to concern themselves with the feelings, motives and desires of others and to look more at what people *do* than at what they *feel* or think (low Psychological Mindedness).

The profile of failure-avoiding students reveals few, if any, redeeming qualities. Nor do they have clear-cut career goals as reflected by the lowest score of all groups on the Vocational Identity scale (Roberts & Covington, 1992). This personality and career configuration mirrors the motivational makeup of failure-avoiders: Being driven to avoid failure without the intellectual skills and confidence to achieve success consistently, they are less likely to break out of a failure loop, certainly in school, and most likely beyond, making their prognosis for successful career entry none too positive. Thus in answer to our second inquiry, the generally negative countenance of failure-avoiding students is not confined solely to their academic life, but permeates all aspects of their existence.

Overstrivers and Failure-Acceptors Revisited

Next, we extended our analysis to those hybrid individuals who otherwise would have remained undifferentiated under a bipolar model but who emerge as distinctive under a quadripolar treatment.

Our third inquiry concerned overstrivers. We already knew a good deal about the behavioral and cognitive consequences of attempting to avoid failure by succeeding—among them, a disposition toward meticulous overpreparation, the presence of devastating anxiety attacks during the retrieval phase of the achievement cycle, and a preoccupation with thoughts of perfection. Now what additional light can be shed on these dynamics by considering personality factors?

We begin by analyzing that cluster of CPI variables that reflects level of maturity and general well-being (Class II), and whose mean values are listed in Table 7.2 by student type. As already noted (see Table 7.1), the tendency to approach success is positively correlated with Self-control and Tolerance scales. Given this fact, it is noteworthy that as a group overstrivers (who in part reflect approach tendencies) are depressed on these two scales, scoring substantially lower than success-oriented persons and differing little, if at all, from failure-avoiders. The same pattern holds for the Good Impression and Well-being scales. Despite the fact that these variables load positively on approach tendencies, overstrivers appear no more willing than failure-avoiders to comply with the wishes of others, even when noncompliance causes friction (low Good Impression), nor are they any freer than failure-avoiders from worries about the future (low Well-being). Overall, these data suggest that maturity and general well-being become casualties when otherwise success-oriented persons tie their sense of worth to achievement competitively defined.

However, this analysis presents us with a puzzle. How is it that overstrivers who are highly disciplined, indeed, overly so, when it comes to academic study (note their relatively high standing on Intellectual Efficiency) can also be described as lacking in self-control, and harboring strong feelings, yet make little attempt to hide them? The key to understanding this apparent paradox rests with the elevated scores posted by overstrivers on several anger scales developed by the co-authors, including Anger-toward-Self and Suppression of Anger. It seems likely that the same fear that drives overstrivers to highly inflexible, rigid and overly disciplined study also generates resentment and anger toward self for feeling incompetent, despite their successes, and toward others for making them feel that way—emotions that are not always easily concealed. When intolerance of others, skepticism, and a lack of emotional control—all unattractive personality features associated with avoidance tendencies (Table 7.1)—are combined with ambitiousness and the kinds of assertiveness reflected in a high Capacity-for-Status (Table 7.2), the result can be an unhealthy confection of arrogance, aggressiveness, and an almost demonic drive to succeed.

Our fourth, and final inquiry concerned narrowing the number of plausible interpretations for the relative absence of both approach and avoidance tendencies. As mentioned earlier our initial and admittedly tentative interpretation of these low standings was that they reflected a state of resignation or indifference toward school brought on by repeated failure experiences which in turn progressively undercut a belief in the individual's ability ever to succeed again. The presumption of apathy is consistent with a finding mentioned earlier

TABLE 7.2

Mean Level Differences on Selected Scales from the California Psychological Inventory (CPI) for Overstriving, Success-oriented, Failure-avoiding, and Failure-accepting Students

CPI Scales	Overstriver	Success-Oriented	Failure-Avoider	Failure-Acceptor	F
Class I					
Capacity-for-status	19.50	20.42	17.71	20.25	6.25*
Social presence	35.73	38.30	33.73	37.35	5.44*
Class II					
Self-control	21.88	25.90	21.00	23.87	6.16*
Tolerance	17.69	20.97	17.65	19.85	6.75*
Good impression	14.79	17.66	12.41	14.51	11.08*
Well-being	30.69	33.26	29.19	32.10	6.35*
Class III					
Achievement via conformance	25.67	27.62	23.78	26.13	7.81*
Achievement via independence	19.43	20.31	18.54	20.87	3.47
Intellectual efficiency	35.81	36.82	32.82	37.59	6.99*
Class IV					
Psychological mindedness	10.64	11.73	9.20	10.77	10.74*
Flexibility	9.67	11.27	10.63	11.64	2.40

Note. Overstrivers score high on both approach and avoidance scales of the AAAQ, success-oriented score high on approach and low on avoidance, failure-avoiders score low on approach and high on avoidance, and failure-acceptors score low on both approach and avoidance. F-test degrees of freedom are (3,212).

*$p < .05$

(Covington & Omelich, 1985) that failure-accepting students display less pride in success and less shame in failure than do most other students. Minimal or flat affective reactions are known to reflect conditions of depression and withdrawal; but whether or not apathy—if apathy it be—is born out of growing suspicions of incompetency (as assumed by self-worth theory) is not clear, especially in light of the self-reports of failure-acceptors that ability status is not a very important source of worth to them. Perhaps the need to be perceived as highly able is simply irrelevant to the self-definition of these individuals.

And, of course, it is possible that what these students are experiencing is not resignation at all. Inaction has many causes. Perhaps inaction merely reflects a passive lifestyle captured by the statement, "I prefer to let others do my worrying for me." Also, inaction can result from ambivalence over the cultural and intellectual values associated with college ("I don't have a clear idea why I came to college"), and in more extreme cases, may manifest itself as an outright rejection of these values, accompanied by feelings of alienation and resentment ("When I see so much hypocrisy and cynicism regarding grades and grading I sometimes just want to give up"). Inaction can also result from being *disconnected*, a term originally employed by Katchadourian and Boli (1985) to describe students who are as yet unclear about their life goals and the part that college might play in achieving them. Finally, it is possible that failure-acceptors are simply outliers whose values cannot be easily captured by a competitive ethos that permeates the traditional meaning of approach and avoidance motives. Such individuals might well be described as "creative," "eccentric," "individualistic," and "unconventional."

What do the personality data tell us? Whatever else can be said, surprisingly enough, failure-acceptors appear quite well adjusted compared to the other two failure-prone groups, if we can judge from the meaning attached by Gough (1987) to an elevated CPI profile. Failure-acceptors compare favorably to success-oriented individuals on such scales as Well-being, Tolerance, Self-control, and Social Presence, despite the fact that these variables are positively associated with the presence of approach tendencies, not with their absence (see Table 7.1). The fact that failure-acceptors can be described as generally self-assured, convivial, self-disciplined, and relatively free of worries renders less tenable the notion that a combination of low approach/avoidance tendencies reflects feelings of alienation, anger, and resentment. Also, the hypothesis that these individuals may have adopted a passive, withdrawn approach to life's challenges fares little better. Failure-acceptors express as much ambition and desire to do well as do success-oriented individuals, as reflected by equally high scores on the Capacity-for-Status scale.

A much more lively, spontaneous and energetic person emerges than would otherwise be surmised from the data on achievement motivation alone. But why should this be? Is it possible that traditional motivation theory simply misses the mark when it comes to capturing the essence of failure-acceptors? But if their source of worth is not to be found in competitive achievement and their apparent inaction not the result of demoralization, then where are we to look? The present data provides us with an important clue. Despite their apparent indifference to the dynamics of success and failure, failure-acceptors nonetheless enjoy high scores on the Intellectual Efficiency, Flexibility, and Achievement by Independence scales, rivaling if not exceeding the mean values of success-oriented individuals. Such an elevated cluster of scores indicates a preference for autonomous striving and for the creative expression of one's imagination (Gough, 1987). By this reckoning these students may be threatened more by boredom than by assaults on their sense of competency. They may see little purpose in scrambling for grades and hence have little to sustain either their interest or their loyalties in an institutional context that all too often values compliance and rewards the blind regurgitation of information on multiple-choice exams.

EDUCATIONAL IMPLICATIONS

We do not intend that our research efforts remain simply an exercise in theory-building. We seek to draw practical lessons from our portraits of student personality and coping styles, lessons that can lead to concrete proposals for educational change based on a motivational analysis. According to self-worth theory, today's crisis in education—student indifference, dropout and lethargy—is less a matter of being unmotivated than of being *overmotivated*, but for the wrong reasons. The real threat to learning occurs when the individual's sense of worth becomes tied to his or her ability to achieve competitively. If pride in success and shame in failure depends largely on self-perceived ability, then student involvement in learning will last only as long as one continues to succeed as a means for aggrandizing ability. But once failure threatens a self-image of competency, with its legacy of shame and anger, students will likely withdraw from learning or, ironically, actually redouble their efforts in a misguided attempt to avoid failure by succeeding.

Given this perspective, we ask how can the threat to learning be *diffused*, on the one hand, so that overstrivers and failure-avoiders feel less vulnerable; yet, on the other hand, how can learning be *infused* with powerful incentives that appeal to all, sufficient to transform both disengagement (failure-acceptors) and defensive vigilance into personal commitment? This question implies changing the system, not changing students. Yet for some students, like success-oriented individuals, no tinkering seems needed; they perform well consistently under a variety of learning conditions, even competitive circumstances (Covington & Omelich, 1987b; Harackiewicz & Manderlink, 1984).

The key to the changes implied here requires shifting the prevailing motives for learning from being failure-prone to success-oriented. Theoretically, this involves adopting a metaphor of *motives-as-goals*, incentives that draw and beguile students toward action, rather than continuing to rely on the traditional view of motives as drives (Covington, 1992). The proper reasons (motives) for learning are scarcely new, but they are noteworthy for being honored more in the breach than in the observance. They include acquiring knowledge for the sake of self-mastery and for gaining control over one's future (e.g., preparation for career); for serving the interest of the group, and of the larger society; and, for purposes of giving expression to one's creative energies and for the satisfaction of curiosity. Our approach to encouraging such goals has taken several distinctive but interlocking research directions.

Nature of the Task

We are exploring the nature of school tasks and have, along with other investigators (e.g., Malone, 1981), concluded that in order to foster intrinsic task engagement, student assignments must provide challenges worthy of significant commitments of time and energy and that demand the highest levels of thinking of which students are presently capable. Recently, we began developing scholastic tasks designed to stimulate such involvement based on three important motivational principles: an opportunity for self-improvement, the challenge of manageable conflict, and the chance for group participation. First, irrespective of subject-matter content—whether it be physics, economics, or political science—intense, personal engagement depends on being able to improve one's performance without penalty, doing things better with practice and overcoming early errors and mistakes. Second, sustained involvement is encouraged by the presence of controversy and uncertainty. Here uncertainty and its resolution translates into a process of clarifying one's objectives, arranging relevant information in a coherent form, and applying problem-solving operations consistent with these objectives. Naturally, uncertainty must be constrained within manageable limits. Sustained involvement depends on a reasonable match being established between the individual's present capabilities and the requirements of the achievement task (Battle, 1965; Woodson, 1975). When students experience a close match between their resources and task demands they learn the most, and this is true for students at all levels of ability. Contrariwise, a mismatch interferes with learning at all ability levels, but for different reasons. Able students who compete against easy standards become bored, whereas less able students for whom too much is required become discouraged and quit. Third, task engagement is further encouraged by the social reinforcers that accompany group or cooperative problem solving (Harris & Covington, 1993; Slavin, 1983, 1984). Any number of students can win when learning is seen as a cooperative venture. When each student achieves his or her goal, then all those with whom the individual is cooperating likewise achieve their goals, an arrangement that maximizes achievement and discourages social loafing.

Interestingly, our evidence suggests that all four student types are equally positive about the prospects of learning in groups. For this reason, many of the tasks currently under development by our staff feature cooperative problem solving. For instance, one task requires groups of undergraduates to rank order the importance of a number of causes of civil unrest and urban rioting of the kind that rocked the Los Angeles area in the early 1990s (after Pfeiffer & Jones, 1971). Using a jigsaw paradigm, each member of the group contributes to the larger solution by becoming expert on one of the potential causes to be ranked. The quality of the group solution (and the corresponding grade that is assigned equally to all members) is determined by comparing the degree of match between the collective student rankings and a separate set of rankings created by a number of social scientists.

Absolute Standards of Excellence

A second focus of our research involves investigating reward systems whose payoff (grades) depends directly on evidence of self-improvement, of helping others, and of being sensitive to new, heretofore unrecognized problems. The rewards associated with intrinsic reasons for learning differ largely from extrinsic payoffs by their absolute nature: Intrinsic rewards depend less on how many other students succeed or fail than on the kinds of tasks chosen—with the most rewards going to the realistic goal-setter—and on whether or not one's performance meets or surpasses prevailing standards of excellence. For example, in the Urban Unrest Problem, as just mentioned, the group grade depends on how close the group's answer matches that of experts. Here, then, any number of groups can play and any number can win. No longer are students necessarily precluded from striving for success because of limited rewards that are distributed disproportionately. Such an arrangement creates a condition of motivational equity (Covington, 1992). Clearly, not every college student is equally bright, but at least we can provide a common (equal) basis in the reasons that all students learn.

One important caveat regarding the concept of motivational equity is the potentially negative consequences of rewards becoming too plentiful. For many students, especially overstrivers, the reinforcing value of grades depends on their scarcity—the fewer the number of As, the more their attainment signals high ability. So what happens when grades are based less on ability per se and more on the skills of cooperation, diligence, and the satisfying of prevailing standards? If there are no clear losers in the learning game, will it be worth playing? More specifically, will overstrivers who have survived, perhaps even flourished, under competitive grading systems resent such a devaluation? The fact that these individuals have tied their sense of worth and individuality to the scarcity of high grades may only intensify their grievance. And what of failure-avoiders who may become confused over receiving an unexpectedly high grade? Are such grades deserved by the individual or are they merely the result of group effort or the humanitarian impulse of an instructor?

Accumulating evidence from our laboratory (Covington & Beery, 1976; Covington & Jacoby, 1983) suggests that the key to diffusing these potentially troublesome concerns is the use of performance standards that increase in difficulty level as the student's grade aspirations rise—that is, requiring a moderate level of performance for a grade of C, more demanding requirements for a B, with the greatest demands reserved for the top grades. Under this so-called *grade-choice arrangement* (Block, 1977), we have found that the academic performance of students is markedly superior to that of comparison groups graded on a competitive basis (Covington, 1985; Covington & Omelich, 1984). Moreover, grades assigned in this manner create little resentment among those students who would have normally succeeded anyway (overstrivers) despite the greater number of high grades awarded. Failure-prone students also feel greater ownership of otherwise unexpected achievements because a grade-choice arrangement fosters a greater sense of personal control over grades than is true under a competitive arrangement. In the latter case, one's grade depends more (quixotically) on how well others do, and less on how well the individual does against publicly available standards of excellence whose attainment demands more measured and predictable amounts of effort.

Intrinsic Involvement and Talent Selection

A third complementary line of research reflects recognition of the fact that despite all the motivation and performance benefits of minimizing competition, competitive sorting in college still remains an entrenched way of life, a practice often justified as an orderly way to distribute individuals proportionately across the available jobs in our society, some of which are more attractive than others (for rebuttals, see Campbell, 1974; Covington, 1992; Deutsch, 1975, 1979). The scramble for top grades in college science courses as a passport to prestigious medical schools is just one manifestation of this competitive ethos. These realities cannot be overlooked or denied. But does this mean that attempting to encourage intrinsic task engagement in college is an exercise in futility, or that individuals cannot pursue intrinsic goals in institutions that rank their performance competitively? Hopefully not. Otherwise, how is it possible for students to declare (as they sometimes do), "I only got a C, but I learned more in that class than in any other." We must recognize that the best learning likely depends on both intrinsic and extrinsic motives, and that the potential for intrinsic involvement coexists in all of us right alongside a potential for responsiveness to external rewards. This view is a dramatic departure from the traditional perspective that intrinsic and extrinsic processes are somehow basically incompatible—witness the time-honored definition of intrinsic motivation as the absence of extrinsic rewards.

We have just begun an extensive investigation of those motives that activate and sustain student work on assignments like the Urban Unrest Problem (Covington & Wiedenhaupt, 1993). Preliminary results indicate, first, that there is an ebb and flow in the reasons for continued engagement, which at times reflect intrinsic engagement ("I want to see how well I measure up to the instructor's standards"), and at other times reflect extrinsic involvement ("It seems an easy way to earn grade points"); and, second, that different kinds of students reflect characteristically different patterns of motivation. As a second phase of this research we plan systematically to alter not only the nature of the learning tasks themselves, say, increasing or decreasing levels of controversy or uncertainty, but also to manipulate reward contingencies in an effort to identify those conditions that promote learning for its own sake in a larger institutional context that pulls for externally regulated talent selection.

REFERENCES

Anderson, J. G., & Evans, F. B. (1974). Causal models in educational research: Recursive models. *American Education Research Journal, 11*, 29–39.

Atkinson, J. W. (1957). Motivational determinants of risk-taking behavior. *Psychological Review, 64*, 359–372.

Atkinson, J. W. (1981). Studying personality in the context of an advanced motivational psychology. *American Psychologist, 36*, 117–128.

Battle, E. S. (1965). Motivational determinants of academic task persistence. *Journal of Personality and Social Psychology, 2*, 209–218.

Beery, R. G. (1975). Fear of failure in the student experience. *Personnel and Guidance Journal, 54*, 190–203.

Berglas, S., & Jones, E. (1978). Drug choice as a self-handicapping strategy in response to noncontingent success. *Journal of Personality and Social Psychology, 36*, 405–417.

Birney, R. C., Burdick, H., & Teevan, R. C. (1969). *Fear of failure.* New York: Van Nostrand.

Block, J. H. (1977). Motivation, evaluation, and mastery learning. *UCLA Educator, 12,* 31–37.

Campbell, D. N. (1974, October). On being number one: Competition in education. *Phi Delta Kappan,* 143–146.

Carver, C. S., & Scheier, M. F. (1988). A control-process perspective on anxiety. *Anxiety Research, 1,* 17–22.

Clark, B. R., & Trow, M. (1960). *Determinants of college student subcultures.* Unpublished manuscript, Center for the Study of Higher Education, Berkeley, CA.

Clark, B. R., & Trow, M. (1966). Determinants of the sub-cultures of college students—The organizational context. In T. M. Newcomb & E. Wilson (Eds.), *College peer groups.* Chicago: Adeline.

Covington, M. V. (1984a). Motivated cognitions. In S. G. Paris, G. M. Olson, & H. W. Stevenson (Eds.), *Learning and motivation in the classroom* (pp. 139–164). Hillsdale, NJ: Lawrence Erlbaum Associates.

Covington, M. V. (1984b). The motive for self-worth. In R. Ames & C. Ames (Eds.), *Research on motivation in education* (Vol. 1, pp. 77–113). New York: Academic Press.

Covington, M. V. (1985). The effects of multiple-testing opportunities on rote and conceptual learning and retention. *Human Learning, 4,* 57–72.

Covington, M. V. (1989). Self-esteem and failure in school: Analysis and policy implications. In A. M. Mecca, N. J. Smelser, & J. Vasconcellos (Eds.), *The social importance of self-esteem.* Berkeley: University of California.

Covington, M. V. (1992). *Making the grade: A self-worth perspective on motivation and school reform.* New York: Cambridge University Press.

Covington, M. V., & Beery, R. G. (1976). *Self-worth and school learning.* New York: Holt, Rinehart & Winston.

Covington, M. V., & Jacoby, K. E. (1983). *Productive thinking and course satisfaction as a function of an independence-conformity dimension.* Paper presented at the meeting of the American Psychological Association, Montreal.

Covington, M. V., & Omelich, C. L. (1979a). Are causal attributions causal? A path analysis of the cognitive model of achievement motivation. *Journal of Personality and Social Psychology, 37,* 1487–1504.

Covington, M. V., & Omelich, C. L. (1979b). Effort: The double-edged sword in school achievement. *Journal of Educational Psychology, 71,* 169–182.

Covington, M. V., & Omelich, C. L. (1981). As failures mount: Affective and cognitive consequences of ability demotion in the classroom. *Journal of Educational Psychology, 73,* 796–808.

Covington, M. V., & Omelich, C. L. (1984). Task-oriented versus competitive learning structures: Motivational and performance consequences. *Journal of Educational Psychology, 76,* 1038–1050.

Covington, M. V., & Omelich, C. L. (1985). Ability and effort valuation among failure-avoiding and failure-accepting students. *Journal of Educational Psychology, 77,* 446–459.

Covington, M. V., & Omelich, C. L. (1987a). "I knew it cold before the exam": A test of the anxiety-blockage hypothesis. *Journal of Educational Psychology, 79,* 393–400.

Covington, M. V., & Omelich, C. L. (1987b). Item difficulty and test performance among high-anxious and low-anxious students. In R. Schwarzer, H. M. van der Ploeg, & C. D. Spielberger (Eds.), *Advances in test anxiety research* (Vol. 5, pp. 127–135), Hillsdale, NJ: Lawrence Erlbaum Associates.

Covington, M. V., & Omelich, C .L. (1988). Achievement dynamics: The interaction of motives, cognitions and emotions over time. *Anxiety Journal, 1,* 165–183.

Covington, M. V., & Omelich, C. L. (1990). *The second time around: Coping with repeated failures.* Unpublished manuscript, Department of Psychology, University of California, Berkeley.

Covington, M. V., & Omelich, C. L. (1991). Need achievement revisited: Verification of Atkinson's original 2 x 2 model. In C. D. Spielberger, I. G. Sarason, Z. Kulcsár, & G. L. Van Heck (Eds.), *Stress and emotion: Anxiety, anger, and curiosity* (Vol.14, pp. 85–105). Washington, DC: Hemisphere.

Covington, M. V., Omelich, C. L., & Schwarzer, R. (1986). Anxiety, aspirations, and self-concept in the achievement process: A longitudinal model with latent variables. *Motivation and Emotion, 10,* 71–88.

Covington, M. V., & Wiedenhaupt, S. (1993). *Interests, habits and the illusion of choice.* Unpublished manuscript, Institute for Personality and Social Research, University of California, Berkeley.

Culler, R. E., & Holahan, C. J. (1980). Test anxiety and academic performance: The effects of study-related behaviors. *Journal of Educational Psychology, 72,* 16–20.

Deffenbacher, J. L. (1977). Relationship of worry and emotionality to performance on the Miller Analogies Test. *Journal of Educational Psychology, 69,* 191–195.

Deffenbacher, J. L. (1986). Cognitive and physiological components of test anxiety in real-life exams. *Cognitive Therapy and Research, 10,* 635–644.

Depreeuw, E. (1990). *Fear of failure: A complex clinical phenomenon.* Belgium: University of Leuven.

Deutsch, M. (1975). Equity, equality, and need. *Journal of Social Issues, 31,* 137–149.

Deutsch, M. (1979). Education and distributive justice. *American Psychologist, 34,* 391–401.

Feather, N. T. (1961). The relationship of persistence at a task to expectation of success and achievement-related motives. *Journal of Abnormal and Social Psychology, 63,* 552–561.

Feather, N. T. (1963). Persistence at a difficult task with an alternative task of intermediate difficulty. *Journal of Abnormal and Social Psychology, 66,* 604–609.

Folsom, C. H., Jr. (1969). An investigation of Holland's theory of vocational choice. *Journal of Counseling Psychology, 16*(3), 260–266.

Gough, G. H. (1957). *Manual for the California Psychological Inventory.* Palo Alto, CA: Consulting Psychologists Press. (Rev. ed. 1964).

Gough, G. H. (1964). Academic achievement in high school as predicted from the California Psychological Inventory. *Journal of Educational Psychology, 55,* 174–180.

Gough, G. H. (1966). Graduation from high school as predicted from the California Psychological Inventory. *Psychology in the Schools, 3,* 208–216.

Gough, G. H. (1968). College attendance among high-aptitude students as predicted from the California Psychological Inventory. *Journal of Counseling Psychology, 15,* 269–278.

Gough, H. G. (1987). *Manual for the California Psychological Inventory.* Palo Alto, CA: Consulting Psychologists Press.

Hagtvet, K. A. (1984). Fear of failure, worry and emotionality: Their suggestive causal relationships to mathematical performance and state anxiety. In H. M. van der Ploeg, R. Schwarzer, & C. D. Spielberger (Eds.), *Advances in test anxiety research* (Vol. 3, pp. 211–224). Hillsdale, NJ: Lawrence Erlbaum Associates.

Harackiewicz, J. M., & Manderlink, G. (1984). A process analysis of the effects of performance-contingent rewards on intrinsic motivation. *Journal of Experimental Social Psychology, 20,* 531–551.

Harris, A. M., & Covington, M. V. (1993). The role of cooperative reward interdependency in success and failure. *Journal of Experimental Education, 61*(2), 151–168.

Heist, P. A., & Yonge, G. (1968). *Manual for the omnibus personality inventory, form F.* New York: Psychological Corporation.

Holland, J. L. (1966). *Psychology of vocational choice.* Waltham, MA: Blaisdell.

Holland, J. L. (1973). *Making vocational choices: A theory of careers.* Englewood Cliffs, NJ: Prentice-Hall.

Holland, J. L., Gottfredson, D. C., & Power, P. G. (1980). Some diagnostic scales for research in decision making and personality: Identity, information, and barriers. *Journal of Personality and Social Psychology, 39,* 1191–1200.

Katchadourian, H. A., & Boli, J. (1985). *Careerism and intellectualism among college students.* San Francisco: Jossey-Bass.

Kirkland, K., & Hollandsworth, J. (1980). Effective test taking: Skills-acquisition versus anxiety-reduction techniques. *Journal of Counseling and Clinical Psychology, 48,* 431–439.

Laux, L., & Glanzmann, P. (1987). A self-presentational view of test anxiety. In R. Schwarzer, H. M. van der Ploeg, & C. D. Spielberger (Eds.), *Advances in test anxiety research* (Vol. 5, pp. 31–37). Hillsdale, NJ: Lawrence Erlbaum Associates.

Liebert, R. M., & Morris, L. W. (1967). Cognitive and emotional components of test anxiety: A distinction and some initial data. *Psychological Reports, 20,* 975–978.

Littig, G. H. (1966). Achievement motivation, expectancy of success, and risk-taking behavior. In J. W. Atkinson & N. T. Feather (Eds.), *A theory of achievement motivation* (pp. 103–115). New York: Wiley.

Litwin, L. W. (1963). Effects of motivation on probability preference. *Journal of Personality, 31,* 417–427.

Malone, T. W. (1981). Toward a theory of intrinsically motivating instruction. *Cognitive Science, 4,* 333–369.

Mandler, G., & Sarason, S. (1952). A study of anxiety and learning. *Journal of Abnormal and Social Psychology, 47,* 166–173.

McClelland, D. C. (1961). *The achieving society.* Princeton, NJ: Van Nostrand.

McClelland, D. C. (1980). Motive dispositions: The merits of operant and respondent measures. In L. Wheeler (Ed.), *Review of personality and social psychology* (Vol. 1, pp. 10–41). Beverly Hills, CA: Sage.

McClelland, D. C. (1985). How motives, skills, and values determine what people do. *American Psychologist, 40,* 812–825.

Moulton, R. W. (1965). Effects of success and failure on level of aspiration as related to achievement motives. *Journal of Personality and Social Psychology, 1,* 399–406.

Osipow, S. H., Ashby, J. D., & Wall, H. W. (1966). Personality types and vocational choice: A test of Holland's theory. *Personnel and Guidance Journal, 45,* 37–42.

Pfeiffer, J. W., & Jones, J. E. (Eds.). (1971). *Structured experiences for human relations training* (Vol. III). Iowa City, Iowa: University Associates Press.

Roberts, B., & Covington, M. V. (1991). *The myth of Hermes.* Unpublished manuscript, Institute of Personality Assessment and Research, University of California, Berkeley.

Roberts, B. W., & Covington, M. V. (1992). *Hope-of-success and Fear-of-failure Predict Vocational Aspirations.* Poster presentation, Fourth Annual American Psychological Society meeting, San Diego.

Salamé, R. (1984). Test anxiety: Its determinants, manifestations and consequences. In H. M. van der Ploeg, R. Schwarzer, & C. D. Spielberger (Eds.), *Advances in test anxiety research* (Vol. 3, pp. 83–119). Hillsdale, NJ: Lawrence Erlbaum Associates.

Schmalt, H. D. (1982). Two concepts of fear of failure motivation. In R. Schwarzer, H. M. van der Ploeg, & C. D. Spielberger (Eds.), *Advances in test anxiety research* (Vol. 1, pp. 45–52). Lisse: Swets & Zeitlinger.

Slavin, R. E. (1983). When does cooperative learning increase student achievement? *Psychological Bulletin, 94,* 429–445.

Slavin, R. E. (1984). Students motivating students to excel: Cooperative incentives, cooperative tasks, and student achievement. *The Elementary School Journal, 85,* 53–64.

Snyder, C. R. (1984, September). Excuses, excuses: They sometimes actually work—to relieve the burden of blame. *Psychology Today, 18,* 50–55.

Solomon, L. J., & Rothblum, E. D. (1984). Academic procrastination: Frequency and cognitive-behavioral correlates. *Journal of Counseling Psychology, 31,* 503–509.

Woodson, C. E. (1975). *Motivational effects of two-stage testing.* Unpublished manuscript, Institute of Human Learning, University of California, Berkeley.

8

Seeking Academic Assistance as a Strategic Learning Resource

Stuart A. Karabenick
Eastern Michigan University

Rajeev Sharma
Allahabad University, India

In his classic book *Teaching Tips*, McKeachie (1986) advised beginning college teachers to create classroom environments that maximize student involvement. An advocate of student-centered learning, he cited considerable evidence that class discussion, compared to lectures, increases motivation and facilitates critical thinking. Discussions afford students the opportunity to evaluate their comprehension of course content and apply concepts. Even instructors of large classes are urged to encourage student comments and questions.

Those who take his advice undoubtedly find many of their classes receptive to opportunities for interaction. In others, however, discussions may never occur or become productive. Furthermore, whereas some students profit from increased involvement, others, even with the best of teacher intentions and inducements, remain silent and passive. This is especially problematic for students who despite being confused take little or no advantage of instructors who not only provide time for discussions and questions in class, but offer other forms of assistance as well. McKeachie (1986) proposed that the lack of interest and knowledge, habitual passivity, fear, and embarrassment are reasons why students do not contribute to class discussions. After all, students do take risks when offering opinions; they can be easily ridiculed as well as rewarded for seeking needed information or clarification in (public) classrooms and even in the privacy of faculty offices (Karabenick, 1990).

Creating effective learning environments means recognizing, and minimizing, such impediments to involvement, which includes increasing students' willingness to seek assistance from others when necessary. Cultural norms that stress independence are part of the problem. More than in most societies "going it alone" is a maxim to which many American parents and undoubtedly many teachers probably subscribe. This is reflected in theoretical perspectives that define the ideal learner as one who accomplishes tasks on his or her own, *without* assistance from others (e.g., Winterbottom, 1958). In their view, seeking assistance from others is antithetical to academic achievement: opposite poles of a single continuum. This chapter reviews evidence suggesting that such a unidimensional approach is too narrow. It fails to distinguish between relying on others as a substitute for involvement and employing them as an important resource in the learning process, that although seeking assistance may manifest dependency, it can also represent an important component of a mature strategic approach to learning. We begin by reviewing theoretical developments that place the seeking of assistance within a broader strategic framework, present by means of a heuristic model the process and major determinants of help-seeking, and describe recent work on college students' classroom questioning.

A STRATEGIC VIEW OF HELP-SEEKING

In an influential review, Nelson-Le Gall (1981) expanded upon earlier suggestions (e.g., Murphy, 1962) that help-seeking can be an autonomous coping strategy that is important for achieving independent competence. Such "instrumental help-seeking" refers to obtaining the minimum assistance necessary to accomplish tasks. Instrumental, mastery-oriented help-seeking is typified by requests for necessary or indirect, as opposed to unnecessary or direct assistance, for example, asking someone for the rule or principle needed to solve a math problem after persistent failures at a solution (Nelson-Le Gall, 1987). By contrast, the intention of "executive help-seeking" is to decrease the cost of goal attainment, for example, asking a classmate for the answer to the problem. Because the goal is to minimize activity and participation, executive help-seeking may be productive in the short run, yet perpetuate dependency by obviating active involvement in the learning process. With greater involvement, instrumental help-seeking is more likely to decrease dependency to the extent that learners acquire knowledge that is transferable to subsequent academic tasks (see also Nelson-Le Gall, 1985; Nelson-Le Gall & Glor-Scheib, 1985; Nelson-Le Gall, Gumerman, & Scott-Jones, 1983).

Ames (1983) characterized help-seeking as an alternative achievement strategy in response to inadequate performance, and Kuhl (1985) viewed it as a coping strategy in the learning process, a means of acquiring environmental control. Similarly, for Rohrkemper and Corno (1988), seeking assistance from teachers and peers represents an adaptive way of changing the situation in response to difficulty or unfamiliarity in school. For Newman (1991), "adaptive help-seeking" is a strategy of self-regulated learners (Paris & Newman, 1990; Zimmerman & Martinez-Pons, 1986; Zimmerman & Schunk, 1989) that increases the likelihood of academic success. Adaptive help-seekers obtain assistance efficiently, for the purpose of learning, and only when necessary. Others (Aberbach, Harold, & Eccles, 1990; Aberbach & Lynch, 1991) linked "appropriate" help-seeking to autonomous learning behaviors (Fennema & Peterson, 1985). In summary, a variety of complementary theoretical approaches propose that help-seeking represents an important strategic resource. Unlike other learning strategies (e.g., rehearsal or elaboration), however, it is inherently interpersonal and potentially public, which renders it susceptible to social influences that can interfere with its effective use.

EVIDENCE SUPPORTING THE STRATEGIC PERSPECTIVE

If help-seeking represents an adaptive, self-regulating, instrumental response to academic difficulties, then learners who adopt such strategies should be more likely to seek help when necessary. For example, Nelson-Le Gall and Jones (1990) reported that young children's (third- and fifth-grade) preferences for independent mastery (Harter, 1983) are related to the likelihood of seeking instrumental (i.e., indirect rather than direct) help. The connection between preferences for challenge and independent mastery and help-seeking appears to be established by middle school (Arbreton & Wood, 1992; Newman, 1990). Its presence in the later grades is suggested by evidence that high school students who used several other self-regulating strategies were more likely to seek assistance from peers, teachers, and adults (Zimmerman & Martinez-Pons, 1986). Ames and Lau (1982) reported that poorly performing college students with beliefs consistent with achievement and mastery orientations were more likely to appear at an exam review session. According to Karabenick and Knapp (1991), the more that college students indicated they would respond to poor performance by increased reliance on approach-oriented achievement activities (e.g., greater effort), the greater their stated likelihood of seeking help from teachers and study skills centers. And those who used more cognitive, metacognitive, and resource-management learning strategies indicative of active approaches to learning also reported having sought more help when needed (Karabenick & Knapp, 1991). Karabenick and Knapp (1986) further indicate that college students' stated likelihood of seeking help from teachers and study skills personnel was directly related to their learning/task and inversely related to their performance/ego orientations (see Dweck, 1986; Nicholls, 1984). In sum, there is evidence that students characterized as having achievement-motivated, active, mastery/task-oriented approaches to learning are more, rather than less, likely to seek help when necessary, which supports the perspective that seeking academic assistance reflects an appropriate, strategic response to learning.

PROCESS AND DETERMINANTS OF HELP-SEEKING

Understanding academic help-seeking is facilitated if viewed as a multi-stage process, represented by the heuristic model shown in Fig. 8.1 (see also Gross & McMullen, 1983; Nelson-Le Gall, Gumerman, & Scott-Jones, 1983; van der Meij, 1986). By way of overview, the self-evaluation that accompanies knowledge acquisition or performance feedback may signal the existence of a problem that seeking help could remedy. Seeking help is conceived as contingent on its benefits outweighing its potential costs, the alternatives to which are continued persistence, self-help, or abandoning the task. Several variables affect the direction that learners take at each of these stages. Although all learners may not construe the stages and its options as modeled in this fashion, or be mindful of them, they are likely to be typical for most help seeking episodes.

Determining that a problem exists and that help is needed

The initiation of help-seeking often follows metacognitive evaluations, through monitoring activities (Markman, 1981), that comprehension is inadequate during knowledge acquisition, for example, not understanding parts of a lecture, or following performance outcomes, such as receiving poor grades on academic assignments. Factors such as the importance of understanding material and/or a student's aspiration level influence the threshold for determining inadequacy (Rosen, 1983). However, whether an academic outcome indicates inadequacy, and therefore a problem, may depend on whether defenses are present that deny its existence, or beliefs that discount it. According to Ames (1983; Ames & Lau, 1982), causal attributions for problems such as a test being too difficult, bad luck, the irrelevance of effort, or poor teaching, are considered "help-irrelevant" beliefs because they foster the conclusion that help would be unproductive. By contrast, "help-relevant" attributions increase the likelihood of help-seeking. These include believing that one is generally capable but is having difficulties in one specific area, that success is contingent on effort, and that help has yet to be utilized. Recognizing that a problem exists still may not prompt help-seeking, however. Among the alternatives is persistence. The decision for learners is whether the continuation of current efforts or assistance from others is the preferred alternative. Another possibility, "self-help," consists of activities that aid in comprehension or skill acquisition without another's assistance, such as consulting a study skills manual rather than a tutor.

Magnitude of need

Intuitively, help-seeking should increase with the degree of perceived need for assistance. However, the evidence does not consistently support a direct relationship, with further complexity due to variation in how need has been operationalized. Examples of how need is manipulated or assessed are: (a) objective indicators of naturally occurring performance (e.g., exam grades, CAT scores), (b) subjective reports (e.g., expected performance, confidence), (c) hypothetical/contingencies (e.g., "What would you do if you needed help?"), and (d) experimentally manipulated performance.

Several laboratory studies, for example, have examined whether children, classified by ability or skill level, sought assistance on verbal tasks, such as selecting the word that best matches a target. In general, lower ability groups opted for more help (hints or answers) (Nelson-Le Gall, 1987; Nelson-Le Gall, DeCooke, & Jones, 1989; Nelson-Le Gall, Kratzer, Jones, & DeCooke, 1990; van der Meij, 1990). The relation is somewhat stronger when based on subjective estimates of need rather than objective performance indicators (Nelson-Le Gall & Jones, 1990; Nelson-Le Gall et al., 1990). Similarly, low-ability elementary school students were observed seeking more help during mathematics instruction (Nelson-Le Gall & Glor-Scheib, 1985), as were kindergarten students asking questions (Good, Slavings, Harel, & Emerson, 1987).

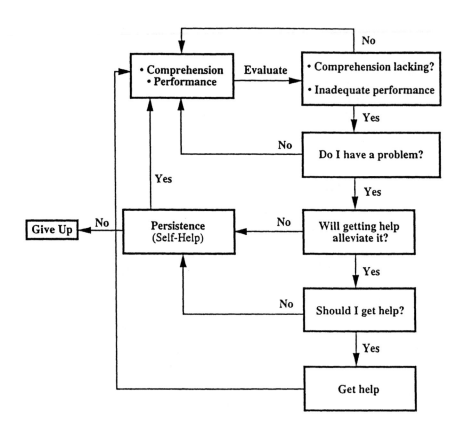

FIG. 8.1. Model of stages and alternatives in the academic help-seeking process.

College students with lower test performance were more likely than high performing students to appear at a remedial review session (Ames & Lau, 1982). There is, therefore, substantial evidence that learners with lower levels of ability, skill, or performance are more likely to seek assistance.

Not all studies, however, have found a direct relation between diagnostic ability level or performance levels and help-seeking. In the study by Good et al. (1987), the incidence of classroom questioning by high school students was *inversely* related to ability level—lower ability students tended to ask *fewer* questions. And Karabenick and Knapp (1988b) reported a non-monotonic relationship in a large sample of college students, in which the self-reported frequency of academic help-seeking (from peers, teachers, & study skills personnel) was highest for students in the middle range of performance (expected semester grade average in the C-, B+ range). One reason for non-monotonicity could have been the sampling of a sufficient number of students with very poor performance (i.e., very high levels of need), whose low rates of help-seeking were a consequence of low ability attributions, passivity, or hopelessness, without which a curvilinear relationship would not have resulted.

Assessing intentions to seek help reveals a different pattern than does observed or reported behavior: students with high rather than low ability, or characteristics indicative of high ability, are more likely to indicate they would seek help when faced with academic difficulties. Newman (1990), for example, reported this pattern with 7th graders (although not for students in the 3rd and 5th grades). Zimmerman and Martinez-Pons (1990) compared the self-regulated learning strategies, when having difficulty with academic work, of gifted and regular 5th-, 8th-, and 11th-grade students. Gifted students indicated they were more likely to seek help from peers, and 5th-grade gifted students indicated being more likely than regular students to seek help from adults. Karabenick and Knapp (1991) reported that college students with higher levels of self-esteem, and we can assume higher self-perceived ability, indicated that when faced with academic difficulty they would be more likely to seek academic assistance from formal sources (e.g., teachers, support services). In sum, lower ability (and higher need) typically translates to greater help-seeking (except perhaps for students with extremely poor performance). However, it appears that students with higher ability levels are more likely to seek help than students with lower ability *when the need arises*, that is, more likely to use help as a strategic resource when necessary.

The decision to seek assistance: A cost–benefit analysis

The benefits of help derive from an increased probability of success and an increase, in the case of instrumental help-seeking, in skills and knowledge that may reduce the need for subsequent assistance. A substantial body of work has examined help-seeking in a broad range of experimental and field settings (DePaulo, Nadler, & Fisher, 1983; Spacapan & Oskamp, 1992) and has identified the major cost factors that influence its likelihood. Among the social psychological factors are the need to reciprocate and indebtedness to the help provider (Greenberg & Westcott , 1983), overcoming culturally prescribed individualism (van der Meij, 1986), public disclosure and embarrassment (Karabenick & Knapp, 1988a; Shapiro, 1983), and most generally, threat to self-esteem (Fisher, Nadler, & Whitcher-Alagna, 1982; Nadler & Fisher, 1986).

Developmentally, by third grade, children are apparently aware of both the benefits and costs of classroom help-seeking (Newman & Goldin, 1990; van der Meij, 1986). Evidence indicates that the association between the perceived benefits of help and help-seeking is also present by the third grade (Newman, 1990). According to Schwager and Newman (1991), third- and seventh-graders' ratings of personal involvement with teachers predicted intentions to seek help from them. Not until the seventh grade, however, do perceived negative consequences appear to inhibit intentions to seek help (Newman, 1990), a period when achievement evaluation takes on greater significance. As suggested by Good et al. (1987), the negative consequences of seeking help may be cumulative and only manifest themselves in the higher grades. There is direct evidence that the perceived threat from seeking help is inversely related to college students' intentions to seek help (Karabenick & Knapp, 1991), to the amount of help sought during an academic term (Karabenick & Knapp, 1986; 1991), and to the likelihood of asking questions in class (Karabenick & Sharma, 1994).

Helping resources

Potential helpers differ in ways that affect both the decision to seek help and the value of help received. An important distinction is whether helping resources are informal (e.g., classmates, friends, family) or formal (e.g., teachers, study skills personnel). Informal, compared to formal resources are generally more available, less costly in terms of access time and money, and typically less threatening. They may, however, be less able to supply the requisite assistance and, except for communal as opposed to exchange relationships (Clark, 1983), result in feelings of indebtedness and/or inferiority (Fisher et al., 1982). Studies suggest that young children prefer teachers to peers for assistance in class, perhaps because peers have less information or expertise (Nelson-Le Gall, Gumerman, & Scott-Jones, 1983; Newman & Goldin, 1990). For older students, the trend is toward more informal assistance. In one study, approximately two-thirds of the college students who expressed a need for help during an academic term sought assistance from more knowledgeable friends, whereas only half approached their instructors, and very few used other institutionally provided sources (Knapp & Karabenick, 1988). In summary, because they are more accessible and less threatening, we prefer approaching people we know for help whenever possible, and target formal sources of assistance to alleviate problems only when necessary.

Seeking help

As with other learning strategies, seeking help is a skill that develops with experience (Nelson-Le Gall, 1981; Nelson-Le Gall et al., 1983). Learners must identify appropriate sources of assistance (e.g., those having the necessary information and/or expertise) that are available, and make the necessary arrangements (often appointments in the case of formal resources). For informal sources this involves making requests that are likely to induce acquiescence, for example, reasons why help is needed that engender sympathetic rather than negative emotions (Reisenzein, 1986). In addition to differences in the goals of help discussed above (e.g., whether necessary, direct, or instrumental), recent work has more closely examined the "timing" of help requests, contrasting appropriate requests with those that are too frequent and/or prior to sufficient independent effort, or inadequate (Aberbach, Harold, & Eccles, 1990; Aberbach & Lynch, 1991).

QUESTION ASKING IN COLLEGE CLASSROOMS

Studies of academic help-seeking have focused primarily on classroom behavior, which consists in large measure of students asking their teachers and peers questions. In addition to Good, Nelson-Le Gall, and Newman and their colleagues in the United States, van der Meij (1986) conducted an extensive investigation of classroom questioning in the Netherlands. We have undertaken a series of studies of college students' tendencies to ask questions in the classroom about which much less is known. As stated at the outset, the rate of student questioning, as in Grades K–12 (Dillon, 1988; Susskind, 1969), is low (Pollio, 1989), an average of 3.3 per hour according to one recent estimate (Pearson & West, 1991). College teachers rather than students ask most of the questions. Although there is increasing use of student-centered approaches that facilitate questioning (Greeson, 1988), the traditional lecture (or lecture/discussion) class structure remains the norm.

In an initial study we examined college students' perceived causes of classroom questioning when teachers are presenting course material (Sharma & Karabenick, 1989). Responses from students in several university classes were classified according to the source (the student, teacher, subject-matter, or peers) and the type of cause (informational, motivational, or procedural). Clearly, most of the reasons students cited for *asking* questions in class reflected the need to increase their understanding of course material (student source/informational type—60%), followed by curiosity (student source/motivational type—15%). Students specified teachers primarily in connection with cognitive factors, such as not presenting information clearly or not adequately answering a previous question (teacher/information—6%), or going too fast (teacher/procedure—5%). Interestingly, virtually none of the students indicated that teachers motivated them to ask questions. The role of classmates was primarily informational as well with 7% indicating they asked questions to help their peers understand the material.

Approximately one third of the reasons given for not asking questions involved anticipated negative consequences—fear of appearing unintelligent and avoiding embarrassment (student/motivation—29%). (This may be an underestimate since the proportion increased to 45% when students were asked why they thought "others in their class" don't ask questions.) Approximately one third (28%) of the reasons were student/informational—not having a question to ask, or, as is often suspected by teachers, not knowing enough to ask questions (see Miyake & Norman, 1979), and 15% mentioned they were too busy taking notes or didn't want to interrupt the lecture (student/procedure). Teachers were typically mentioned in connection with procedure, with 8% stating that they probably wouldn't see the student's raised hand or answer the question, or moved on before the question could be formulated. The predominant mention of peers was as an alternative source of information to asking in class, and only occasionally as a motivational determinant (possible embarrassment).

The picture that emerges is consistent with evidence from other studies. Insufficient knowledge prompts questioning and presumably initiates the questioning process, whereas both motivational (perceived negative consequence) and cognitive factors (lack of a question to ask) inhibit questioning. That teachers weren't mentioned frequently as either facilitating or inhibiting questioning is unexpected, because we have typically assumed that teachers are important determiners of classroom questioning. However, we may have underestimated teacher influences by conservatively categorizing the student as the source unless another source (teacher, subject-matter, or peer) was stated explicitly, that is, students may have been implicitly citing teacher sources when indicating fear or embarrassment. Another possibility is that students may not be fully aware or capable of spontaneously reporting situational (i.e., teacher) influences on questioning (see Nisbett & Wilson, 1977). Because such reports might not reveal the full extent of teacher influences on students' motivation to ask questions, we conducted additional studies that used a different approach—directly assessing student perceptions of teacher support of classroom questioning.

Teacher influences on questioning have typically been studied either from a socio-linguistic perspective (Dillon, 1990; Morine-Dersheimer, 1985) or as one of several factors affecting classroom questioning (e.g., Newman, 1990; van der Meij, 1986); moreover, ratings of whether students are encouraged to ask questions are part of several existing student evaluations of teacher effectiveness (e.g., the "group interaction" dimension of Marsh's 1984 Students' Evaluations of Educational Quality—SEEQ). Nevertheless, the specific effects of this dimension on students' tendencies to ask questions have not been studied extensively. Schwager and Newman (1991) reported that children's perceptions of teacher encouragement predicted their intentions to seek help from teachers, which included asking them questions. We did not, however, find a similar relationship among college students (Sharma & Karabenick, 1989). Although it is possible that adults differ from children in this respect, other evidence from that study suggests alternatives. First, because perceived teacher support was inversely related to students' level of confusion, students who perceived their teachers as more supportive might have had fewer questions, in effect canceling their increased tendency to ask. Furthermore, because perceived teacher support of questioning was inversely related to students' hesitation to ask questions, its influence on the likelihood of asking questions might be indirect—perceived support affects hesitation, which in turn influences questioning.

We explored these possibilities by embedding perceived teacher support within a structural model, shown in Fig. 8.2a, that specifies both direct and indirect teacher influences on questioning (Karabenick & Sharma, 1994). Based on our previous results, generic models of help-seeking (Gross & McMullen, 1983; Nelson-Le Gall et al., 1983), and of questioning in particular (Flammer, 1981; van der Meij, 1986), students' perceptions of teacher support for questioning were expected to influence question asking by directly affecting (positively) whether they have a question to ask (see van der Meij, 1990) and (negatively) their reluctance to ask, that is, inhibition. "Confusion" conceptualizes students' awareness of need, which we anticipated would directly influence (positively) whether students have a question to ask. Furthermore, given evidence that more confused students are more threatened by asking a question (Karabenick & Knapp, 1991; Newman, 1990), confusion was directly linked (positively) to inhibition. No causal priority was assumed between the exogenous variables of perceived teacher support and confusion, nor between the endogenous variables having a question and inhibition. The model was evaluated with information obtained from college students in small- to moderate-size classes, the results of which are also shown in Fig. 8.2.

Analyses were conducted both with individual students (with scores standardized separately for each class and pooled across classes) and classes (i.e., class means) as the unit of analysis. Using students as the unit of analysis ($N = 1327$) we found once again that perceived teacher support of questioning was not significantly related to students' reported likelihood of asking questions. However, based on a maximum likelihood evaluation (LISREL) of the proposed structural model, shown in Fig. 8.2b, perceived support did, as expected, appear to affect questioning indirectly through its influence on inhibition. In addition, perceived support was inversely related to confusion, and the scenario within classes can be described as follows. Students who perceived their teachers as more supportive were not as confused when their teachers were presenting material. As a consequence they needed and had fewer questions but were less hesitant to ask them. Students perceiving less

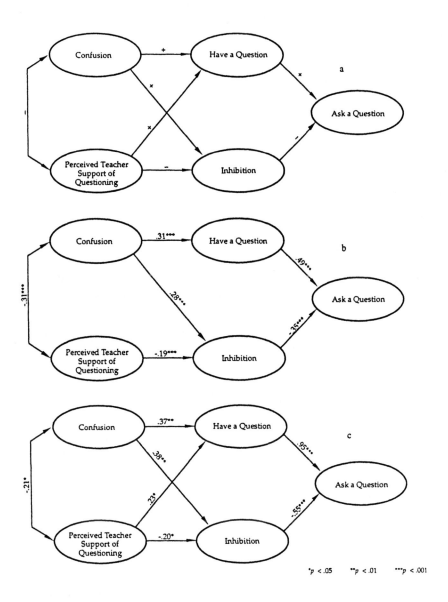

FIG. 8.2. Questioning behavior in the classroom: Proposed (a) model, and LISREL solution based on within-classroom (b) and between-classroom (c) variation.

teacher support, on the other hand, were more confused and had more questions, but they were also more hesitant to ask those questions. Perceived teacher support of questioning was thus not related to the reported likelihood of asking questions within classes because of offsetting mediating effects rather than an absence of influence.

Unlike students analyzed individually, classes that perceived their teachers as more supportive reported being more likely to ask questions. As shown in Fig. 8.2c, this appears to be a function of the effect of perceived support on the likelihood that students had questions, a path not present in the within-class model. Thus, classes that perceived their teachers as more supportive had more questions to ask in addition to lower levels of inhibition, whereas those perceiving less support had fewer questions and were more inhibited. We cannot conclude from this analysis alone that students of more supportive teachers generated more questions, because students as well as teachers varied across classes (Abrami, Leventhal, & Dickens, 1981). However, because the within-class analysis was conducted to reflect only student effects, and the model based on class means reflects both student and teacher effects, we can attribute to teacher influences those paths present in the between-class model not present in the within-class model. The only such effect is between teacher support and question generation. We submit, therefore, that students of teachers who were perceived as more supportive generated more questions to ask (controlling for confusion). This would be important if confirmed by other studies given the value of question generation for increased comprehension (see Dole, Duffy, Roehler, & Pearson, 1991). The multivariate structural modeling approach presents a more complete understanding of how perceived teacher support affects students' questioning tendencies. In conjunction with similar modeling studies (e.g., Newman, 1990) it also casts doubt on conclusions drawn from univariate and nonstructural multivariate analyses that may underestimate effects of teacher support by not taking into consideration students' levels of need or indirect effects (e.g., Aitken & Neer, 1991).

Additional studies reveal ways that perceived support relates to other characteristics that are important determinants of learning (Karabenick & Sharma, 1994). Results suggest that students whose motivational tendencies and use of learning strategies can be characterized as self-regulating (Corno, 1989) are more likely to perceive their teachers as supportive of classroom questioning. It is possible that more successful self-regulating students perceived more support because they encountered more rewarding teacher interactions. Alternatively, their previous successes may result in classroom behaviors that increase the likelihood of positive teacher interactions (i.e., a self-fulfilling prophecy effect). Third, they may bias their perceptions in a manner that is consistent with their self-schemas. Whatever the process involved, less successful students with fewer self-regulating tendencies perceive their teachers as less supportive, which makes them more hesitant to ask questions that would increase their chances of success.

FACILITATING STRATEGIC ACADEMIC HELP-SEEKING

Increasing students' adaptive, instrumental help-seeking is likely to involve some combination of their greater awareness of the need for assistance, help-relevant attributions, higher perceived benefits and lower perceived cost (e.g., threat to self-esteem), and the skills to acquire help from appropriate sources. In addition to teachers creating more conducive classrooms, for example, by being more supportive and less threatening, more comprehensive approaches are possible. One approach, similar to that employed by McKeachie and his colleagues (McKeachie, Pintrich, & Lin, 1985), provided students in a university orientation course with instruction in theory and research related to academic help-seeking (Collins-Eaglin & Karabenick, 1992). Topics included comprehension monitoring, attribution theory, and the perceived negative consequences of seeking assistance. Students also engaged in classroom role-play, then applied their instruction to an actual interaction with one of their instructors. Qualitative evaluation indicated reductions in perceived negative consequences, greater willingness to seek assistance, and considerable enthusiasm about the utility of the experience. Other evidence suggests that even a less targeted approach may be beneficial. According to Walter, Smith, and Hagen (1992), first-term college students' intentions to seek help from instructors, tutors, and other students increased for those participating in a freshman study skills course, but decreased for students who received no support. Thus, some features of comprehensive strategy courses have implications for academic help-seeking as well as other strategies, although we are unable to specify the critical components of those experiences.

CONCLUSIONS AND DIRECTIONS FOR FUTURE RESEARCH

Given over a decade of research and theoretical development we know more about the characteristics of learners, and of instructional settings, that affect the incidence of academic help-seeking. In general, we can conclude that utilizing personal resources effectively when necessary is an important strategic component of an adaptive, self-regulated, mastery-oriented approach to learning. And the supportive interpersonal learning environments that McKeachie advises college faculty to create (and that he, himself fosters in interactions with colleagues as well as students!) will facilitate the appropriate use of that strategy. More recent research on the type and timing of help-seeking (Arbreton, 1993) is likely to improve our understanding of this important learning strategy. Further studies are also needed on the social impact of help-seeking, and questioning in particular, in social contexts. Although we know that help-seeking is more likely when students believe it is normative (i.e., other students have sought assistance), possible moderating influences (e.g., the perceived ability level of other students who have sought help) have yet to be explored. There is also evidence to suggest that questioning influences others' metacognitive judgments of comprehension (Karabenick, 1993). Additional studies are required to determine the conditions under which this takes place.

The impact on assistance-seeking by increasingly ubiquitous computer-mediated and computer-facilitated learning environments also requires further examination (for recent work on question asking in CAI contexts see Graesser, Person, & Huber, 1993). For example, there are several features of computer-mediated communication (i.e., E-mail or computer conferencing) that facilitate involvement by virtue of reduced threat as a consequence of decreases in time pressure and anonymity (Karabenick, 1987; Karabenick & Knapp, 1988a; Moore & Karabenick, 1992). Even without anonymity, when students' responses are identified, the lack of face-to-face contact appears to facilitate expression and disclosure. The exponential increase in information available to learners is also placing greater reliance on strategies that improve the efficiency of database searches, a context in which seeking assistance is of particular relevance. Computer assistance (e.g., using various expert systems) makes searching easier, and the increased privacy they provide should facilitate certain requests for assistance that would be threatening if made in person. Nevertheless, students must now acquire these new skills, and especially in the initial phases of information searching, may yet find themselves sitting at a terminal wondering whether to ask that reference librarian for help. We suggest that models of the information search process (e.g., Kulthau, 1990) would be more complete if additional psychological determinants were taken into consideration (Keefer & Karabenick, 1992). The kind of learning environment that Bill McKeachie suggests that we create for students in the classroom would apply to computer-mediated contexts as well.

REFERENCES

Aberbach, A. J., & Lynch, S. (1991, April). *When getting help is helpful: Age and gender differences in children's autonomous help-seeking.* Paper presented at the biennial meeting of the Society for Research in Child Development, Seattle, WA.

Aberbach, A. J., Harold, R., & Eccles, J. S. (1990, April). *Parental helping behaviors and children's autonomous learning behaviors in the classroom.* Paper presented at the annual meeting of the American Educational Research Association, Boston, MA.

Abrami, P. C., Leventhal, L., & Dickens, W. J. (1981). Multidimensionality of student ratings of instruction. *Instructional Evaluation, 6,* 12–17.

Aitken, J. E., & Neer, M. R. (1991). *Variables associated with question-asking in the college classroom.* Paper presented at the 77th annual meeting of the Speech Communication Association, Atlanta, GA.

Ames, R. (1983). Help-seeking and achievement orientation: Perspectives from attribution theory. In B. M. Depaulo, A. Nadler, & J. D. Fisher (Eds.), *New directions in helping: Vol. 2. Help-seeking* (pp. 165–186). New York: Academic Press.

Ames, R., & Lau, S. (1982). An attributional analysis of help seeking in academic settings. *Journal of Educational Psychology, 74,* 414–423.

Arbreton, A. (1993). *When getting help is helpful: Developmental, cognitive, and motivational influences on students' academic help seeking.* Unpublished doctoral dissertation, University of Michigan, Ann Arbor.

Arbreton, A., & Wood, S. (1992). *Help-seeking behavior and children's learning preferences in the middle school years.* Paper presented at the biennial meeting of the Society for Research on Adolescence, Washington, DC.

Clark, M. (1983). Reactions to aid in communal and exchange relationships. In B. M. Depaulo, A. Nadler, & J. D. Fisher (Eds.), *New directions in helping: Vol. 2. Help-seeking* (pp. 205–229). New York: Academic Press.

Collins-Eaglin, J., & Karabenick, S. A. (1992, April). *Teaching students of color the strategy of seeking academic assistance as a critical component of the freshman year experience.* Paper presented at the Conference on the Freshman Year Experience, Lexington, KY.

Corno, L. (1989). Self-regulated learning: A volitional analysis. In B. J. Zimmerman, & D. H. Schunk (Eds.), *Self-regulated learning and academic achievement* (pp. 111–141). New York: Springer-Verlag.

DePaulo, B. M., Nadler, A., & Fisher, J. D. (Eds.). (1983). *New directions in helping: Vol. 2. Help-seeking.* New York: Academic Press.

Dillon, J. T. (1988). The remedial status of student questioning. *Journal of Curriculum Studies, 20,* 197–210.

Dillon, J. T. (1990). *The practice of questioning.* New York: Routeledge.

Dole, J. A., Duffy, G. G., Roehler, L. R., & Pearson, P. D. (1991). Moving from the old to the new: Research on reading comprehension instruction. *Review of Educational Research, 61,* 239–264.

Dweck, C. (1986). Motivational processes affecting learning. *American Psychologist, 41,* 1040–1048.

Fennema, E. H., & Peterson, P. L. (1985). Autonomous learning behavior: A possible explanation of gender-related differences in mathematics. In L. C. Wilkinson, & C. B. Marrett (Eds.), *Gender influences in classroom interaction* (pp. 17–35). New York: Academic Press.

Fisher, J. D., Nadler, A., & Whitcher-Alagna, S. (1982). Recipient reactions to aid. *Psychological Bulletin, 91,* 27–54.

Flammer, A. (1981). Toward a theory of question asking. *Psychological Research, 43,* 407–420.

Good, T. L., Slavings, R. L., Harel, K. H., & Emerson, H. (1987). Student passivity: A study of question asking in K–12 classrooms. *Sociology of Education, 60,* 181–199.

Graesser, A. C., Person, N. K., & Huber, J. D. (1993). Question asking during tutoring and in the design of educational software. In M. Rabinowitz (Ed.), *Cognitive science foundations of instruction* (pp. 149–172). Hillsdale, NJ: Lawrence Erlbaum Associates.

Greenberg, M. S., & Westcott , D. R. (1983). Indebtedness as a mediator of reactions to aid. In J. D. Fisher, A. Nadler, & B. M. DePaulo (Eds.), *New directions in helping: Vol. 1. Recipient reactions to aid* (pp. 85–112). New York: Academic Press.

Greeson, L. W. (1988). College classroom interaction as a function of teacher- and student-centered instruction. *Teacher and Teacher Education, 4,* 305–315.

Gross, A. E., & McMullen, P. A. (1983). Models of the help-seeking process. In B. M. DePaulo, A. Nadler, & J. D. Fisher (Eds.), *New directions in helping: Vol. 2. Help-seeking.* (pp. 45–70). New York: Academic Press.

Harter, S. (1983). Developmental perspectives on the self-system. In P. Mussen (Ed.), *Handbook of child psychology: Socialization, personality and social development* (Vol. 4, pp. 275–385). New York: Wiley.

Karabenick, S. A. (1987). *Computer Conferencing: Its impact on academic help-seeking.* Presented at the Symposium on Computer Conferencing and Allied Technologies. University of Guelph, Guelph, Ontario.

Karabenick, S. A. (1990). When students need help. *Journal of Professional Studies, Winter,* 41–56.

Karabenick, S. A. (April, 1993). *Social mediation of metacognition: Effects of others' questions on comprehension monitoring.* Paper presented at the annual meeting of the American Educational Research Association, Atlanta, GA.

Karabenick, S. A., & Knapp, J. R. (1986). *Incidence and correlates of academic help-seeking.* Unpublished manuscript, Eastern Michigan University.

Karabenick, S. A., & Knapp, J. R. (1988a). Effects of computer privacy on help-seeking. *Journal of Applied Social Psychology, 18,* 461–472.

Karabenick, S. A., & Knapp, J. R. (1988b). Help seeking and the need for academic assistance. *Journal of Educational Psychology, 80,* 406–408.

Karabenick, S. A., & Knapp, J. R. (1991). Relationship of academic help seeking to the use of learning strategies and other instrumental achievement behavior in college students. *Journal of Educational Psychology, 83,* 221–230.

Karabenick, S. A., & Sharma, R. (1994). Perceived teacher support of student questioning in the college classroom: Its relation to student characteristics and role in the classroom questioning process. *Journal of Educational Psychology, 86,* 90-103.

Keefer, J. A. & Karabenick, S. A. (1992, May). *Help-seeking and the library reference/instruction setting: A social-psychological perspective.* Paper presented at the 20th annual LOEX Library Instruction Conference, Ypsilanti, MI.

Knapp, J. R., & Karabenick, S. A. (1988). Incidence of formal and informal help-seeking in higher education. *Journal of College Student Development, 29,* 223–227.

Kuhl, J. (1985). Volitional mediators of cognition-behavior consistency: Self-regulatory processes and action versus state orientation. In J. Kuhl, & J. Beckmann (Eds.), *Action control: From cognition to behavior* (pp. 101–128). Berlin: Springer-Verlag.

Kulthau, C. C. (1990). Validating a model of the search process: A comparison of academic, public and school library users. *Library and Information Science Research, 12,* 5–31.

Markman, E. M. (1981). Comprehension monitoring. In W. P. Dickson (Ed.), *Children's oral communication skills* (pp. 61–84). New York: Academic Press.

Marsh, H. W. (1984). Students' evaluations of university teaching: Dimensionality, reliability, validity, potential biases, and utility. *Journal of Educational Psychology, 76,* 707–754.

McKeachie, W. J. (1986). *Teaching tips: A guidebook for the beginning college teacher* (8th ed.). Lexington, MA: Heath.

McKeachie, W. J., Pintrich, P. R., & Lin, Y. (1985). Teaching learning strategies. *Educational Psychologist, 20,* 153–160.

Miyake, N., & Norman, D. A. (1979). To ask a question, one must know enough to know what is not known. *Journal of Verbal Learning and Verbal Behavior, 18,* 357–364.

Moore, M. A., & Karabenick, S. A. (1992). The effect of computer communications on the reading and writing performance of fifth-grade students. *Computers in Human Behavior, 8,* 27-38.

Morine-Dersheimer, G. (1985). *Talking, listening, and learning in elementary classrooms.* New York & London: Longman.

Murphy, L. (1962). *The widening world of childhood.* New York: Basic Books.

Nadler, A., & Fisher, J. D. (1986). The role of threat to self-esteem and perceived control in recipient reactions to help: Theory development and empirical validation. In L. Berkowitz (Ed.), *Advance in experimental social psychology* (pp. 81–123). New York: Academic Press.

Nelson-Le Gall, S. (1981). Help-seeking: An understudied problem-solving skill in children. *Developmental Review, 1,* 224–246.

Nelson-Le Gall, S. (1985). Help-seeking behavior in learning. In E. W. Gordon (Ed.), *Review of research in education* (Vol. 12), (pp. 55–90). Washington, DC: American Educational Research Association.

Nelson-Le Gall, S. (1987). Necessary and unnecessary help-seeking in children. *Journal of Genetic Psychology, 148,* 53–62.

Nelson-Le Gall, S., & Glor-Scheib, S. (1985). Help seeking in elementary classrooms: An observational study. *Contemporary Educational Psychology, 10,* 58–71.

Nelson-Le Gall, S., Gumerman, R., & Scott-Jones, D. (1983). Instrumental help-seeking and everyday problem-solving: A developmental perspective. In B. Depaulo, A. Nadler, & J. Fisher (Eds.), *New directions in helping: Vol. 2. Help-seeking* (pp. 265–283). New York: Academic Press.

Nelson-Le Gall, S., & Jones, E. (1990). Cognitive-motivational influences on the task-related help-seeking behavior of black children. *Child Development, 61,* 581–589.

Nelson-Le Gall, S., Kratzer, L., Jones, E., & DeCooke, P. (1990). Children's self-assessment of performance and task-related help seeking. *Journal of Experimental Child Psychology, 49,* 245–263.

Newman, R. S. (1990). Children's help-seeking in the classroom: The role of motivational factors and attitudes. *Journal of Educational Psychology, 82,* 71–80.

Newman, R. S. (1991). Goals and self-regulatory learning: What motivates children to seek academic help. In M. L. Maehr, & P. R. Pintrich (Eds.), *Advances in motivation and achievement: Goals and self-regulatory processes* (Vol.7, pp. 151–183). Greenwich, CT: JAI Press.

Newman, R. S., & Goldin, L. (1990). Children's reluctance to seek help with schoolwork. *Journal of Educational Psychology, 82,* 92–100.

Nicholls, J. G. (1984). Conceptions of ability and achievement motivation. In R. Ames & C. Ames (Eds.), *Research on motivation in education: Student motivation* (Vol. 1) (pp. 39-73). New York: Academic Press.

Nisbett, R., & Wilson, T. D. (1977). Telling more than we can know: Verbal reports on mental processes. *Psychological Review, 84,* 231–259.

Paris, S. G., & Newman, R. S. (1990). Developmental aspects of self-regulated learning. *Educational Psychologist, 25,* 87–102.

Pearson, J. C., & West, R. (1991). An initial investigation of the effects of gender on student questions in the classroom: Developing a descriptive base. *Communication Education, 40,* 22–32.

Pollio, H. R. (1989). *Any questions please* (Knoxville: Teaching–learning issues). Learning Research Center, University of Tennessee, Knoxville.

Reisenzein, R. (1986). A structural equation analysis of Weiner's attribution-affect model of helping. *Journal of Personality & Social Psychology, 50,* 1123–1133.

Rohrkemper, M., & Corno, L. (1988). Success and failure on classroom tasks: Adaptive learning and classroom teaching. *The Elementary School Journal, 88,* 297–312.

Rosen, S. (1983). Perceived inadequacy and help-seeking. In B. M. DePaulo, A. Nadler, & J. D. Fisher (Eds.), *New directions in helping: Vol. 2. Help-seeking* (pp. 73–107). New York: Academic Press.

Schwager, M. T., & Newman, R. S. (1991, April). *Children's perceptions of the classroom in relation to help-seeking.* Paper presented at the annual meeting of the American Educational Research Association, Chicago, IL.

Shapiro, E. G. (1983). Embarrassment and help-seeking. In B. M. Depaulo, A. Nadler, & J. D. Fisher (Eds.), *New directions in helping: Vol. 2. Help-seeking* (pp. 143–163). New York: Academic Press.

Sharma, R., & Karabenick, S. A. (1989, August). *Students' questioning in the classroom and its relationship to help-seeking.* Paper presented at the 97th annual convention of the American Psychological Association, New Orleans, LA.

Spacapan, S., & Oskamp, S. (Eds.). (1992). *Helping and being helped.* Newbury Park, CA: Sage.

Susskind, E. (1969). The role of questioning in the elementary school classroom. In F. Kaplan, & S. Sarason (Eds.), *The psycho-educational clinic* (pp. 130–151). New Haven, CT: Yale University Press.

van der Meij, H. (1986). *Questioning: A study of the questioning behavior of elementary school children.* The Hague: SVO.

van der Meij, H. (1990). Question asking: To know that you do not know is not enough. *Journal of Educational Psychology, 82,* 505–512.

Walter, T. L., Smith, J., & Hagen, J. (1992, February). *The effects of academic support upon student help seeking and learning skills.* Paper presented at the annual meeting of the Freshman Year Experience Conference, Columbia, SC.

Winterbottom, M. (1958). The relation of need for achievement to learning experiences in independence and mastery. In J. W. Atkinson (Ed.), *Motives in fantasy, action, and society* (pp. 453–478). Princeton, NJ: Van Nostrand.

Zimmerman, B. J., & Martinez-Pons, M. (1986). Development of a structured interview for assessing student use of self-regulated learning strategies. *American Educational Research Journal, 23,* 614–628.

Zimmerman, B. J., & Martinez-Pons, M. (1990). Student differences in self-regulated learning: Relating grade, sex, and giftedness to self-efficacy and strategy use. *Journal of Educational Psychology, 82,* 51–59.

Zimmerman, B. J., & Schunk, D. H. (Eds.). (1989). *Self-regulated learning and academic achievement: theory, research, and practice.* New York: Springer-Verlag.

9

Situated Motivation

Scott G. Paris
University of Michigan

Julianne C. Turner
Pennsylvania State University

Consider the implications of three statements about motivation and education:

1. I've got so many unmotivated students in my class!
2. My students are only motivated to get good grades.
3. She was a great teacher, a real motivator.

The first statement implies that students come to class with high or low motivation and that teachers cannot help "unmotivated" students learn. Motivation is a personal characteristic, state, or trait in this view. The second statement indicates that students can have good or bad motivation and implies that extrinsic rewards, such as grades, are not virtuous incentives for learning. The third statement describes a teacher as someone who displays leadership and enthusiasm. She probably elicits hard work and success from her students but her talents are perceived as part of her personality rather than her teaching techniques. All three statements reflect popular views in education that motivation is a characteristic of people or a property of events; some teachers and some events are motivating and others are not. In this chapter, we criticize such monolithic characterizations of motivation. Instead, we argue that analyses of motivation should consider the characteristics of individuals in specific situations because a person's motivational beliefs and behavior are derived from contextual transactions.

A TRIBUTE TO WILBERT MCKEACHIE

The arguments for a "persons in contexts" view of motivation has many roots but we want to connect some of our ideas to Bill McKeachie's prescience about psychological theories. A review of Bill's fifty years of psychological research reveals a wealth of information on a variety of topics. In addition to being a prolific researcher, Bill has several trademarks to his career that are excellent models for new researchers. One characteristic is his anticipation of major theoretical constructs on many fronts. For example, his writings in the 1950s and 1960s include references to schema theory, learner-centered instruction, higher order thinking strategies, test anxiety, and many other emerging constructs that became central themes in psychology. A second trademark of Bill's work is his ability to see the panoramic landscape of issues while focusing on specific details. Thus, his individual studies are set in broad theoretical frameworks. A third trademark is the bridge between theoretical and practical uses of psychology. Bill's impact on teaching has been worldwide, from his book on instructional "tips for teaching" to systems of evaluation of teaching effectiveness to the establishment of undergraduate courses on "learning how to learn." The fourth trademark of his research, and the focus of this chapter, is his emphasis on the interactions between persons and situations. Like Kurt Lewin and Jack Atkinson, Bill believes that motivation is constructed by the individual in a cognitively dynamic context. In his 1961 Nebraska Symposium chapter, Bill said,

> At the same time that the individual's motives are being activated, he is choosing a strategy, such as maximizing satisfaction or minimizing regret. Since the student is involved in several courses as well as in extracurricular, social, and other activities, his strategy must involve assessment of the potential rewards and punishments and their probabilities of attainment in all of these situations. Whatever his strategy, its choice also involves an assessment of his habits and skills in relation both to the possible satisfactions in the situation and to the types of behavior necessary to achieve these satisfactions. From these dual assessments comes an estimate of the amount and kind of satisfaction and the probability of attaining it in each class. This

combination of subjective expectancies of affect and of probability of affect is what I call motivation. (p. 116)

WHAT MAKES MOTIVATION "SITUATED"?

The quotation from McKeachie calls attention to the choices and assessments that individuals make about themselves and possible courses of action. It provides an introduction to four critical characteristics of students' personal motivation in different situations, or what we have termed *situated motivation*. First, motivation is a consequence of the *cognitive assessments* that individuals provide in situations; in this quotation, it is the expectancies, values, and probabilities of potential goals, rewards, and satisfactions. Thirty years later these concepts have been articulated in a variety of theories emphasizing the motivational consequences of cognitive attributions (Weiner, 1992), judgments about expectancies and values (Atkinson & Feather, 1966), cognitive interpretations of self-efficacy (Bandura, 1986), and self-serving rationalizations (Covington, 1992). Undoubtedly, this cognitive bias toward motivation needs to be balanced with noncognitive and affective aspects of motivation but the predominant models of motivation, and particularly academic motivation, have been based on cognitive self-appraisals.

Second, cognitive interpretations of events are *constructed*, which means that they are open to distortion by virtue of age, bias, and defensive interpretation. This is a consequence of constructivist models in developmental, educational, and social psychology during the past 20 years and places attention squarely on individual differences in constructed interpretations of the world. Our special concern is how children conceptualize, and sometimes misconstrue, the meanings of classroom activities and how those concepts influence their motivation to learn. Third, motivation is necessarily *contextualized* because individuals create unique cognitive interpretations of events, goals, and probabilities in different situations. For example, the presence of a competitive versus noncompetitive peer may alter one's effort and persistence (i.e., the social facilitation effect) and perhaps the degree of disappointment or satisfaction following the task. The people present, the physical status of the individual, and competing motives are some of the extenuating circumstances that may influence a person's performance in a specific context. It is the fit of the individual to the contextual circumstances that determines the course and vigor of the actions, hence, situated motivation.

This bears closely on the fourth characteristic; situated motivation is necessarily *unstable*. We do not think that goals remain the same for all individuals in all settings nor are their perceptions of their own efficacy or competence always the same. When motivation is cast in terms of desirable characteristics such as intrinsic motivation or mastery goal orientations, attention is directed toward enduring characteristics of individuals rather than features of situations that elicit such orientations. This subtle distinction has different implications for research. The first view is *typological*; it leads to identification of individuals by type of motivation and subsequent descriptions of their behavior. The latter view is *contextual*; it examines the person in context and identifies intra-individual variability as well as situations that elicit different kinds of motivation. We believe that motivation waxes and wanes according to one's history of success and failure and the relative incentives provided in different situations. The same tasks do not always elicit the same motivation nor are people uniformly motivated across situations. This means that we should avoid categorizing people according to types or degrees of motivation that they display and also avoid identifying environmental events as motivating or not because neither alone is sufficient to predict motivation across contexts or people.

A focus on the motivational interactions of persons in situations is consistent with today's emphasis on self-referenced systems of motivation, situated cognition, and anchored instruction. We find these approaches provocative for developmental and educational psychology because they examine differences across individuals in terms of their cognitive constructions of situations rather than enduring limitations of their cognitive abilities or motivational styles. Previous theories of motivation have often emphasized how young children are constrained by schedules of rewards and punishments and only gradually are they able to make plausible evaluations of choices, goals, and courses of action. Newer cognitive theories of motivation give more credit to young children's ability to consider how they might act in various situations. In a similar manner, traditional motivational theories have examined personality traits and characteristics that constrain reasoning and motivation. This would include such constructs as inner- versus outer-directed children, impulsive and reflective learning styles, and dependent versus independent children. Newer theories emphasize personalized evaluations of events in situations and how those settings can be changed to encourage different motivational orientations.

When motivation is analyzed as a cognitive, constructive, and contextualized set of interpretations, it is not simply a hyper-rational system of action. Thoughts and feelings can be irrational and discordant as well as contextually inappropriate thereby leaving individuals to act in less than optimal ways in different situations. But whether actions are derived from rational or irrational cognitions, one's behavior in a situation reflects a cumulative set of motivational beliefs that drive learning and self-assessment of one's performance that in turn determine the affective consequences of one's action. Thus, situated motivation may be regarded as the engine of self-regulated learning. Because students' autonomy is an important goal of both development and education, it is critical for researchers to identify how and why some situations evoke positively motivated behaviors and some do not.

The purpose of this chapter is to show how tasks and situations in school influence students' motivation. We begin with a description of some empirical evidence of children's literacy because research in this area has shown how the situations and activities created by teachers can have profound impact on students' motivation. Next we describe four important characteristics of situated motivation: students' choice, challenge, control, and collaboration. Finally, we provide implications of situated motivation on classroom activities of learning, teaching, and assessment.

SITUATED MOTIVATION IN SCHOOL

School provides multiple tasks and opportunities for students to learn, yet some situations are more motivating for some students than others. When academic tasks involve repeated drill on low-level skills, when the activities are detached from meaningful purposes for students, and when the focus of the activity is on "getting the work done" or "doing the procedures right" rather than substantive cognitive outcomes, students do not use critical thinking skills (Doyle, 1983). This sentiment has been echoed by critics of decontextualized knowledge practices in school. For example, Resnick (1987) said, "Indeed, evidence is beginning to accumulate that traditional schooling's focus on individual, isolated activity, on symbols correctly manipulated but divorced from experience, and on decontextualized skills may be partly responsible for the school's difficulty in promoting its own in-school learning goals" (p. 18).

One way to study the contexts of learning created by different educational practices and philosophies is to compare how children respond to whole language and traditional basal instruction in language arts (Goodman, 1989; Pearson, 1989). Whole language instruction focuses on constructing meaning for authentic purposes. For example, five- and six-year-olds in whole language classrooms typically use oral language to bridge their knowledge of familiar topics to reading and writing activities in which spelling, grammar, and accuracy are less important than comprehension and expression of meaning. In contrast, language arts instruction in a skills-oriented classroom typically requires children to practice phonics, sentence completion, and word identification activities on workbook pages that emphasize high levels of success rather than the process of constructing meaning. Advocates of whole language instruction argue that their methods are more interesting and motivating for young children, whereas advocates of skills-oriented instruction argue that without the ability to decode print, young children are frustrated and anxious about literacy. These opposing claims provide an appropriate arena in which to examine situated motivation because we can investigate how different kinds of classroom environments influence students' behavior.

Fisher and Hiebert (1990) analyzed 180 literacy tasks that they observed in second- and sixth-grade classrooms that were classified as either literature-based (LB) or skills-oriented (SO). (LB classrooms are characteristic of whole language instruction and SO classrooms are typical of traditional basal reading instruction so we will use these labels in our discussions.) There were striking differences in the kinds of learning activities provided to students in the two situations. LB classrooms had extensive opportunities for students to write about and discuss their literacy experiences with others in the classroom. Students often chose their reading and writing tasks and shared their interpretations with classmates. Students in SO classrooms had more passive roles because the tasks were more specified by teachers. Their tasks were relatively simple to complete. Fisher and Hiebert (1990) observed similar kinds of LB and SO tasks at both grade levels. The authors argued that the kinds of tasks in which children engage are powerful determiners of their motivation and thoughtfulness. The authors estimated that students complete approximately 10 tasks per day and more than 20,000 separate tasks in 12 years of schooling. As they put it, "If the majority of the 20,000 tasks that make a school career are teacher specified, cognitively simple, and done either by oneself or involve listening to the monologue of an adult, educators should wonder why so many students stay in school rather than wonder, as they now do, why some students drop out of school" (Fisher & Hiebert, 1990, p. 15).

Turner (1992) provided detailed analyses of children's literacy tasks and their motivated behaviors and found similar consequences of situations for learning. She analyzed students' responses to different kinds of tasks in first-grade classrooms, some of which might be labeled LB and others SO. The purpose of this study was to provide behavioral indicators of motivated literacy as opposed to children's speculative responses to surveys about how they might feel and how they might act in various circumstances. Eighty-four children were observed in six different classrooms of each type and four kinds of motivated behavior were recorded. First, children's use of *reading strategies*, including decoding and comprehension strategies, were targeted because the observations occurred during literacy instruction and reflected motivation to understand the text meaning (and follow the teachers' directions). Second, *general learning strategies*, such as rehearsal, elaboration, and organizational tactics were also recorded. Third, children's *persistence* on a task despite having difficulty or making errors was included as an index of student's effort. Fourth, *volitional control* was recorded when students took actions to ignore distractions or maintain their engagement on a task. These four categories of behavior indicate deliberate effort and strategic behavior designed to focus children's attention and accomplish the task purpose. One question addressed in the study was whether there were more motivated behaviors observed during instruction in LB or SO classrooms.

There was a broad spectrum of tasks and learning opportunities provided to students in the 12 classrooms. Indeed, the variability among classrooms was greater than the variability between LB and SO classrooms and, thus, main effects of classroom type were obscured. This is because some of the teachers in classrooms identified as LB actually spent a great deal of time teaching skills and other teachers identified as SO classrooms actually involved students in many thought-provoking activities with reading and writing. Therefore, the observations were organized according to the qualities of the learning tasks, which were classified as either "Open" or "Closed." Open tasks allowed students to select relevant information, to structure the problem, and to choose their course of action. They included such tasks as selecting recreational reading, writing journals or original stories, or reading with partners. In contrast, Closed tasks specified both the desirable operations and solutions. For example, Closed tasks included worksheet exercises such as matching words and filling in blanks.

The frequencies of Open and Closed tasks differed significantly between LB and SO classrooms. Basically, teachers who adhered to a whole language philosophy were more likely to include Open tasks in their instruction, although several SO teachers included more Open tasks than Closed tasks. The nature of tasks was the best predictor of student's motivation because reading strategies, persistence, and volitional control were all more frequent in Open versus Closed tasks. Eighty-one percent of all reading strategies occurred during Open tasks; 63% of all observations of persistent literacy behavior occurred in Open tasks; and 70% of the observations of volitional control occurred during Open tasks. Clearly, students displayed more desirable, active, strategic efforts for learning when engaged in Open tasks. The greater incidence of strategic and motivated behavior occurred regardless of students' gender or whether students were in LB or SO classrooms.

What does this mean? In first grade, students used reading strategies more often when engaged in tasks like partner reading, reading individual trade books, and writing their own compositions. The tasks required greater autonomy, more choices, and richer thinking strategies in order to read and write. In contrast, Closed activities such as worksheets were done in a rote fashion. Persistence and volitional control showed similar patterns. Children often selected, tried out, monitored, and revised their own strategies because Open tasks were more challenging. One child made more than 25 attempts to arrange the words in a sentence so that they made sense. Many students knew how to manage their own behavior to achieve their literacy goals. Some selected quiet places in the classroom to work removed from the commotion of other students; others asked neighbors to be quiet, such as the child who demanded, "Shut up, Brian. I am *trying* to work. Do you mind?"

Students' responses to Open-ended interview questions revealed differences in understanding and motivation. For example, when students worked on Closed activities typical in many of the basal reading lessons, they reported that their learning goal was primarily procedural (e.g., "how to write the letters," "trying to find the words"). While working on Closed tasks, students were less likely to focus on the lesson content and more likely to identify sources of difficulty such as identifying unfamiliar letters and sounds or following directions rather than understanding the meaning of text. They also reported a greater incidence of "Don't know" responses and, "I guessed it" than students in Open tasks.

This study illustrates that students' learning strategies and motivation are a consequence of their engagement with different kinds of tasks. Complex and challenging tasks afford more opportunities for self-regulated learning than activities that are highly specified by the teacher. But it is not the teacher or the educational philosophy alone that determines student motivation because students' effort and strategies were diminished in LB classrooms when teachers used Closed tasks and motivated behaviors were enhanced in SO classrooms when teachers used Open tasks. Nicholls and Thorkildsen (1989) found that elementary school students have emerging "theories of curriculum" and are able to distinguish procedural from substantive learning. When the instructional focus is on practice, rote application of rules, and adherence to teacher-specified activities, students place little value on the tasks and display less motivation. Clearly, students are constructing their cognitions within the context of the classroom to provide appropriate learning strategies and effort in different situations.

CHARACTERISTICS OF ACADEMIC TASKS THAT MOTIVATE LEARNING

We are intrigued with the concept of situated motivation for several reasons. First, it emphasizes the characteristics of situations that elicit different courses of action, different emotions, and different cognitive interpretations of events. The analytical focus is upon properties of tasks, activities, and contexts that elicit specific reactions from individuals. In the research just reviewed, there are clearly some tasks and situations that promote children's strategic learning and effort more than others. We examine those characteristics in more detail later but for now, it is worth noting that this is a claim about main effects of situations. We believe that some situations have prototypical characteristics that are generally more motivating than other situations but we hasten to add that the person by situation interaction provides greater information about who is motivated by different situations and why. The tensions between generalizable claims about motivation and idiosyncratic claims about a contextualist view of motivation can be reconciled when the different levels of analysis are considered. Therefore, a focus on task features or situational characteristics is not contrary to a person by environment perspective as long as both levels of analysis are pursued.

A second reason why we think that situated motivation is a heuristic construct is because it emphasizes that meaning is highly personalized; it does not reside in the environment or the person alone but rather is constructed by people in specific situations. Therefore, external events are not uniformly motivating or unmotivating for people, nor are there generalizable traits or dispositions to be motivated by particular stimuli. This is not to deny extrinsic reinforcement or individual differences in motivational orientation; rather, it is meant to place those concepts of motivation in subservient roles to the person by situation interaction. Whereas some motivational theories have postulated noncognitive concepts such as drives, habits, and incentives, other theories have gone to the opposite extreme and have created such complex systems of action tendencies that cognitive consternation overwhelms a course of action. Situated motivation falls between these extremes and emphasizes the constructive representation of one's field of action and considers the decision processes that the individual uses within that field.

We highlight four significant characteristics of a person's decisions within a field of action to illustrate when decisions are goal oriented and motivated. These characteristics were evident in the Open literacy tasks observed by Turner (1992) and are consistent with the LB classrooms observed by Fisher and Hiebert (1990). In the following sections we consider the importance of choice, challenge, control, and collaboration. When students are involved in tasks that include ample opportunities for each of these characteristics, they are more likely to display independent, strategic, and motivated behavior for learning.

Choice

The essence of motivated action is the ability to choose among alternative courses of action, or at least, the freedom to choose to expend varying degrees of effort for a particular purpose. A choice of goals and effort investment reflect the personal interest of an individual. Interest in a topic involves both feeling-related characteristics, such as enjoyment and involvement, and value-related characteristics, such as attributing significance to an activity (Schiefele, 1991). When students attribute positive values and feelings to particular courses of action, they are likely to choose them and pursue them vigorously. Studies of middle school students (Pintrich & DeGroot, 1990) and upper elementary students (Meece, Blumenfeld, & Hoyle, 1988) have shown that students who believe that their schoolwork is interesting and important are cognitively engaged in trying to learn and understand the material.

Intrinsic value, which is the foundation for personal choice, is also an important component in students' decisions about whether or not to become and remain cognitively engaged in academic work. Pokay and Blumenfeld (1990) and Nolen (1988) found that task value significantly predicted the extent to which students voluntarily used strategies in learning situations. Students who perceived their tasks to be interesting and worthwhile also reported more self-regulation and persistence (Pintrich & DeGroot, 1990). Wigfield and Eccles (1992) found that students' perceived value for math predicted their later decisions to take additional math courses, especially for girls.

Schiefele (1991) investigated student interest in learning text specifically. Results from his studies of high school and college students indicated that interest in text significantly influenced students' text processing, their use of learning strategies, and the quality of their learning experiences in academic classes. Students who showed greater interest processed text more deeply; they used more elaboration, critical thinking, and information-seeking strategies. They also invested greater amounts of time and effort and reported higher intrinsic motivation, self-esteem, skill, and potency in those subjects. Interest predicted the quality of the learning experience, whereas achievement motivation and ability were nonsignificant predictors. Thus, general motivational orientation and past success are not necessarily the best predictors of students' interest and choices.

When students make personal choices about the books they read, the stories they write, and the projects they pursue, they are more likely to be thoughtfully engaged in the tasks. Choice leads to commitment, deep involvement, and strategic thinking with tasks. The freedom to choose particular goals is captured by the labels "intrinsic motivation" and "mastery goal orientation." Selections of goals are not made consciously but rather are part of a seamless "flow experience" where actions and awareness merge, according to the theory of intrinsic motivation posited by Csikzentmihalyi (1975). When teachers allow students to pursue personal goals, they promote interest by making their own competence salient, by helping students orient to the learning processes that are required, by helping them concentrate on their performance, and by providing ongoing feedback about their level of success (Harackiewicz & Sansone, 1991). When young children's literacy is based on literature or whole language, teachers evidently promote individual choices among activities of personal interest as the vehicles for students to engage in and practice literacy skills. This may be why students exhibit more motivated behavior in these kinds of Open activities in classrooms. Conversely, when teachers control students' choices and goals, it may jeopardize their feelings of self-determination (Ryan & Grolnick, 1986) and their sense of independence.

Challenge

Educators often promote the old adage that "nothing succeeds like success" but current motivation theory does not support this slogan. Success without effort is a cheap reward and quickly loses its value in the classroom. Indeed students may interpret success that comes without challenge or risk-taking as an indication of the lower expectations held by others for their own level of achievement. When they think that other people hold low expectations for them or feel pity, that may reinforce their perception of their own low ability (Weiner, 1992).

Motivating tasks are in fact moderately difficult (Clifford, 1991). Like the old ring toss game used to evaluate an individual's need for achievement, moderate difficulty where the expectation for success is reasonably high imposes the greatest risk to students. Students gauge the degree of challenge provided by tasks and, depending on the audience and the payoff, may choose to complete difficult tasks in order to confirm or enhance perceptions of their competence and self-efficacy (Bandura, 1986; Schunk, 1989).

The benefits of moderate risk taking are evident in Csikzentmihalyi's (1975) theory of motivation as well. He hypothesizes that people cannot be truly engaged in activities unless the challenges are in balance with their skills or abilities to respond. When challenges exceed skills, frustration, worry, and anxiety will result. The activity invites boredom and detachment when there is no challenge. Instruction in the classroom requires continual adjustment of task difficulty, depending on the students' progress and reactions to learning, in order to provide new challenges that are inviting.

Other theorists emphasize that the value of risk taking depends on the interpretation of failure. Students judge success and failure subjectively in order to balance their interpretations of the reasons for their performance with their interpretation of the consequences of their performance. Usually, these interpretations operate to preserve a sense of self-worth and optimism and to avoid self-blaming (Covington, 1992). For example, Clifford (1991) describes "constructive failure" as opportunities for students to learn the value of persistence and alternative strategies to accomplish a goal. Failure then is not interpreted as a limitation of ability or effort, but rather as a less than optimal use of strategies that should evoke reappraisal rather than frustration or withdrawal. Students' positive adjustments to failure events have been referred to as *adaptive learning* because the experiences can lead to stronger beliefs about one's efforts and strategies that can be enacted and lead to new levels of perceived efficacy and competence (Paris & Oka, 1986; Rohrkemper & Corno, 1988). In this view, "optimum challenge" elicits strategic responses and greater effort to overcome temporary setbacks. Rohrkemper and Corno (1988) describe how students can adjust tasks that are too easy (i.e., boring) or too difficult (i.e., frustrating) by changing their orientations and goals or changing the nature of the task. Both are situational adjustments that provide challenges appropriate for each individual and both require active control by the person.

Control

Once students have chosen personally interesting and challenging tasks, they must exhibit control and autonomy to reach those goals in classrooms. However, this often proves difficult because teachers cannot grant total freedom nor control. Many research studies have shown that there is a positive relation between the autonomy-orientation of the classroom environment and students' own intrinsic motivation (e.g., deCharms, 1968; Grolnick & Ryan, 1987). For example, Ryan and Grolnick (1986) found that children who perceived their classrooms as more autonomy-promoting reported greater interest in their schoolwork, greater perceived confidence in school, and generally positive views of their self-worth. Despite these benefits of student control and autonomy, teachers often provide little genuine freedom in classrooms. This may be partly due to issues of behavior management and partly due to pressure on both students and teachers to progress through the curriculum and perform well on periodic tests.

Thoughtful engagement in academic tasks requires volitional control. This includes strategies that control intentions and impulses during academic learning in order to avoid distractions and remain committed to one's selected goal (Corno, 1989). Volitional control strategies can be used to monitor one's own actions as well as actions of others in group situations. Control then can become interpersonal, such as asking other students for help or quiet, as well as an internalized component of self-regulated learning. The extent to which students exercise these volitional control strategies depends very much on their interpretation of what is appropriate in specific situations.

Collaboration

In many classrooms, instruction is given to groups of children but most of their work is completed alone. Individual seat work is intended to supply opportunities for practice and successful completion of tasks but recent conceptualizations of learning question this view (e.g., Rogoff, 1990). They describe learning as an apprenticeship relation in which an adult guides the child through active participation to expand one's knowledge and level of performance. Social guidance and cooperation in classrooms have now been recognized as fundamental for motivation.

Social interaction is motivational in several ways. First, peer comments and ideas introduce elements of surprise that pique students' curiosity and encourage further exploration. Attention to other perspectives and lateral thinking are encouraged. Second, peers provide models of expertise that others can emulate. They may be more attentive to peer models and more willing to try to emulate them. Third, peers provide benchmarks for monitoring one's own level of accomplishment which may in turn increase the belief in self-efficacy. The standards and feedback provided by peers are often more powerful than the information provided by teachers. Fourth, persistence is enhanced when working with others because there is an obligation to the group and a collaborative goal. Situations that encourage productive social interaction promote positive concepts about the activity and increase effort allocation from individuals.

In summary, motivational research has shown that classrooms in which students have genuine choices, challenging tasks, control over their own learning, and opportunities to collaborate with others all enhance students' determination, effort, and thoughtful engagement. One goal of educational research is to identify classroom tasks and situations that allow for choice, challenge, control, and collaboration because they promote students' motivational beliefs and behavior but an equally important goal, on a more specific level of analysis, is to identify the fit between individuals and tasks to determine the appropriateness of different situations for different students.

IMPLICATIONS OF SITUATED MOTIVATION

The construct of situated motivation draws attention to episodes and activities in classrooms that may be brief but have long-lasting consequences on students' orientation to school and their beliefs about themselves. The main implication for research may be the analysis of individual differences among students in the context of classroom events, analyses that can only be made of persons in situations, not of one or the other alone. We consider some of the pragmatic consequences of situated motivation for learning, instruction, and assessment in the following sections.

Consequences for Learning

The high road to thoughtfulness and mindfulness in the classroom must follow a route that allows students choices, challenges, control, and collaboration. The value of such tasks has been vividly illustrated in studies of early literacy by Turner (1992) and Fisher and Hiebert (1990). Similar outcomes have been observed for older children in a variety of academic domains (Blumenfeld & Meece, 1988). The benefits of open-ended classroom activities can be translated into a variety of frameworks. We briefly describe three broad theoretical perspectives for interpreting the importance of situated motivation for academic learning: metacognitive theories of learning, self-referenced theories of motivation, and ownership models of learning. All of them emphasize how skill and will, the cognitive and motivational aspects of self-regulated learning, are fused in some learning situations and not others (Paris & Cross, 1983).

One framework for interpreting situated motivation is provided by self-regulated learning because it includes checking, monitoring, and directing one's goal-directed behavior (Zimmerman, 1989). Likewise, various descriptions of students' metacognition about learning emphasize self-reflection and self-management of behavior (Paris & Winograd, 1990). As research has enlarged the notion of metacognition to overlap motivational constructs, it has become evident that there is no clear demarcation between assessing one's thinking and assessing one's goals, self-perceptions, or attributions because these are also cognitions. This perspective brings to an analysis of situated motivation a wide range of cognitive strategies for learning that are natural companions to motivational strategies such as volitional control or goal declarations.

A second perspective for examining situated motivation is derived from the many varieties of self-referenced systems of motivation including self-efficacy, self-competence, self-concept, self-control, and self-worth. For example, individuals may feel pride in a certain situation because they used a study strategy successfully to learn something new. The consequences of learning include the interpretation that the individual provides for success in that situation (which may vary over time and audiences) and the ways that the individual approaches a similar task in the future. Expectancies, values, attributions, and feelings of self-worth are intermediaries in cycles of task engagement and learning and require analyses according to repeated experience because each situation is different from the preceding one. Only by understanding the differences across situations can changes in the individual's motivated behavior be understood. Students construct interpretations of their psychological well-being that are dynamic calculations of their talents and values in different social groups and in different situations. Thus, self-worth is situated, constructed, cognitive, and contextual.

A third perspective, especially relevant for literacy learning, is reflected in the term *students' ownership of learning* (Au, Scheu, Kawakami, & Herman, 1990). The fundamental aspect of "ownership" is that students internalize the responsibility to make their own choices, direct their own behavior, and attribute the consequences of their actions to their behavior. In literacy, this may mean that children who select their own books for recreational reading, choose their partners and settings for learning, identify their favorite authors and books, and control the pace and sequence of their learning demonstrate a high degree of personal ownership over literacy. These characteristics of "ownership" are context-dependent and thus part of the general notion of situated motivation. Each of these three perspectives provides a holistic interpretation of student motivation that integrates students' understanding of goals, tasks, self, and others, in situations that help to determine possible courses of action.

Consequences for Teaching

Teachers create environments to foster learning but embedded within these environments are a variety of tasks and activities that may or may not prove motivating for students. Selections of educational activities cannot be predicated on a cognitive agenda alone because repeated practice, mastery learning, and memorization of facts and concepts are difficult activities to sustain when the ostensible purpose is only to display that understanding on a later test. Learning for the sake of evaluation gives rise to a bartering orientation on the part of students whereby they perform for a grade and negotiate the degree of effort required for the value of the grade. When students' performance is oriented toward extrinsic reinforcement or based on the least amount of effort in the situation, students are unlikely to use effective learning strategies, help-seeking, or persistence (Blumenfeld & Meece, 1988).

As McKeachie (1990) said in his reprise of educational psychology, "We now know that intrinsic motivation and a sense of self-efficacy have much to do with learning strategies and the mindfulness of student learning; in the next decade, we will gain a better understanding of the kinds of instructional methods that facilitate such motivation and that integrate learning with basic values" (p. 197). These teaching methods include flexible and multiple groupings for different tasks, the use of peers and cross-age tutors in partner learning, the use of technology such as television and computers to enhance learning, and other instructional techniques that encourage student inquiry, research, and cooperation for authentic learning goals. We briefly describe project-based learning as one example of innovative teaching methods that enhance motivation and learning by creating situations that promote students' choices, challenges, control, and collaboration.

Project-based learning has several key characteristics (cf. Blumenfeld et al., 1991). First, there is a driving question that helps to organize students' efforts and search for information. The question is designed to be open-ended and to elicit curiosity and controversy. Second, project-based learning requires actively searching for information in a variety of text and nontext sources. Students are encouraged to interview other people, to use library resources, and to find information in classroom sources independently. Third, project-based learning is collaborative because work is divided among various students who allocate tasks and assign responsibility. They also must integrate the knowledge required by individuals into a group presentation, performance, or project that demonstrates the synthesis of their individual efforts. Fourth, project-based learning extends across time and domains in the curriculum. Problems are posed by teachers that may require weeks of work and serve to bridge students' skills in science, math, and literacy. Fifth, project-based learning has authentic goals but multiple routes to reach them. Students themselves establish their primary purposes and choose how to demonstrate their knowledge or answer the driving question. The solution of the problem and the public demonstration of knowledge must be meaningful to the students to engage their sustained interest.

Project-based learning capitalizes on all the resources within the school and the community. It expands the boundaries of learning beyond seat work, textbooks, and isolated activities. Project-based learning requires creative teachers who act as coaches or mentors or resources for students in their quest for information. Because projects provide highly individualized approaches to learning that may take the teachers and students in unknown directions, flexibility and willingness to give up control are required. Highly skilled teachers know how to structure projects so that students have choices but within a limited arena. That is, they have multiple avenues to accomplish their purposes but each avenue can be worthwhile. Likewise, they are free to choose different tasks and activities to meet their individual levels of challenge and risk taking but they are not free to avoid choices and challenges altogether. Some might argue that effective teachers create "illusions" of choice, challenge, and control because the opportunities are constrained. Yet it is the perceptions of students in these situations that is paramount and if they perceive that they have choice and control, and if they take responsibility for reaching their goals, then indeed they can display appropriate and continued motivation.

Consequences for Assessment

Some might ask how one evaluates students' project-based learning when it reflects collaborative work. Others might argue that there is no comparability of assessment if students work on different projects and do not master or encounter the same information. More generally, some people may feel that the outcomes of learning, not the motivational antecedents, should be assessed. These traditional views of evaluation of learning are based on the notion of individual and independent accomplishments gauged against a comparative and uniform standard. Usually this means that all students master the same material and are evaluated on the same tests. But *performance assessment* eschews normative comparisons and evaluates students' learning activities and processes against established criteria or personal growth. This permits individual differences in the products that are evaluated but not the standards of excellence. Performance assessment allows for a variety of tasks to be used as indicators of learning processes, some done collaboratively and some done independently. Performance assessment is consistent with project-based learning and places value on the demonstrations of student's choices, risk taking, volitional control strategies, and ability to work with others. In these situations, motivation is assessed along with learning, as part of the interaction of skill and will in a situation, not as a confounding variable, but as an important educational outcome in its own right.

The reason that authentic assessment is so important is that traditional assessment often stultifies students' motivation for learning. Working for grades can redefine students' educational objectives as high test scores. Not only does this minimize a student's educational purposes, it often creates testing situations that are discordant with learning situations. When students know information about a topic but are unable to display it in a testing situation, they become frustrated and may discount the validity of the test or the value of learning. McKeachie (1961) in his Nebraska Symposium chapter said, "Entering into the student's performance on the examination is not only his knowledge or other learning ostensibly assessed by the examination but also his motivation in the testing situation and his skills in taking examinations. One of the really oppressive thoughts which worries me is that some variable may work in opposite ways in the learning and examination situations" (p. 119).

Our research (Paris, Lawton, Turner, & Roth, 1991) on students' views of standardized achievement testing confirms McKeachie's concerns. For example, we found that 8- to 10-year olds are enthusiastic about taking tests. They try to do their best but by 15–16 years of age, many students report decreased effort invested on standardized achievement tests and increased use of counterproductive strategies such as making designs on their answer sheets or filling in the blanks without thinking. Their lack of effort may be due to the perceived unimportance of the test or it may be a defensive coping tactic so that their score is not regarded by them as a true indication of their ability. As Covington (1992) notes, most students learn to try halfheartedly, and keep excuses handy in order to avoid attributions that their performance indicates either their maximum level of effort or ability. High school students also show greater cynicism toward the purposes of the test, the uses of the test by teachers, and the validity of the test scores. They show greater anxiety and frustration over the test and report using more inappropriate strategies, such as answering questions without reading passages or taking guesses when they get bored. Our research indicates that these deleterious test-taking strategies and motivational orientations are even more pronounced among low-achieving students who may feel the most threatened by the test. Thus, testing situations that are comparative, evaluative, and not genuine, can elicit counterproductive motivation and learning from students.

Some educators believe that the solution to better test scores is to train test-taking strategies to students throughout the year, and especially before the tests, so they encourage teachers to give students practice tests. Test-wiseness also may include training on managing anxiety, focusing attention, and eliminating possible wrong answers from multiple choices. These tactics increase students' test-wiseness and possibly test scores but the cost in motivation may be too great to bear if students interpret this focus in the curriculum to mean that the primary value of education, the main purpose for learning, and the primary assessment of knowledge are simply high test scores.

The development of disillusionment over testing and evaluation create specific, negative situations of student's motivation that impact directly on their learning behaviors in the classroom. How do we know that the negative effects are "situated" rather than just symptomatic of adolescent dissatisfaction with all grading or schooling? We compared students' views of standardized achievement tests with their views of teacher-made tests that covered the regular school curriculum and found that high school students differentiated the two kinds of evaluations (Wong & Paris, 1993). Standardized tests evoked more negative affect and were perceived as less important than regular tests. The differentiation of the two kinds of tests begins by Grade 5 when social comparative information is becoming more prevalent and more consequential in the classroom but becomes more distinctive with repeated high-stakes testing endured by students in each year of school. A strong emphasis on the "accountability" and the "authority" of externally imposed achievement tests to measure the relative and normative accomplishments of students reduces the teachers' leverage for learning to promises of extrinsic rewards, threats of sanctions, and authoritative demands. None of these sustain thoughtfulness and high level task engagement. Assessment that does not include genuine goals and does not elicit positive motivational orientations from students actually undermines students' learning and future motivation.

CONCLUSIONS

The empirical research on students' motivation shows that classroom tasks for learning and assessment can have significant influences on students' motivation and learning. Research also shows that different philosophies of instruction and different curricula, such as language arts instruction based on literature and whole language versus basal readers and component skills, have profound influences on students' learning strategies, help-seeking, and volitional control strategies. We believe that students' perceptions of choice, challenge, control, and collaboration in the classroom activities given to them are critical for their sustained motivation. Methods of instruction and assessment that support these aspects of motivation promote students' sense of ownership, responsibility, and self-regulated learning.

The term *situated motivation* is neither redundant, obvious, nor glib. Historically, educational psychology has been dominated by theories of motivation that regard motivation as a trait of the individual or a property of the environment, not the interaction of the two. For those who consider the term obvious, we would ask you to reflect on the implicit theories of motivation held by lay people who usually refer to human motivation in terms such as *lazy, hard-working, or unmotivated* and the surprising lack of data on the motivation of students (a) in different subject areas, (b) while learning the same content under various conditions, and (c) while engaging in the same activities repetitively over weeks and years. We hope the term evokes the same enthusiasm that greeted *situated cognition* and the concept of *domain-specific learning* because they are tightly welded in our view (Brown, Collins, & Duguid, 1989). Children's self-regulated learning is fueled by the intertwined set of beliefs, their skill and will, that children construct about themselves over time. We believe that their theories about themselves and schooling emerge developmentally as a consequence of their interactions with school tasks and activities (Paris & Newman, 1990). Thus, analyses of situated motivation—the thoughts, feelings, and actions of students in specific contexts—can help us create optimal situations that promote every students' learning and self-worth.

REFERENCES

Atkinson, J. W., & Feather, N. T. (Eds.). (1966). *A theory of achievement motivation.* New York: Wiley.

Au, K. H., Scheu, J. A. Kawakami, A. J., & Herman, P. A. (1990). Assessment and accountability in a whole language curriculum. *The Reading Teacher, 43,* 574–578.

Bandura, A. (1986). *Social foundations of thought and action: A social cognitive theory.* Englewood Cliffs, NJ: Prentice-Hall.

Blumenfeld, P. C., & Meece, J. L. (1988). Task factors, teacher behavior, and students' involvement and use of learning strategies in science. *Elementary School Journal, 88,* 235–250.

Blumenfeld, P. C., Soloway, E., Marx, R. W., Krajcik, J. S., Guzdial, M., & Palincsar, A. S. (1991). Motivating project-based learning: Sustaining the doing, supporting the learning. *Educational Psychologist, 26,* 369–398.

Brown, J. S., Collins, A., & Duguid, P. (1989). Situated cognition and the culture of learning. *Educational Researcher, 18,* 32–42.

Clifford, M. M. (1991). Risk taking: Theoretical, empirical, and educational considerations. *Educational Psychologist, 26,* 263–297.

Corno, L. (1989). Self-regulated learning: A volitional analysis. In B. J. Zimmerman & D. H. Schunk (Eds.), *Self-regulated learning and academic achievement* (pp. 111–141). New York: Springer-Verlag.

Covington, M. V. (1992). *Making the grade: A self-worth perspective on motivation and school reform.* Cambridge: Cambridge University Press.

Csikzentmihalyi, M. (1975). *Beyond boredom and anxiety.* San Francisco: Jossey-Bass.

deCharms, R. (1968). *Personal causation.* New York: Academic Press.

Doyle, W. (1983). Academic work. *Review of Educational Research, 53,* 159–199.

Fisher, C. W., & Hiebert, E. H. (1990). Characteristics of tasks in two approaches to literacy instruction. *Elementary School Journal, 91,* 3–18.

Goodman, K. (1989). Whole-language research: Foundations and development. *Elementary School Journal, 90,* 207–221.

Grolnick, W. S., & Ryan, R. M. (1987). Autonomy in children's learning: An experimental and individual difference investigation. *Journal of Personality and Social Psychology, 52,* 890–898.

Harackiewicz, J. M. & Sansone, C. (1991). Goals and intrinsic motivation: You can get there from here. In M. Maehr & P. Pintrich (Eds.), *Advances in motivation and achievement* (Vol. 7, pp. 21–49). Greenich, CT: JAI Press.

McKeachie, W. J. (1961). Motivation, teaching methods, and college learning. In M. R. Jones (Ed.), *Nebraska symposium on motivation* (pp. 111–142). Lincoln: University of Nebraska Press.

McKeachie, W. J. (1990). Research on college teaching: The historical background. *Journal of Educational Psychology, 82,* 189–200.

Meece, J. L., Blumenfeld, P. C., & Hoyle, R. H. (1988). Students' goal orientations and cognitive engagement in classroom activities. *Journal of Educational Psychology, 80,* 514–523.

Nicholls, J. G., & Thorkildsen, T. A. (1989). Intellectual conventions versus matters of substance: Elementary school students as curriculum theorists. *American Educational Research Journal, 26,* 533–544.

Nolen, S. B. (1988). Reasons for studying: Motivational orientations and study strategies. *Cognition and Instruction, 5,* 269–287.

Paris, S. G., & Cross, D. R. (1983). Ordinary learning: Pragmatic connections among children's beliefs, motives, and actions. In J. Bisanz, G. Bisanz, & R. Kail (Eds.), *Learning in children* (pp. 137–169). New York: Springer-Verlag.

Paris, S. G., Lawton, T. A., Turner, J. C., & Roth, J. L. (1991). A developmental perspective on standardized achievement testing. *Educational Researcher, 20,* 12–20.

Paris, S. G., & Newman, R. S. (1990). Developmental aspects of self-regulated learning. *Educational Psychologist, 25,* 87–102.

Paris, S. G., & Oka, E. R. (1986). Children's reading strategies, metacognition, and motivation. *Developmental Review, 6,* 25–56.

Paris, S. G., & Winograd, P. W. (1990). How metacognition can promote academic learning and instruction. In B. Jones & L. Idol (Eds.),

Dimensions of thinking and cognitive instruction (pp.15–51). Hillsdale, NJ: Lawrence Erlbaum Associates.

Pearson, P. D. (1989). Reading the whole-language movement. *Elementary School Journal, 90,* 203–241.

Pintrich, P. & DeGroot, E. (1990). Motivational and self-regulated learning components of classroom academic performance. *Journal of Educational Psychology, 82,* 33–40.

Pokay, P., & Blumenfeld, P. (1990). Predicting achievement early and late in the semester: the role of motivation and use of learning strategies. *Journal of Educational Psychology, 82,* 41–50.

Resnick, L. (1987). Learning in school and out. *Educational Researcher, 16,* 13–20.

Rogoff, B. (1990). *Apprenticeship in thinking.* New York: Oxford University Press.

Rohrkemper, M., & Corno, L. (1988). Success and failure on classroom tasks: Adaptive learning and classroom teaching. *Elementary School Journal, 88,* 297–312.

Ryan, R. M., & Grolnick, W. S. (1986). Origins and pawns in the classroom: Self-report and projective assessments of individual differences in children's perceptions. *Journal of Personality and Social Psychology, 50,* 550–558.

Schiefele, U. (1991). Interest, learning, and motivation. *Educational Psychologist, 26,* 299–323.

Schunk, D. H. (1989). Social cognitive theory and self-regulated learning. In B. J. Zimmerman & D. H. Schunk (Eds.), *Self-regulated learning and academic achievement* (pp. 83–110). New York: Springer-Verlag.

Turner, J. C. (1992). *Situated motivation in literacy instruction.* Unpublished doctoral dissertation, University of Michigan, Ann Arbor.

Weiner, B. (1992). *Human motivation: Metaphors, theories, and research.* Newbury Park, CA: Sage.

Wigfield, A., & Eccles, J. S. (1992). The development of achievement task values: A theoretical analysis. *Developmental Review, 12,* 265–310.

Wong, C. A., & Paris, S. G. (1993). *Students' perceptions of different types of tests*. Paper presented to the American Educational Research Association, Atlanta.

Zimmerman, B. J. (1989). A social-cognitive view of self-regulated academic learning. *Journal of Educational Psychology, 81*, 329–339.

10

Investigating Self-Regulatory Processes and Perceptions of Self-Efficacy in Writing by College Students

Barry J. Zimmerman
Rafael Risemberg
Graduate School of the City University of New York

Among his many interests in the field of collegiate instruction, Wilbert McKeachie has devoted special attention to increasing students' active participation in the teaching-learning process. He has investigated the effectiveness of a wide variety of instructional methods designed to enhance students' role in this process and their self-perceptions of it. His pioneering contributions have provided a solid foundation for current research on students' sense of agency over their academic achievement and their use of self-regulatory processes, which refer to metacognitive, motivational, and behavioral efforts to control their own learning (Zimmerman, 1989, 1990).

In this chapter, we survey McKeachie's findings and insights—particularly as they bear on the issue of academic self-regulation. We describe three recent studies that examine college students' self-regulation and perceptions of self-efficacy in their academic writing, or their confidence that they can perform this task (Zimmerman & Bandura, 1994). Finally, McKeachie's recommendations for improving college students' self-regulatory processes and metacognitive skills are considered in terms of their impact on the students' motivation and sense of academic agency as well as their educational accomplishment.

CONTRIBUTIONS OF WILBERT MCKEACHIE TO COLLEGE TEACHING

In January 1993, the American Psychological Society's (APS) flagship publication, the *APS Observer*, ran a front-page article featuring that organization's efforts to stress the importance of the teaching of psychology. The source of interest in this topic was traced to a "recent surge of enthusiasm in improving undergraduate education and teaching" ("APS to Showcase," 1993, p. 1). No individual has contributed more to public awareness of the importance of this topic or to its scientific development than McKeachie. From the publication of his initial book on teaching psychology, *Teaching Tips* (McKeachie & Kimble, 1951), to the present, he has been an articulate spokesman for improving the quality of undergraduate courses in psychology and a leader in the development of new and innovative instructional methods. His introductory book, *Psychology* (McKeachie & Doyle, 1966) was a leading text in the field for a number of years. For these personal and professional contributions, he has been awarded numerous prestigious honors by the American Psychological Association (APA), the APS, and the American Educational Research Association (AERA).

McKeachie is especially well known for his insightful reviews of research on instructional psychology, college teaching, teaching effectiveness, and teaching of psychology. He has twice contributed to the *Annual Review of Psychology* on instructional psychology (McKeachie, 1974; Pintrich, Cross, Kozma, & McKeachie, 1986). In the most recent chapter, he and colleagues traced the impressive growth and progress in the field of instructional psychology to the influence of cognitive theory and research. His own investigations have evolved from studies of general principles of instructional design (Guetzkow, Kelly, & McKeachie, 1954) to an in-depth analysis of the role of students' prior experiences, strategies, and information-processing characteristics during learning (Naveh-Benjamin, McKeachie, Lin, & Tucker, 1986).

ENHANCING COLLEGE STUDENTS' SENSE OF AGENCY DURING LEARNING

From the beginning of McKeachie's professional career, he has displayed a deep interest in studying the teaching-learning process from the perspective of the student. His research has focused extensively on approaches or variables that students might perceive as personally advantageous such as individualized teaching (McKeachie, Forrin, Lin & Teevan, 1960), problem-oriented teaching (McKeachie & Hiler, 1954), teacher warmth (McKeachie, Lin, Milholland, & Issacson, 1966), teacher–student compatibility (Lin, McKeachie, Wernander, & Hedegard, 1970), and facilitative teaching (McKeachie, Lin, Moffett, & Daugherty, 1978). Implicit in all these instructional approaches is the simple assumption that how one teaches can make a substantive difference in how students respond to the experience of learning, that is, to their sense of personal agency about the process of learning.

His choice of dependent measures also reflected a deep concern about students' cognitive and emotional self-reactions to the teaching-learning process—measures such as student ratings of faculty teaching (McKeachie & Solomon, 1958), student ratings of debilitative anxiety (McKeachie, 1951), and cognitive indices of motivation (McKeachie, Isaacson, Milholland, & Lin, 1968). He has viewed students' learning in more *personal* terms than mere assimilation of knowledge: Their learning includes their cognitive and emotional reactions to the very process through which their knowledge was acquired. In this sense, McKeachie anticipated the purposive, strategic, and self-regulative dimensions of learning that are themes of much current research.

Many of his early studies involve comparisons of different instructional processes, such as student-centered versus teacher-centered teaching approaches (McKeachie, 1954). Instead of being content with conducting simple outcome studies, he decided to include student process variables, such as perceived school anxiety, that might mediate instructional outcomes (e.g., McKeachie, 1958). He was among the first researchers to investigate what has been called *attribute-treatment interactions*, a label drawn from the use of a two-factor analysis of variance model to test for the presence of a process attribute that might mediate the effects of a particular form of instruction.

In the 1970s and 1980s, McKeachie began to focus on the role of students' cognitive processes during instruction, including their cognitive structures (Lin et al., 1970), cognitive schemas (Biela, Lingoes, Lin, & McKeachie, 1989) and levels of information processing (McKeachie, 1984). This line of research revealed many benefits when instructors taught directly toward students' metacognitive understanding of procedures, skills, and strategies. Rather than creating simple prescriptions for instructional improvements, McKeachie has sought to discover a schema that will help teachers to interact effectively with unique students in various classroom settings.

McKeachie's years of research on student ratings of faculty bespeak his commitment to finding practical ways to improve the quality of undergraduate education (e.g., Lin, McKeachie, & Tucker, 1984; McKeachie & Solomon, 1958). Although he acknowledged the role of achievement outcomes in evaluating faculty instruction, he (McKeachie, 1990) placed particular emphasis on students' motivation and mindfulness in learning. Research has shown that college students' ratings of their motivation and interest in the course are reliable indicators of the quality of faculty instruction (Marsh, 1984, 1987). Not only are such attitudinal measures valuable in their own right, they are predictive of students' future decisions to major in the discipline (Guetzkow et al., 1954).

In addition, McKeachie (1990) advocated the creation of a system of student self-ratings that would foster greater self-awareness of learning strategies or problem-solving processes and would prompt students to monitor and evaluate their gains in thinking and knowledge. Students could be given self-report forms that include such self-perception items as "I am learning how to think more clearly about this course" or such progress-toward-goal items as "developing skill in expressing myself orally or in writing." Faculty were encouraged to use the results of such instruments to understand the effectiveness of their courses on student problem-solving and self-monitoring processes. Also recommended to faculty were speak-aloud measures and inventories like the *LASSI: Learning and Study Strategies Inventory* (Weinstein, Schulte, & Palmer, 1987) to provide evidence of the impact of their course on students' learning strategies and to tie these strategy outcomes to specific classroom instructional activities.

In recent years, McKeachie (McKeachie, Pintrich, & Lin, 1985) has turned his attention to the issue of teaching learning strategies to students who are at academic risk. His results led him to caution that presenting such strategies to these students was not enough to enable them to become self-regulating: Their motivation also appeared to play a key role. So during an era when theorizing about student learning has often become preoccupied with narrow psychological issues or topics, he has been a prominent spokesman for the need for more multifaceted psychological accounts that are at once cognitive, motivational, and behavioral. Only such descriptions can fully capture students with distinctive self-perspectives and changing levels of motivation—such as learners who are often but not always purposive about learning, learners who are sometimes but not consistently strategic about their approach, and learners who feel self-efficacious about their chances of success under certain instructional conditions but not others.

In a review of research on college teaching, McKeachie (1990) summarized various historical trends and offers a number of recommendations for future research based on insights he has gained from more than four decades of teaching and research experience. Throughout this review, he calls attention to the increasing complexity with which research on college students has been conducted. A shift in focus from behavioral and product variables to an emphasis on more cognitive, process-oriented constructs has led to a richer theoretical picture of the college teaching-learning experience.

One area that McKeachie (1990) emphasized as crucial to the learning process is metacognition—the ability to think about one's own thinking and to actively select appropriate strategies for various learning situations. Another important area that he stressed is the motivational component of learning, in particular improving students' intrinsic motivation and self-efficacy, both of which propel them to optimize strategy selection and to continue learning. To achieve these outcomes, McKeachie recommended that instructors teach thinking and motivation in addition to course content. Students should be trained not only to utilize strategies but also to know how to choose those that are the most effective. To improve intrinsic motivation and perceptions of self-efficacy, students should learn to monitor and evaluate their strategy choices and academic outcomes in order to enhance awareness of their gains in thinking and knowledge. Finally, McKeachie stressed the context-specific nature of instruction: Students' knowledge of learning strategies should include knowing which strategies are most effective personally, with which academic material, and for which goals.

COLLEGE TEACHING AND STUDENTS' SELF-REGULATION OF LEARNING

Many of McKeachie's insights and recommendations in this area pertain specifically to the study of self-regulated learning. As we noted earlier, students who self-regulate are described as metacognitively, motivationally, and behaviorally active participants in their own learning (Zimmerman 1989, 1990). Metacognitive processes include strategic planning and self-monitoring. Motivationally, these students self-initiate activities and display effort and persistence until the task is completed. Behaviorally, these students restructure their environment for optimal learning, and they seek out information from external sources. These self-regulatory processes depend in turn on perceptions of self-efficacy or a person's confidence that he or she can perform a particular task in a given set of circumstances (Bandura, 1977). Perceptions of self-efficacy are viewed as a key source of student motivation. In accord with this belief, students with higher self-efficacy will choose more challenging tasks and will persist on these tasks longer than students with lower self-efficacy (Bandura, 1993; Schunk, 1984). Indeed, there is compelling evidence that self-perceptions of academic efficacy are critical in motivating students to self-regulate their learning (Zimmerman & Martinez-Pons, 1992).

McKeachie's interest in studying self-regulated learning phenomena can be traced to his beliefs about the significance of the active individual who takes charge of the learning process by setting goals, choosing strategies for learning, and self-evaluating the attainment of these goals. In addition, he has stressed the importance of the motivational components of learning and the intricate interactions among cognitive constructs that influence learning. Finally, he recognized the specificity of self-regulatory responses to academic task contexts, and the need to teach contextual awareness as a specific form of knowledge to students.

Now we turn our attention to the field of academic writing, a skill that poses special demands for students to self-regulate. For example, writing is generally performed alone, it must be carried out over a sustained period of time, and it is often revised in response to evaluation standards. Hence, the study of writing provides an appropriate task to launch into the examination of self-regulatory processes. These processes are the focus of three studies of the acquisition of writing skill, conducted in the McKeachie tradition with college students.

THREE STUDIES OF COLLEGE STUDENTS' SELF-REGULATION OF WRITING

The first study (Zimmerman & Bandura, 1994) sought to assess the influence of a number of self-regulated learning variables on the development of writing proficiency. Subjects were 95 freshmen from a highly selective university. These students were enrolled in eight writing courses, half of which were considered "advanced," and the other half "regular" (placement into the advanced classes was contingent on the student receiving a high score on an advanced placement test). At the beginning of the academic semester, subjects were administered four instruments measuring different constructs related to self-regulation. At the end of the semester, students' final grades served as the outcome measure of writing proficiency.

Descriptions of the four instruments are as follows. Two of these were self-efficacy scales. The first, the Writing Self-Regulatory Efficacy scale, assessed students' perceived capability to carry out a variety of self-regulatory behaviors associated with writing, among them planning, revising, generating good topics, time management, and motivation for writing. This scale contained 25 items written in declarative form (e.g., I can refocus my concentration on writing when I find myself thinking about other things), to which subjects indicated how well they could perform the task using a 7-point Likert scale, with choices ranging between *not well at all* and *very well*. In the second instrument, Self-Efficacy for Academic Achievement, students rated the strength of their conviction that they could achieve each of 12 possible academic grades (A, A-, B+, . . . , F) in the writing course they were currently taking. Again, the strength of their self-efficacy was expressed on a 7-point scale, with choices ranging between *high uncertainty* and *high certainty*. For the third instrument, Grade Goals scale, subjects were asked to indicate which of 12 academic grades they were striving for in the writing course using a scale that ranged from A to F, with plus and minus gradations in between. Finally, in the Self-Evaluative Standards scale, students were asked to rate how satisfied they would be to attain each of the 12 possible final grades for their performance in their writing course using a 7-point scale that ranged from *very dissatisfied* to *very satisfied*.

Results showed a number of positive correlations between process and outcome variables. Final course grade was found to be significantly correlated with self-efficacy for academic achievement, grade goals, and self-evaluative standards, as well as verbal aptitude (subjects' verbal Scholastic Aptitude Test scores). In addition, all of the process variables—self-regulatory efficacy for writing, self-efficacy for academic achievement, grade goals, and self-evaluative standards— were significantly correlated with each other.

A path model was created in order to assess causal relations among the processes that led to the final course outcome. To simplify the presentation of this model, nonsignificant paths were deleted from Fig. 10.1. As shown in Fig. 10.1, students' class membership was linked to verbal aptitude scores, but neither of these variables directly influenced final course grades. Rather, verbal aptitude affected writing outcome indirectly via its effects on self-evaluative standards, which in turn influenced grade goals. Perceived self-regulatory efficacy for writing influenced both academic self-efficacy and self-evaluative standards, both of which in turn affected grade goals. Perceived academic self-efficacy and grade goals were the two constructs that had the greatest impact on writing outcome. The combined predictive variables accounted for 35% of the variance in writing outcome.

In summary, the two types of perceived self-efficacy played a key role in the development of writing proficiency. Both of these types of self-efficacy raised the goals that students set for themselves, one directly and the other indirectly through self-evaluative standard setting. Indeed, these variables played no less an important role in course grade attainment than did verbal ability, which had its effects only indirectly via self-evaluative standards.

The other two studies (Risemberg, 1993) have as their focal point college students' expository writing. In Study 1, a descriptive study, subjects were 71 undergraduates at a 4-year urban college. These subjects each read two source texts, one on Martin Luther King, Jr. and the other on Malcolm X, and were then asked to write a comparison/contrast essay based on these texts. They carried out this task in two steps: first reading the texts and taking preliminary notes, then using the texts and the notes to write a first draft of the essay. During both phases, subjects also had access to three additional texts: two model comparison/contrast essays and a set of guidelines for writing good comparison/contrast essays. None of these three texts were "required" reading but were made readily available to subjects.

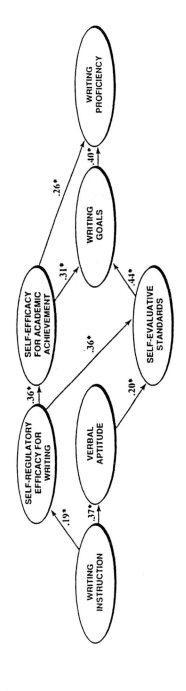

FIG. 10.1 Path coefficients for the significant paths of influence between variables in the model of self-regulation and final academic grades (*ps < .05). From "Impact of self-regulatory influences on development of writing proficiency" by B. J. Zimmerman and A. Bandura, unpublished manuscript. Copyright by B. J. Zimmerman and A. Bandura. Reprinted by Permission.

Three writing process scores, a reading background score, and a writing product score were assessed for all subjects. Reading ability was assessed by use of a standardized multiple-choice test that also served as each subject's college reading placement exam. The three writing process instruments each measured a different self-regulated learning construct. The first, the Self-Efficacy for Writing Questionnaire, was adapted from the previously cited Writing Self-Regulatory Efficacy scale (Zimmerman & Bandura, 1994), modified to be more specific to the particular writing task, but in all other respects identical. Its purpose was to assess each subject's confidence in being able to write a good comparison/contrast essay. The second writing process variable was level of organizing/transforming. Subjects' pre-writing notes were assessed for the extent to which they ordered content into superordinate and subordinate categories or created ordered visual displays, and the degree to which subjects made gist statements out of the original text. Scores ranged from the lowest level of *copying text; no particular order* (score of 1) to the highest level of *well organized outline or chart* (score of 6). The last process variable was labeled self-directed information seeking, and it was assessed surreptitiously by computer. The score for information seeking was defined as the total amount of time students spent reading the three additional, unrequired texts, all of which were available on the screens of personal computers placed before each subject. Finally, each essay was scored for writing quality according to primary trait scoring, an assessment method specific to a particular writing task. In this case, the two primary traits for assessment were comparison/contrast text structure and comparison/contrast topic sentences with supporting details. Each of the primary traits was scored from 0 to 4, and then the subscores were added together for a final writing quality score.

Two sets of analyses were conducted on the data in this descriptive study. First, a correlation matrix of the process and product variables showed writing quality to positively correlate significantly with each of the four process variables. Reading was the most highly correlated with writing outcome (not surprisingly, because this was a read-to-write task), followed by organizing, self-efficacy for writing, and information seeking. Among the process variables themselves, only one correlation was statistically significant: reading ability with organizing. Self-efficacy for writing was weakly correlated with reading ability, organizing, and information seeking. Likewise, information seeking was weakly correlated with reading ability and organizing. Information seeking was then divided into its two phases: pre-writing and writing. Results showed that information seeking during pre-writing was positively correlated with writing quality. In contrast, information seeking during the writing phase was negatively, although not significantly, correlated with writing quality. Thus, it was information seeking during pre-writing, and not during the writing task itself, that was associated with writing outcome. Information seeking in neither phase was significantly correlated with any of the other process variables.

Next, a series of regressions were carried out, beginning with four simple regressions, using each of the four main process variables as separate predictors of the outcome variable writing quality. In each case, these variables by themselves significantly predicted writing quality. In order to test the hypothesis that the three writing process variables would each contribute uniquely to writing quality, a multiple regression was carried out, with writing quality once again as the dependent variable. Results indicated that each of the three variables did, indeed, contribute uniquely to writing quality.

In Study 2, Risemberg (1993) went one step further by training subjects in a particular writing strategy. In this study, 71 undergraduates from a 4-year urban college (but different subjects from the ones in Study 1) participated. These subjects were randomly assigned to two groups. One group, the experimental group, was taught to use graphic organizers for the purposes of a pre-writing task. Graphic organizers are a diagrammatic display of information that are a combination of visual and verbal elements, organized to integrate information into a meaningful whole (see Fig. 10.2). They are as highly structured as outlines but contain an added visual element. Originally intended as an aid for reading comprehension, graphic organizers are now utilized for writing tasks as well. The graphic organizers taught in this study were specific for the comparison/contrast essay text structure. For example, Catholicism and Voodoo religions could be compared and contrasted on such common features as priesthood, rituals, beliefs in God, and populations of followers. Subjects in the control group were not taught any pre-writing strategy but spent time carrying out freewriting activities.

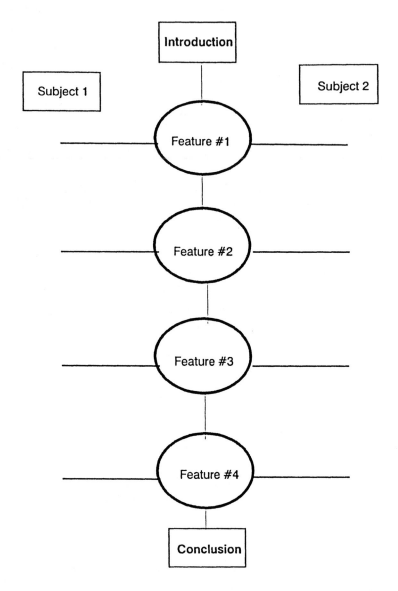

FIG. 10.2   The structure of a graphic organizer.   From *Self-regulated strategies of organizing and information seeking when writing expository text from sources* by Rafael Risemberg, 1993, unpublished dissertation, City University of New York.   Copyright by Rafael Risemberg.   Adapted by permission.

After the training phase, subjects carried out the same tasks as did the subjects in Study 1. They filled out the Self-Efficacy for Writing Questionnaire, then read two source texts, then spent time pre-writing, and finally wrote a first draft of a comparison/contrast essay based on the sources they had read. As in Study 1, subjects also had access to model comparison/contrast essays, and their computers secretly recorded the amount of time they spent accessing these additional texts. One procedural difference from that of Study 1 was that in Study 2, experimental subjects were told to construct graphic organizers during the pre-writing phase; control subjects, untrained in the use of graphic organizers, were told to take notes in whatever form they wished. Measured variables, as in Study 1, were reading ability, self-efficacy for writing, organizing/transforming, information seeking, and final writing outcome.

Results showed that the graphic organizing training was successful: All but 3 of the experimental group's 36 subjects wrote graphic organizers for the pre-writing task. The effect of graphic organizer training on all of the writing variables was analyzed next, through a series of *t* tests. In support of the author's hypothesis, the experimental group outperformed the control group on three of the four measures: self-efficacy for writing, organizing, and writing product. For the remaining variable, information seeking, *t* tests showed that experimental subjects spent significantly less time seeking information than did control subjects; this was particularly true during the pre-writing phase.

Correlational results were similar to those of Study 1. When data from both groups were combined, writing quality was found to be positively correlated with three of the four process variables: organizing, reading ability, and self-efficacy for writing. Only information seeking was not significantly associated with writing outcome. Among the process variables themselves, organizing, self-efficacy for writing, and reading ability were all significantly intercorrelated. In contrast, information seeking was not significantly correlated with any of the process variables.

Next, in order to substantiate the hypothesis that each of the main process variables would contribute uniquely to writing quality, a multiple regression was carried out. The predictor variables under consideration were reading, self-efficacy for writing, organizing, information seeking, and four interactions: Training x Reading,

Training x Self-efficacy, Training x Organizing, and Training x Information Seeking. Results indicated that only the two major treatment variables contributed uniquely to writing quality: Organizing and Training x Organizing.

In summary, the latter two studies examined college students' use of two self-regulated learning strategies: organizing/transforming and self-directed information seeking. In the descriptive study, use of each of these strategies led to a better writing product. However, in the training study, in which half the subjects were taught a graphic organizer strategy, information seeking declined among the trained subjects. This unexpected finding should caution teachers that instructing students to use one type of self-regulation strategy may influence their use of another type. Finally, self-efficacy for writing was once again shown to be a meaningful construct. In the descriptive study, self-efficacy significantly predicted writing outcomes; and in the training study, experimental subjects improved both their self-efficacy for writing and their writing product.

CONCLUSION

These three studies provide further support for McKeachie's career-long emphasis on the importance of increasing students' active participation in the teaching-learning process. His hypothesis about the importance of students' metacognitive skills was validated in Risemberg's (1993) studies, in which students' organizing and information-seeking strategies, both metacognitive in nature, were shown to influence writing outcomes. McKeachie's belief in complex motivational factors playing a role in learning was made evident in all three studies. Such self-regulative constructs as self-efficacy for writing, self-efficacy for academic achievement, grade goals, and self-evaluative standards were all implicated as being important intermediary variables for predicting writing product, in some cases surpassing verbal ability in their predictiveness (Zimmerman & Bandura, 1994).

In light of the accumulated evidence, greater priority in the college curriculum must be given to McKeachie's recommendations to teach "thinking about thinking" and to enhance students' motivation and interest in learning. Students can be taught to use metacognitive as well as other self-regulatory processes, such as goal setting and self-evaluation, through special courses in learning strategies or as part of their regular classes (Zimmerman, Greenberg, & Weinstein, 1994).

When metacognitive and other self-regulative strategies are internalized together, students will improve not only their immediate performance in school but also their self-efficacy beliefs and motivation to reach their ultimate academic goals.

ACKNOWLEDGMENTS

The initial section of this chapter was drawn from a paper presented by Barry J. Zimmerman at the annual meeting of the American Educational Research Association, April 1993 as part of a symposium entitled "College Students' Cognition and Motivation: A Symposium in Honor of Wilbert J. McKeachie." He would like to express his appreciation to Sabastian Bonner and Diana J. Zimmerman for their assistance in preparing that paper.

REFERENCES

APS to showcase the teaching of psychology. (1993). *APS Observer, 6*(1), 1.

Bandura, A. (1977). Self-efficacy: Toward a unifying theory of behavioral change. *Psychological Review, 84,* 191–215.

Bandura, A. (1993). Perceived self-efficacy in cognitive development and functioning. *Educational Psychologist, 28,* 117–148.

Biela, A., Lingoes, J. C., Lin, Y.-G., & McKeachie, W. J. (1989). Cognitive schemas in social perception. *Multivariate Behavioral Research, 24,* 195–208.

Guetzkow, H. S., Kelly, E. L., & McKeachie, W. J. (1954). An experimental comparison of recitation, discussion, and tutorial methods in college teaching. *Journal of Educational Psychology, 45,* 193–209.

Lin, Y.-G., McKeachie, W. J., & Tucker, D. G. (1984). The use of student ratings in promotion decisions. *The Journal of Higher Education, 55,* 583–589

Lin, Y.-G., McKeachie, W. J., Wernander, M., & Hedegard, J. (1970). The relationship between student-teacher compatibility of cognitive structure and student performance. *Psychological Record, 20,* 513–522.

Marsh, H. W. (1984). Students' evaluations of teaching: Dimensionality, reliability, validity, potential biases, and utility. *Journal of Educational Psychology, 76,* 707–754.

Marsh, H. W. (1987). *Student's evaluations of university teaching: Research findings, methodological issues and directions for future research.* Elmsford, NY: Pergamon.

McKeachie, W. J. (1951). Anxiety in the college classroom. *Journal of Educational Research, 45,* 135–160.

McKeachie, W. J. (1954) Student-centered vs. instructor-centered instruction. *Journal of Educational Psychology, 45,* 143–150.

McKeachie, W. J. (1958). Students, groups, and teaching methods. *American Psychologist, 7,* 503–506.

McKeachie, W. J. (1974). Instructional psychology. In *Annual review of psychology* (Vol. 25). Palo Alto, CA: Annual Reviews Inc.

McKeachie, W. J. (1984). Does anxiety disrupt information processing or does poor information processing lead to anxiety? *International Review of Applied Psychology, 33,* 187–203.

McKeachie, W. J. (1990). Research on college teaching: The historical background. *Journal of Educational Psychology, 82(2),* 189–200.

McKeachie, W. J., & Doyle, C. (1966). *Psychology.* Reading, MA: Addison-Wesley.

McKeachie, W. J., Forrin, B., Lin, Y.-G., & Teevan, R. (1960). Individualized teaching in elementary psychology. *Journal of Educational Psychology, 51,* 285–291.

McKeachie, W. J., & Hiler, W. (1954). The problem-oriented approach to teaching psychology. *Journal of Educational Psychology, 45,* 143–150.

McKeachie, W. J., Isaacson, R. L., Milholland, R. L., & Lin, Y.-G. (1968). Student achievement motives, achievement cues, and academic achievement. *Journal of Consulting and Clinical Psychology, 32,* 26–29.

McKeachie, W. J., & Kimble, G. (1951). *Teaching tips: A guidebook for the teaching of general psychology.* Ann Arbor: Author.

McKeachie, W. J., Lin, Y.-G., Milholland, J. E., & Isaacson, R. L. (1966). Student affiliation motives, teacher warmth, and academic achievement. *Journal of Personality and Social Psychology, 4,* 457–461.

McKeachie, W. J., Lin, Y.-G., Moffett, M. M., & Daugherty, M. (1978). Effective teaching: Facilitative vs. directive style. *Teaching Psychology, 54*, 193–194.

McKeachie, W. J., Pintrich, P. R., & Lin, Y.-G. (1985). Teaching learning strategies. *Educational Psychologist, 20*, 153–160.

McKeachie, W. J., & Solomon, D. (1958). Student ratings of Instructors: A validity study. *Journal of Educational Research, 51*, 379–383.

Naveh-Benjamin, M., McKeachie, W. J., Lin, Y.-G., & Tucker, D. G. (1986). Inferring students' cognitive structures and their development using the "ordered tree technique" *Journal of Educational Psychology, 78*, 130–140.

Pintrich, P. R., Cross, D. R., Kozma, R. B., & McKeachie, W. J. (1986) Instructional psychology. In *Annual review of psychology* (Vol. 37). Palo Alto, CA: Annual Reviews Inc.

Risemberg, R. (1993). *Self-regulated strategies of organizing and information seeking when writing expository text from sources.* Unpublished doctoral dissertation, Graduate Center of the City University of New York, New York.

Schunk D. H. (1984). The self-efficacy perspective on achievement behavior. *Educational Psychologist, 19*, 119–218.

Weinstein, C. E., Schulte, A. C., & Palmer, D. R. (1987). *LASSI: Learning and study strategies inventory.* Clearwater, FL: H & H Publishing.

Zimmerman, B. J. (1989). A social cognitive view of self-regulated learning. *Journal of Educational Psychology, 81*, 329–339.

Zimmerman, B. J. (1990). Self-regulated learning and academic achievement: An overview. *Educational Psychologist, 25*(1), 3–17.

Zimmerman, B. J., & Bandura, A. (1994.). Impact of self-regulatory influences on writing course attainment. *American Educational Research Journal*, in press.

Zimmerman, B. J., Greenberg, D., & Weinstein, C. E. (1994). Self-regulating academic study time: A strategy approach. In D. H. Schunk & B. J. Zimmerman (Eds.), *Self-regulation of learning and performance: Issues and educational applications.* Hillsdale, NJ: Lawrence Erlbaum Associates.

Zimmerman, B. J., & Martinez-Pons, M. (1992). Perceptions of efficacy and strategy use in the self-regulation of learning. In D. H. Schunk & J. Meece (Eds.), *Student perceptions in the classroom: Causes and consequences* (pp. 185–207). Hillsdale, NJ: Lawrence Erlbaum Associates.

11

Strategic Learning/Strategic Teaching: Flip Sides of a Coin

Claire E. Weinstein
University of Texas at Austin

The research and development work of Wilbert J. McKeachie has had a profound impact on conceptualizations, research, and practices in the field of higher education. In the 1950s, Bill was already publishing articles and chapters with titles like: "How Do Students Learn?," "Motivating Students' Interest," "The Interactions Between Student Anxiety and Teaching Approach in Learning Mathematics," "Student Centered Instruction Versus Instructor Centered Instruction," and "Relieving Anxiety in Classroom Examinations." In a number of papers and publications over the past 40 years, Bill has made it clear that he regards himself as a student of college teaching and learning. He has conducted extensive studies dealing with how students view instructional events, the impact of different types of instruction, the interaction of student characteristics and individual differences with instructional events, the characteristics of different types of instruction, and the roles of affective variables in education. Bill has also worked to develop alternate dependent measures of educational outcomes as well as measures of students' cognition, metacognition, motivation, and affect. Bill's contributions in these areas have had a tremendous impact on my own and my students' research and development efforts.

The focus of this chapter is on four areas of our work that have either derived from or benefited greatly from Bill's work: conceptions of the critical components of strategic learning, assessment of student learning strategies, interventions designed to enhance students' strategic learning, and the implications of this work for helping college instructors and faculty to be more strategic teachers.

A CONCEPTION OF STRATEGIC LEARNING

The development of our model of strategic learning proceeded interactively with our development of a model of strategic teaching. Building on the work of Paris (Paris, Lipson, & Wixson, 1983; Paris & Newman, 1990), Pintrich (Pintrich & DeGroot, 1990; Pintrich & Garcia, 1991), Pressley (Pressley, Borkowski, & Schneider, 1987), Schunk (1989), Wittrock (1986, 1992), Zimmerman (1986, 1990; Zimmerman & Schunk, 1989), and others, these models combine skill, will, and self-regulation components. The nature of skilled functioning in academic contexts is quite complex. What does it mean to be an expert, strategic learner? First, expert learners have a variety of different types of knowledge that can be loosely classified into five basic categories: (a) knowledge about themselves as learners; (b) knowledge about different types of academic tasks; (c) knowledge about strategies and tactics for acquiring, integrating, applying, and thinking about new learning; (d) prior content knowledge; and (e) knowledge of both present and future contexts in which the knowledge could be useful. The first category includes what students know about their learning strengths and weakness, their preferences, their better and worse times of day, their academic likes and dislikes, and their goals (Biggs, 1987; Entwistle, 1992; Marton, 1988; Schmeck, 1988). This type of knowledge is most important for helping students to be able to schedule their time as well as identify and allocate needed resources, such as a study group, or tutor. The second category, knowledge about different types of academic tasks, includes what students know about the different types of academic tasks they might be expected to perform as part of their classes, such as reading for understanding, taking notes, observing a demonstration, listening to a lecture, and taking tests (Biggs, 1987; Entwistle, 1992; Jones & Idol, 1990; McKeachie, 1993; Menges & Svinicki, 1991; Weinstein, Goetz, & Alexander, 1988). It is impossible to know if you have reached a learning goal if you are not clear about the nature of the goal. Students must understand the nature of academic tasks and the appropriate outcomes so that they can monitor and control their attainment of learning goals. Knowledge about strategies and tactics for acquiring, integrating, thinking about, and applying new learning is the third category (Biggs, 1987; Entwistle, 1992; McKeachie, 1993; Menges & Svinicki, 1991; Weinstein et al., 1988; Weinstein & Mayer, 1986; Wittrock, 1992; Zimmerman, 1986, 1990; Zimmerman & Schunk, 1989). Learning and thinking strategies and skills are the tools we use to meet our learning goals. They help us to generate meaning, monitor our learning progress, and store new information in ways that facilitate future recall or application. The fourth category, prior content knowledge, refers to using existing knowledge to help build meaning, either directly or through generating analogies, for new content (Alexander & Judy, 1988). Finally, knowledge of both present and future contexts in which the knowledge could be useful, is important for generating meaning, organizing new knowledge, as well as generating and maintaining motivation to learn.

However, clearly these different aspects of relevant knowledge are not sufficient for expertise. Expert learners must also know how to use these various types of knowledge to meet their learning goals and how to monitor their own progress so they can adjust what they are dong if a problem occurs. They need to know how to use self-assessment or self-testing to determine if they are or are not meeting their learning goals so that they can modify their strategies on a timely basis (Brown, 1987; Brown, Bransford, Ferrara, & Campione, 1983; Flavell, 1979; Garner & Alexander, 1989; Weinstein, 1988). Students must also want to learn—effective learning requires the integration of skill and will components (Paris, Lipson, & Wixson, 1983).

Motivation and positive affect for learning derive from many components and interact with and result from many factors. These factors include things such as goal setting, goal analysis and goal using, efficacy expectations, outcome attributions, interest, valuing, perceptions of self-worth and instrumentality, and utility value (Ames & Archer, 1988; Locke & Latham, 1990; McCombs, 1989; McCombs & Marzano, 1990; Pintrich & DeGroot, 1990; Pintrich & Garcia, 1991; Schunk, 1989; Zimmerman, 1990; Zimmerman & Schunk, 1989).

However, these different types of knowledge and the will to reach learning goals are still not sufficient for expertise. Strategic learners also have metacognitive awareness and control strategies they can use to orchestrate and manage their studying and learning. This involves a number of interacting activities. Each activity interacts and dynamically impacts all other components. On the macro level, relevant activities include time management and using a systematic approach for studying and learning (Weinstein, 1988). A systematic approach includes: setting a learning or study goal; creating a plan to reach the goal; selecting the specific strategies or methods to use to achieve the goal; implementing the methods selected to carry out the plan; monitoring progress on both a formative and a summative basis; modifying the plan, the methods, or even the original goal, if necessary; and evaluating what was done to decide if this would be a good way to go about meeting similar goals in the future. Evaluating this whole process helps students to build up a repertoire of strategies that can be called upon more automatically in the future when a similar situation arises. Developing systematic approaches to different academic tasks is effortful and time-consuming initially, but somewhat automatic once a student has developed an effective repertoire (Anderson, 1990). On the microlevel self-regulation involves facilitating metacognitive awareness, monitoring strategy use, and monitoring understanding on a continuous basis (Brown, 1987; Brown et al., 1983; Flavell, 1979; Garner & Alexander, 1989).

ASSESSING STRATEGIC LEARNING

Bill has always been interested in methods to diagnose student characteristics and approaches to learning, studying, and taking tests. His most recent work in this area has been with Pintrich and others on the development of the Motivated Strategies for Learning Questionnaire (Pintrich et al., 1991). Our own work in this area has led to the development of the Learning and Study Strategies Inventory (LASSI; Weinstein, Palmer, & Schulte, 1987).

The LASSI is a 77-item diagnostic/prescriptive self-report measure of strategic learning that focuses on thoughts and behaviors that can be changed and enhanced through educational interventions. It helps students identify their learning and studying strengths and weaknesses so that they and their instructors know where to concentrate their efforts to become more expert, strategic learners. The LASSI has now been used in about 1,300 colleges and universities in the United States in a variety of ways, including as a pretest or pretest/posttest measure in learning-to-learn courses. The LASSI provides standardized scores (percentile score equivalents) and national norms for 10 different scales (there is no total score because this is a diagnostic measure): Attitude, Motivation, Time Management,

Anxiety, Concentration, Information Processing, Selecting Main Ideas, Study Aids, Self Testing, and Test Strategies.

The Attitude scale contains items addressing students' attitude toward and interest in college, as well as their general motivation for succeeding in school (sample item: I feel confused and undecided as to what my educational goals should be). The Motivation scale addresses students' diligence, self-discipline, and willingness to work hard at academic tasks (sample item: When work is difficult I either give up or study only the easy parts). Time Management items address students' use of time management principles and methods to help them organize and control their time (sample item: I only study when there is the pressure of a test). Anxiety scale items address the degree to which students worry about school and their performance (sample item: Worrying about doing poorly interferes with my concentration on tests). The Concentration scale items address students' ability to direct their attention to academic tasks, including study activities (sample item: I find that during lectures I think of other things and don't really listen to what is being said). Items on the Information Processing scale address how well students can use imaginal and verbal elaboration, organization strategies, and reasoning skills to help build bridges between what they already know and what they are trying to learn and remember (sample item: I translate what I am studying into my own words). The Selecting Main Ideas scale items measure students' skills at selecting important information to concentrate on for further study (sample item: Often when studying I seem to get lost in details and can't see the forest for the trees). Items on the Study Aids scale measure students' ability to use or create study aids that support and increase meaningful learning (sample item: I use special helps, such as italics and headings, that are in my textbooks). The Self Testing scale items address comprehension monitoring methods such as reviewing and practicing (sample item: I stop periodically while reading and mentally go over or review what was said). Items on the last scale, Test Strategies, address students' use of test preparation and test-taking strategies (sample item: I have difficulty adapting my studying to different types of courses).

A new measure we have developed, the Assessment of Readiness for Training (ART; Weinstein & Palmer, in press), is designed to be a diagnostic/prescriptive self-report measure of strategic learning to be used in training settings in business and industry. Tremendous amounts of money are spent by U.S. businesses and industries for training new employees to perform their specific job tasks, upgrading and enhancing the knowledge and skills of existing employees, providing opportunities for job upgrading and the development of managerial skills, introducing employees to new technologies and job tasks, and providing opportunities for personal growth and development. Any training activity must be examined from two perspectives: effectiveness and efficiency. Effectiveness variables impact training outcomes, such as amount of learning and level of proficiency, whereas efficiency variables impact cost factors such as time (duration of training) and cost of materials or consultants.

Most interventions designed to increase either the effectiveness or efficiency of training focus on instructional materials, methods, and teaching strategies. A critical component that is often ignored in most of these approaches is the degree to which the individual is ready and able to interact with the instruction in ways that will result in meaningful and enduring learning. Using a model of strategic learning applied to a business/industrial context, the ART was developed to assess trainees' strengths and weaknesses in eight different areas: Anxiety, Attitude Toward Training, Motivation, Concentration, Identifying Important Information, Knowledge Acquisition, Monitoring Learning, and Time Management.

HELPING STUDENTS TO BECOME MORE STRATEGIC LEARNERS: AN ADJUNCT COURSE APPROACH

Much of Bill's work has focused on helping students to be more successful learners. For years at the University of Michigan he has developed and taught a course in applying psychological principles and findings to helping students learn more about how to study, process new information, store it in meaningful ways, and use their new knowledge in creative and thoughtful manners. Building upon some of Bill's work and using our own model of strategic learning, we have developed a course at the University of Texas designed to help students develop greater expertise as strategic learners. Initially, this course was introduced in the Department of Educational Psychology to serve as an applied laboratory for the research being conducted as part of the Cognitive Learning Strategies Project that I direct and to provide a service for students experiencing difficulty succeeding academically at the university. Over time, as a result of research conducted as part of the Cognitive Learning Strategies Project, as well as other research in this area, this course has evolved into a class in strategic learning.

The formal title of this course is EDP310 Introduction to Educational Psychology: Individual Learning Skills. The course is not required for any degree plan and is considered a free elective. It is a 3-credit, semester-long (14 weeks) course taken for a grade.

Student population

Three broad categories of students register for this course. The first group is composed of students who are predicted to be at-risk for failure or low achievement at their time of entry into the University of Texas. Some of these students enter the university through special admissions programs while others are identified through admissions tests or diagnostic tests, and recommendations from academic advisors. Whatever the means of selection, these students are identified as having some of the same characteristics as students who have not succeeded in the past. The second group includes students who enter the university under regular admissions procedures but experience academic difficulties at some point in their program. The last group includes students who are not experiencing academic problems but simply want to improve their grades, students preparing for graduate work, and those who believe this course might be an "easy A" (although they soon learn this is not the case). Although the course is listed as a lower division class, it is also taken by a large number of juniors and some seniors. Currently, there are 16 sections of 25 students each during the two long semesters and 3 sections during each of two summer sessions.

Instructors

The class is taught by graduate students in the Department of Educational Psychology, many of whom audit the course the semester before they teach it. Students teaching this class must also complete a course on university teaching that, of course, uses Bill's book about college teaching (McKeachie, 1994). New instructors are assigned to mentors (graduate students with at least one year of experience in teaching the course) during their first year of teaching. Weekly meetings are held with all instructors together to go over the next week's curriculum, review and critique the past week's classes, and discuss any problems. In addition, instructors are observed and receive feedback from peers and the faculty administrator. Instructors also have access to a file of teaching ideas and materials for each course topic (this is an evolving file that is added to each semester by instructors in the course).

Curriculum

The curriculum is designed to help students gradually improve their learning strategies and skills, knowledge, attitudes, and motivation so that they can become more strategic learners. The first three days of the course focus on introductions and pretesting. The pretest data help both the instructors and the students identify students' strengths and weaknesses so that individualization of assignments and priorities can be made over the span of the semester. This pretest data also helps to increase students' awareness of their strengths and weaknesses outside of a graded context. The measures are only used for diagnostic assessment and help create a baseline against which to measure future growth and achievements. These scores do not directly affect a student's grade. The specific measures used in any given semester will vary depending on the evaluation or research questions being addressed that semester. However, a measure of learning and study skills, as well as a measure of reading comprehension, is always used.

After an initial orientation to the course, the first week or so is devoted to presenting a model of the students as managers of their own learning. This analogy is used to help make the concept of a strategic learner who is able to self-regulate his or her own learning more meaningful and memorable to the students. The knowledge, metacognitive, motivation, and executive control components are all introduced. Relevant academic context and social climate variables, such as time constraints, teacher expectations, and forms of social support, are also described and discussed. The students are told that they will learn how to generate management plans for common academic tasks such as taking notes in a lecture or from a book, listening in class, completing projects, giving presentations, preparing for and taking exams, and completing semester projects. As a part of this process it is explained that strategic learners are goal-directed and use strategies in pursuit of their goals. To help them get started, the next topic is setting, using, and analyzing goals.

Being able to establish and use realistic yet challenging academic goals is a central theme in the course. This theme of setting and using goals is returned to many times in a variety of contexts. When this topic is first introduced, students are urged to examine existing goals and to generate new goals for their personal, social, academic, and occupational lives. They are then guided through a series of steps and activities designed to help them clarify their goals (as well as distinguish them from wishes and dreams), prioritize them, and use them to identify the utility value of different academic tasks. Analyzing and balancing goals, as well as using them to motivate oneself, is practiced over the course of the semester.

The discussion about establishing and using goals leads nicely into other topics related to motivation and positive affect toward learning. For example, efficacy expectations, valuing, attributions, and utility value are all discussed as components of motivation that are under the students' control.

Throughout the course all topics are related back to the model of strategic learning. This provides students with a schema they can use to make sense of new information and to refine as their understanding deepens. Specific topics covered in the second half of the course include: knowledge-acquisition strategies; pre-, during-, and postreading strategies; time management; dealing with procrastination; attention and concentration; note taking; listening skills; preparing for and taking tests; the relationship between understanding and long-term memory; and dealing with academic stress. The last portion of the course is reserved for integrating the model and adapting it to various learning contexts, learner characteristics, learning goals, and situational variables.

A wide variety of content materials and instructional methods are used in this course. This is because the strategies and skills being taught are useful in a variety of courses but, like any learning method, they must be applied in specific content areas to be learned. The range, or domain of applicability, of a particular strategy varies. A strategy that generalizes to more than one content area is more generic, such as a reading comprehension method, whereas a strategy that is specific to one content area, such as learning to find the area of a triangle, is more content-dependent. This course focuses on more generic strategies. However, learning a generic strategy still requires experience with it in a variety of content domains. These experiences help students learn the domain of applicability for that particular strategy and how to adapt and use the strategy with different content materials and tasks.

The final week of the class is again devoted to assessment so that students can see where they improved. Students also receive feedback about areas they might want to continue working on through the university's learning skills center or other special help programs in some of the individual colleges.

Assessment

A variety of different measures are used depending on research needs or course development needs being addressed in any given semester. However, a measure of strategic learning and a reading comprehension measure are always used so that students can get individual feedback about their strengths and weaknesses that can be used to help target priority areas for individualization of assignments and homework. A measure of reading comprehension that has been used is the Nelson-Denny Reading Test (Brown, Bennett, & Hanna, 1981). The measure of strategic learning that is used is the LASSI (Weinstein, Palmer, & Schulte, 1987) described earlier.

The results obtained in the course assessments have been very significant. Not only do students generally evidence improvements of 10 percentile points and more on both the reading measures and the scales of the LASSI, but they also evidence significant improvements in their gradepoint averages that are maintained across at least five semesters (the longest follow-up we have conducted).

Clearly, a course like this can impact on student success in many ways. However, these effects can be magnified by embedding the teaching of learning-to-learn strategies and skills within content classes. This is called the *metacurriculum approach*. For both more generic as well as domain-specific strategies, incorporating modeling and guided practice with feedback into the classroom provides students with opportunities to expand, deepen, and transfer the use of their repertoire in varied and appropriate contexts.

STRATEGIC TEACHING: THE METACURRICULUM APPROACH

A large portion of Bill's work in the past few decades has focused on improving college teaching (it is interesting to point out that Bill himself is the winner of numerous teaching awards, including the national award given by the American Psychological Association). The investigation of strategic teaching, and its interaction with strategic learning, is also another emphasis of our work. There are tremendous implications of the research and development work in strategic learning for helping college instructors and faculty to be more strategic teachers (e.g., McKeachie, 1994; Menges & Svinicki, 1991; Weinstein & Meyer, 1991). It is unfortunate that for so long the study of college teaching was divorced from the study of student learning. Strategic teaching is the flip side of strategic learning. Strategic teachers need to know about their students, such as their knowledge about themselves as learners, their understanding of the nature and target outcomes for different academic tasks, their existing content knowledge, and their repertoires of learning strategies and study skills. Strategic teachers also need to know about different teaching methods and how these interact with their personalities, learning goals, and prior knowledge, as well as with the educational context in which they teach and their students. They need to understand determinants of students' achievement motivation and know how to use instructional activities that can provide a positive context for learning. Academic learning involves a negotiation between the instructor and the student. Strategic teaching contributes to the development of strategic learners—and it is the transfer of responsibility for learning to the individual that is the ultimate outcome of education.

College students must perform a variety of academic tasks, such as: reading textbooks or original sources, listening to lectures, watching demonstrations or a film, writing papers or homework assignments, preparing for and taking tests, and completing projects. Strategic learners need to understand the nature of each of these tasks. What are the characteristics of different tasks? What is required to complete individual tasks? What standards of performance are required? How will I be asked to demonstrate what I have learned? Many students are unclear about the nature of many academic tasks. Students often do not understand procedural aspects of common tasks such as how to select out the important ideas and information in a textbook.

There is much that college faculty can do to help students understand the nature and requirements of academic tasks. Students are required to participate in or complete a number of different academic tasks throughout a course. To both facilitate student learning from these tasks, as well as to facilitate the development of strategic learning, it is important that faculty clearly define and explain the nature of each task. For example, early in a course, when the textbook or other written sources are introduced, instructors could highlight the characteristics of the material and their expectations for what students must learn from it. In an introductory course, particularly if the instructor is not sure if students are familiar with reading skills in this content area, they might model ways to help identify and focus on the important ideas and information. If professors use the lecture method in their courses, they might bring in an overhead projector for a couple of classes and take notes on their own presentations, explaining why they have recorded some things and not others. Again, all of these methods are designed to help students understand the nature and requirement of the different tasks in a course.

In addition to understanding academic tasks, students must also learn to monitor their progress toward completing academic tasks and reaching their learning goals (Brown, 1987). Without checking actively on their progress, many students fall victim to what has been called the illusion of knowing (Glenberg, Wilkinson, & Epstein, 1982). Students may not realize there are holes in their understanding until they receive their grade on a test. Taking the test may be the first time they checked on their new knowledge in a way that would identify gaps or misunderstandings.

Monitoring understanding can be as simple as trying to paraphrase what we have been trying to learn, or as complex as trying to analyze and evaluate how it fits in with our prior knowledge. Many learning strategies also can be used to test understanding. For example, if students try to paraphrase in their own words what they are reading in a textbook, this can help them to help build meaning for the new information and can also help them to identify gaps or errors in their understanding. One of the benefits of homework assignments and class projects is to give students an opportunity to apply their knowledge. If students have difficulty completing their assignments, or if they cannot explain what they are learning to someone else, they would also know that they have comprehension problems. Checking on our understanding is an important part of strategic learning that fosters self-regulation. Students must be aware of their problems in our understanding, or gaps in our knowledge, before they can do something about it.

Professors can help students to monitor their understanding as well as helping them to learn why this is important and how they can do it on their own. For example, at the beginning of a class, an instructor could take a few moments and ask students to summarize in their own words the main ideas that were generated in the last class period.

When presenting a new principle, they could stop and ask the students to generate potential situations where it would be applicable.

One particularly useful method for helping students to check their understanding and which also helps students learn a variety of learning strategies is the use of cooperative learning. Cooperative learning is a method that builds on the best of peer tutoring and the benefits of trying to teach something to someone else. It is now widely accepted that in many traditional tutoring situations, it is the tutor and not the student receiving the tutoring, who benefits the most. When preparing for the tutoring sessions, and while doing the tutoring, tutors process the content in ways that help them to both consolidate and integrate their own content knowledge. In attempting to diagnose their tutees' problems and teach adaptively to meet the needs of their students, tutors also learn a great deal about how to learn. The tutor needs to diagnose the tutee's learning problem, or knowledge gap, in order to help them overcome it. Cooperative learning provides an opportunity for students to benefit from playing both roles—tutor and tutee.

In one form of cooperative learning, two students take turns being the tutor. For example, if two students were going over the notes for a course, the first student would paraphrase and explain the first page of notes. Then they would switch and the second member of the pair would go over the next section. The student paraphrasing and explaining on each turn is called the reciter. The other student, however, does not just listen passively. His or her task is to be the critiquer, the one who checks on the reciter's accuracy and completeness. If there is a problem or gap in the reciter's description, the critiquer would either correct it or help the reciter to understand the misconception. Thus, each student gets a chance to increase and consolidate their content knowledge and get help with their learning skills. Numerous studies have shown the effectiveness of this method for learning and for learning how to learn (Dansereau, 1988).

Instructors can use cooperative learning in a variety of ways. Sometimes, when covering particularly difficult material, professors will allocate the first 10 minutes of class for students to work in cooperative learning groups to review the material already presented. Although it might appear that this would reduce class time, it actually helps to make the rest of the class period more productive. If the students are better prepared, then they will be in a better position to benefit from the rest of the instructional presentation. Another way some college instructors use this method is to set up study buddies for their class. These are pairs of students who meet outside of class for 1 to 2 hours per week. Sometimes participation in study buddy pairs is required as part of the course and sometimes it has been used on a voluntary basis, perhaps giving extra credit to students who participate. This is also a particularly effective method when there is a lab or recitation section.

These are just some examples of ways in which the work of Bill McKeachie and many other researchers in educational psychology, cognitive psychology, and higher education has been applied to college teaching. For more extensive discussions, see McKeachie (1994) and Menges and Svinicki (1991).

A PERSONAL NOTE

I have tried to give an overview in this chapter of my work in areas that relate to Bill's interests, as well as the many ways in which it has been influenced by the conceptions and research conducted by Bill McKeachie. However, I also want to acknowledge Bill's role as a mentor and friend in my life. Whether it has been to offer professional advice, to bring me a wonderful sandwich from Zingerman's deli in Ann Arbor, to advise some school that they really did want me as a consultant, to review a paper, to introduce me to a wonderful restaurant, to sponsor me for the Spencer Fellowship from the National Academy of Education, to talk over ideas, or to stop in the middle of a conference to pack my bags and send me home on a plane because my mother took critically ill, Bill and Ginny McKeachie have always been there for me with unconditional friendship, love, and support. The world truly is a better place because of people like Bill and Ginny McKeachie . . . thank you!!!

REFERENCES

Alexander, P. A., & Judy, J. E. (1988). The interaction of domain-specific and strategic knowledge in academic performance. *Review of Educational Research, 58*(4), 375–404.

Ames, C., & Archer, J. (1988). Achievement goals in the classroom: Students' learning strategies and motivational processes. *Journal of Educational Psychology, 80*(3), 260–267.

Anderson, J. R. (1990). *Cognitive psychology and its implications.* New York: Freeman.

Biggs, J. B. (1987). *Student approaches to learning and studying.* Melbourne: Australian Council for Educational Research.

Brown, A. L. (1987). Metacognition, executive control, self-regulation, and other more mysterious mechanisms. In F. E. Weinert & R. H. Kluwe (Eds.), *Metacognition, motivation, and understanding* (pp. 65–116). Hillsdale, NJ: Lawrence Erlbaum Associates.

Brown, J. I., Bennett, J. M., & Hanna, G. (1981). *Nelson-Denny Reading Test Forms E and F.* Chicago: Riverside.

Brown, A. L., Bransford, J. D., Ferrara, R. A., & Campione, J. C. (1983). Learning, remembering, and understanding. In J. H. Flavell & E. M. Markman (Eds.), *Cognitive development (Vol. III) Handbook of child psychology* (pp. 77–166). New York: Wiley.

Dansereau, D. F. (1988). Cooperative learning strategies. In C. E. Weinstein, E. T. Goetz, & P. A. Alexander (Eds.), *Learning and study strategies: Issues in assessment, instruction, and evaluation* (pp. 103–120). New York: Academic Press.

Entwistle, N. J. (1992). Student learning and study strategies. In B. R. Clark & G. Neave (Eds.), *Encyclopedia of higher education.* Elmsford: Pergamon.

Flavell, J. H. (1979). Metacognition and cognitive monitoring: A new era of cognitive-developmental inquiry. *American Psychologist, 34,* 906–911.

Garner, R., & Alexander, P. A. (1989). Metacognition: Answered and unanswered questions. *Educational Psychologist, 24*(2), 143–158.

Glenberg, A. M., Wilkinson, A. C., & Epstein, W. (1982). The illusion of knowing: Failure in the self-assessment of comprehension. *Memory and Cognition, 10*(6), 597–602.

Jones, B. F., & Idol, L. (Eds.). (1990). *Dimensions of thinking and cognitive instruction.* Hillsdale, NJ: Lawrence Erlbaum Associates.

Locke, E. A., & Latham, G. P. (1990). *A theory of goal setting and task performance.* Englewood Cliffs, NJ: Prentice-Hall.

Marton, F. (1988). Describing and improving learning. In R. R. Schmeck (Ed.) *Learning strategies and learning styles* (pp. 53–82). New York: Plenum.

McCombs, B. L. (1989). Self-regulated learning and academic achievement: A phenomenological view. In B. J. Zimmerman & D. H. Schunk (Eds.), *Self-regulated learning and academic achievement* (pp. 51–82). New York: Springer-Verlag.

McCombs, B. L., & Marzano R. J. (1990). Putting the self in self-regulated learning: The self as agent in integrating will and skill. *Educational Psychologist, 25*(1), 51–69.

McKeachie, W. J. (1994). *Teaching tips: A guidebook for the beginning college teacher* (9th Ed.). Lexington, MA: Heath.

Menges, R. J., & Svinicki, M. S. (Eds.). (1991). College teaching: From theory to practice. In *New Directions for Teaching and Learning* (Vol. 45). San Francisco: Jossey-Bass.

Paris, S. G., Lipson, M. Y., & Wixson, K. K. (1983). Becoming a strategic reader. *Contemporary Educational Psychology, 8*, 293–316.

Paris, S. G., & Newman, R. S. (1990). Developmental aspects of self-regulated learning. *Educational Psychologist, 25*, 87–105.

Pintrich, P. R., & DeGroot, E. V. (1990). Motivational and self-regulated learning components of classroom academic performance. *Journal of Educational Psychology, 82*, 33–40.

Pintrich, P. R., & Garcia, T. (1991). Student goal orientation and self-regulation in the college classroom. In M. Maehr & P. R. Pintrich (Eds.), *Advances in motivation and achievement: Goals and self-regulatory processes* (Vol. 7, pp. 371–402). Greenwich, CT: JAI Press.

Pintrich, P. R., Smith, D. A. F., Garcia. T., & McKeachie, W. J. (1991). *A manual for the use of the motivated strategies for learning questionnaire (MSLQ).* Ann Arbor, MI: NCRIPTAL, The University of Michigan.

Pressley, M., Borkowski, J. G., & Schneider, W. (1987). Cognitive strategies: Good strategy users coordinate metacognition and knowledge. *Annals of Child Development, 4*, 89–129.

Schmeck, R. R. (Ed.). (1988). *Learning strategies and learning styles.* New York: Plenum.

Schunk, D. H. (1989). Social cognitive theory and self-regulated learning. In B. J. Zimmerman & D. H. Schunk (Eds.), *Self-regulated learning and academic achievement* (pp. 83–110). New York: Springer-Verlag.

Weinstein, C. E. (1988). Executive control processes in learning: Why knowing about how to learn is not enough. *Journal of College Reading and Learning, 21,* 48–56.

Weinstein, C. E., Goetz, E. T., & Alexander, P. A. (Eds.). (1988). *Learning and study strategies: Issues in assessment, instruction, and evaluation.* New York: Academic Press.

Weinstein, C. E., & Mayer, R. E. (1986). The teaching of learning strategies. In M. C. Wittrock (Ed.), *Handbook of research on teaching* (3rd ed., pp. 315–327). New York: Macmillan.

Weinstein, C. E., & Meyer, D. K. (1991). Cognitive learning strategies and college teaching. *New Directions for Teaching and Learning (45).* San Francisco: Jossey-Bass, Inc.

Weinstein, C. E., & Palmer, D. R. (in press). *The assessment of readiness for training.* Clearwater, FL: H & H Publishing.

Weinstein, C. E., Palmer, D. R., & Schulte, A. C. (1987). *LASSI: Learning and Study Strategies Inventory.* Clearwater, FL: H & H Publishing.

Wittrock, M. C. (1986). Students' thought processes. In M. C. Wittrock (Ed.), *Handbook of research on teaching* (3rd ed.) (pp. 297–314). New York: Macmillan.

Wittrock, M. C. (1992). An empowering conception of educational psychology. *Educational Psychologist, 27,* 129–141.

Zimmerman, B. J. (1986). Development of self-regulated learning: Which are the key subprocesses? *Contemporary Educational Psychology, 16,* 307–313.

Zimmerman, B. J. (1990). Self-regulated learning and academic achievement: An overview. *Educational Psychologist, 23*(1), 3–17.

Zimmerman, B. J., & Schunk, D. H. (Eds.). (1989). *Self-regulated learning and academic achievement: Theory, research, and practice.* New York: Springer-Verlag.

12

Teaching Dialogically: Its Relationship to Critical Thinking in College Students

Susan N. Reiter
Washtenaw Community College

College students' critical thinking skills remain an area of grave concern (Association of American Colleges, 1985; National Institute on Education, 1984), and instructional methods to promote them continue to challenge educators. Within the last decade, researchers have dispelled notions that critical thinking skills are natural "by-products" of encountering conventional college subject matter (deBono, 1983; Fischer & Grant, 1983; Glaser, 1985; McPeck, 1981; Nickerson, 1987), conventional course tasks (Quellmalz, 1987), or conventional instructional methods (Nickerson, 1987).

Today, experts call for "direct" critical thinking methods, or instruction that places higher order objectives at center stage and where thinking skills are taught explicitly (Beyer, 1985; Fischer & Grant, 1983; Jackson, 1986; Nickerson, 1987; Quellmalz, 1987; Swartz, 1987; Worsham & Stockton, 1986; Woods, 1987).

Direct critical thinking methods might make students aware of the mental processes they use (McKeachie, Pintrich, Lin, Smith, & Sharma, 1990; Woods, 1990); instruct students in employing thinking skills (Bereiter, 1984; Beyer, 1985, 1987; Swartz, 1987); give students practice in thinking using a diverse array of examples and domains (Beyer, 1985; Perkins, 1987); or ask students to apply thinking skills to entirely new contexts (Lipman, 1987; Quellmalz, 1987; Sadler & Whimbey, 1985).

Although calls from the research community for "direct" critical thinking instruction have been strong, their use in college classrooms remains limited. Even when critical thinking is an intended goal of classroom instruction, indirect critical thinking methods (such as discussion) are employed much more frequently than direct critical thinking methods (such as asking students to apply thinking skills in entirely new contexts) (Beyer, 1985; Chipman, Segal, & Glaser, 1985; Johnson & Johnson, 1988; Keeley, Browne, & Kreutzer, 1982).

Educational research has yet to substantiate which specific types of direct critical thinking methods are most effective for college students. Without clear signals of what strategies to try, instructors are wary to experiment with direct critical thinking methods for fear that their students' learning might decrease instead of increase under the innovation. More work is needed on identifying the precise techniques that "maximize positive change" in critical thinking skills among the college student population (McMillan, 1987, p. 11).

To this end, this chapter examines the relationship between college students' critical thinking and one direct method of critical thinking instruction—namely, dialogical instruction.

DIALOGICAL INSTRUCTION

Definition

Dialogical instruction (Paul, 1987, 1992) is a discussion technique in which an instructor uses classroom questioning to encourage students to argue course issues from several different points of view, particularly those that oppose their own. Through the process of arguing for and against several positions, and advocating conclusions different from one's own, a student begins to think "dialogically."

Dialogical instruction is a direct (rather than indirect) critical thinking method because it requires that students use a number of explicit critical thinking skills (see Table 12.1).

It incorporates many specific recommendations in the critical thinking literature including: (a) eliciting multiple perspectives through instructor questioning (Glaser, 1984; Presseisen, 1986); (b) requiring that students weigh various alternatives through role-playing techniques (Brookfield, 1987; Daloz, 1986; Duncombe & Heikkinen, 1989; Resnick, 1987); and (c) asking students to devise arguments against positions that they favor (Brookfield, 1987; Daloz, 1986).

TABLE 12.1

Critical Thinking Skills Required in Dialogical Instruction

Dialogical Instruction Steps	Required Skills
To state and defend one's position	Provide evidence based on fact (not opinion) to support one's own position
To identify mutliple viewpoints	Exhibit openness to a variety of viewpoints, and not discount perspectives simply because they differ from one's own
To assume an opposing position and argue from it	Exhibit flexibility in reasoning, and argue objectively/nondefensively a position opposing one's own
To present arguments for two points of view simultaneously (i.e., carry on a self-dialogue)	Remain clear in one's thinking amid complexity
To render a final judgment after considering evidence presented from a number of perspectives	Evaluate information brought to the table

The Role of Dissonance

Dialogical instruction is based on the notion that the presentation of multiple viewpoints in the classroom creates "cognitive dissonance" in the learner and acts as a motivator for continued critical thought and analysis until the dissonance is relieved. Daloz (1986) suggested that instructors "toss bits of disturbing information . . . that raise questions about their students' current world views and invite them to entertain alternatives, to close the dissonance, accommodate their structures, *think afresh*" (p. 223).

In dialogical instruction, the dissonance appears on two levels: (a) the student is exposed to multiple perspectives in the classroom when many students are asked to state their own views (external conflict between students and peers); and (b) the student is asked to argue from a point of view opposing his or her own (internal conflict).

A number of dissonance-based teaching methods have gotten recent press (Clarke, 1988; Duncombe & Heikkinen, 1989; Fredericks & Miller, 1990; Johnson & Johnson, 1979, 1985; Spracher, 1983). With the exception of Johnson and Johnson (1979, 1985), few studies examine relationships to critical thinking outcomes per se. Also, to date, most studies have examined dissonance in which the student's views are pitted against an entity external to oneself (e.g., learner versus subject matter, Clarke, 1988; learner versus peers, Spracher, 1983). Studies in which the dissonance is centered internally (e.g., learner versus self) have been notably absent.

This chapter examines the dissonance instruction–critical thinking question at a micro level—that of the individual learner versus his or her attitudes, beliefs, and views—with respect to critical thinking outcomes.

DESIGN

Questions and Hypotheses

In this study, the central question is "What is the relationship between dialogical instruction and critical thinking?"

First, the researcher hypothesized that treatment subjects (in classes including dialogical instruction) would score significantly higher than control subjects (in lecture/discussion classes) on critical thinking performance. Second, the researcher hypothesized treatment subjects would rate themselves significantly higher than control subjects on self-report critical thinking. Third, the researcher hypothesized that there would be significant two-way interactions between the treatment and self-report critical thinking, when moderated by motivation.

Definitions

Critical thinking

Critical thinking is defined here as having two major components: (a) *higher order thinking* (the ability to use analysis, synthesis, and evaluation skills) and (b) *multilogical thinking* (the ability to reason objectively from multiple viewpoints).

Traditionally, critical thinking was simply equated with higher order cognitive skills such as analysis, synthesis, and evaluation (Bloom, 1956). More recent interpretations, however, have extended the definition to include critical attitudes (DeNitto & Strickland, 1987; Ennis, 1987; Furedy & Furedy, 1985; McPeck, 1981; Paul, 1987; Ruggiero, 1988; Siegel, 1980; Swartz, 1987). The definition employed here encapsulates both.

Defined further, *higher order thinking* means the ability to break a problem into manageable parts and select relevant/valid information (analysis); the ability to combine information meaningfully from a variety of sources (synthesis); and the ability to make a judgment based on evidence and criteria (evaluation) (Fischer & Grant, 1983).

Multilogical thinking hinges on the learner's ability to exhibit three major critical attitudes: (a) openness (remaining open-minded, considering and respecting multiple viewpoints) (Ennis, 1987; Ruggiero, 1988); (b) inquisitiveness (intellectual curiosity, and a persistent and diligent commitment to "thinking things through") (Ruggiero, 1988); and (c) objectivity (an ability to entertain opposing views non-defensively, to critique one's own position, and to change one's view should evidence warrant) (DeNitto & Strickland, 1987; Ruggiero, 1988; Swartz, 1987).

Motivation

The researcher selected four motivational theoretical constructs hypothesized to have moderating effects: (a) intrinsic goal orientation (the subject's preference for course material that challenges or arouses curiosity, regardless of the grade acquired); (b) task value (the interest, importance, and utility that the subject associates with course tasks); (c) self-efficacy (the subject's certainty or confidence that he or she can learn and understand course concepts); and (d) expectancy for success (the subject's belief that he or she will perform well on course tasks).

Study Design

Using a control-treatment design, the researcher studied three instructors. Each taught a control semester and a treatment semester of a course in one of three disciplines (for a total of six classes). In the control semester, each instructor used his or her typical teaching style comprised of lecture and discussion. In the treatment semester (occurring one semester later), each instructor also included dialogical instruction.

Different students were enrolled in control and treatment semesters of the same course. Within-course control-treatment comparisons were conducted to control for across-course variation in implementing dialogical instruction and "teacher effect."

Sample

A 4-year comprehensive Research I university and a community college, located in two small adjacent midwestern cities, were selected. Three courses were sampled: children's literature (baccalaureate—literature), ecology (baccalaureate—ecology), and philosophy (community college—philosophy).

The total sample ($N = 204$), spanning treatment and control semesters, was predominantly Caucasian (97%) and female (68%). Control and treatment ns, respectively, for the three courses were: literature (36, 45), ecology (28, 43), and philosophy (24, 28).

In order to identify differences between control and treatment groups at pretest, t tests were performed using a questionnaire of motivational and learning strategies (Motivated Strategies for Learning Questionnaire—MSLQ, Pintrich, Smith, Garcia, & McKeachie, 1989). (See upcoming Measures section for a description of the instrument.)

Eleven scales on the instrument were analyzed including: (a) 4 motivational scales (intrinsic motivation, alpha = .66; task value, alpha = .88; self-efficacy, alpha = .79; and expectancy for success, alpha = .84); (b) 4 cognitive engagement scales (rehearsal, alpha = .62; elaboration, alpha = .76; organization, alpha = .75; and metacognition, alpha = .78); (c) 2 resource management scales (time/study management, alpha = .78; and effort management, alpha = .62); and (d) critical thinking, alpha = .72.

T tests suggested that treatment subjects ($n = 110$) exceeded control subjects ($n = 88$) on 3 of 11 pretest scales: (a) organization (the subject selects key ideas and then uses outlines, charts, and other tools to arrange them meaningfully) ($p < .06$), (b) time/study management (the subject allocates sufficient time to studying and selects sites conducive to study) (p < .01), and (c) pretest critical thinking (the subject questions assertions made in course material, seeks supporting evidence, and develops his or her own ideas related to those presented in class) (p < .05).

A "subsample," employed to gather more in-depth information on the subjects, was created and consisted of 5 randomly selected subjects per class per semester (n = 30). T tests revealed no significant differences between the subsample (n = 30) and total sample (n = 174) on any of the 11 motivational or cognitive scales on the self-report measure at pre- or posttest.

Course Descriptions for the Control Semester

Children's literature was a 200-level baccalaureate course designed to increase a student's knowledge and appreciation of fiction written for children and adolescents. The course was required for students seeking a teaching certificate. Ecology was a 400-level baccalaureate course designed to provide students with an understanding of basic ecological concepts and systems. Philosophy was a 100-level community college course designed to introduce students to basic philosophical principles and thinkers, and to explore the value of studying philosophy in one's daily life.

All three instructors used a combination of lecture and discussion in the control semester.

Training Procedures

Each instructor received the following background material: (a) general information about college student cognitive growth (Perry, 1988); (b) a chapter on dialogical thinking (Paul, 1987); (c) a training packet including step-by-step written instructions for classroom application; and (d) a series of exercises tailoring dialogical instruction to individual course topics. The training packet and exercises were withheld until after the completion of the control semester to lessen the likelihood for infusion of the treatment technique into control semester instruction.

Preceding the treatment semester, each instructor engaged in an individualized training session where he or she practiced the technique using simulated exercises.

Course Descriptions for the Treatment Semester

The common thread running throughout all three courses in the treatment semester was the practice of presenting multiple viewpoints in the classroom, and then asking students to argue from various points of view (particularly those that opposed their own). However, the technique's application varied widely in each of the three courses.

In the literature course, students were asked to: (a) defend or oppose the appropriateness of using select course texts in an elementary school curricula (e.g., some students were asked to argue that a text promoted delinquent behavior, and therefore should not be used; other students were asked to argue that the same text promoted responsible behavior, and therefore should be used); and (b) analyze course texts from diverse literary traditions (e.g., first a Marxist, then a feminist perspective).

In the ecology course, (a) some students were asked to defend either photosynthesis as the earth's initial primary oxidizing source, other students were asked to defend photorespiration as the earth's initial primary oxidizing source; and (b) students who personally supported hunting were asked to argue that hunting is "poor ecological practice," students who personally opposed hunting were asked to argue that hunting is "good ecological practice."

In the philosophy course: (a) some small groups were asked to supply evidence supporting the position that Socrates a great man, whereas other small groups were asked to supply evidence supporting the opposing view; and (b) students were asked to state whether all adults were entitled to a college education, and then to argue the opposing view.

Documentation of Intervention Use

First, all three instructors were asked to submit a log documenting each application of dialogical instruction by describing: (a) the activity; (b) the level and quality of student response; (c) the amount of time on intervention; and (d) lessons that he or she learned from the current implementation that could be applied to future implementations. Second, 2 to 3 class sessions per course per semester were videotaped for documentation purposes.

MEASURES

Higher Order Thinking

Subsample subjects received an essay performance measure to test higher order thinking: The Test of Thematic Analysis (Winter & McClelland, 1978). The higher order measure tapped a subject's ability to organize six short but complicated vignettes by developing meaningful categories and identifying overarching similarities across categories. It measured a variety of reasoning skills including drawing valid comparisons and recognizing qualifications (analysis), identifying themes from discrete information sources (synthesis), and basing judgements on fact rather than affective and subjective criteria (evaluation). Thus, the instrument appeared to be a face-valid measure of higher order thinking.

The researcher administered the measure to the subsample (n = 30) within the last week of class (posttest only). Participants had 25 minutes to complete the task.

Subsample subjects were scored on nine criteria. They received points for drawing valid comparisons, identifying overarching themes, and recognizing qualifications; they were penalized for drawing erroneous comparisons and basing judgements on affective or subjective criteria. Total points possible per subject ranged from -3 to +6.

Each subsample subject received a total score. Class means were derived by averaging the total scores of the five subjects per class.

Two independent coders (one blind) scored within one point of each other on 91.6 % of the data. A perfect match was achieved on 58.3% of subjects. The nonblind coder's score was recorded when disagreements between the two coders surfaced.

Multilogical Thinking

Subsample subjects received an essay performance measure to test multilogical thinking: The Analysis of Argument Test (Stewart, 1977). This instrument tapped a subject's "intellectual flexibility," or the ability to reason clearly and objectively from multiple viewpoints when dealing with controversial and emotionally charged issues. Therefore, it appeared to be a face-valid measure of the objectivity component of multilogical thinking. Stewart (1977) reported slight positive correlations between the Analysis of Argument Test and standard aptitude measures (e.g., SAT r = .20), and no relationship to "objective concept formation" or reasoning measures.

The researcher administered the instrument to the subsample (n = 30) within the last week of the semester (posttest only). Subsample subjects were instructed to read a 300-word stimuli passage that expressed an extreme position on childrearing practices, and then to write a 5-minute response arguing against the author's position. When time had elapsed, and without warning, subjects were directed to write a 5-minute response supporting the author's position. Participants had 15 minutes to complete the total exercise.

The test penalized, with a negative score, those subjects who allowed emotionality and bias to interfere with reasoning from multiple perspectives (and who therefore respond less convincingly to the stimulus) and rewarded, with a positive score, those subjects who responded objectively from multiple perspectives.

Subsample subjects were rated on six criteria in scoring the "attack" response and on four criteria in scoring the "defense" response including: breaking down positions into separate elements, evaluating arguments on the basis of merits instead of emotionally-charged opinions or beliefs, and developing coherent and logical responses under both test conditions. Total points possible per subject ranged from -5 to +5.

Each subsample subject received a total score. Class means were derived by averaging the total scores of the five subjects per class.

Two independent coders (one blind) scored within two points of each other on 93.3% of subjects, and within one point of each other on 73.3% of subjects. A perfect match was achieved on 33.3% of subjects. The nonblind coder's scores were recorded when disagreements between the two coders arose.

Critical Thinking

Subjects received the MSLQ (Pintrich et al., 1989), an 85-item instrument designed to assess students' motivational orientations and use of study skills and learning strategies in a specific course. The instrument included a 5-item critical thinking scale describing various critical thinking behaviors including seeking supporting evidence and questioning assumptions and assertions (see Table 12.2). Subjects rated statements on a 7-point scale (*not at all like me* —1—to *very much like me* —7—).

Each instructor administered the MSLQ to the total sample (N = 204) at pretest (within the first week of class) and at posttest (within the last week of class). The mean of the scale was calculated by averaging all five items. Means were derived for all six classes. The alpha for the critical thinking scale was .72.

LIMITATIONS

The study's limitations fall into two major groups: (a) measure validity, and (b) power.

The first limitation involves the multilogical thinking performance measure. Recall that in this study multilogical thinking was defined as capturing the attitudinal or dispositional side of critical thinking, and the researcher outlined three major types of critical attitudes (openness, inquisitiveness, and objectivity) (see Definitions section). However, the Analysis of Argument Test tapped only the latter type of critical attitude, objectivity. Critical attitudes such as inquisitiveness and openness may be better assessed via observations or self-report measures. Clearly, they were not tapped in the Stewart (1977) performance measure.

Therefore, serious questions arise as to whether the multilogical performance instrument measured the full scope of multilogical thinking that it was intended to measure, thereby calling into question the validity of this measure.

A second key limitation is the small number of subjects receiving the study's performance measures. As noted, only the subsample (5 subjects per class per semester, n = 30) received the higher order thinking and multilogical thinking performance measures. (In contrast, all 204 subjects received the MSLQ self-report measure, pre- and post-). Thirty subjects, across the two semesters, is a small number on which to generalize the study's performance data.

No significant differences emerged between the subsample and total sample at pre- or posttest on the 11 scales of the self-report measure (see Sample section). Nevertheless, problems of low power plagued the study.

RESULTS

T tests, regression analyses, and two-way analyses of variance were conducted to test for mean differences between control and treatment groups on higher order thinking performance, multilogical thinking performance, and self-report critical thinking.

TABLE 12.2
Items on the Critical Thinking Scale of the MSLQ[a]

42. I often find myself questioning things I hear or read in this course to decide if I find them convincing.

51. When a theory, interpretation, or conclusion is presented in class or in the readings, I try to decide if there is good supporting evidence.

55. I treat the course material as a starting point and try to develop my own ideas about it.

70. I try to play around with ideas of my own related to what I am learning in this course.

75. Whenever I read or hear an assertion or conclusion in this class, I think about possible alternatives.

[a]Pintrich et al., 1989

Higher Order and Multilogical Thinking

On higher order thinking performance data, *t* tests were conducted to assess mean differences in the control-treatment subsample (n = 30). Control and treatment means were in the directions predicted when all three courses were combined, and in the literature and ecology courses (see Table 12.3). However, control and treatment means were not in the directions predicted in the philosophy course (note: the standard deviation suggested more variance with the philosophy treatment group). Mean differences were statistically significant in the literature course only.

On multilogical thinking performance data, *t* tests were conducted to assess mean differences in the control-treatment subsample (n = 30). Control and treatment means were in the directions predicted in the literature and ecology courses (see Table 12.4). Again, however, control and treatment means were not in the directions predicted in the philosophy course. Mean differences were not statistically significant in any of the three courses.

Overall, the pattern of data for higher order and multilogical thinking performance supports the researcher's hypotheses in the literature and ecology courses, suggesting a positive treatment effect for these courses.

Critical Thinking

On the critical thinking scale of the self-report measure, first, *t* tests were conducted to analyze control-treatment mean differences of the total sample (n = 162). Treatment and control means were in the directions predicted in each of three courses individually and combined (see Table 12.5). Although mean differences were not statistically significant, nevertheless, the probability of a treatment mean exceeding a control mean in 4 out of 4 groups is 1 in 8 (and the combined probability is approximately .01). Therefore, a trend favoring the treatment group emerged.

Second, two-way analysis of variance was performed to test the relationship between the treatment and critical thinking, moderated by four motivational variables (intrinsic motivation, task value, self-efficacy, and expectancy for success). All variables were self-report and posttest.

Subjects were divided into two groups (high and low) on each of the four moderating variables (e.g., low intrinsic, high intrinsic; low task value, high task value, etc.). Groups were split at the median. (Note:

TABLE 12.3
Course Means on the Higher Order Thinking Performance Test[a]

Course	C/T[b]	n	Posttest mean[c]	SD	One-tail prob
Combined	C	15	2.067	1.163	0.121
	T	15	2.867	1.552	
Bac—Lit	C	5	1.600	1.342	0.050*
	T	5	3.200	0.837	
Bac—Eco	C	5	2.400	1.517	0.713
	T	5	2.800	1.789	
CC—Phl	C	5	2.200	0.447	0.817
	T	5	2.000	1.826	

[a]Winter & McClelland, 1978

[b]C = control, T = treatment

[c]Range = -3, +6

* p < .05. ** p < .01. *** p < .001.

TABLE 12.4
Course Means on the Multilogical Thinking Performance Test[a]

Course	C/T[b]	n	Posttest mean[c]	SD	One-tail prob
Combined	C	15	-1.133	1.846	0.910
	T	15	-1.200	1.320	
Bac—Lit	C	5	-1.800	1.304	0.453
	T	5	-1.200	1.095	
Bac—Eco	C	5	-0.400	2.408	0.731
	T	5	0.000	0.707	
CC—Phl	C	5	-1.200	1.789	0.329
	T	5	-2.250	0.957	

[a]Stewart, 1977

[b]C = control, T = treatment

[c]Range = -5, +5

* $p < .05$. ** $p < .01$. *** $p < .001$.

TABLE 12.5

Course Means on the Critical Thinking Scale of the MSLQ[a]

Course	C/T[b]	n	Posttest mean[c]	SD	One-tail prob
Combined	C	68	4.4794	1.098	0.126
	T	94	4.7707	1.251	
Bac—Lit	C	26	4.1231	1.032	0.117
	T	38	4.6105	1.309	
Bac—Eco	C	26	4.4769	0.891	0.381
	T	40	4.7212	1.214	
CC—Phl	C	16	5.0625	1.304	0.627
	T	16	5.2750	1.140	

[a]Pintrich et al., 1989

[b]C = control, T = treatment

[c]Range = +1, +7

* p < .05. ** p < .01. *** p < .001.

cell distributions were often unequal, and in the case of the philosophy course, produced extremely low *n*s.) (See Tables 12.6–12.9.)

Main effects

A number of main effects of motivation on self-report critical thinking emerged including: (a) a main effect of *intrinsic motivation* in the literature, ecology, and combined courses (p < .05, see Table 12.6); (b) a main effect of *task value* in the ecology and combined courses (p < .05, see Table 12.7); and (c) a main effect of *self-efficacy* in the literature, ecology, and combined courses (p < .05, see Table 12.8). A main effect of *expectancy for success* approached statistical significance in the ecology course (p < .06, see Table 12.9). These findings suggest that subjects who report higher motivation also report higher critical thinking. This trend held true regardless of a subject's control or treatment status.

Two-way interactions

Several significant two-way interactions emerged. When all three courses were combined, among subjects who rated themselves *high on task value*, treatment subjects tended to rate themselves *higher* than control subjects *on critical thinking* [t(61) = 2.99, p = .004], whereas among subjects who rated themselves *low on task value*, control and treatment subjects tended to rate themselves *similarly on critical thinking* [t(90) = .50, p = .618]. (See Table 12.7 and Fig. 12.1.)

Likewise, in the literature course, among subjects who rated themselves *high on task value*, treatment subjects tended to rate themselves *significantly higher* than control subjects *on critical thinking* [t(24) = 3.53, p = .002], whereas among subjects who rated themselves *low on task value*, control and treatment subjects tended to rate themselves *similarly on critical thinking* [t(35) = .30, p = .768]. (See Table 12.7 and Fig. 12.2.) Also in the literature course, among subjects who rated themselves *high on self-efficacy*, treatment subjects tended to rate themselves *significantly higher* than control subjects *on critical thinking* [t(32) = 2.52, p = .017], whereas among subjects who tended to rate themselves *low on self-efficacy*, control and treatment subjects tended to rate themselves *similarly on critical thinking* [t(27) = .29, p = .774]. (See Table 12.8 and Fig. 12.3.)

In the ecology course, among subjects who rated themselves *high on expectancy for success*, treatment subjects tended to rate themselves *significantly higher* than control subjects *on critical thinking* [t(12) = 2.60, p = .023], whereas among subjects who rated themselves *low on*

TABLE 12.6
Two-Way Interactions Between the Treatment and Critical Thinking, Moderated by Intrinsic Motivation, on the MSLQ[a]

	Control Critical Thinking Posttest Mean[b]		Treatment Critical Thinking Posttest Mean		F Main Effect Intr Moto	F Main Effect Treatment	F Two-Way Interaction
	Low Intr Moto Grp	High Intr Moto Grp	Low Intr Moto Grp	High Intr Moto Grp			
Combined							
	n = 36	n = 32	n = 52	n = 35	36.28***	3.35	2.002
	4.12	4.89	4.22	5.48			
Bac—Lit							
	n = 16	n = 10	n = 21	n = 16	16.41***	2.49	2.56
	3.90	4.48	3.97	5.45			
Bac—Eco							
	n = 15	n = 11	n = 26	n = 14	16.89***	1.66	1.30
	4.19	4.87	4.28	5.54			
CC—Philosophy							
	n = 5	n = 11	n = 5	n = 5	1.33	.165	.034
	4.60	5.27	4.92	5.40			

[a]Pintrich et al., 1989
[b]Range = +1, +7
+ $p < .06$. * $p < .05$. ** $p < .01$. *** $p < .001$.

TABLE 12.7

Two-Way Interactions Between the Treatment and Critical Thinking, Moderated Task Value, on the MSLQ[a]

	Control Critical Thinking Posttest Mean[b]		Treatment Critical Thinking Posttest Mean		F Main Effect Task Value	F Main Effect Treatment	F Two-Way Interaction
	Low Task Value Grp	High Task Value Grp	Low Task Value Grp	High Task Value Grp			
Combined	$n = 39$	$n = 29$	$n = 53$	$n = 47$			
	4.39	4.59	4.28	5.42	15.83***	2.26	6.70*
Bac—Lit	$n = 14$	$n = 12$	$n = 23$	$n = 14$			
	4.37	3.83	4.24	5.21	1.20	2.97	6.23*
Bac—Eco	$n = 16$	$n = 10$	$n = 25$	$n = 15$			
	4.29	4.78	4.21	5.57	17.10***	1.08	2.93
CC—Phl	$n = 9$	$n = 7$	$n = 5$	$n= 5$			
	4.62	5.63	4.76	5.56	3.94	.007	.046

[a]Pintrich et al., 1989
[b]Range = +1, +7
+ $p < .06$. * $p < .05$. ** $p < .01$. *** $p < .001$.

TABLE 12.8

Two-Way Interactions Between the Treatment and Critical Thinking, Moderated by Self-Efficacy, on the MSLQ[a]

	Control Critical Thinking Posttest Mean[b]		Treatment Critical Thinking Posttest Mean		F Main Effect Self-Effi	F Main Effect Treatment	F Two-Way Interaction
	Low Self-Effi Grp	High Self-Effi Grp	Low Self-Effi Grp	High Self-Effi Grp			
Combined	$n = 36$	$n = 34$	$n = 50$	$n = 37$			
	4.28	4.68	4.28	5.32	17.13***	2.74	3.081
Bac—Lit	$n = 11$	$n = 15$	$n = 18$	$n = 19$			
	4.09	4.15	3.98	5.21	6.87***	3.39	4.05*
Bac—Eco	$n = 18$	$n = 8$	$n = 27$	$n = 13$			
	4.40	4.65	4.31	5.58	11.00***	.819	3.56
CC—Phl	$n = 5$	$n = 11$	$n = 5$	$n = 5$			
	4.28	5.42	5.28	5.04	1.28	.168	1.90

[a]Pintrich et al., 1989

[b]Range = +1, +7

+ $p < .06$. * $p < .05$. ** $p < .01$. *** $p < .001$.

TABLE 12.9

Two-Way Interactions Between the Treatment and Critical Thinking, Moderated by Expectancy for Success, on the MSLQ[a]

	Control Critical Thinking Posttest Mean[b]		Treatment Critical Thinking Posttest Mean		F Main Effect Expt Succ	F Main Effect Treatment	F Two-Way Interaction
	Low Expt Succ Grp	High Expt Succ Grp	Low Expt Succ Grp	High Expt Succ Grp			
Combined							
	n = 40	n = 28	n = 46	n = 41			
	4.42	4.56	4.41	5.08	5.36*	1.35	1.98
Bac—Lit							
	n = 13	n = 13	n = 13	n = 24			
	4.18	4.06	4.34	4.76	.335	2.11	.721
Bac—Eco							
	n = 21	n = 5	n = 31	n = 9			
	4.50	4.40	4.45	5.64	5.25*	.706	3.90+
CC—Phl							
	n = 6	n = 10	n = 2	n = 8			
	4.70	5.28	4.20	5.40	2.10	.005	.228

[a]Pintrich et al., 1989

[b]Range = +1, +7

$+ p < .06.$ $* p < .05.$ $** p < .01.$ $*** p < .001.$

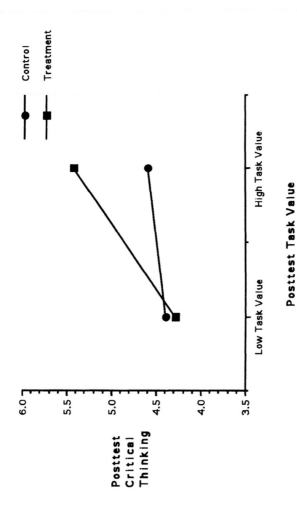

Fig. 12.1. Posttest critical thinking by posttest task value and treatment on the MSLQ, all courses combined.

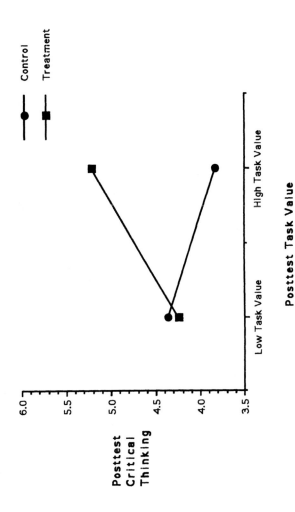

Fig. 12.2. Posttest critical thinking by post-test task value and treatment on the MSLQ, literature course.

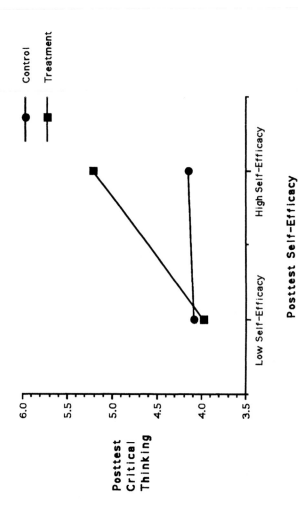

Fig. 12.3. Posttest critical thinking by posttest self-efficacy and treatment on the MSLQ, literature course.

expectancy for success, control and treatment subjects tended to rate themselves *similarly on critical thinking* [t(50) = .14, p = .891]. (See Table 12.9 and Fig. 12.4.)

In the philosophy course, none of the interactions between the treatment and critical thinking (moderated by motivation) was statistically significant. (See Tables 12.6–12.9.)

In summary, the two-way interaction data suggest that the treatment works only with students who report that they are highly motivated. Specifically, positive treatment effects on self-report critical thinking surfaced when task value, self-efficacy, and expectancy for success variables were taken into account. That is, the treatment tends to make a difference in self-report critical thinking among subjects who value course tasks highly (literature, combined courses); who are highly efficacious (literature); and who have high expectancy for success (ecology). The most profound treatment effects on self-report critical thinking occurred in the literature course when moderated by task value (see Fig. 12.2), suggesting that the treatment has the strongest positive effect on literature students who value course tasks highly.

DISCUSSION AND IMPLICATIONS

Treatment Effects: The Relationship between Dialogical Instruction and Higher Order and Multilogical Thinking Performance

On performance data, control and treatment means were in the directions predicted, on both types of thinking (higher order and multilogical), in the literature and ecology courses (see Tables 12.3–12.4). Although mean differences were significant in the literature course only, the pattern of these data suggest a positive relationship between dialogical instruction and students' performance on tests requiring analysis, synthesis, evaluation, and objective reasoning from multiple perspectives.

Main Effects: The Motivation-Critical Thinking Connection

Significant main effects surfaced for all 4 motivational variables (intrinsic motivation, task value, self-efficacy, and expectancy for success) on self-report critical thinking, suggesting a strong link between motivation and critical thinking.(see Tables 12.6–12.9). That is, subjects who reported high motivation tended to report high critical thinking, whether or not they received dialogical instruction. These findings support a growing

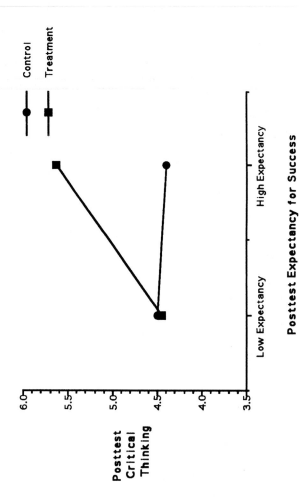

Fig. 12.4. Posttest critical thinking by posttest expectancy for success and treatment on the MSLQ, ecology course.

body of literature which suggests important interactions between motivational and cognitive spheres of learning (McKeachie et al, 1990; Pintrich, 1988, Resnick, 1987). Specifically, these data suggest that four aspects of motivation tend to be consistent with high student self-ratings of critical thinking: (a) a strong desire for mastery of course concepts (intrinsic motivation); (b) viewing course tasks as highly important, useful, and interesting (task value), (c) a high certainty that one can learn and understand course material (self-efficacy), and (d) a high expectation for course success (expectancy).

Interaction Effects: The Moderating Effects of Motivation in Dialogical Instruction

Motivation-treatment interactions proved to be important in understanding which students benefit most from dialogical instruction. Using self-report critical thinking as the dependent variable, no main effects emerged. However, several significant interactions surfaced between the treatment and self-report critical thinking when moderated by task value, self-efficacy, and expectancy for success. The relationship was positive: higher motivation and higher critical thinking went hand-in-hand.

The strongest of these effects was among literature subjects who rated themselves high on task value (see Table 12.7 and Fig. 12.2). These data suggest that the greatest positive treatment effects in self-report critical thinking occur with treatment subjects who perceive course material as highly interesting, important, and useful to learn. One explanation for this finding is that high task value students appear to operate under the belief that understanding course material is important, and thereby may be willing to engage in dialogical instruction as a means of enhancing understanding. Low task value students appear to operate under a different set of beliefs in which understanding course material is not as important, and thereby their willingness to engage in a technique that promotes deeper understanding may also be lower. Therefore, underlying beliefs in course task value may shape a student's decision to engage in dialogical instruction, and enhance or diminish its effect on his or her critical thinking.

Dreyfus, Jungwirth, & Eliovitch (1990) conclude that for students who perceive school knowledge as distinct from practical, everyday knowledge "the efficacy of an otherwise meaningful conflict may be impaired" because they fail to connect with it (p. 568). Dreyfus et al.

make a clear connection between the perceived utility of the task and the ability of the task to stimulate the desired cognitive dissonance. Similarly, the utility of dialogical instruction as a method of critical thinking hinges on the notion that, in fact, it creates a dissonance in the learner. The perception by students that course tasks used in dialogical instruction have little utility or value may lead to student apathy and disengagement. Instead of creating dissonance within the student, the student may simply remain disengaged and unmoved by the stimulus. As a result, dialogical techniques used with the "low-task value student" may fail to create the state of dissonance the techniques were designed to create.

Differences in Treatment Effects Across Courses: Instructional Factors in Successful Dialogical Instruction Designs

Treatment effects were not consistent across the three courses. For example, the data tended to confirm the researcher's hypotheses in the literature and ecology courses, and most consistently in the literature course. In the following sections, three possible explanations are posited to explain why the results are most consistent with hypotheses in the literature course: time on treatment, rewards for thinking, and instructor role modeling.

Time on Treatment

A first factor distinguishing between the literature course and the other two courses is time on treatment. Instructor self-reports revealed that the greatest number of minutes devoted to dialogical instruction occurred in the literature course (525 minutes of instructor-logged time)—approximately two times the amount devoted in the other two courses.

Quellmalz (1987) suggested that in order for classroom inquiry approaches (like dialogical instruction) to be successful, students must engage in "*sustained* inquiry," if they are to acquire "strategic patterns" in critical thinking (p. 95, italics added). Sustained inquiry may entail infusing dialogical instruction, at some level, as part of every class period (e.g., asking students to begin each class period by stating a position and then articulating an opposing one). Likewise, dialogical thinking skills might become a required element in all out-of-class assignments such as papers and projects. Imagine a paper in which the entire exercise was to demonstrate that one had traversed through all five stages of dialogical thinking: from stating and supporting one's position, to critiquing it, to generating alternatives, to rendering a final judgment after consideration of multiple perspectives.

For maximum effect, dialogical thinking should be infused in as many learning activities as possible—in class as students engage in discussion about course issues, and out-of-class as students read, consider, and actively apply course material. Even with such a "total" approach to dialogical instruction, the effects that instructors and researchers can expect dialogical instruction to reap if contained within a single course are limited, particularly if rote learning/drill-and-practice instructional methods are used in all other courses. Ideally, direct critical thinking methods would be sustained across several courses (Quellmalz, 1987), or across clusters of courses in a student's academic program. Had the same students enrolled in all three courses that included dialogical instruction (literature, ecology, and philosophy—i.e., a cross-curricular approach), the results may have favored the treatment more overwhelmingly. All in all, the positive treatment effects in the literature course support Quellmalz' arguments for sustained approaches to critical thinking interventions.

Rewards for thinking

A second factor distinguishing between the literature course and the other two courses is reward structure. A review of course tasks in the three courses studied revealed that less than 25% of graded course tasks required higher order thinking and less than 10% required multilogical thinking. Although the percentages were quite low across all three courses, again, the highest percentages fell in the literature course.

Extrinsic rewards for demonstrating critical thinking should be carefully considered when using direct critical thinking interventions like dialogical instruction. Clearly, it sends one message to students to encourage dialogical thinking in class discussions. It sends quite another to also require dialogical thinking skills on the assignments, papers, projects and exams that constitute a student's final grade.

Assuming that students do well on critical thinking tasks, the effects of explicitly stated and high-extrinsic rewards for critical thinking may serve as a motivator for engagement in dialogical instruction, and lead ultimately to greater positive treatment effects. Re-running the experiment in which the percentages of graded course tasks requiring higher order and lower order skills were reversed (i.e., where lower order thinking skills were required in only 25% of graded course tasks, and higher order and multilogical thinking skills on the other 75%), and examining differences in treatment effects would test this explanation.

A review of videotapes taken during the control and treatment semesters of instruction showed that each of the three instructors utilized some verbal praise during dialogical instruction to encourage student participation (e.g., "that's good," "keep going"). Therefore, some informal reward mechanisms for critical thinking were present in classroom discourse. However, the fact that critical thinking was not reinforced through more formal means in graded tests and assignments may have diluted the effectiveness of informal reward mechanisms, and thereby in stimulating student critical thinking overall.

To the extent that the literature course had the highest extrinsic rewards for critical thinking overall (25% for higher order thinking), the data suggests that direct critical thinking methods have the best chance for success in classrooms that reward heavily for demonstrating critical thinking skills.

Instructor role modeling

A third critical element distinguishing between the literature course and the other two courses was the consistent use of instructor role modeling. In log entries kept during the treatment semester, the literature instructor repeatedly reported using some form of role modeling in which he demonstrated the precise dialogical thinking behaviors in which he would ask his students to engage. Modeling often took the form of "playing devil's advocate" where a student stated a personal view and the instructor stated an opposing one.

In one logged report, the literature instructor indicated some concern with this approach, fearing that he was "giving students the answer." However, role modeling proved to be an important first step toward educating the students to new classroom norms and to new ways of thinking.

Consistent with scaffolding models of instruction (see Palinscar, 1986), the amount of instructor guidance in the literature course gradually decreased as students' exposure to the method and their familiarity and facility with it increased. The scaffolding approach is evident in the literature instructor's log entries which show the preponderance of instructor role modeling within the first three weeks of entries. In later entries, such references virtually disappeared.

An important observation was that instructor role modeling need not be flawless to be effective. One might assume that an awkwardly handled role modeling episode would be more detrimental than no modeling at all (i.e., a mis-handled role modeling session might lead a student to think: If the instructor-expert cannot think dialogically, how can I?) In fact, the opposite appears to be true. Based on instructor logs and videotapes of treatment semester instruction, student participation seemed to rise rather than fall after role modeling sessions, whether handled awkwardly or well.

This finding is consistent with Schunk, Hanson, & Cox's (1987) research favoring coping models in which the modeler encounters difficulties, and in the process, demonstrates strategies for overcoming the obstacles faced. Likewise, the data from the dialogical thinking study suggest that instructor role modeling need not be done perfectly, it simply needs to be done.

Role modeling may be an important step in the dialogical instruction process for two other reasons. First, dialogical instruction is a sophisticated, complex, and intellectually demanding technique requiring that students think not only at high cognitive levels (e.g., analyze, synthesize, and evaluate) but also in new ways (e.g., from multiple perspectives). By modeling each step, instructors may help students grasp the intricacies of this complex process.

Second, through modeling, instructors demonstrate to students that they are willing to take the same risks of failure, embarrassment, and critical examination of positions that they are asking students to assume. Studies show that Socratic forms of classroom inquiry can be anxiety-producing (see Tribe & Tribe, 1987) and laden with social risk (Resnick, 1987). Role modeling is the instructor's show of good faith that he or she, too, is fully engaged in the process, and that all members of the classroom share equally in the technique's benefits and risks.

Role modeling may be an important variable in the success of any instructional method or process. However, its importance may well increase with a teaching technique's complexity, divergence from traditional classroom practices and expectations, and element of risk. To be sure, dialogical instruction clearly ranks high on all three criteria. Overall, the literature instructor's consistent use of role modeling may have contributed to the positive treatment effects in the literature course.

SUMMARY

In summary, dialogical instruction appears to work with students who value course tasks highly, are efficacious, and expect to do well in the course. Treatment subjects with these motivational attributes tended to report higher critical thinking than their control counterparts. However, the results tended to vary by course, suggesting that treatment effects of dialogical instruction rest not only with whether dialogical instruction was implemented, but for how long and in what ways. An analysis of the three courses suggested that dialogical instruction has positive effects on critical thinking when used regularly, when students are rewarded for demonstrating critical thinking on graded tests an assignments, and when supported by consistent instructor role modeling.

This study suggests that direct critical thinking methods have the best chance for success when the teaching method is one part of an entire instructional design working in concert to achieve critical thinking aims. Future designs should see that a number of instructional processes, beyond the teaching method proper, are aligned to support critical thinking goals, for example, (a) critical thinking objectives, as opposed to knowledge acquisition objectives, serve as the cornerstone of the course, (b) course texts that promote higher order thinking and that present multiple perspectives on single issues are selected, and (c) graded tests and assignments are weighted heavily toward analysis, synthesis, evaluation, and multilogical thinking skills.

One recommendation of this study is that researchers and educators continue to try direct critical thinking methods like dialogical instruction, but not before they lay the proper groundwork for these innovations. With more holistic approaches to the design of interventions, direct critical thinking methods have a fair chance at success.

ACKNOWLEDGMENT

The research discussed in this chapter was conducted at the Teaching and Learning Program of the National Center for Research to Improve Postsecondary Teaching and Learning (NCRIPTAL) under the kind and astute direction of Dr. Wilbert J. (Bill) McKeachie. The initial idea for the study was greatly influenced by Bill, who has dedicated several decades to studying the art and science of teaching as it relates to student learning. I am unsure whether I am more grateful to Bill for *his science* or *his art*. I thank him for taking an interest in the ideas of those of us around him, for supporting us as we developed our ideas, and for challenging us to unravel and re-think them.

REFERENCES

Association of American Colleges. (1985) *Integrity in the college curriculum: A report to the academic community.* Washington, DC: Association of American Colleges.

Bereiter, C. (1984). How To keep thinking skills from going the way of all frills. *Educational Leadership, 42*(1), 75–77.

Beyer, B. K. (1985). Teaching critical thinking: A direct approach. *Social Education, 49*(1), 303.

Bloom, B. S. (Ed.). (1956). *Taxonomy of educational objectives, Handbook I: Cognitive domain.* New York: Longmans, Green.

Brookfield, S. (1987). *Understanding and facilitating adult learning* (3rd ed.). San Francisco: Jossey-Bass.

Chipman, S., Segal, J., & Glaser, R. (1985). *Thinking and learning skills* (Vol. III). Hillsdale, NJ: Lawrence Erlbaum Associates.

Clarke, J. (1988). Designing discussions as group inquiry. *College Teaching 36*(4), 140–143.

Daloz, L. A. (1986). *Effective teaching and mentoring.* San Francisco: Jossey-Bass.

deBono, E. (1983). The direct teaching of thinking as a skill. *Phi Delta Kappan 64*(10), 104.

DeNitto, J., & Strickland, J. (1987). Critical thinking: A skill for all seasons. *College Student Journal, 21*(2), 201–204.

Dreyfus, A., Jungwirth, E. & Eliovitch, R. (1990). Applying the "cognitive conflict" strategy for conceptual change--some implications, difficulties, and problems. *Science Education, 74*(5), 555–69.

Duncombe, S., & Heikkinen, M. (1989). Role playing for different viewpoints. *College Teaching, 36*(1), 3–5.

Ennis, R. (1987). A taxonomy of critical thinking dispositions and abilities. In J. Baron & R. Sternberg (Eds.), *Teaching thinking skills: Theory and practice* (pp. 9–26). New York: Freeman.

Fischer, C. G. & Grant, G. E. (1983). Intellectual levels in college classrooms. In C. Ellner & C. Barnes (Eds.). *Studies of college teaching* (pp. 47–59). Lexington, MA: Heath.

Fredericks, M., & Miller, S. I. (1990). Paradoxes, dilemmas, and teaching sociology. *Teaching Sociology, 18*(18), 347–355.

Furedy, C., & Furedy, J. (1985). Critical thinking: Toward research and dialogue. *Using Research to Improve Teaching: New Directions in Teaching and Learning, 23,* 51–69.

Glaser, R. (1984). Education and thinking: The role of knowledge. *American Psychologist, 39*(2), 93–104.

Glaser, R. (1985). Critical thinking: Educating for responsible citizenship in a democracy. *National Forum, 65,* 24–27.

Jackson, R. M. (1986, May). Thumbs up for direct teaching of thinking skills. *Educational Leadership,* 32–36.

Johnson, D. W., & Johnson, R. T. (1979). Conflict in the classroom: Controversy and learning. *Review of Educational Research, 49,* 51–61.

Johnson, D. W., & Johnson, R. T. (1985). Classroom conflict: Controversy vs. debate in learning groups. *American Educational Research Journal, 22,* 237–256.

Johnson, D. W., & Johnson, R. T. (1988). Critical thinking through structured controversy. *Educational Leadership, 45*(8), 58–64.

Keeley, S. M., Browne, N. M., & Kreutzer, J. S. (1982). A comparison of freshmen and seniors on general and specific essay tests of critical thinking. *Research in Higher Education, 17*(2), 139–154.

Lipman, M. (1987). Some thoughts on the foundation of reflective education. In J. B. Baron & R. J. Sternberg (Eds.), *Teaching thinking skills: Theory and practice* (pp. 151–161). New York: Freeman.

McKeachie, W. J., Pintrich, P. R., Lin, Y., Smith, D. A., & Sharma, R. (1990). *Teaching and learning in the college classroom: A review of the research literature* (2nd ed.). Ann Arbor: University of Michigan Regents.

McMillan, J. H. (1987). Enhancing college students' critical thinking: A review of studies. *Research in Higher Education, 26*(1), 3–29.

McPeck, J. E. (1981). *Critical thinking and education.* New York: St. Martin's Press.

National Institute of Education. (1984). *Involvement in learning: Realizing the potential of American higher education* (Stock No. 065-000-00213-2. Final report of the study group on the conditions of excellence in

American higher education). Washington, DC: Superintendent of Documents.

Nickerson, R. S. (1987). Why teach thinking? In J. B. Baron & R. J. Sternberg (Eds.), *Teaching thinking skills: Theory and practice* (pp. 27–40). New York: Freeman.

Palinscar, A. S. (1986.) The role of dialogue in providing scaffolded instruction. *Educational Psychologist, 21*(1–2), 73–98.

Paul, R. (1987). Dialogical thinking: Critical thought essential to the acquisition of rational knowledge and passions. In J. B. Baron & R. J. Sternberg (Eds.), *Teaching thinking skills: Theory and practice* (pp. 127–148). New York: Freeman.

Paul, R. (1992). *Critical thinking: What every person needs to survive in a rapidly changing world* (2nd ed.). Santa Rosa, CA: Foundation for Critical Thinking.

Perkins, D. N. (1987). Thinking frames: An integrative perspective on teaching cognitive skills. In J. B. Baron & R. J. Sternberg (Eds.), *Teaching thinking skills: Theory and practice* (pp. 41–61). New York: Freeman.

Perry, W. G., Jr. (1988). Cognitive and ethical growth: The making of meaning. In A. W. Chickering & Associates (Eds.), *The modern American college* (pp. 76–116). San Francisco: Jossey-Bass.

Pintrich, P. R. (1988). A process-oriented view of student motivation and cognition. In J. S. Stark and L. A. Mets (Eds.), Improving teaching and learning through research. *New directions for institutional research, 57,* (pp. 65–79). San Francisco: Jossey-Bass.

Pintrich, P. R., Smith, D. A., Garcia, T., & McKeachie, W. J. (1989). *Motivated Strategies for Learning Questionnaire* (OERI/ED). Ann Arbor: NCRIPTAL.

Presseisen, B. Z. (1986). *Thinking skills.* Washington, DC: National Education Association.

Quellmalz, E. S. (1987). Developing reasoning skills. In J. B. Baron & R. J. Sternberg (Eds.), *Teaching thinking skills: Theory and practice* (pp. 86–105). New York: Freeman.

Resnick, L. B. (1987). *Education and learning to think.* Washington, DC: National Academy Press.

Ruggiero, V. R. (1988). *Teaching thinking across the curriculum.* New York: Harper & Row.

Sadler, W. A., Jr. & Whimbey, A. (1985). A holistic approach to improving thinking skills. *Phi Delta Kappan, 67*(3), 199–203.

Schunk, D. H., Hanson, A. R., & Cox, P. D. (1987). Peer-model attributes and children's achievement behaviors. *Journal of Educational Psychology, 79*(1), 54–61.

Siegel, H. (1980). Critical thinking as an educational ideal. *The Educational Forum, 45,* 7–23.

Spracher, W. C. (1983). Teaching through informal debate. *NEWS for Teachers of Political Science, 3.*

Stewart, A. (1977). *Analysis of argument test: An empirically derived measure of intellectual flexibility.* Boston: McBer.

Swartz, R. J. (1987). Teaching for thinking: A developmental model for the infusion of thinking skills into mainstream instruction. In J. B. Baron & R. J. Sternberg (Eds.), *Teaching thinking skills: Theory and practice* (pp. 106–126). New York: Freeman.

Tribe, D. M. & Tribe, A. J. (1987). Lawteach: An interactive method for effective large group teaching. *Studies in Higher Education, 12*(3), 299–309.

Winter, D. & McClelland, D. (1978). Thematic analysis: An empirically derived measure of the effects of liberal education. *Journal of Educational Psychology, 70,* 8–16.

Woods, D. R. (1987). How might I teach problem solving? In J. E. Stice (Ed.), *Developing critical thinking and problem solving abilities. New Directions for Teaching and Learning* (No. 30). San Francisco: Jossey-Bass.

Worsham, A., & Stockton, A. (1986). *A model for teaching thinking: The inclusion process.* Bloomington, IN: Phi Delta Kappan.

13

Competition, Achievement, and Gender: A Stress Theoretical Analysis

Marita Inglehart
Donald R. Brown
Mina Vida

University of Michigan

The relationship between competition and achievement might seem to educational psychologists an issue resolved some time ago. After all, everybody "knows" that competitive situations are inferior to cooperative settings when it comes to letting students fulfill their potential (see Johnson & Johnson, 1975; Johnson, Maruyama, Johnson, Nelson, & Skon, 1981). Why would this chapter then revisit this issue?

One general reason for considering this issue one more time can be seen when looking at the title of this volume: *Student Motivation, Cognition, and Learning*. This title captures an understanding of student achievement as not just being driven by students' potentials and abilities or given opportunities for learning; it also implies that all learning is influenced by subjective factors, specifically by the way we feel and think about subject matters and learning. The way we feel and think about competitive settings is just one instance in which the significance of these factors can—and will be—demonstrated.

A more specific reason for this chapter relates to the frequency with which competition comes up when talking with undergraduate women about their career decision making. It is well documented that women do not persist to the same degree as male students in such undergraduate concentration areas as medicine (Inglehart, Brown, & Malanchuk, 1993). When talking with women who changed their concentration from pre-med to another area, quite frequently the stress of competing for top grades is mentioned as one reason for changing fields. This leads to the interesting research question of whether competition might have a different meaning for male than for female students and, as a result influences men's and women's performances in highly competitive settings differently.

With this specific interest and the general programmatic idea of "motivation, cognition, and learning" in mind we revisit the topic of competition and achievement. Our main hypothesis is that different ways of thinking about competition will influence student motivation and thus academic achievement. And we argue that there might be a tendency for the gender of a person to be connected with different ways of thinking about competition. The data presented are part of a longitudinal study of men and women in an integrated AB–MD program at the University of Michigan, the Inteflex Program, to examine (a) men's/women's relationships with competition, (b) the relationship between competition and achievement in general, and then (c) how men's and women's approach to competition might influence their achievement differently.

MEN, WOMEN, AND COMPETITION

"Women Join the Ranks of Science but Remain Invisible at the Top" (Angier, 1991) and "Analyzing the Managerial Gender Gap" (Cannings, 1991) are just two of many articles published during the last years that point to the filtering process that keeps women from getting into the most competitive (and prestigious and highest paid) positions in science and management. Economists or sociologists might look at this situation with Weber's notion of closure in mind—"the process by which social collectives seek to maximize rewards by restricting access to resources and opportunities to a limited circle of eligibles" (Parkin, 1979, p. 44). As psychologists we examine women's relationship with competition as one factor contributing to this filtering out of women on the way to the top. However, two notes of caution should be put at the outset of this endeavor. First and quite obviously, many other sociopsychological and structural factors are involved in this filtering process (see, e.g., Eccles, 1987; Paludi, 1990; Hall, 1982). Second, a "blame-the-victim" approach is unjustified when considering these issues. If women's appraisal of competition in an environment might lead to a decrease in their performance, then there is no reason to think of this as either the only reason or as demonstrating that women's ways of thinking cause the inequality in the job market. Instead it should contribute to understanding one aspect of the dynamic of this filtering process that keeps women from living up to their potentials and it should allow us to make suggestions to foster women's potential success.

When analyzing men and women's relationships with competition, it might be worthwhile to start with activities early on in life, namely with gender differences in playing activities. There is evidence that from early on in life consistent and substantial gender differences in playing activities can be found across a variety of species and cultures (Lever, 1978). *Rough-and-tumble play*—a term used to describe behaviors displayed during exuberant arousal that mimic more intentionally aggressive actions (DiPietro, 1981)—was found to be clearly a function of gender. The complexity of children's games also seems to be a function of gender with boys engaging more in play in larger groups and with a higher degree of interdependence between the players (Lever, 1978). Connections between these play activities early in life and later interaction styles and reactions to different environments have been reported by Coats and Overman (1992) who describe how women's childhood play experiences are related to women's choices of traditional versus nontraditional careers.

Gender differences are also found when analyzing adult men's and women's sports- and work-related activities and attitudes. Male athletes score higher on competitiveness and "win orientation" than female athletes (Gill, 1988), and female but not male athletes show increasing levels of competition-state anxiety the closer an actual competition comes. In a study of cooperative and competitive attitudes from Grades 2 through 12 girls showed consistently more positive attitudes toward cooperation in schools and boys showed consistently more positive attitudes toward competition (Ahlgren & Johnson, 1979). Similar studies with undergraduates report comparable results (see, e.g., Bohlmeyer, Burke, & Helmstadter, 1985). Furthermore, when studying attributions about the gender of participants in competitive versus cooperative interactions, it becomes obvious that there is a shared gender stereotype that associates competitive behavior with masculinity (King, Miles, & Kniska, 1991).

Looking at these and related studies, it can be argued that men and women differ in the way they approach competition. Men on the average are likely to value competition more highly than women. Furthermore, other gender differences in values—such as women scoring higher on person-related values than men and men scoring higher than women on mastery-related values (see Inglehart and Brown, 1989; Inglehart et al., 1993)—might relate to evaluations of competition and might shape how men and women appraise competitive settings. Women might view competition more in person-related terms and thus perceive these competitive situations in a more negative light, namely as situations that cast persons against each other instead of situations that aim at cooperation and giving social support. Men, on the other hand, might approach competition in a more positive way. Their mastery-orientation values might lead to their appraisal of competition as more positive and as a challenge they want to live up to.

In summary, we argue that, on the average, women tend to relate to competition more negatively than men. In connection with other gender differences in values, these differential appraisals of competition have consequences for men's and women's performance in competitive settings. For women, experiencing settings as competitive can be negative and thus be a handicap that keeps them from living up to their potentials. For men, competition might be seen as a challenge and thus provide the stimulation to really strive to perform at one's best.

Competition and Achievement

Since the 1920s, research has been conducted to investigate the influence of competition on achievement. This question intrigued social as well as educational psychologists for obvious reasons. Social psychologists were interested in this issue as part of their research of processes within groups and between groups (see, e.g., Deutsch, 1949; Kelley & Thibaut, 1969). Educational psychologists addressed this question in the larger framework of how to structure learning environments in such a way that they allow students to live up to their potentials (see, e.g., Johnson & Johnson, 1974, 1975).

A number of review articles were written that examine the effects of cooperative, competitive, and individualistic efforts on achievement (Hayes, 1976; Johnson & Johnson, 1974, 1975; Johnson et al., 1981; Michaels, 1977; Miller & Hamblin, 1963; Sharan, 1980; Slavin, 1977). One of the major controversies that resulted from these reviews is concerned with whether cooperation or competition promotes higher achievement. Whereas some psychologists argue that competition leads to greater achievement than does cooperation (see Michaels, 1977), others find evidence for the opposite effect (Sharan, 1980). The most comprehensive and sophisticated meta-analysis of research concerning this question was conducted by Johnson et al. (1981). This analysis shows that 109 of the 122 studies examined address the issue of whether competition or cooperation leads to a superior performance. Of these studies, 36 are inconclusive, 65 provide evidence that cooperation leads to a higher achievement than competition, and 8 demonstrate the opposite effect. The authors conclude that cooperation is clearly superior in its effect on achievement over competition.

One might argue that such a sophisticated and comprehensive statistical meta-analysis as the one conducted by Johnson et al. (1981) is exactly what is needed when research concerning a certain question remains inconclusive after years and dozens of studies. Undoubtedly, such a meta-analysis is extremely informative. However, at the same time, it is useful to think about the psychological processes that might be hidden behind the pure numbers reported in a meta-analysis. Specifically, one wonders why competition was superior to cooperation in 8 of the studies discussed, and why 36 studies were inconclusive in regard to this question (cf. Johnson et al., 1981). Starting with these questions in mind, we attempt to examine the psychological processes in a person working in a competitive environment and analyze their effects on achievement.

Our analysis starts with the assumption that a person in a competitive situation experiences stress. The resources a person perceives as having might be appraised as being not sufficient to gain the desired end results—due to the competition. This is exactly the situation that leads to the rise of stress. Since Lazarus entered the field of stress research in the 1960s (see Inglehart, 1991, for an overview), it has become widely accepted that stress is not primarily the function of an objective situation, but that a person's appraisal of this situation is crucial in determining his or her reactions. An example of this would be a situation in which 50 persons apply for 20 places in a clinical psychology program. If we assume that all 50 applicants know these numbers, one might argue that—objectively—they are in the same situation and should thus experience the same amount of stress due to this competition. However, according to Lazarus, one would have to consider exactly how these 50 applicants appraise this situation in order to understand how much stress each one will experience. Factors such as the person's appraisal of this situation as a challenge versus a threat, considerations of one's own resources and other options, will clearly influence the amount of stress that each of these applicants will experience.

Which forms could an appraisal of competition in an academic setting take? Lazarus (Lazarus and Folkman, 1984) argued that persons usually engage in a primary appraisal which is concerned with the person's subjective well-being in a situation with a stressor. In this sense, we would expect that the more a person appraises a situation as a challenge instead of as a potential harm, the better off the person will be. In a competitive academic setting this would imply that the more students actually value competition and see it as a challenge to show their real potential, the better off they should be academically. Accordingly, we hypothesize that the more our subjects, the Inteflex students, value competition, the better their achievement should be in a competitive situation (Hypothesis 1).

Two arguments can be given that support the reasoning leading to this hypothesis. First, it seems as if a person-environmental fit issue might be involved in this process. Persons who value competition highly have a better fit with a highly competitive environment, and thus, might outdo persons who do not value competition highly and who feel alienated in such a setting. There might be less of a problem for a competitive person to go along with the demands and challenges of a competitive environment than for a less competitive person.

Furthermore, a person who values competition highly might also be more achievement-oriented, or at least more clearly goal-structured and more highly motivated to perform well in a competitive setting, compared with a person who does not value competition highly. For both of these reasons, it seems important to consider the degree to which a person endorses competition as a moderating variable in such a situation.

The second way in which a competitive situation might be appraised is concerned with the degree to which relevant others in such a situation (faculty, administrators, other students) endorse competition as a value. From research on the significance of social support in stressful settings we know that social support can buffer negative effects of stress (see Inglehart, 1991, for an overview).

Perceiving others as highly competitive might be interpreted as a lack of social support and thus as detrimental for a person's performance. Accordingly, we expect that the more a person perceives relevant others as valuing competition highly—and thus as not being supportive—the less well a person will achieve (Hypothesis 2).

To summarize our ideas concerning the influence of competition on achievement, we argue that the effect that competition has on achievement depends on the appraisal processes that take place in a person when encountering competition. If the person focuses on the positive value of competition and appreciates achievement and competition, this person's achievement will be increased. On the other hand, if a person focuses on the degree to which relevant others in these situations value competition, the competition might be appraised as a lack of social support and one's performance should suffer. It is important to note that these two processes would be relevant for men and women, and that, for both men and women, the same appraisals should lead to the same outcomes. However, the degree to which men and women engage in these two types of appraisals might be different and thus the outcomes might differ as well.

Competition, Achievement, and Gender

There is evidence from research on the effects of classroom climates that there are gender-specific reactions to competition. These studies show that competitive classroom climates are detrimental to girls' achievement when compared with boys' achievement (Casserly, 1980; Kahle, 1984; Fennema & Peterson, 1986; Eccles, McIvor, & Lange, 1986). The girls' achievement decreased as more competitive interactions in the classrooms took place. Peterson and Fennema (1985) demonstrated for example that girls' cognitive gain scores are negatively related to the number of competitive interactions in a classroom and that they are positively related to the number of opportunities for cooperative and/or individualized learning.

If differential reactions to competition are based on differential appraisal processes of men and women, then the more both men and women value competition, the better they will perform, and the more both men and women perceive others as being competitive, the less well they will perform (Hypotheses 1 and 2 differentiated for gender). However, we would expect that when men and women look at a competitive environment, they focus on different aspects of this situation: Men focus more on the achievement-related, challenge aspect of this situation than women. In an extreme case, they might welcome the competition as a chance to live up to the challenge and demonstrate how great their potential is. Women, on the other hand, focus more on the person-related issues. They might, for example, miss relaxed get-togethers with their fellow students or supportive mentoring conversations with their superiors or instructors. Accordingly, we expect that the more women perceive an environment as competitive the less well they should do, and the more men perceive an environment as competitive the better they should do (Hypothesis 3).

METHOD

These hypotheses are tested on a sample of 534 (330 male and 204 female) students of an integrated AB–MD program (Inteflex Program) at the University of Michigan. They entered this program between 1975 and 1985. In the *second* year of this program, they answered a self-administered questionnaire that included three sets of 21 items concerning (a) the importance that they themselves place on such values as responsibility, empathy, conformity, and competition; (b) their evaluation of the importance that the faculty/administrators in the program; and (c) that other students in this program place on these values. Furthermore, this questionnaire also contained one set of 12 items concerned with the atmosphere in the medical school. These items asked such questions as how competitive, serious, hard-working and scientific was the ambience of the medical school. The questions and the alternatives used in the analyses are found in Table 13.1.

A principal axis factor analysis with Varimax rotation was conducted separately for each of these four sets of items. In each of the three analyses concerning the 21 items, one of the resulting factors had the items "conformity," "competition," "materialistic things," "good grades," and "adherence to rules" loading on it (see Table 13.2 for the results of these factor analyses). The sums of the respondents' answers to these five items for each of the three subsets were used as indices of (a) the students' own evaluation of competition, (b) their perception of the faculties'/administrators' evaluation of competition, and (c) the other students' evaluation of competition.

A factor analysis of the answers to the 11 items used to measure the students' evaluation of the medical school setting was also conducted. It resulted in a factor "competition" that had five items

TABLE 13.1
Questions Used to Measure the Different Aspects of Competition Studied Here

Scale 1: *How well do you think each of the following phrases describes the tone in the medical school?*

1a.   Intellectually stimulating
1b.   Competitive, grade conscious
1e.   Intense atmosphere, high standards
1h.   Scientific, research-oriented
1i.   Serious, hard-working

Answers: 1 = "not at all" to 5 = "very much"

Scales 2 to 4: *How much importance do you think is placed on these values by*

> — the faculty and administrators of the program?
> — the students in the program?
> — yourself?

Faculty:	*Students:*	*Self:*	
2a	3a	4a	Conformity
2b	3b	4b	Competition
2c	3c	4c	Materialistic things
2h	3h	4h	Good grades
2p	3p	4p	Adherence to rules

Answers: 1 = "none" to 5 = "very much"

Achievement indicators:

(a)   Grade point average scores (year 4 / year 6) (= GPA4 / GPA6) A (3.9-4.0) = 1; A- (3.5 - 3.8) = 2; B+ (3.2-3.4) = 3; B (2.9 - 3.1) = 4; B- (2.5 - 2.8) = 5; C+ (2.2 - 2.4) = 6; C (1.9 - 2.1) = 7; C- (1.8 or <) = 8

(b)   Total scores in the National Boards of Medical Examinations I (NBME–I) and II (NBME–II)

(c)   Medical Science total grade point average (Medical Science GPA); Grade point average at the end of the program(GPA total)

TABLE 13.2
Results of the Factor Analyses

Results of the Factor Analysis of Scale 1:
Factor loadings of the five items that load on a factor
"perceived competitiveness of the Medical School"

		Factor
1a.	Intellectually stimulating	.73
1b.	Competitive, grade conscious	.65
1e.	Intense atmosphere, high standards	.87
1h.	Scientific, research-oriented	.85
1i.	Serious, hard-working	.90

Results of the Three Factor Analyses of Scales 2 to 4:
Factor loadings of the five items that load on a factor of "perceived
competitiveness" in each of the three factor analyses

	Faculty Item:		*Students Item:*		*Self Item:*	
Conformity	2a:	.58	3a:	.32	4a:	.63
Competition	2b:	.74	3b:	.79	4b:	.80
Materialistic things	2c:	.63	3c:	.66	4c:	.62
Good grades	2h:	.68	3h:	.78	4h:	.63
Adherence to rules	2p:	.54	3p:	.36	4p:	.32

loading on it (see Table 13.2 for the exact results). The answers to these five items were summed up and this sum score was used as an indicator of a student's perception of the competitiveness of the medical school setting in general.

Six indicators of the students' achievement were used, namely their grade point average scores at the end of the fourth and the sixth year of the program (GPA 4 score and GPA 6 score), their total GPA and their medical science GPA at the end of the 7-year program, plus their total scores in the National Board of Medical Examination I (NBME–I) (given in the fourth/fifth year of the program) and II (NBME–II) (given at the sixth/seventh year of the program). It is important to note that the GPA scores are inversely coded to the GPAs: A high GPA of 4 is the best possible value, and a high GPA score of 8 would be the worst score. (See Table 13.1 for the exact descriptions of these measures).

It is crucial to realize that all four competition measures (the students' own values of competition, their evaluations of the faculty / administrators' values concerning competition, their evaluations of the other students' evaluation of competition, plus their evaluation of the competitiveness of the tone in the medical school) were collected in the *second* year of the program, while all the outcome variables—the students' achievement—were measured in the *later* years of the program.

RESULTS

We found clear support for Hypotheses 1 and 2. As predicted in Hypothesis 1, the more the students—both men and women—valued competition in the second year of the program, the better was their academic achievement in the following years [GPA 4 score males: r = .25; ($p < .001$); females: r = .28; ($p < .001$); GPA 6 score males: r = .11; p = .118; females: r = .21; ($p < .05$); Medical Science GPA males: r = -.22; ($p < .001$); females: r = -.14; ($p < .05$); total GPA males: r = -.26; ($p < .001$); females: r = -.24; ($p < .001$); NBME–I males: r = -.16; ($p < .01$); females: r = -.04, ns; NBME–II males: r = -.13; ($p < .10$); females: r = -.20; ($p < .05$)] (See Table 13.3).

TABLE 13.3
Regression Analyses of the Impact of Perceived and Experienced Competitiveness on Academic Achievement of Male and Female Students

	NBME–I/II		GPA 4/6		GPA: Medical/Total	
	male	*female*	*male*	*female*	*male*	*female*
Predictor:						
Hypothesis 1:						
Evaluation of own	-.16*	-.04	.25***	.28***	-.22***	-.14+
competitiveness	-.13+	-.20*	.11	.21*	-.26***	-.24**
Hypothesis 2:						
Perceived competitiveness	.18**	.21**	-.12*	-.11	.24***	.04
of the faculty	ns	.20*	-.13+	-.03	.26***	.09
Perceived competitiveness	.17**	.17*	-.11+	.01	.17**	.04
of the other students	.08	.12	-.10	.02	.17**	.04
Hypothesis 3:						
Competitiveness of	ns	.15+	ns	-.21**	.00	.12+
Medical School	-.16*	.14	.08	-.19+	-.10	.14

$^+(p < .10)$; $^*(p < .05)$; $^{**}(p < .01)$; $^{***}(p < .001)$.

This result clearly supports our argument that the more a person— be it a man or a woman—values competition, the better this person's performance will be.

As predicted in Hypothesis 2, the more these students perceived in the second year that the faculty/administrators of the program value competition highly, the worse was their later achievement. As can be seen in Table 13.3, this result holds for both male and female students [GPA 4 score males: -.12; ($p < .05$); females: -.11 ns; GPA 6 score males: r = -.13; ($p < .10$); females: ns; Medical Science GPA males: $r = .24$; ($p < .001$); females: ns; total GPA males: $r = .26$; ($p < .001$); female: ns; NBME–I males: $r = .18$; ($p < .01$); females: $r = .21$; ($p < .01$); NBME–II males: ns; females: $r = .20$; ($p < .001$)].

Furthermore, the more these students perceived in the second year of the program that other students in this program value competition highly, the worse was their later achievement [GPA 4 score males: r = -.11; ($p < .10$); females: ns; GPA 6 scores males: r = -.10 ns; females: ns; Medical Science GPA males: $r = .17$; ($p < .01$); females: ns; total GPA males: $r = .18$; ($p < .001$); females: ns; NBME–I score males: $r = .17$; ($p < .01$); females: $r = .17$; ($p < .05$); NBME–II males: ns; females: ns.] (See Table 13.3).

The crucial test of our considerations comes when analyzing the impact that these students' general evaluations of the competitiveness of the medical school environment had on their later performances. We predict here that for women the more competitive they perceive the environment to be, the less well they do (because they focus more on the person-related issues of competition), whereas the more men perceive the environment as competitive, the better they should perform (because they focus more on the achievement-related aspects of competition).

This expectation was also supported by the data: As can be seen in the second part of Table 13.3, men lived up to their potential the more they perceived the environment as competitive [NBME–II: $r = -.16$; ($p < .05$)], while women were handicapped in their performance the more they perceived the environment as competitive [GPA 4 score: $r = -.21$; ($p < .01$); GPA 6 score: $r = -.19$; ($p < .05$) ; Medical Science GPA: $r = .12$; ($p < .10$); total GPA: $r = .21$; ($p < .01$); NBME–I: $r = .15$; ($p < .05$)].

As can be seen in Table 13.4, the stepwise regression analyses also support our hypotheses as predicted.

TABLE 13.4
Stepwise Regression Analyses of the Four Competition Indicators on Academic Achievement

Predicting the NBME–I total score:

male students:

Step	R-square	Standard error	Variable	Partial	Signif.
1	.034	105.68	faculty/adm.	.184	.002
2	.068	103.98	self	-.188	.002
3	.084	103.30	other students	.129	.033

female students:

Step	R-square	Standard error	Variable	Partial	Signif.
1	.042	90.53	faculty/adm.	.206	.012
2	.073	89.39	self	-.178	.031

Predicting the NBME–II total score:

male students:

Step	R-square	Standard error	Variable	Partial	Signif.
1	.034	129.92	tone2 (7)	-.185	.007

female students:

Step	R-square	Standard error	Variable	Partial	Signif.
1	.065	76.785	faculty/adm.	.256	.009

Predicting GPA 4 score:

male students:

Step	R-square	Standard error	Variable	Partial	Signif.
1	.045	1.30	faculty/adm.	-.21	.000
2	.099	1.26	self	.24	.000
3	.120	1.25	other students	-.15	.007

female students:

Step	R-square	Standard error	Variable	Partial	Signif.
1	.056	1.31	tone	-.24	.002
2	.105	1.28	self	.23	.003

(continued)

Predicting GPA 6 score:

male students:

Step	R-square	Standard error	Variable	Partial	Signif.
1	.069	1.32	self	.26	.000
2	.100	1.30	other students	-.18	.003
3	.114	1.30	faculty/adm.	-.13	0.42

female students:

1	.095	1.13	self	.31	.000
2	.148	1.10	tone	-.24	.003
3	.185	1.08	faculty/adm.	-.21	.011

Predicting Medical GPA:

male students:

1	.062	6.64	faculty/adm.	.25	.000
2	.125	6.42	self	-.26	.000
3	.137	6.39	other students	.12	.037

female students:

1	.029	11.30	self	-.17	.024

Predicting Total GPA:

male students:

1	.069	4.45	self	-.26	.000
2	.155	4.24	faculty/adm.	.30	.000
3	.174	4.20	other students	.15	.010

female students:

1	.069	4.14	self	-.26	.001
2	.119	4.04	tone	.23	.002
3	.140	4.01	faculty/adm.	.15	.047

Note: The "faculty/adm." variable is the sum of the answers in the second year of the program to questions 2a, 2b, 2c, 2h, and 2p (wording of all questions see Table 14.1). The "other students" variable is the sum of the answers to questions 3a, 3b, 3c, 3h, 3p. The "self" variable is the sum of the answers to questions 4a, 4b, 4c, 4h, and 4p. "Tone" is the sum of the answers to questions 1a, 1b, 1e, 1h, and 1i.

CONCLUSION

Interpreting competition as a source of stress and analyzing reactions to competition with this analogy in mind proved to be helpful in understanding the relationship between competition and achievement in men and women. The practical implications of these findings suggest that by supporting a person's appreciation of competition as a challenge and by reducing the interpersonal lack of social support that accompanies stressful situations, productivity might be enhanced.

This general implication leads to concrete suggestions such as the following: In order to allow persons to optimally perform in competitive situations, the focus in these situations should be changed to a positive evaluation of competition. Specifically, if one is concerned with women's achievement there are several possible ways to avoid damaging effects of women's perceptions of competition in an environment. First, it might be useful to focus a woman's attention on the task at hand and away from the fact that the environment is competitive. Strengthening intrinsic motivation and reducing the salience of a competitive environment might help women to perform better. The second approach to this problem might be to provide women with adequate social support. Such social support could come at several levels. It could take the form of mentoring relationships, or of cooperative work groups consisting of peers, or it could even consist of support on a more general level given by academic and professional organizations. Finally, it might also be beneficial to change women's attitudes toward competition and thus their appraisal of competitive situations. In this regard it would be helpful to understand that being competitive is not a masculine trait, but a way of behaving that men and women can accept or reject to the same degree and with the same social consequences.

In summary then, it is important to ascertain the effects of the perception of academic settings on achievement. Approaching this issue with a person–environmental fit perspective, it seems important to consider the values held by students and those connoted by the demands of the task, the field of study and the setting. The closer the fit of a person's values and the demands of a situation is, the more a student should be able to live up to his or her potential.

This becomes especially important when considering the performance differences between men and women in the natural science fields that are commonly seen as having a "demand value" of being competitive. A potential effect of this model of achievement can also be seen in results found when comparing the achievement of the Inteflex students with the achievement of students in a control group. These are students who had applied to the Inteflex program, but were not accepted, and thus enrolled in the College of Literature, Science and Arts (LS&A) at the University of Michigan with a pre-medical orientation. Sixty-five percent of the male students in this control group, but only 28% of the female students persist in pre-med and eventually go to medical school. At the same time, there is no difference in the attrition rate of men and women in the Inteflex Program that is less competitive due to the fact that these students were already accepted into the medical school program when entering the program. Nevertheless, the value connotations of the biomedical areas of the curriculum still result in lower performance of the female students when compared with the male students.

We believe that considering academic achievement in the context of students' cognitions and motivations have characterized the work of Wilbert McKeachie and are happy to acknowledge his influence on our work.

ACKNOWLEDGMENTS

We want to thank all those who have been involved in the organization of this ongoing study since it started in 1972, under the direction of Donald R. Brown. We are especially grateful to William Moore, June Brown, and Penelope Morris.

REFERENCES

Ahlgren, A., & Johnson, D. W. (1979). Sex differences in cooperative and competitive attitudes from the 2nd through the 12th grades. *Developmental Psychology, 15,* 45–49.

Angier, N. (1991, May 21). Women join the ranks of science but remain invisible at the top. *The New York Times,* pB5(N) pC1(L).

Bohlmeyer, E. M., Burke, J. P., & Helmstadter, G. C. (1985). Differences between education and business students in cooperative and competitive attitudes, emotional empathy, and self-esteem. *Psychological Reports, 56,* 247–253.

Cannings, K. (1991). An interdisciplinary approach to analyzing the managerial gender gap. *Human Relations, 44,* 679–695.

Casserly, P. (1980). An assessment of factors affecting female participation in advanced placement programs in mathematics, chemistry, and physics. In L. H. Fox, L. Brody, & D. Tobin (Eds.), *Women and the mathematical mystique* (pp. 138–163). Baltimore: Johns Hopkins University Press.

Coats, P. B., & Overman, S. J. (1992). Childhood play experiences of women in traditional and nontraditional professions. *Sex Roles, 26,* 261–271.

Deutsch, M. (1949). A theory of cooperation and competition. *Human Relations, 2,* 129–151.

DiPietro, J. A. (1981). Rough and tumble play: A function of gender. *Developmental Psychology, 17,* 50–58.

Eccles, J. (1987). Gender roles and women's achievement related decisions. *Psychology of Women Quarterly, 11,* 135–172.

Eccles, J., Mac Iver, D., & Lange, L. (1986). *Classroom practices and motivation to study math.* Paper presented at the annual meeting of the American Educational Research Association, San Francisco.

Fennema, E., & Peterson, P. (1986). *Autonomous learning behaviors and classroom environments.* Paper presented at the annual meeting of the American Educational Research Association, San Francisco.

Gill, D. L. (1988). Gender differences in competitive orientation and sport participation. *International Journal of Sport Psychology, 19,* 145–159.

Hall, R. M. (1982). *The classroom climate: A chilly one for women?* (Project on the Status and Education of Women). Washington, DC: Association of American Colleges.

Hayes, L. (1976). The use for group contingencies for behavioral control: A review. *Psychological Bulletin, 83,* 628–648.

Inglehart, M. R. (1991). *Reactions to critical life events—A social psychological explanation.* New York: Praeger.

Inglehart, M., & Brown, D. R. (1989, August). *Self-development and academic achievement: A longitudinal analysis.* Paper presented at the annual meeting of the American Psychological Association, New Orleans.

Inglehart, M. R., Brown, D. R., & Malanchuk, O. (1993). The professional development of women physicians: Attending the

University of Michigan Medical School in the 1970s—Working in the 1990s. In K. Hulbert & D. Schuster (Eds), *Women's lives through time* (pp. 374–391). San Francisco: Jossey-Bass.

Johnson, D. W., & Johnson, R. (1974). Instructional structure: Cooperative, competitive, or individualization. *Review of Educational Research, 44,* 213–240.

Johnson, D. W., & Johnson, R. (1975). *Learning together and alone: Cooperation, competition, and individualization.* Englewood Cliffs, NJ: Prentice-Hall.

Johnson, D. W., Maruyama, G., Johnson, R., Nelson, D., & Skon, L. (1981). Effects of cooperative, competitive, and individualistic goal structures on achievement: A meta-analysis. *Psychological Bulletin, 89,* 47–62.

Kahle, J. (1984). *Girl-friendly science.* Paper presented at the annual meeting of the American Association for the Advancement of the Sciences, New York.

Kelley, H. H., & Thibaut, J. W. (1969). Group problem solving. In G. Lindzey & E. Aronson (Eds.), *The handbook of social psychology* (2nd ed., Vol. 4). Reading, MA: Addison-Wesley.

King, W. C., Miles, E. W., & Kniska, J. (1991). Boys will be boys (and girls will be girls): The attribution of gender role stereotypes in a gaming situation. *Sex Roles, 25,* 607–623.

Lazarus, R. S., & Folkman, S. (1984). *Stress, appraisal and coping.* New York: Springer.

Lever, J. (1978). Sex differences in the complexity of children's play and games. *American Sociological Review, 43,* 471–483.

Michaels, J. (1977). Classroom reward structures and academic performance. *Review of Educational Research, 47,* 87–99.

Miller, L., & Hamblin, R. (1963). Interdependence, differential rewarding, and productivity. *American Sociological Review, 28,* 768–778.

Paludi, M. A. (1990). Sociopsychological and structural factors related to women's vocational development. *Annals of the New York Academy of Sciences, 602,* 157–168.

Parkin, F. (1979). *Marxism and class theory: A bourgeois critique.* Columbia University Press.

Peterson, P. L., & Fennema, E. (1985). Effective teaching, student engagement in classroom activities, and sex-related differences in learning mathematics. *American Educational Research Journal, 22*, 309–335.

Sharan, S. (1980). Cooperative learning in teams: Recent methods and effects on achievement, attitudes, and ethnic relations. *Review of Educational Research, 50*, 241–272.

Slavin, R. (1977). Classroom reward structure: Analytical and practical review. *Review of Educational Research, 47*, 633–650.

14

Research on College Student Learning and Motivation: Will It Affect College Instruction?

Marilla D. Svinicki
University of Texas at Austin

This chapter focuses on a different aspect of educational research than the others in this volume. It is obvious to see that although most of the other authors represent the impact Wilbert McKeachie has had on the field of educational research, I represent the other side of the coin, the impact that he has had on the rest of higher education. I am one of those in the trenches trying to make changes in college teaching and learning from the inside out. We are the consumers of the research and procedures that McKeachie and the others generate. As the director of the faculty development center at a major research university with 48,000 students, 2,500 faculty, and 2,700 teaching assistants, I can speak from first-hand experience about the degree to which McKeachie and others like him have made inroads into the everyday life of the college classroom. Therefore, this chapter looks not so much at the research itself, but rather at why that research has the potential for influencing college teaching and learning to a far greater degree than any that has preceded it, a potential that may never be realized unless some action is taken by researchers and practitioners alike.

One could propose that on one hand educational psychology has been a major source of change in college teaching and learning, and on the other hand educational psychology has had little impact on college instruction overall. Each of those statements could be argued effectively.

On the first side, if there's been any change at all in college instructional practices, much of it comes as a result of the kind of work that McKeachie and his colleagues have done and from their willingness to reach out to the rest of the academic community and share what they know, unlike too many other researchers. On the second side, however, those changes have been long and slow in coming; and we still have an uphill battle to convince the rest of the academy that the traditions they hold so dear fly in the face of all that is now known about learning.

A HISTORICAL EXAMPLE: SOMETHING CAN MAKE A DIFFERENCE

Future predictions notwithstanding, it is best to begin with the positive side and say why the research and theory being discussed in this volume has so much potential for changing higher education. To put it boldly, psychology has done more to change the face of college instruction than any other force at work within the academy to date, except perhaps state legislatures or the economy.

Consider this. For centuries college instruction remained fairly constant in form, consisting primarily of a scholar relating his specialized knowledge to students who transcribed his words and then dropped their coins in the folds of his hood as they left the lecture hall. Perhaps this last part about the coins has changed to automatic pay deposits, but some of those medieval scholars would feel right at home in the lecture halls of today's college and universities.

Nevertheless there has been change in college instruction in the last 30 years and quite a bit of it is due to the changes in psychological thinking in the postwar era. If we were to be honest, we would have to say that what change has come to college teaching has usually (although not always) been a result of psychology tinkering with the system. Consider the following example.

There can be little disagreement that one of the first cracks in the marble facade of the academy was the result of a shift in the psychological zeitgeist toward a behavioral emphasis, which then spilled over into the design of college instruction. From that tradition came several separate innovations that have significantly changed college teaching and learning.

First was the innovation of programmed instruction, a method solidly based on this shift toward a behavioral emphasis. Although programmed instruction itself did not survive very long, its components did. Those components include (a) specification of desired outcomes in the form of objectives; (b) the breaking down of large instructional units into smaller, more easily assimilated chunks; (c) the sequencing of instruction in a logical order; (d) the requirement of active responding and immediate feedback; (e) the insistence on mastery before proceeding; (f) the eventual development of branching instruction, and so on. All of these ideas were unheard of or at least not practiced in concert prior to that time. They represented a very significant shift away from the traditional notions of education.

At the same time that programmed instruction was flowering, two other revolutionary systems derived from psychological theories were also being proposed: mastery learning and self-paced instruction. These two have the same deep structure and philosophical underpinnings as programmed instruction, but are usually associated with different aspects of that structure. For example, mastery learning puts the emphasis on having the students move to progressively more advanced material only when they have demonstrated competence on basic material; its focus is on building learner competence. Self-paced instruction puts the emphasis on the differential time required to learn by different learners; its focus is on allowing students as much time and practice as necessary to master the content. Programmed instruction puts the emphasis on structuring the material to facilitate learning; its focus is on the organization of learning. And yet all three support the others, and they were frequently found together as instructional innovations.

One does not see too much print-based programmed instruction these days or many full-fledged mastery or self-paced instruction systems, but one can hardly turn around without tripping over some form of their successor, computer-assisted instruction. Of all the instructional innovations that have come along over the years, there is little doubt that computer-based instruction is one that will continue and expand in use for the foreseeable future. It is being accepted by faculty in all disciplines, even the humanities. Whether they realize it or not, those instructors who adopt computer-assisted instruction are following in the footsteps of those psychologists who pioneered programmed instruction, mastery learning and self-pacing because computers have made possible the promise of those systems. The computer-based programs allow instruction to meet the criteria that were pioneered by the earlier systems. They allow for self-paced, individualized, branched instruction that monitors progress and does not allow a student to proceed without mastering the basics. They provide for active learning and immediate feedback, and they are a lot more entertaining than Holland and Skinner's programmed introductory text ever was.

More important than the mechanics of these behaviorally based methods, however, was the shift in thinking about learning and teaching that they represented. These three innovations would forever change the way teaching and learning were conceptualized by those who tried them. This shift in thinking, although not seismic in proportion, moved the foundation of college teaching from a content base toward a student base just enough to crack the walls of the academy and open the possibility for the even greater shift that would come with the advent of cognitive psychology and the focus on student learning that is the focus of the research of McKeachie and his colleagues today.

THE IMPACT OF THE COGNITIVE MOVEMENT

It is hard for someone steeped in the cognitive tradition and believing in the value of learning strategies and student motivation research to understand just what an earthquake-size event it represents for the average faculty member to contemplate the ideas embodied in this philosophy. That is why I believe that this research has the potential of having an even greater impact on college teaching and learning than the behavioral models that proceeded it. It will have that great impact for two reasons: it can be aimed at the students, allowing them for the first time to participate in their own education more effectively; and it has a great deal of intuitive appeal for the faculty, so that they are more likely to accept it than they have other theories of learning.

The Impact of Reaching the Students

The kind of work described in the other chapters of this volume touches an audience that the previous behavioral work did not and that audience is the students. The older, behavioral paradigm still focused on changing the teaching rather than the learning, an idea very consistent with the basic assumptions of behavioral theory. All one needed to do was manipulate the way the material was taught and all students would learn. The student, like the laboratory animal, need not get involved. The responsibility for improving learning rested on the instructor, just as it had before; we simply had a better way to present the content. The majority of the actors in the classroom drama, the students, were not a resource to be tapped.

Enter the cognitive model and it became a whole new balance of power in the teaching/learning equation. The learning-based programs pioneered by McKeachie and the other authors in this volume are designed to have a direct effect on the ability of students to cope with the learning demands placed on them in their college classes. They are no longer the passive recipients of instruction, but potentially active partners in the process. A whole new resource for the improvement of college education is activated, and a self-renewing resource at that.

Consider what a revolutionary proposal it is to acknowledge the role of the learner in the educational process. The implications of this idea go far beyond mere mechanics; this change has philosophical, political, and social implications as well. Philosophically, the cognitive movement in education, particularly the constructivists with their emphasis on the role of the learner, implies an approach to understanding that contradicts the received knowledge premise on which most of education is based. Politically, it implies that the paternalistic approach to instruction that has predominated, in which the teacher/master knew best and the function of education was to create clones of the power structure, needs to be scrapped in favor of a more participatory process in which learning is negotiated between teacher and student. Socially, this shift to learner participation means a new role for the teacher away from authority and even facilitator toward resource. Although many of these points have been made by essayists over the years, they have had primarily a political or philosophical base rather than a research or theory base. The advent of cognitive psychology with its research on learner effects provides new support for these positions.

Moving away from the political ramifications of the shift representing by this research, however, the potential for impact on higher education is greatly enhanced by the emphasis on students as active participants in the learning process. The research presented in this volume offers a way of expanding the influence of psychology beyond the instructor. By developing ways of involving students in the educational process as more than passive recipients, cognitive research increases its influence on what happens in the college classroom in two ways.

The most obvious impact will be on the students themselves. Research on learning strategies and motivation is already suggesting ways in which students can improve their own learning. The area of self-regulation is based on the premise that students can become better learners if they become more aware of their learning and then choose to act on that awareness. When students become better learners, teachers will be able to spend less time on management of learning and more on expanding learning opportunities. For example, if students were aware of the value of comprehension monitoring and would/could engage in it without constant prodding by the instructor, the instructor would only need to make monitoring opportunities available (rather than required) and could skip all the administrative fuss that accompanies required assignments. This would leave more time for developing content enrichment materials or individual assistance to those with special needs.

A second impact on education would result from having more sophisticated consumers of teaching. When students know more about learning, they may become more discriminating about the way teaching occurs. For example, students who knew that active processing of ideas leads to better learning might demand more opportunities to discuss the content themselves rather than listen passively to a lecture each period. Currently, students accept the way higher education is conducted because that is the way it has always been conducted and there has been no compelling reason to change. Evidence that this reliance on a teacher-managed learning system is not consistent with optimal learning should provide support for student demands that the system change.

Effects on the Faculty

Tapping student potential is promising, but tapping faculty potential offers an equally encouraging possibility of long-term change in higher education. One of the first impressions that this shift to a cognitive perspective is making on the faculty is the concept of active learning. Whether this idea came more from a behavioral or a cognitive tradition is hard to say, but college instructors are slowly coming around to the idea that students need to be involved actively in their learning . . . and not in the superficial way represented by repetitious drill and practice, but a way that promotes deep processing and cognitive restructuring. They may not be doing this because they have adopted the theoretical underpinnings on which these methods are based, but there has been an increase in instructional methods that have active participation as part of the model, such as problem-based learning, case studies, simulations, inquiry and collaborative learning.

The upsurge in instructional methods using active participation, regardless of the motives behind it, is encouraging. It is resulting in a subtle redefinition of what is "normal" in the college classroom. In the past, instructors would have felt uncomfortable doing anything other than lecturing in their classes. In fact many of the instructional evaluation forms in use today are based on the concept of the lecture format and ask questions that would only be appropriate for that format. Even the physical structure of the classrooms is set up to support the lecture, teacher-centered method. Now, however, the dominance of teacher talk is slipping somewhat as more and more instructors are experimenting with alternative student activities.

However, the adoption of instructional methods derived from research on learning strategies and motivation represents a far more profound change than simply more activity on the part of learners. Such methods require a renegotiation of the role of the instructor and the student. Under the old system, the instructor was the source of knowledge, the organizer of the learning, the motivator, the central figure.

Enter cognitive psychology and the student becomes the central figure. What the students learn depends on their goals, their prior knowledge, how they perceive new information, process it, organize it, relate it to what they know. The most important instructional activity an instructor can provide is not a crystal-clear lecture but an opportunity for the students to work with the content on their own or in groups.

This is a difficult transition for the college faculty and students to make. For both parties it requires learning a new set of behaviors and attitudes. Faculty who incorporate active learning strategies in their classes must contend with student resistance to the new techniques as well as their own fears of inadequacies. Students must be able to trust the instructor to salvage the situation if things go wrong, and they must be willing to move beyond performance goals ("What will be on the test?") to the riskier, learning goals inherent in the more free-form student-centered instruction methods.

Faculty are making the change in dribs and drabs. Those who hear about the idea embodied in instruments like the MSLQ are intrigued by the possibilities it represents for a variety of reasons. They have long felt frustrated by their inability to "cover all the content," while at the same time watching the amount of content they feel they must cover grow beyond the ability of their students to absorb it. It is no wonder they are drawn to the idea of students becoming more efficient and effective learners. It represents a potential solution to a real problem they face every day.

They have also felt frustrated by their apparent inability to "motivate" the students to work and learn. In our work with faculty, we hear a constant complaint about students wanting to be "spoonfed," a complaint that is probably a mislabeling of the students' request, but that reflects an irritation faculty feel with the student need for structure. An educational philosophy which holds that responsibility for learning should rest more in the hands of students and less in the hands of the faculty has an inherent appeal to a beleaguered instructor, however reactionary that might sound.

There is also a great deal of face validity in the idea of differences in learning styles, strategies and motivations. Faculty respond positively to the idea that different people learn in different ways and will benefit from different teaching methods. In my own work I have never seen anything make quicker inroads into a stubborn reliance on lecture than the idea that some students do not know how to process information that way. Faculty may be skeptical about a lot of educational research, but this is one concept that intrigues and excites them.

Finally, the idea that the focus of instruction should be on learning and that there is actually something an instructor might be able to do to impact that learning taps a scholar's intellectual curiosity as well. Teaching becomes more than telling; it becomes a puzzle with a solution; a problem to be solved. The researcher in all of them is engaged. Evidence for this concept is seen in the popularity of the Classroom Research concept. Being able to have some control over the course of learning in their students is an attractive option for faculty.

For all these reasons and probably more that I have not included, the research on student learning and motivation has the possibility of making great changes in college teaching first because it reaches the students and opens the possibility of their contributing to those changes and second because if the faculty embrace it, it will forever change the assumptions about learning and teaching upon which they base their instructional decisions.

GETTING THE WORD TO THE PRACTITIONERS

Now we are faced with the question "if this is such wonderful news about learning, how do we get every faculty member to adopt it?" And that may be where McKeachie above all his colleagues has had and continues to have his most profound impact, as a translator and mediator between the world of the researcher and the world of the college teacher. All the most wonderful research and theory in the world will be so much mental gymnastics if it is never conveyed to those who need it most, the faculty and students. We must find ways for these concepts of learning and motivation to get into the everyday parlance of the college instructor.

Here McKeachie has led the way most decisively. The first publication of *Teaching Tips* is dated 1951. I don't know what was in that original version, but subsequent editions have been filled with the wisdom of research and practice. That book has probably been read by more faculty than any other book on higher education and probably with more effect as well. The very concept of the book and the other publications that he has authored, such as the more recent compendia of research from NCRIPTAL, says that there is much that the members of the academy can learn about learning. Part of teaching may be an art, but there is a lot of science to inform the practice. And it behooves the practitioner to become schooled in that science.

McKeachie was also one of the first people who advocated such training in teaching for college faculty and who supported the idea of evaluating teaching for improvement. He was one of the first to offer some systematic training for the graduate students who were serving as teaching assistants, a movement which has expanded to unbelievable proportions in recent years. His has been a significant voice in the faculty development movement from its very beginnings in the 1970s.

McKeachie has been one of the most effective spokesmen for the idea that teaching is more than an inborn talent. He has had the courage to speak to his fellow faculty about research on learning and teaching. And they listen to what he has to say. There are some specific reasons for this beyond the fact that his message is a good one.

First, he has the courage to speak about the everyday concerns and questions faced by a college instructor. He does not hide behind qualifiers and hedgers as so many theorists and researchers do; if he believes in the research, he says so and is willing to put it to the test of practice. He does it in his own teaching and recommends it to others.

Second, he has enormous credibility to faculty members because he is a colleague. He is a faculty member, a teacher, first and foremost. One can see it in the examples he uses and the interest he shows in teaching, not only his own but that of others as well. The Center for Research on

Learning and Teaching at Michigan was one of the earliest faculty development programs in the country to try to make a difference in college instruction. The rest of us in the field are just following along behind.

Third, he has enormous credibility as a researcher. He and those with whom he has worked have done first-rate research with great integrity. When he makes a recommendation, it has a solid base in reality.

Finally, and perhaps most important, he has enormous credibility as a person. There is no arrogance of the researcher who knows the right answer and touts it in the face of all evidence to the contrary. There is no false modesty. There is just an open and honest inquiring mind and the model of a gentleman and a scholar, which invites others to be as open and as inquiring in return. It is no wonder that he has been able to speak to the higher education community so effectively.

But he cannot do it alone. That brings me back to my opening claim that research such as that discussed in this volume has had both a profound effect on college instruction, and none at all. When it is discovered by faculty and used, it makes a difference. But in spite of all that has been learned about learning, the vast majority of college instruction is carried out under the old models and has not been affected by the recent advances at all.

Why is that? There are not enough Bill McKeachies around, individuals who are willing to step out of their building and talk to someone from the Physics department or the College of Engineering or the Music department. Researchers in learning talk to one another, just like researchers in other fields do. And so the physicists learn about learning from another physicist, the engineers from another engineer and the musicians from other musicians.

Higher education needs more people who are willing to translate from research to practice and back, from one discipline to another and back. It needs researchers who do not define the end of a project as the day the results are accepted for publication; and we need practitioners who are willing to stretch their understanding of theory and research beyond popular psychology. Most faculty developers have that inclination to serve as mediators, but suffer pangs of guilt every time they have to simplify and possibly compromise a theory in order to fit it to an application. We need everyone, researchers and practitioners alike, to follow McKeachie's lead and knock down the walls that separate our theoretical knowledge about learning from the everyday practice of teaching. If we do so, perhaps the potential of the research on cognition and motivation to redefine and re-energize college teaching and learning will be reached.

15

Concluding Remarks

Wilbert J. McKeachie
University of Michigan

INTRODUCTION

To be honored by a Festschrift is a wonderful thing, and my gratitude is enhanced by the stimulation and pleasure I have received from reading each of the contributions.

Reading the preceding chapters, I am struck by the extent to which some aspect of *similarity* and *difference* enters into a number of the contributions. In this chapter I shall try to trace some aspects of that theme through the contributions as they relate to the themes of cognition, motivation, and instruction.

The classical use of similarity in psychology has been in theories dealing with the role of similarities and differences in affecting transfer of learning. Clearly, people and animals use learning in new situations; yet more often than not when we attempt to measure transfer of learning, learners fail to transfer in many situations where we had hoped transfer would occur.

I have argued elsewhere (McKeachie, 1987) that all learning and memory involves transfer; we never use learning in exactly the same situation in which it was learned. At any later period in time, we have changed, and the situation is no longer the same. We simply label the transfer as *memory* if the situation provides ample cues to the situations in which learning occurred. If the new situation is a little different from the original ones we describe the outcome as *near transfer*; if it is more different, we call it *far transfer* [or in Salomon and Perkins' neat metaphor, "high road transfer" involving decontextualization of a principle (Salomon & Perkins, 1989)]; if the situation is still more different we speak of *problem solving*; and if the new situation bears little resemblance to the situations in which relevant previous learning occurred, we talk about *creativity*.

All of these involve the use of prior learning in new situations; the difference is in the apparent similarity of the situations to the situations in which the original learning occurred, and often in the degree to which the new situation requires integration of formerly disparate episodes of learning.

But what do we mean by "similarity"? When I was a graduate student, the best we could do was to use Thorndike's theory of identical elements. We now know that simply identifying elements of the situation is not sufficient because the same situation may be perceived quite differently by different individuals with differing past experiences and motivation and even by the same individual at different times. This does not mean that "similarity" is solely in the mind of the perceiver. There are respects in which independent observers will agree that two situations are similar (cf. Medin, Goldstone, & Gentner, 1993).

What is transferred depends not only on the original learning and the transfer situation, but also upon the person, task, goals and context in which transfer may or may not occur. Sometimes the transfer is not appropriate or optimal, as is illustrated in the discussion of the representativeness heuristic by Kevin Biolsi and Ed Smith. People underweight prior probabilities and make judgments based on similarity to prototypes even in professional judgments such as medical or legal decisions.

As the preceding chapters indicate, I have always had both an intrinsic interest in research in cognition and motivation and a practical interest in how the theory and findings can be used to promote better instruction. In the following sections I shall highlight some of the ways in which the themes of similarity and transfer emerge in each of the chapters as they relate to the improvement of teaching and learning. Basically my argument is that in teaching we need to help students to be aware of critical dimensions of similarity and difference in order that the concepts and skills we attempt to teach will be transferred appropriately in situations after they leave our classes.

COGNITION

This volume begins with Moshe Naveh-Benjamin and Yi-Guang Lin's description of methods of assessing cognitive structures. "What does this have to do with your theme of similarity?" you may ask. My answer is that when we build conceptual structures or schemas linking previously unrelated facts, we gain the ability to see similarities that were previously unrecognized and to make discriminations that were previously amorphous. Salomon and Perkins' "high road transfer" involves the abstraction of concepts and principles. When we relate facts and concepts to one another, we gain greater possibilities for retrieval and appropriate use in new situations. As Naveh-Benjamin and Lin indicate, much of education involves the development of more and more highly organized conceptual structures that become increasingly similar to those of experts in the field of study. As students develop more complex cognitive structures, they have greater potential for recognizing similarities and differences—a key to effective transfer.[1]

Jan Donald's studies of the conceptual structures and goals of teachers are thus important, for they illustrate how much the experts in different disciplines differ. In each of the three disciplines she studied (Physics, Engineering, and Psychology), there was an emphasis upon teaching thinking, but the sort of thinking involved differed, with the physicists emphasizing logical problem solving, the engineers emphasizing analytic, independent thinking, and the psychologists emphasizing abstraction and concept formation. There are clear similarities in their descriptions, but the differences are sufficiently great that one might not expect great transfer from one field to the other.

Concept formation, categorization, and verbal labels can help (or hinder) transfer, as is illustrated in the chapters by Kevin Biolsi and Ed Smith and by Scott VanderStoep and Colleen Seifert. Kevin and Ed enriched my understanding of similarity by pointing out the relevance

---

[1]It is still not clear to me whether the terms "schema" or "structure" are appropriate ways to describe storage of information. The connotations of these terms are probably more static than we would wish. Yet we need some way of tying the dynamics of memory down long enough to aid teaching and learning. Both Jan Donald's and Naveh-Benjamin and Lin's methods are heuristic for teaching and for understanding the use of memory in new situations.

of prototype theory and the representativeness heuristic in determining our transfer of learning to new problem situations. Concepts enable us to go beyond the information given in a new situation—to link our percepts to beliefs, feeling and action (Smith, 1988).

Susan Reiter suggests that thinking depends upon dissonance—again the issue of similarity or difference, in this case difference between what is already in our heads and new information. But such thinking can probably not take place if the student does not know enough to recognize the dissonance. Students need to develop cognitive structures if they are to see the similarities and differences necessary for appropriate transfer or for thinking about how to integrate or evaluate different points of view.

Some years ago the magazine, *Psychology Today*, developed an introductory textbook in which each chapter was written by a different author, and chapters could be assigned in any order. Thus students might move from Skinnerian behaviorism to Freudian psychoanalysis without any cues from the text that these points of view might not be compatible. One hopes that teachers helped students do more than memorize such terms as *reinforcement* and *Oedipus Complex*, but I suspect that in many introductory courses students did not benefit from the challenge of reconciling the dissonances between the two theoretical positions because they didn't recognize that they were incompatible.

Studies of adult language learning suggest that interference between two languages is reduced if one language is learned relatively well before beginning the other. May this be a hint to us about what strategies to use in introducing comparisons to create dissonance and thinking? Perhaps conflicting ideas are confusing when one lacks a clear understanding of both, but when one idea is already clearly structured, its difference from a new viewpoint may provide the challenge needed to stimulate thinking.

But how then can we fit in Jan Donald's finding that the discrepancy between the physicists' view and that of students is a barrier to learning—a view vividly presented in Sheila Tobias's 1990 book, *They're Not Dumb; They're Different?* We have a similar phenomenon in the new calculus course that I am now evaluating—students who have had calculus in high school seem to have more difficulty in coping with the new approach than those who have had no previous calculus. For both the physics student and the math student, their present structure is probably not well-developed so that relevant similarities and differences between their views and that of the instructor are not clearly perceived. Restructuring a schema is not easy. Very likely the relationship between perceived difference and thinking is curvilinear; small differences can be assimilated, but large differences may seem impossible to understand. Thus students may fail to try to transfer skills or knowledge from one course to another because they perceive them to be in different domains.

If a teacher can recognize and take account of an existing schema, frame of reference, or epistemology, teaching strategies can be used to facilitate thinking that brings about constructive change. But if the existing conceptual structure is ignored and the new is not compared to the old, the dissonance may lead students to reject or misinterpret the new viewpoint.

Currently one of the major themes in education, both in this country and others, is teaching thinking. As I see it, the advocates of teaching thinking want to promote greater transfer of learning to new situations—better problem solving, more effective decision making. One of the assumptions of those who teach thinking is that one is more likely to think in the future if one practices thinking now. In short, if we want our students to think better, they need to practice it now. This is certainly reasonable, but the results of practice probably depend a great deal upon the knowledge available for thinking and the kind of practice undertaken. VanderStoep and Seifert indicate that building conceptual structures such as those described by Naveh-Benjamin and Lin and by Donald, may enable one to use analogies for problem solving. But simply having the appropriate schemas is not sufficient; practice with multiple analogs increases the likelihood of accessing an appropriate solution schema. So, to go back to our earlier question about the necessity of comparisons, explicit comparisons should help.

The idea of making explicit comparisons brings up the important issue of awareness and consciousness. What is the role of consciousness in learning and transfer of learning? Claire Ellen Weinstein helps students develop a repertoire of learning skills that can be used strategically in dealing with a variety of learning situations. In her course and in my own course, Learning to Learn, we try to teach students to be metacognitive—to be aware of their own learning and thinking— and to match their approaches to the demands of the situation. As Claire Ellen points out, to be strategic requires that one be able to differentiate and categorize situations and to choose an appropriate approach taking account of the situation and one's own goals and skills. Yet metacognition takes cognitive capacity and thus may sometimes interfere with learning and thinking.

Can strategic thinking be automatized so that it takes little capacity? The problem is that for novices, automatized judgments of similarity may be based on surface features. Thus learning may be transferred to situations that are superficially similar to those in which one learned a skill, but where the skill is not appropriate or optimal. I am reminded of the great interest in studies of rigidity in the late 1940s and early 1950s—studies often stimulated by Luchins' classic Einstellung demonstration showing that most of us will continue using a method that has worked in the past even in situations where an easier method could be used (Luchins, 1942). (Herb Simon had not yet pointed out the prevalence of satisficing.) In training students to be more mindful of their approaches to learning situations, our hope is that they will be more likely to analyze the situation and their goals more effectively and be less likely to generalize inappropriately or ineffectively.

We want our students to be capable of thinking consciously about their learning. We can't teach everything students need for coping effectively with every situation. They need to create their own strategies as they develop new skills and encounter new situations. A conceptual framework for understanding and thinking about the transferability of previous learning should facilitate successful strategizing and problem solving.

I suspect that an important basis for this kind of mindful transfer is that during learning the learner becomes conscious of the processes used, as in the technique of writing out actions described by Jan Donald. Then, as Weinstein suggests, the learner needs to think about future contexts for use of the learning, a point further elaborated in the chapters by Paul Schutz and by Paul Pintrich and Teresa Garcia.

MOTIVATION

Naveh-Benjamin and Lin suggest that students who have poorly developed schemas may be motivated by seeing the discrepancy between their own concept structure and that of their instructor. I assume that cognitions always have some tinge of affect. Some are positive; some negative; some highly charged affectively; others less so. Thus the ease of change is likely to depend not only on how tightly structured a schema is but also on the degree to which it is dear to the learner. Presumably the conceptual structures in college courses are not among the most highly charged. From Reiter's results it seems likely that if the student sees a course as having high value, the structure of the instructor (and presumably of the experts in the field) should have positive value.

Motivation theory suggests that mild discrepancies from our existing level of adaptation or frame of reference arouse curiosity, interest, and thinking; large discrepancies arouse anxiety and retreat (Berlyne, 1960). When a new situation or a new theoretical position is quite similar to those in which we have learned and used our learning, transfer can occur mindlessly and effortlessly; when the difference is greater, we may need to think about the similarities and differences; but when there is great incompatibility, our response may simply be rejection. In many respects Vigotsky's zone of proximal development represents this principle. Marty Covington makes a similar point with respect to the fact that optimal motivation involves realistic learning objectives slightly above the learner's current capacity.

The other motivation chapters also involve our theme of similarity and difference. Pintrich and Garcia and Schutz point out that self-regulation depends on knowing where you are in relation to where you'd like to be; that is being aware of the similarities and differences between the *present* situation and your *present* self and a *possible* situation and *possible* self (cf. Markus & Nurius, 1986). Surely if discrepancies between relatively non-affective schemas, such as those studied by Naveh-Benjamin and Lin, are motivating, then differences in self-schemas must be much more motivating, a theme that is developed in detail by Pintrich and Garcia. Possible selves involve the internalized standards for achievement that Barry Zimmerman and Rafael Risemberg have found to be important.

Both Weinstein and Schutz emphasize the role that goals play in organizing schemas, plans, and self-efficacy, but where do the goals come from? How do they get activated? Presumably this takes some appraisal of the present situation and some awareness of a possible situation that is different. Atkinson and Birch (1970) suggested that we are always motivated and that the problem of motivation is not to activate a static organism, but rather to change the direction of motivation. Thus we presumably must do some sort of calculus involving comparing the potential goals in possible situations and the probabilities of attaining them with the potential satisfactions of the present activity. But, as Biolsi and Smith point out, human beings are often motivated to minimize effort, a point that has been elaborated in the research on effort-avoidance by Brigitte Rollett (1987) of the University of Vienna.

Yet in Marty Covington's fourfold table only the "failure accepters" would be characterized by effort-avoidance in academic situations. In fact his "overstrivers" are characterized by high effort possibly motivated by a very salient negative possible self. Presumably his "success-oriented" are the ideal—able to estimate accurately the amount of effort needed to achieve good learning outcomes.

In some respects these success-oriented students appear to be like Stu Karabenick and Rajeev Sharma's high ability students in that they are able to judge fairly accurately what is needed to move from their present situation to the desired one. Karabenick and Sharma's high ability students seek help when they need it but don't seek help when they don't need it. This may account for the lack of information seeking by the trained subjects in the experiment described by Zimmerman and Risemberg.

It seems to me that there are probably three reasons why students don't ask for help even when they recognize a discrepancy between what they know and what they need to know. The first may simply be embarrassment; asking for help may be seen as an admission of incompetence. A second may be a simple failure to recognize the need for help; but a third may be a lack of skill in asking good questions, an inability to identify what is needed in terms that elicit appropriate help. If one has asked for help without success, it is not surprising that this strategy is not used. In short, help-seeking, like effort avoidance, depends both on the individual and the situation.

Asking good questions requires a certain level of prior knowledge about a task or subject matter discipline. I think I can ask appropriate questions about most areas of psychology, but when it comes to asking about how to deal with my lawnmower or car when they malfunction, I am not very good. Can we teach generalizable help-seeking skills that can be applied in both novice and non-novice areas?

If we do try to develop help-seeking as a useful learning strategy, we also need to take account of gender differences in help-seeking. From the findings of Marita Inglehart, Don Brown, and Mina Vida, I would expect women's help seeking to be dependent upon the presence of perceived support to a greater degree than for men. In our studies in the 1960s (McKeachie, Lin, Milholland, & Isaacson, 1966) we found that women's achievement (as compared with men's) was more consistently affected positively by teacher warmth. If one takes teacher warmth as being likely to lead to student perception of support, our results support those of Inglehart, Brown, and Vida.

INSTRUCTION

What is the role of instruction? Scott Vanderstoep and Colleen Seifert showed that explicit instruction in differences in applicability of similar rules to transfer situations helped learners make appropriate transfer of the rules. Should we introduce comparisons and labels? Can you build up a concept without any comparisons, at least implicitly?

Picard (1992) demonstrated that one should begin building a conceptual structure with object-oriented sequencing of material; that is by learning aspects of one theory first, then aspects of another theory, and finally comparisons of the aspects of the theories. Teaching the similarities and differences between two theories aspect by aspect from the beginning seemed to be less effective for novices in the subject matter. This fits with concept formation research going back as far as Hull (1920), Heidbreder, (1946), and Hovland (Hovland & Weiss, 1953) indicating that positive instances generally help more than negative instances in forming concepts initially. If labels help in developing concepts or prototypes, when should they be introduced? From the first positive instance? Or only after some experience with what goes into the concept or prototype? As Kevin Biolsi and Ed Smith indicate, similarities to prototypes may be so easily accessed that they may preclude the use of other important information. Maybe we shouldn't try to be efficient in developing them. Or, more likely, maybe we should be developing means of preventing their misuse. What can we do to facilitate appropriate transfer while guarding against inappropriate transfer?

CHOICE, CHALLENGE, CONTROL, AND COLLABORATION: IMPLICATIONS FOR LEARNING

Scott Paris and Julie Turner's four C's—Choice, Challenge, Control, and Collaboration—provide a nice framework both for their own work and for summing up some common elements in all the papers.

Choice gives learners the opportunity to assess their values, their knowledge, skills, and strategies available in the present situation, and their likelihood of achieving success. Paris and Turner's study of "open tasks" involving learner choice and autonomy could be replicated, I believe, in college classrooms. In fact the teachers described in our earlier research as "student centered" or "facilitative" teachers had classes that could well have been described in terms of learner choice and autonomy (McKeachie, 1954; McKeachie et al., 1978). The difference in terminology between the 1950s and 1990s illustrates how the focus of educational research has shifted from the teacher to the learner.

Challenge is represented in Donald's and Naveh-Benjamin and Lin's discussion of the challenge to teachers and learners in bridging the gap between the learner's prior conceptual structure and that of the teacher, who presumably represents the structure of the discipline. We find challenge also in Reiter's description of the value of dialogical teaching in stimulating better thinking and in Covington's program to design tasks with "manageable conflict."

Control is represented in all of the papers, as each describes ways of training learners to develop better cognitive, motivational, and volitional skills and strategies that will thereby give them greater control of their own learning. As students develop a greater repertoire of skills, increased ability to diagnose learning tasks, and better awareness of their own goals and standards, they gain greater autonomy as learners.

In addition to the cognitive values of cooperative learning described by Weinstein and others, *Collaboration* gives students the social support necessary for taking the risk of assuming greater responsibility for their own learning. As Inglehart, Brown, and Vida show, collaborative learning is particularly effective for students with positive attitudes toward cooperation and negative feelings about competition. Although such attitudes are particularly prevalent among women, they also characterize many men. As Covington points out, intense engagement with learning depends upon being able to improve on early mistakes without penalty—a condition more likely to obtain in small cooperative groups than in competitive classes. In cooperative situations even highly anxious students feel freer to learn in more effective ways. Everyone can win!

WHAT OF THE FUTURE?

The prophets of the Old Testament were not so much fortune tellers who foretold the future, as moralists who called the nation to adhere to higher values. I am no prophet, and I am more often optimistic than given toward prophesies of doom. Because I have learned in psychology that the best predictor of future behavior is likely to be past behavior, I shall point toward some current trends that seem to me to portend a good future. And perhaps I shall preach a few values that I believe to be important for that future.

First of all is the fact, illustrated in this volume, that there are clear links between basic psychological research and educational practice. The gap between the laboratory and the classroom is no longer a chasm, but rather has been bridged by many researchers and theorists who are comfortable in crossing back and forth. I believe that we will meet the challenge posed by Marilla Svinicki; educational research will increasingly stimulate and contribute both to basic theory and to educational practice. I value both laboratory research and research in natural settings. None of us can reach final truth, but we can come closer if we respect and communicate with one another.

Second, research on teaching and learning at the college and university level will continue to develop and flourish. When Harold Guetzkow and our group of teaching fellows in introductory psychology carried out our first study of methods of teaching in 1946, there were probably only half a dozen other psychologists doing such research. For several years after finishing my Ph.D., I invited Ben Bloom of the University of Chicago, Ron Levy from Roosevelt University, Don Elliot from Wayne State University, and Don Johnson and Henry Clay Smith from Michigan State University to come to Ann Arbor for an annual conference on research in classroom processes. At that time our group represented well over half of all the researchers in the world dealing with university teaching. Year after year I turned down offers for administrative positions because I felt that no one else would do the research I was doing if I were to leave.

Now research on college learning and teaching is a flourishing subdivision of educational and instructional psychology. I expect its growth to continue, and as Marilla Svinicki recommends, there will be more and more opportunities for students, as well as teachers, to learn about that research and to apply it for improved learning. We may not have a revolution, but change is occurring.

A third trend is the shift in focus from teaching to learning. This movement, facilitated by the dominance of cognitive psychology, is a healthy one, I believe. The emphasis on learning has helped us recognize that much, perhaps most, learning goes on outside the classroom. This has had the desirable consequence that we recognize that some of the most important aspects of teaching are in the planning, preparation, coaching, and feedback that go on outside the classroom.

Yet I trust that teaching will not be neglected. I still find the dynamics of classroom interactions endlessly fascinating. The continuous flow of activities requiring teachers and students alike to monitor the actions and reactions of a variety of individuals with diverse interests and experiences and to shift strategies as the situation changes from moment to moment—this is certainly among the most complex and challenging tasks human beings encounter. What a tragedy that sometimes the potential excitement deteriorates into boredom for both teacher and student! I hope that future research will increase the moments of joy and decrease the moments of emptiness.

Another consequence of the shift from teaching to learning has been our realization of the importance of motivation. True, we have always recognized that learning was influenced by motivation, but as long as we focused upon the classroom, our attention was directed to such motivational devices as the role of examples and visual aids in maintaining interest in lectures. Now we know that it is not enough to provide momentary motivational devices but that we need even more to motivate student thinking and behavior outside the classroom, and after the course is ended.

A final consequence of the trend from teaching to learning is just beginning to appear. I hope and predict that learning settings will change. We already have seen some changes in laboratories, computerized classrooms, and experiential learning. But at the University of Michigan seats are still tied in rows by pipes bolted across sets of movable chairs, with the presumed goal of keeping students facing the teacher. I had to go through three administrative levels of "No's" before the Provost authorized removal of the pipes so that my students could work in small groups. Future classrooms, I pray, will be learner centered.

A fourth set of trends is in the area of research methodology. We now have a clearer sense of our ethical obligations, a broader array of methodologies, and a greater sense of the importance of context. Our

1946-1947 experiment was the best-controlled study I have ever been involved in. We had matched groups, carefully monitored differentiation of teaching methods, and multiple measures of processes and outcomes (McKeachie, 1951; Guetzkow, Kelly, & McKeachie, 1954). I now believe that it is not proper to restrict teachers' freedom to adjust as they see best for the education of their students.

Further if one takes student time for research, it must have value for them educationally or motivationally. Because of these ethical constraints research in college courses is inevitably less controlled than a purist would like; we are never able to measure all the variables we would like to. (In fact if we administered every pre-post and interim measure that would be desirable, there would be no time left for teaching!)

A good deal has been made of the shift from input-output to process-product research designs and from process-product to student mediation research. These are important trends (although I would note that we used trained observers to get at classroom processes in our studies in the 1940s and Ben Bloom was using stimulated recall to get at student thinking over 40 years ago). It seems to me that we need to integrate rather than denigrate alternate ways of carrying out educational research.

I hope that conflict between quantitative and qualitative methodologists will not last as long as the Arab-Israeli or North Ireland conflicts. I see the growing use of qualitative methods as enriching our understanding rather than as a conquest by the barbarians. Those of us doing research in natural settings need all the help we can get; at best in each study we make only small gains in reducing the vastness of unknown complexities.

Some of the challenges of the post-modernists with respect to the subjectivity of all research seem to me appropriate; however, a completely relativistic position is ultimately self-defeating. In an article in the *Educational Psychologist*, Jack Carroll (1993) pointed to the enormous human problems faced by the Third World countries and the need to address literacy and educational provisions in these countries. The challenge he describes is enormous, but it must be met. I believe our field will become increasingly international, and one of the positive results of this will be the opportunities it will give us to determine how much of what we know is really conditioned by Western culture and how much is truly generalizable across cultures and historical periods.

"Situated cognition" and "design experiments" challenge our old ways of thinking about single-variable, cause-effect, research designs. I believe that these concepts point us in the right direction. I reject a strongly relativistic view of what we can do in educational research, but I believe that in any one study we only decrease uncertainty a small amount. Nonetheless, I believe that we are building a science that is cumulative.

This book provides evidence that we not only can carry out interesting research, but that that research also provides a solid foundation for those who follow us. It also demonstrates that concepts developed from basic research can be usefully transferred to the practical problems of improving teaching and learning, despite the differences between laboratories and classrooms.

We've come a long way in the last half-century; progress in the years ahead should be even more exciting!

REFERENCES

Atkinson, J. W., & Birch, D. (1970). *The dynamics of action.* New York: Wiley.

Berlyne, D. E. (1960). *Conflict, arousal, and curiosity.* New York: McGraw Hill.

Carroll, J. B. (1993). Educational psychology in the 21st century. *Educational Psychologist, 28*(2), 89–95.

Guetzkow, H., Kelly, E. L., & McKeachie, W. J. (1954). An experimental comparison of recitation, discussion, and tutorial methods of teaching. *Journal of Educational Psychology, 45,* 224–232.

Heidbreder, E. (1946). The attainment of concepts: II. The problem. *Journal of Genetic Psychology, 35,* 191–223.

Hovland, C. I., & Weiss, W. (1953). Transmission of information concerning concepts through positive and negative instances. *Journal of Experimental Psychology, 45,* 173–182.

Hull, C. L. (1920). Quantitative aspects of the evolution of concepts: An experimental study. *Psychological Monographs, 28* (Whole No. 123).

Luchins, A. (1942). Mechanization in problem solving: The effect of Einstellung. *Psychological Monographs, 54*(6) (Whole No. 248).

Markus, H., & Nurius, P. (1986). Possible selves. *American Psychologist, 41,* 954-969.

McKeachie, W. J. (1951). Anxiety in the college classroom. *Journal of Educational Research, 45,* 135-160.

McKeachie, W. J. (1954). Student-centered vs. instructor-centered instruction. *Journal of Educational Psychology, 45,* 143-150.

McKeachie, W. J., Lin, Y.-G., Milholland, J. E., & Isaacson, R. L. (1966). Student affiliation motives, teacher warmth, and academic achievement. *Journal of Personality and Social Psychology, 4,* 457-461.

McKeachie, W. J., Lin, Y.-G., Moffett, M. M., & Daugherty, M. (1978). Effective teaching: Facilitative vs. directive style. *Teaching of Psychology, 5,* 193-194.

McKeachie, W. J. (1987). Cognitive skills and their transfer: Discussion. *International Journal of Educational Research, 2*(6) 707-712.

Medin, D. L., Goldstone, R. L., & Gentner, D. (1993). Respects for similarity. *Psychological Review, 100*(2) 254-278.

Picard, E. (1992). *Construction of knowledge structures in repeated reading* (Forschungsberichte. No. 59). Deutsches Institut fur Fernstudien an der Universitat Tubingen.

Rollett, B. A. (1987). Effort avoidance and learning. In E. DeCorte, H. Lodewijks, R. Parmentier, & P. Span *Learning and instruction: European research in an international context* (Vol. 1). Oxford: Leuven University Press and Pergamon.

Salomon, G., & Perkins, D. (1989). Rocky roads to transfer: Rethinking mechanisms of a neglected phenomenon, *Educational Psychologist, 24,* 113-142.

Smith, E. E. (1988). Concepts and thought. In R. Sternberg & E. Smith (Eds.), *The psychology of human thought.* Cambridge University Press.

Tobias, S. (1990). *They're not dumb, they're different.* Tucson, AZ: Research Corporation.

CURRICULUM VITA

Wilbert J. McKeachie

Current Positions

1946-	Department of Psychology, The University of Michigan Teaching Fellow to Professor, 1946- Chairman, 1961-1971
1975-	The Center for Research on Learning and Teaching, The University of Michigan Research Scientist, 1975- Director, 1975-1983

Degrees	Dates	University
B.A.	1942	Michigan State Normal College
M.A.	1946	The University of Michigan
Ph.D.	1949	The University of Michigan

Honorary Degrees:
LL.D., University of Cincinnati
Sc.D., Denison University
LL.D., Eastern Michigan University
Litt.D., Hope College
Sc.D., Northwestern University

Other Honors

1955	Alumni Award for Distinguished Teaching, The University of Michigan
1969	Faculty Intramural Athlete of the Year, The University of Michigan (1st awardee)

1969   Alumni Honors Award, Eastern Michigan University

1973   American College Testing-American Education Research
             Association Award for
             Outstanding Research

1977   National Academy of Education Member

1985   American Psychological Foundation Award for Distinguished
             Teaching of Psychology

1987   American Psychological Association Award for Distinguished
             Career Contributions to
             Education and Training in Psychology

1988   Edward L. Thorndike Award for Outstanding Research,
             American Psychological
             Association, Division of Educational Psychology

1990   Recipient of the American Educational Research Association
             Special Interest Group on Faculty Evaluation and Development;
             Career Achievement Award and announcement that the annual
             award will henceforth be called the Wilbert J. McKeachie
             Award.

1990   The University of Michigan Distinguished Faculty
             Governance Award

1992   Centennial Award for Outstanding Contributions, American
             Psychological Association

Academic and Professional Experience

July-Nov., 1942 Mathematics teacher and Methodist minister, Trout
    Lake, Michigan

1942-1945   United States Navy, Deck and Radar Officer, U.S.S.
    Guest, (DD 472) Pacific Theater

Membership and Offices in Professional Societies

American Psychological Association
    1975-76   President

Michigan Psychological Association
    1953-54   President

American Association for the Advancement of Science
    1976   Chairman, Section J (Psychology)

American Council on Education
    1973-84   Committee on Institutional Research
                                Program
    1978-79   Board of Directors

American Association for Higher Education
    1978-79   President

American Institutes for Research in the Behavioral Sciences
    1979-   Board of Directors

American Psychological Foundation
    1980-82   President

Canadian Psychological Association
    1977-   Honorary Life Fellow

International Association of Applied Psychology
    1982-86   Founding President, Division of
                                Educational, Instructional,
                                and School Psychology

National Academy of Education
    1983-85   Chairman of Section III, The
                                Psychology of Education

Other Associations
    1990-91   President, Center for Social Gerontology

Community and National Service

1965-67	Moderator, First Baptist Church, Ann Arbor
1966-70	Board of Directors, Washtenaw County Community Mental Health Center
	American Baptist Campus Foundation President 1972-74, 1978-1985
1967-72	Special Medical Advisory Group, Veterans Administration
1971-73	National Academy of Science-National Research Council Panel on the Impact of Information on Drug Use and Misuse
1976-80	National Advisory Council, National Institute of Mental Health.

BIBLIOGRAPHY

BOOKS and SEPARATES

Readings in introductory psychology. (Ed.) with D. Beardslee, D. Dulany, et al., Ann Arbor: George Wahr Publishing Company, 1951, xiii-347.

A review outline of general psychology (Ed.). Ann Arbor: George Wahr, 1951. 2nd Edition, Ann Arbor: George Wahr, 1955.

A review outline of general psychology (with S. Komorita, A. Neel, & M. Wagman). Paterson, NJ: Littlefield, Adams, 1962.

Teaching tips: Strategies, Research, and Theory for College and University Teachers (9th Ed.). Lexington: D. C. Heath, 1994.

Improving undergraduate instruction in psychology (with D. Wolfle, et al.). New York: The MacMillan Co., 1952, pp. vii-60.

Man in his world: Human behavior. Ann Arbor: University of Michigan Extension Service, 1952.

The appraisal of teaching in large universities (Ed.). Ann Arbor: University of Michigan, 1959.

Undergraduate curricula in psychology (with J. E. Milholland). Scott, Foresman and Company, 1961.

Psychology (3rd Ed. with C. Doyle & M. M. Moffett). Reading, MA: Addison-Wesley, 1976.

Some thoughts about teaching the beginning course in psychology (with E. L. Walker). Belmont, CA: Brooks/Cole, 1967.

Translated into Spanish and Portuguese, Brooks/Cole, 1968.

The importance of teaching: A memorandum to the new college teacher (with Committee on Undergraduate Teaching). New Haven, CT: The Hazen Foundation, 1968.

Research on college teaching: A review. Washington, DC: ERIC Clearinghouse on Higher Education, 1970.

XIP readings in psychology. Lexington, MA: Xerox College Publishing, 1972.

Psychology: The short course (with C. Doyle). Reading, MA: Addison-Wesley, 1972.

Postsecondary education: Research opportunities for NIE (with J. Stephens). Washington, DC: National Institute of Education, 1976.

Learning, cognition, and college teaching (Ed.). New Directions for Teaching and Learning, No. 2. San Francisco: Jossey-Bass, Inc., 1980.

Joint Hampton-Michigan program for training minority and women researchers, Vols. I & II (Project No. 8-1154, with B. M. Morrison, R. L. Braithwaite, C. M. Jagacinski, & C. Kaczala). Washington, DC: National Institute of Education, 1980.

Improving undergraduate education through faculty development (with K. E. Eble). San Francisco: Jossey-Bass Publishers, 1985.

Cognitive psychology and education. Science and Public Policy Seminars. Washington, DC: Federation of Behavioral, Psychological and Cognitive Sciences, 1986.

Teaching and learning in the college classroom: A review of the research literature (with P. R. Pintrich, Y. G. Lin, & D. A. F. Smith). Ann Arbor, MI: The Regents of the University of Michigan, National Center for Research to Improve Postsecondary Teaching and Learning, 1986. (Second Edition, 1990.)

Teaching psychology: A handbook (edited with James Hartley). Hillsdale, NJ and London: Hove and Erlbaum, 1990.

Teaching Tips for Users of the Motivated Strategies for Learning Questionnaire (with G.R. Johnson, J.A. Eison, R. Abbott, G.T. Meiss, K. Moran, J.A. Gorgan, T.L. Pasternack, & E. Zaremba). Ann Arbor, MI: The Regents of the University of Michigan, National Center for Research to Improve Postsecondary Teaching and Learning, 1991.

A Manual for the Use of the Motivated Strategies for Learning Questionnaire (with P.R. Pintrich, D.A. Smith, & T. Garcia). Ann Arbor, MI: The Regents of the University of Michigan, National Center for Research to Improve Postsecondary Teaching and Learning, 1991.

CHAPTERS IN BOOKS

Past, present, and future in the relation of psychology to general education. Galesburg, IL.: Knox College, 1954.

Group dynamics: Implications from research for instruction and for instructional programs. In G. K. Smith (Ed.), Current issues for higher education. Washington Association for Higher Education, 1956.

The joy of teaching. In D. L. Sharp (Ed.), Why teach? New York: Henry Holt, 1957.

How do students learn? In R. Cooper (Ed.), The two ends of a log. Minneapolis: The University of Minnesota, 1958.

Motivating students' interest. In R. Cooper (Ed.), The two ends of a log. Minneapolis: The University of Minnesota, 1958.

The interactions between student anxiety and teaching approach in learning mathematics. In R. Feirabend & P. DuBois (Eds.), Psychological problems and research methods in mathematics training. St. Louis: 1959.

The interaction of personality variables with teaching methods affecting college learning. In R. Feirabend & P. DuBois (Eds.), Psychological problems and research methods in mathematics training. St. Louis: 1959.

Appraising teaching effectiveness. In W. J. McKeachie (Ed.), The appraisal of teaching in large universities. Ann Arbor: University of Michigan, 1959.

College teachers and the learning process. In J. W. Gustad (Ed.), Faculty preparation and orientation. Winchester, MA: New England Board of Higher Education, 1960.

The instructor. In G. Finch (Ed.), USAF-NAS-NRC-Symposium: Education and Training Media, 1960, 789, 22-23.

Recitation and discussion. In O. Lancaster (Ed.), Achieve learning objectives. University Park, PA: Pennsylvania State University, 1960, 1-37.

The role of the faculty in improving the instructional program. In W. Blaketor (Ed.), Proceedings, 1960 Judson College Faculty Workshop. Marion, AL: Judson College, 1960.

Studies of teaching effectiveness. In J. K. Folger (Ed.), Proceedings, Institute on Institutional Research.
Atlanta, GA: Southern Regional Educational Board, 1960.

Teaching methods. In W. Blaketor (Ed.), <u>Proceedings, 1960 Judson College Faculty Workshop</u>. Marion, AL: Judson College, 1960.

The value of effective teaching in liberal arts colleges. In W. Blaketor (Ed.)., <u>Proceedings, 1960 Judson College Faculty Workshop</u>. Marion, AL: Judson College, 1960.

What do the research findings from behavioral science suggest concerning the improvement of teaching and learning? In G. Smith (Ed.), <u>Current issues in higher education</u>. Washington, DC: NEA, 1960.

The psychology of learning as applicable to effective college teaching. <u>A regional faculty orientation program</u>. Harrisburg, PA: Pennsylvania Association of Colleges and Universities, 1961.

What do research findings reveal that might increase the effectiveness of teaching? In A. Henderson (Ed.), <u>The annual conference on higher on higher education in Michigan</u>. Ann Arbor: University of Michigan, 1961.

Recitation and discussion. In O. Lancaster (Ed.), <u>Achieve learning objectives</u>. University Park, PA: Pennsylvania State University, 1961, 1963.

Teaching scientific psychology in the denominational college: Comments. In A. A. Schneiders & P. J. Center (Eds.), <u>Selected Papers from the ACPA Meetings of 1960, 1961</u> (Fordham University). New York: American Catholic Psychological Association, 1962.

Procedures and techniques of teaching. A survey of experimental studies. In N. Sanford (Ed.), <u>The American college</u>. New York: Wiley, 1962.

Internships in college teaching. In D. L. Delaka & R. R. Taylor (Eds.), <u>On the threshold to academic careers</u>. Madison: University of Wisconsin, 1962.

Psychological content in high school social studies. In B. Berelson (Ed.), <u>The social sciences and the social studies</u>. New York: Harcourt, Brace & World, 1962.

College teaching and student motivation. In H. A. Estrin & R. W. Van Houten (Eds.), <u>Higher education in engineering and science</u>. New York: McGraw-Hill, 1963.

Problems and perils in controlled research in teaching. In E. R. Sternberg (Ed.), <u>Needed research in the teaching of English</u>. Washington, DC: U.S. Office of Education, (Coop. Res. Monograph No. II), 1963.

Psychological characteristics of adults and instructional methods in adult education. In R. G. Kuhlen (Ed.), <u>Psychological backgrounds of adult education</u>. Chicago: Center for the Study of Liberal Education for Adults, 1963.

Research on college teaching. In N. Gage (Ed.), <u>Handbook of research on teaching</u>. Rand-McNally, 1963.

Needed research on psychological factors in learning as related to the social studies. In R. A. Price (Ed.), <u>Conference on needed research in the teaching of the social studies</u>. Syracuse University, NY: Sagamore Conference Center, 1963.

Approaches to teaching. In N. Sanford (Ed.), <u>College and character</u>. New York: Wiley, 1964.

The college teacher and creativity. In D. Schwartz (Ed.), <u>Creativity in its classroom context</u>. Lexington: Bulletin of Bureau of School Service, University of Kentucky, 1964.

Psychology and college teaching: A survey of recent experimental studies with implications for the future. In M. Whiffen (Ed.)., <u>The teaching of architecture</u>. Washington, DC: The American Institute of Architects, 1964.

Psychology. In H. N. Rivlin (Ed.), <u>The first years in college</u>. Boston: Little, Brown, 1965.

Effective teaching: The relevance of the curriculum. In L. E. Dennis & J. F. Kauffman (Eds.), <u>The college and the student</u>. Washington, DC: American Council on Education, 1966, 189-191.

Research in teaching: The gap between theory and practice. In Improving college teaching: Aids and impediments. Washington, DC: American Council on Education, 1966, 28-56.

Higher education. In P. H. Rossi & B. J. Biddle (Eds.), The new media and education. Chicago: Aldine, 1966.

The teacher in higher education. Changing dimensions and demands of the profession. Los Angeles: California Teachers Association, 1966.

Significant student and faculty characteristics relevant to personalizing higher education. In J. W. Minter (Ed.)., The individual and the system. Boulder, CO: Western Interstate Commission for Higher Education, 1967, 21-35.

The means of achieving educational objectives in the classroom. In E. Foreman (Ed.), The improvement of instruction: The instructional process. Macomb: Western Illinois University, 1967.

The faculty: Who they are, what they do. In Southern Regional Educational Board, The college campus in 1969. Atlanta, GA: SREB, 1969.

Field experience in the psychology curriculum. In W. C. Sheppard (Ed.), Proceedings: Conference on Instructional Innovations in Undergraduate Education. Eugene: University of Oregon, 1969, 113-123.

Attitude change: Resistances and conflicts. In W. L. Heimstra (Ed.), Dynamic Christian growth. Proceedings of the Seventeenth Annual Convention, Christian Association for Psychological Studies. Grand Rapids, MI, 1970.

The teaching learning process: Teaching. In Plumtree, et al. (Eds.), University teaching and learning. Waterloo, Ontario: University of Waterloo, 1971.

A tale of a teacher (An autobiography). In T. W. Krawiec (Ed.), The psychologists. New York: Oxford University Press, 1972.

Reprinted in part as: "Academician Wilbert J. McKeachie." Psychology Today, September, 1972, 6, 63-67.

Instinct. In World Book Encyclopedia, 1973 and later editions.

Intelligence. In World Book Encyclopedia, 1973 and later editions

I. Q. In World Book Encyclopedia, 1973 and later editions.

Evaluating drug information programs. Report of the Panel on the Impact of Information on Drug Use and Misuse, Phase II. Assembly of Behavioral and Social Sciences. National Research Council - National Academy of Sciences, Washington, DC, 1973.

Instructional psychology. Annual Review of Psychology, Annual Reviews, 1974.

The evaluation of teachers in higher education, (with J. A. Kulik). In F. N. Kerlinger (Ed.), Review of research in education, Vol 3. Itasca, IL: Peacock, 1975.

Effective college teaching (with J. A. Kulik). In F. N. Kerlinger (Ed.), Review of research in education, Vol. 3. Itasca, IL: Peacock, 1975.

Assessing teaching effectiveness: Comments and summary. In B. Massey (Ed.), Proceedings: International Conference on Improving University Teaching. Heidelberg, Germany: University of Maryland, European Division, 1975.

Preparing for a course. In Chancellor's Advisory Committee on Instructional Development, Ohio Board of Regents, Teaching in higher education: Critical readings. Delaware, OH: Ohio Wesleyan University, 1975.

Examinations. In Chancellor's Advisory Committee on Instructional Development, Ohio Board of Regents, Teaching in higher education: Critical readings. Delaware, OH: Ohio Wesleyan University, 1975.

The impact of NTL on the theory and practice of learning. In A tribute to Lee Bradford. University of Cincinnati, 1976.

Reactions from a former department chairman. In J. C. Smart & J. R. Montgomery (Eds.), Examining departmental management. Jossey-Bass, 1976.

Has the psychology of instruction progressed in this century? Talks to teachers, 1892 and 1976. In T. B. Massey (Ed.), Proceedings: Second International Conference on Improving University Teaching. Heidelberg University and University of Maryland, 1976.

The state of the art in improving learning and teaching. In T. B. Massey (Ed.), Proceedings: Third International Conference on Improving University Teaching. Newcastle-upon-Tyne Polytechnic and University of Maryland, 1977.

A challenge to change. Evaluation for the Veterinary Profession. Proceedings: Seventh Symposium on Veterinary Medical Education. West Lafayette, IN: Purdue University, 1978, 129-131.

Teaching-learning improvement: The state of the art. In T. B. Massey (Ed.), Proceedings: Fourth International Conference on Improving University Teaching. Aachen, F. R. Germany. University of Maryland, University College, 1978, 24-39.

Approaches to teaching. In N. Sanford & J. Axelrod (Eds.), College and Character. Berkeley, CA: Montaign, 1979, 203-215.

Perspectives from psychology: Financial incentives are ineffective for faculty. In D. R. Lewis & W. E. Becker (Eds.), Academic Rewards in Higher Education. Cambridge, MA: Ballinger Publishing Co., 1979, 1-10.

Advances in faculty development. In T. B. Massey (Ed.), Proceedings: Fifth International Conference on Improving University Teaching. The City University London and University of Maryland, 1979.

Improving lectures by understanding students' information processing. In W. J. McKeachie (Ed.), Learning, cognition, and college teaching. New Directions for Teaching and Learning. San Francisco: Jossey-Bass, Inc., 1980.

Implications of cognitive psychology for college teaching. In W. J. McKeachie (Ed.), Learning, cognition, and college teaching. New

Directions for Teaching and Learning. San Francisco: Jossey-Bass, Inc, 1980.

Teaching psychology of today from a developmental point of view. In I. Synn (Ed.), The pursuit of excellence in higher education. Daegu, Korea: Keimyung University, 1980.

Problem solving: Groups versus individuals. In L. T. Benjamin, Jr. & K. D. Lowman (Eds.), Activities handbook for the teaching of psychology. Washington, DC: American Psychological Association, Inc., 1981, 92-94.

Summary. Documentation report of the Ann Arbor symposium. National Symposium on the Applications of Psychology to the Teaching and Learning of Music, The University of Michigan, Ann Arbor, Michigan, 1978-79. Reston, VA: Music Educators National Conference, 1981.

Teaching and learning (with S. C. Ericksen). In D. K. Halstead (Ed.), Higher education: A bibliographic handbook, Vol. II. Washington, DC: National Institute of Education, 1981.

What to do when survival is threatened or how to reconcile educational effectiveness with cost effectiveness in staff development. In T. B. Massey (Ed.), Proceedings: Seventh International Conference on Improving University Teaching. Tsukuba, Japan. University of Maryland University College and The University of Tsukuba, 1981.

Teaching and learning in staff development. In T. B. Massey (Ed.), Proceedings: Seventh International Conference on Improving University Teaching. Tsukuba, Japan. University of Maryland University College and The University of Tsukuba, 1981.

The rewards of teaching. In J. Bess (Ed.), New directions for teaching and learning: Motivating professors to teach effectively, No. 10. San Francisco: Jossey-Bass, 1982.

Academic performance: Anxiety as cause and effect. In Proceedings of the Eighth International Conference, Improving University Teaching. West Berlin. College Park, MD: University of Maryland University College and Fachhochschule fur Sozialarbeit und Sozialpadagogik Berlin, 1982, 160-163.

Faculty as a renewable resource. In R. G. Baldwin & R. T. Blackburn (Eds.), College faculty: Versatile human resources in a period of constraint, New Directions for Institutional Research. San Francisco: Jossey-Bass, Inc, 1983, 57-66.

Research on learning. In Proceedings of the Ninth International Conference, Improving University Teaching. Dublin, Ireland. College Park, MD: University of Maryland University College and National Institute for Higher Education Dublin, 1983, 317-319.

Meeting student needs with technology. In Proceedings of the Tenth International Conference, Improving University Teaching. College Park, MD: University of Maryland University College, 1984, 125-131.

Spatial strategies: Critique and educational implications. In C. D. Holley & D. F. Dansereau (Eds.), Spatial learning strategies: Techniques, applications, and related issues. San Diego: Academic Press, Inc., 1984, 301-312.

Improving the teaching-learning process through multiple sources of feedback: A Norwegian case study. In Proceedings of the Eleventh International Conference, Improving University Teaching. Utrecht, The Netherlands. College Park, MD: The University of Maryland University College and The State University of Utrecht, 1985, 108-113.

Learning to learn (with P. R. Pintrich & Y. G. Lin). In G. d'Ydewalle (Ed.), Cognition, information processing and motivation. North Holland: Elsevier Science Publishers, 1985, 601-618.

Tips on teaching. In M. P. Zanna & J. M. Darley (Eds.), The compleat academic: A practical guide for the beginning social scientist. New York: Random House, 1986, 87-113.

Teaching Psychology: Research and Experience. In V.P. Makosky (Ed.), The G. Stanley Hall Lecture Series, Vol. 6. Washington, D.C.: American Psychological Association, 1986.

Instructional psychology (with P. R. Pintrich, D. R. Cross, & R. B. Kozma). In Annual Review of Psychology, Vol. 37. Palo Alto, CA: Annual Reviews, Inc., 1986, 611-651.

Using student ratings: Lessons learned. In <u>Proceedings of Faculty Evaluation and Development: Lessons Learned</u>. Manhattan, KS: National Issues in Higher Education, Kansas State University, 1986, 17-30.

A response to teaching critical thinking in psychology. In J. S. Halonen & L. S. Cromwell (Eds.), <u>Teaching critical thinking in psychology</u>. Milwaukee, WI: Alverno Productions, 1986, 183-185.

The new look in instructional psychology: Teaching strategies for learning and thinking. In E. De Corte, H. Lodewijks, R. Parmentier, & P. Span (Eds.), <u>Learning and instruction. European research in an international context</u>, Vol. 1. Oxford: Pergamon Books Ltd./Leuven University Press, 1987, 443-456.

Discussion. In R. E. Snow & M. J. Farr (Eds.). <u>Aptitude, learning and instruction. Vol. 3: Conative and affective process analyses</u>. Hillsdale, NJ: Lawrence Erlbaum Associates, Inc., 1987, 327-331.

Teaching and learning (with P. R. Pintrich & K. P. Cross). In K. Halstead (Ed.), <u>Higher education bibliography yearbook 1987</u> (1st ed.). Washington, DC: Research Associates of Washington, 1987, 1-8.

Can evaluating instruction improve teaching? In L. M. Aleamoni (Ed.), <u>Techniques for evaluating and improving instruction</u>. New Directions for Teaching and Learning. San Francisco: Jossey-Bass, Inc., 1987, 3-7.

Cognitive skills and their transfer: Discussion. In E. De Corte (Ed.), <u>Acquisition and transfer of knowledge and cognitive skills: International Journal of Educational Research, Vol. II, No. 6</u>, 1987, 707-712.

The need for study strategy training. In C. E. Weinstein, E. T. Goetz, & P. A. Alexander (Ed.), <u>Learning and study strategies: Issues in assessment, instruction, and evaluation</u>. Orlando, FL: Academic Press, 1988, 3-9.

Teaching and learning (with P. R. Pintrich & K. P. Cross). In K. Halstead (Ed.), <u>Higher education bibliography yearbook 1988</u>

(2nd ed.). Washington, DC: Research Associates of Washington, 1988, 1-7.

Psychology and adult cognition. In R. A. Fellenz (Ed.), <u>Cognition and the adult learner</u>. Bozeman, MT: Montana State University, Center for Adult Learning Research, 1988, 1-12.

Studies of motivation, learning strategies, and critical thinking. In <u>Proceedings of the Fourteenth International Conference, Improving University Teaching</u>. Umea, Sweden. College Park, MD: The University of Maryland University College and The University of Umea, 1988, 87-95.

Teaching that helps anxious students. In <u>Proceedings of the Fifteenth International Conference on Improving University Teaching</u>. Vancouver, Canada. College Park, MD: The University of Maryland University College, 1989.

La nueva imagin de la psicologia instrucional: Ensenando estragias para el aprendizaji y el pensiamento. In Sandra Castaneda F. y Miguel Lopez O., <u>Antologia: La Psicologia Cogniscitiva Del Aprendizaje</u> (with P. R. Pintrich and Y-G. Lin), Mexico, D.F. Universidad Nacional Autonoma de Mexico, 1989.

Faculty Development: The State of the Art in 1990. In <u>Proceedings of the Sixteenth International Conference on Improving University Teaching</u>. Yogyakarta, Indonesia. College Park, MD: The University of Maryland University College, 1990, 11-13

Using Student Ratings to Evaluate Faculty Development. In <u>Proceedings of the Sixteenth International Conference on Improving University Teaching</u>. Yogyakarta, Indonesia. College Park, MD: The University of Maryland University College, 1990, 147-148.

Learning, Teaching, and Learning from Teaching. In J. Nyquist, R. Abbott, D. Wulff and J. Sprague (Eds.), <u>Preparing the Professoriate of Tomorrow to Teach</u>. Dubuque, IA: Kendall/Hunt Publishing Company, 1991, 223-231.

How Administrators Can Improve Teaching. In <u>Proceedings of the Seventeenth International Conference on Improving University Teaching</u>.

Glasgow, Scotland. College Park, MD: The University of Maryland University College, 1991, 86-92.

Enhancing Intrinsic Rewards for Teaching. In <u>Proceedings of the Seventeenth International Conference on Improving University Teaching</u>. Glasgow, Scotland. College Park, MD: The University of Maryland University College, 1991, 105-109.

The Utopian University. In <u>Proceedings of the Seventeenth International Conference on Improving University Teaching</u>. Glasgow, Scotland. College Park, MD: The University of Maryland University College, 1991, 138-142.

What Theories Underlie the Practice of Faculty Development. In K. Zahorski (Ed.), <u>To Improve the Academy: Resources for Student, Faculty & Institutional Development</u>, Vol. 10. Stillwater, OK: The Professional and Organizational Development Network in Higher Education, New Forum Press, Inc., 1991 3-8.

Evolution of Faculty Development Effects (with K.E. Eble). In M.J.Finkelstein (Ed.), <u>ASHE Reader on Faculty and Faculty Issues in Colleges and Universities</u>, 2nd Edition, 1991.

Motivation and Learning Strategies: Cross-cultural Comparisons. In Motokai, H., Misumi, J. and Wilpert, B., (Eds.), <u>Social, Educational, and Clinical Psychology Proceedings of the 22nd International Congress of Applied Psychology</u>. Hillsdale, N.J.: Erlbaum, 1992.

Halonen, J.S. "I Was Just Lucky": An Interview with Model Teacher Wilbert J. McKeachie. In A.E. Puente, J.R. Matthews & C.L. Brewer (Eds.), <u>Teaching Psychology in America: A History</u>. Washington, D.C: American Psychological Association, 1992.

Approaches to Accountability: U.S.A. In Proceedings of the 18th International Conference on Improving University Teaching, Schwabisch Gmund, Germany, July 1993. College Park, M.D.: University of Maryland, University College.

The Complete Scholar: Faculty Development for Those Who Teach Psychology (with B.R. Fretz, A.M. Garibaldi, L.M. Glidden, J.N. Moritsiegue, K. Quina, J.N. Reich, & B. Sholley). In T.V. McGovern (Ed.), <u>Handbook for Enhancing Undergraduate Education in</u>

Psychology. Washington, D.C.: American Psychological Association, 1993.

RESEARCH AND SCHOLARLY ARTICLES

Anxiety in the college classroom. Papers Michigan Academy, 1950, 36, 343-349.

Anxiety in the college classroom. Journal of Educational Research, 1951, 45, 135-160.

Lipstick as a determiner of first impressions of personality. Journal of Social Psychology, 1952, 36, 241-244.

A rating-ranking scale for goals in life (with H. Guetzkow). Religious Education, 1952, 47, 25-27.

Effects of different instructions in multiple choice examinations (with R. C. Teevan). Papers Michigan Academy, 1953, 39.

An experimental comparison of recitation, discussion and tutorial methods in college teaching (with H. Guetzkow & E. L. Kelly). Journal of Educational Psychology, 1954, 45, 224-232.

Individual conformity to attitudes of classroom groups. Journal of Abnormal and Social Psychology, 1954, 49, 282-289.

Objectives of the general psychology course (with R. DeValois, et al.). American Psychologist, 1954, 9, 140-142.

The problem-oriented approach to teaching psychology (with W. Hiler). Journal of Educational Psychology, 1954, 45, 143-150.

Student-centered instruction vs. instructor-centered instruction. Journal of Educational Psychology, 1954, 45, 143-150.

Relieving anxiety in classroom examinations (with D. Pollie & J. Speisman). Journal of Abnormal and Social Psychology, 1955, 50, 93-98.

Reprinted in:

H. W. Krohne (Ed.), <u>Angst bei shulern und studenten</u>. Hamburg, Germany: Hoffmann und campe verlag, 1976.

The teaching of psychology: A survey of research since 1942 (with R. Birney). <u>Psychological Bulletin</u>, 1955, <u>51</u>, 51-68.

Retention of general psychology (with D. Solomon). <u>Journal of Educational Psychology</u>, 1957, <u>48</u>, 110-112.

Student ratings of faculty: A research review. <u>Improving College & University Teaching</u>, 1957, <u>5</u>, 4-8.

Students, groups, and teaching methods. <u>American Psychologist</u>, 1958, <u>13</u>, 580-584.

Student ratings of instructors: A validity study (with D. Solomon). <u>Journal of Educational Research</u>, 1958, <u>51</u>, 379-383.

Teaching psychology by telephone (with R. Cutler & E. McNeil). <u>American Psychologist</u>, 1958, <u>13</u>, 551-552.

Personality and independent study (with K. Koenig). <u>Journal of Educational Psychology</u>, 1958, <u>50</u>, 132-134.

Changes in scores on the Northwestern Misconceptions Test in six elementary psychology courses. <u>Journal of Educational Psychology</u>, 1960, <u>51</u>, 240-244.

The improvement of instruction. <u>Review of Educational Research</u>, 1960, <u>30</u>, 351-360.

Individualized teaching in elementary psychology (with B. Forrin, Y. G. Lin, & R. Teevan). <u>Journal of Educational Psychology</u>, 1960, <u>51</u>, 285-291.

Motivation, teaching methods and college learning. In M. R. Jones (Ed.), <u>Nebraska Symposium on Motivation, 1961</u>. Lincoln: University of Nebraska Press, 1961, <u>9</u>, 111-142.

Translated as:

Motivation, Lehrethoden and Lerne in Hochschulen. In Franz Weinert (Ed.), Pedogogische Psychologie. Koln & Berlin: Keipenhuer & Witsch, 1967.

Current research on teaching effectiveness. Improving College & University Teaching, 1962, 10, 15-19.

Correlation of teacher personality variables and student ratings (with R. L. Isaacson & J. E. Milholland). Journal of Educational Psychology, 1963, 54, 110-117.

Religion, sex, social class, probability of success and student personality (with R. W. Carney). Journal for Scientific Study of Religion, 1963, 3, 32-42.

Dimensions of student evaluations of teaching (with R. L. Isaacson, J. E. Milholland, Y. G. Lin, M. Hofeller, J. W. Baerwaldt, & K. L. Zinn). Journal of Educational Psychology, 1964, 55, 344-351.

Personality, sex, subject matter, & student ratings (with R. E. Carney). Psychological Record, 1966, 16, 137-144.

Student affiliation motives, teacher warmth, and academic achievement (with Y. G. Lin, J.E. Milholland, & R. L. Isaacson). Journal of Personality and Social Psychology, 1966, 4, 457-461.

Cooperative versus competitive discussion methods in teaching introductory psychology (with D. B. Haines). Journal of Educational Psychology, 1967, 386-390.

New developments in teaching. New Dimensions in Higher Education, #16. United States Office of Education, April, 1967.

Student achievement motives, achievement cues, and academic achievement (with J. E. Milholland, R. L. Isaacson, & Y. G. Lin). Journal of Consulting and Clinical Psychology, 1968, 32, 26-29.

Psychology at age 75: The psychology teacher comes into his own. American Psychologist, 1968, 23(8), 551.

The interaction of achievement cues and facilitating anxiety in the achievement of women. Journal of Applied Psychology, 1969, 53(2), 147-148.

Student ratings of faculty. American Association of University Professors Bulletin, 1969, 55(4), 439-444.

Achievement standards, debilitating anxiety, intelligence and college women's achievement (with Y. G. Lin). The Psychological Record, 1969, 19, 457-459.

Aptitude, anxiety, study habits, and academic achievement (with Y. G. Lin). Journal of Counseling Psychology, 1970, 17(4), 306-309.

The relationship between student-teacher compatibility of cognitive structure and student performance (with Y. G. Lin, M. Wernander, & J. Hedegard). Psychological Record, 1970, 20, 513-522.

Goals and activities of male and female college students (with Y. G. Lin). College Student Journal, 1971, 5, 12-16.

Student ratings of teacher effectiveness: Validity studies (with Y. G. Lin & W. Mann). American Educational Research Journal, 1971, 8, 435-445.

Sex similarity in personality correlates of test anxiety (with Y. G. Lin). Psychological Reports, 1971, 29, 515-520.

Sex differences in student response to college teachers: Teacher warmth and teacher sex (with Y. G. Lin). American Educational Research Journal, 1971, 8, 221-226.

Research on college teaching. Educational Perspectives, 1972, 11, 3-10.

Correlates of student ratings. In A. L. Sockloff (Ed.), Proceedings: Faculty effectiveness as evaluated by students. Measurement & Research Center, Temple University, Philadelphia, PA, 1973.

Student characteristics related to achievement in introductory psychology courses (with Y. G. Lin). The British Journal of Educational Psychology, 1973, 43, 70-76.

The decline and fall of the laws of learning. Educational Researcher, 1974, 3(3), 7-11.

Multiple discriminant analysis of student ratings of college teachers (with Y. G. Lin). The Journal of Educational Research, 1975, 68, 300-305.

Psychology in America's bicentennial year. American Psychologist, 1976, 31, 819-833.

An experimental investigation of factors affecting university promotion decision: A brief report (with T. A. Salthouse & Y. G. Lin). The Journal of Higher Education, 1978, 49, 177-183.

A small study assessing teacher effectiveness: Does learning last? (with Y. G. Lin & C. N. Mendelson. Contemporary Educational Psychology, 1978, 3, 352-357.

Effective teaching: Facilitative vs. directive style (with Y. G. Lin, M. M. Moffett, & M. Daugherty). Teaching of Psychology, 1978, 5(4), 193-194.

A factor analytic study of the Alpert-Haber achievement anxiety test (with Y. G. Lin). Academic Psychology Bulletin, 1979, 1(1), 23-27.

Student ratings of faculty: A reprise. Academe, 1979, 65, 384-397.

A note on validity of student ratings of teaching (with Y. G. Lin). Educational Research Quarterly, 1979, 4(3), 45-47.

Using student ratings and consultation to improve instruction (with Y. G. Lin, M. Daugherty, M. M. Moffett, C. Neigler, J. Nork, M. Walz, & R. Baldwin). British Journal of Educational Psychology, 1980, 50, 168-174.

The role of colleagues in the evaluation of college teaching (with P. A. Cohen). Improving College and University Teaching, 1980, 28(4), 147-154.

Effects of instructor/course evaluations on student course selection (with J. Coleman). Journal of Educational Psychology, 1981, 73(2), 224-226.

Test anxiety: Deficits in information processing (with M. Benjamin, Y. G. Lin, & D. P. Holinger. Journal of Educational Psychology, 1981, 73(6), 816-824.

Does anxiety disrupt information processing or does poor information processing lead to anxiety? International Review of Applied Psychology, 1984, 33, 187-203.

The use of student ratings in promotion decisions (with Y. G. Lin & D. G. Tucker). The Journal of Higher Education, 1984, 55(5), 583-589.

Teaching learning strategies (with P. R. Pintrich & Y. G. Lin). Educational Psychologist, 1985, 20(3), 153-160.

Relaxation-induced anxiety: Additional findings. Psychological Reports, 1985, 57, 1277-1278.

Inferring students' cognitive structures and their development using the "ordered tree technique" (with M. Naveh-Benjamin, Y. G. Lin, & D. G. Tucker). Journal of Educational Psychology, 1986, 78(2), 130-140.

Teaching a course in learning to learn (with P. R. Pintrich & Y. G. Lin). Teaching of Psychology, 1987, 14(2), 81-86.

Two types of test-anxious students: Support for an information processing model (with M. Naveh-Benjamin & Y. G. Lin). Journal of Educational Psychology, 1987, 79(2), 131-136.

Ensenar a aprender. Nuestro Tiempo, 1987, 70(399), 31-33.

Teaching, teaching teaching, and research on teaching. Teaching of Psychology, 1987, 14(3), 135-139.

Self-scoring: A self-monitoring procedure (with L. C. Light & Y. G. Lin). Teaching of Psychology, 1988, 15(3), 145-147.

Cognitive schemas in social perception (with A. Biela, J. C. Lingoes, & Y.-G. Lin). Multivariate Behavioral Research, 1989, 24(2), 195-208.

Development of cognitive structures in three academic disciplines and their relations to students' study skills, anxiety, and motivation: Further use of the ordered-tree techniques (with M. Naveh-Benjamin & Y.-G. Lin). Journal of Higher Education Studies, 1989, 4, 10-15.

Use of the ordered-tree technique to assess students' initial knowledge and conceptual learning (with M. Naveh-Benjamin & Y.-G. Lin). Teaching of Psychology, 1989, 16(4), 182-187.

The Multisource Nature of Learning: An Introduction (with A. Iran-Nejad, & D.C. Berliner). Review of Educational Research, 1990, 60, 509-515.

Learning, thinking, and Thorndike. Educational Psychologist, 1990, 25(2), 127-141.

Research on college teaching: The historical background. Journal of Educational Psychology, 1990, 82(2),
189-200.

Judgements of ingroups and outgroups by members of three denominations in the United States and Poland
(with A. Biela, Y-G. Lin, and J. Lingoes), Journal of Psychology and Christianity, 1993, 12(3), 225-235.

OTHER ARTICLES

Summary of Second Annual Conference on Research in the Teaching of Psychology. Newsletter Committee on Teaching Social Psychology, SPSSI, 1950.

What about the church? Young People, January 22, 1950, 4-6.

The church can use science. The Churchman, August, 1951.

Group decision makes democracy work. Religious Education, 1951, 46, 90-91.

A program for training teachers of psychology. American Psychologist, 1951, 6, 119-121.

Teaching psychology on television. <u>American Psychologist</u>, 1952, <u>7</u>, 503-506.

This I believe. <u>The Michigan Daily</u>, November 14, 1952.

Church groups and mental health. <u>Pulpit</u>, 1954, <u>25</u>, 342-343.

College teaching and student motivation. <u>Improving College and University Teaching</u>, 1954, <u>2</u>, 39-41.

The structure of the state psychological association. <u>American Psychologist</u>, 1954, <u>9</u>, 810.

From the president's desk. <u>The Michigan Psychologist</u>, Winter, 1954, 4-8.

Current enrollment trends and college teaching. <u>Improving College and University Teaching</u>, 1955, <u>3</u>, 87-88.

Improving your teaching. <u>Adult Leadership</u>, 1955, <u>3</u>, 14-16.

Religion and social science. <u>Religious Education</u>, 1955, <u>50</u>, 306-307.

Three problems of general education. <u>Improving College and University Teaching</u>, 1955, <u>3</u>, 42.

Mental health & ministers (with W. Allinsmith & L. Berman). <u>The Pulpit</u>, 1956, <u>27</u>, 4-17.

Research training in the graduate curriculum. <u>Psi Chi Newsletter</u>, January, 1958, 18-21.

TV for college instruction. <u>Improving College and University Teaching</u>, 1958, <u>6</u>, 84-88.

Group decision makes democracy work. <u>Religious Education</u>, 1959, <u>46</u>, 90-91.

Conceptions of human nature. In L. F. Miller (Ed.), <u>Digest of Proceedings</u>, Institute for Employee Development Officers, U.S. Civil Service Commission, 1959.

A program for training teachers of psychology, Mark II (with R. L. Isaacson). American Psychologist, 1959, 14, 658-659.

Behavioral sciences can improve college teaching. NEA Journal, 1960, 49, 79-81.

Certification of psychologists. American Psychologist, 1960, 15, 51-52.

An honors program in psychology. Journal of General Psychology, 1960, 63, 179-183.

The instructor faces automation. Improving College and University Teaching, 1960, 8, 91-95.

Problems of the minister's home. Church Management, 1960, 37, 38-41.

Textbooks to come. Contemporary Psychology, 1960, 5, 11.

To be good, teaching should be fun (with E. Bordin). Senate Affairs, 1960, 7, 3-4.

Size of class and institution as a factor in enjoyment of teaching (with E. Bordin). Journal of Higher Education, 1961, 32, 339-342.

Teaching effectiveness. Senate Affairs, 1961, 8, 1-3.

Understanding the learning process. Journal of Engineering Education, 1961, 51, 405-408.

Motives and learning. Sound Seminars, Cincinnati, OH: (a recording), 1964.

Ambivalence in graduate education. American Psychologist, 1964, 19, 682-683.

A look at the teaching machine. Toledo Blade Sunday Magazine, March 15, 1964, 4-5.

The faculty's role in policy making. The Michigan Daily, January 26, 1965.

Automation: New media in education--Concerns and challenges. College and University Bulletin, 1965, 18(3), 1-5.

The discussion group. Memo to the Faculty, No. 14. University of Michigan, Center for Research on Learning and Teaching, 1965.

Functions of APA. American Psychologist, April, 1966, 21(4), 372-374.

The case for multiple models. The Clinical Psychologist, 1967, 20, 108-110.

Interaction affecting achievement in introductory psychology. Ontario Psychological Association Quarterly, 1968, 21, 1-11.

Memo to new department chairmen. Educational Record, 1968, 49, 221-227.

Academic Professional Development Associates. The department chairman--His many roles and functions. Chicago, APDA, 1970.

J. Brann, & T. A. Emmet (Eds.), The academic department or division.

R. J. Wolotkiewicz (Ed.), The college administrator's handbook. Allyn & Bacon, Inc., 1980.

Report of the recording secretary. American Psychologist, 1968, 23, 854-856.

The organization of a large department of psychology. American Psychologist, 1969, 24(7), 659-661.

State associations: A view from the board (of directors of the APA). Michigan Psychologist, April, 1969, 28, 8-12.

A public policy conference for psychologists. American Psychologist, 1969, 24, 6.

Toward an educational psychology of higher education. Educational Psychologist, 1969, 2, 13-14.

Report of the recording secretary. American Psychologist, 1970, 25, 9-12.

Report of the recording secretary. American Psychologist, 1971, 26, 19-21. Proceedings of the American Psychological Association for 1970, 22-49.

APA's organizational state may be critical but not in extremes. Professional Psychologist, 1971, 2, 33-34.

Conflict and style in the college classroom - An intimate study (with B. Ringwald, R. Mann, & R. Rosenwein). Psychology Today, February 1971, 4(9), 45-49, 76-79.

Justice for freshmen. Building a new program. College and University Bulletin, 1971, 24(3), 3-4.

The revival of the textbook. Change, May-June, 1971.

Research on college teaching. Memo to the Faculty, No. 44. University of Michigan, Center for Research on Learning and Teaching, May, 1971.

The psychology department and society. Social Action, 1972, 5(1), 10.

Effective college teaching: Research on student-teacher interactions. ORA Research News, December 1972, 23(6), 1-10.

Admission to graduate work in psychology. American Psychologist, 1972, 27, 1078.

A study of admissions procedures to a Ph.D. program in psychology (with E. J. Lewis). American Psychologist, 1973, 28, 186-187.

Resistances to evaluation of teaching. Occasional Paper No. 2, The Center for the Teaching Progressions, Northwestern University, September, 1973.

In search of an executive officer, APA Monitor, 1974, 8(11), 2.

Organizing effective discussion. In A. B. Smith (Ed.), Institutional research council: Modules on effective college teaching. University of Florida, 1974.

Ph.D. orals. <u>Change</u>, 1975, <u>7</u>(1), 5.

Changing teacher behavior to improve instruction. In D. W. Allen, M.
 A. Melnik, & C. C. Peele (Eds.), <u>Improving university teaching:</u>
 <u>Reform, renewal, reward</u>. Amherst, MA: Clinic to Improve
 University Teaching, 1975, 75-84.

Hashing out the specifics: A dialogue on teaching. <u>Dividend</u>, Spring,
 1975, 18-21.

Textbooks: Problems of publishers and professors. <u>Teaching of</u>
 <u>Psychology</u>, 1976, <u>3</u>(1), 29-30.

With honor and anxiety. <u>APA Monitor</u>, 1976, <u>7</u>(2), 2.

APA: Who needs it? (with C. Kiesler). <u>APA Monitor</u>, 1976, <u>7</u>(3), 2.

Effective college teaching: Current trends in psychology. <u>MATEP</u>
 <u>Newsletter</u>, 1976, <u>1</u>, 13-19.

College grades: A rationale and mild defense. <u>AAUP Bulletin</u>, 1976,
 <u>62</u>, 320-322.

Retire--or take a cut in pay. <u>The Chronicle of Higher Education</u>,
 April 18, 1977, 21.

More on college grades. <u>AAUP Bulletin</u>, 1977, <u>63</u>, 55-56.

Class size, large classes, and multiple sections. <u>Academe</u>, 1980, <u>66</u>, 24-
 27.

Testing, testing, testing. <u>LSA</u>, 1980, <u>4</u>(1), 10-12.

The Institute as a community of learners. <u>Gazette</u> (Official Journal of
 the Western Australian Institute of Technology), 1980, <u>13</u>(2).

Recent developments in research on learning and teaching. <u>Chinese</u>
 <u>University of Hong Kong (CUHK) Educational Journal</u>, 1980, <u>8</u>(1), 97-
 106.

National symposium on the applications of psychology to the teaching
 and learning of music. <u>American Psychologist</u>, 1981, <u>36</u>(4), 408-410.

Faculty/personnel evaluation. Evaluation Notes, Nos. 2 & 3. University of San Francisco, 1981.

Enhancing productivity in post-secondary education. Journal of Higher Education, 1982, 53(4), 460-464.

Undergraduate education in the next decade: Discussion. Teaching of Psychology, 1982, 9(1), 62-63.

Motivation in the college classroom. Innovation Abstracts (National Institute for Staff and Organizational Development, North American Consortium, The University of Texas at Austin), 1982, IV(12).

Mismatches between faculty and student models of teaching. Instructional Evaluation, 1982, 7(1), 17-20.

Student anxiety, learning and achievement. Engineering Education, 1983, 73(7), 724-730.

The role of faculty evaluation in enhancing college teaching. National Forum, 1983, 63(2), 37-39.

The role of testing in student learning. Insurance Educators Letter, 1983, September, addendum pp. 1-3.

Women in the classroom: A response. AAHE Bulletin, 1983, 36(2), 9.

Older faculty members: Facts and prescriptions. AAHE Bulletin, 1983, 36(3), 8-10.

The effect of emotional state on validity of student ratings. Teaching of Psychology, 1983, 10(3), 172-173.

National symposium on the applications of psychology to the teaching and learning of music: Session 3, motivation and creativity. American Psychologist, 1983, 38, 855-857.

The student's role in the community of learners. Advice (Michigan Student Assembly), 1983, 8.

"U" should invest in social responsibility. The Michigan Daily, 1984, January 20, 4.

Qualitative studies of college teaching and learning. The PEN (Postsecondary Education Newsletter) (AERA), 1984, July.

Lessons to be learned from large behavioral research organizations (with O. G. Brim, Jr.). American Psychologist, 1984, 39(11), 1254-1255.

An alternative to forced retirement. Academe, 1985, 71(1), 41.

Instructional evaluation: Current issues and possible improvements. Journal of Higher Education, 1987, 58(3), 344-350.

Tactics and strategies for faculty development. The Department Advisor, 1987, Winter, 2(3).

Teaching thinking. NCRIPTAL Update, 1988, Sept., 2(1), 1.

A letter from Bill McKeachie (1991). Lead article in Cooperative Learning and College Teaching, 1, (2). 1-2.

Recent research on university learning and teaching: Implications for practice and future research. Academic Medicine, 1992, 10, 584-587.

Psychology and education. American Psychologist, 1992, 47, 843-844.

Author Index

Subject Index